D1071585

There You Are

Writings on Irish and American
Literature and History

There You Are
Writings on Irish and American Literature and History

Thomas Flanagan

PREFACE BY
Seamus Heaney

EDITED AND WITH AN INTRODUCTION BY
Christopher Cahill

NEW YORK REVIEW BOOKS

nyrb
New York

THIS IS A NEW YORK REVIEW BOOK

PUBLISHED BY THE NEW YORK REVIEW OF BOOKS

THERE YOU ARE: WRITINGS ON IRISH AND AMERICAN
LITERATURE AND HISTORY
by Thomas Flanagan
Copyright © 2004 by the Estate of Thomas Flanagan

Preface © 2004 by Seamus Heaney

Introduction © 2004 by Christopher Cahill

Copyright © 2004 by NYREV, Inc.

All rights reserved.

This edition published in 2004
in the United States of America by
The New York Review of Books
1755 Broadway
New York, NY 10019
www.nybooks.com

Distributed to the trade by Publishers Group West

Library of Congress Cataloging-in-Publication Data

Flanagan, Thomas, 1923–
    There you are : writing on Irish and American literature and history /
Thomas Flanagan ; edited and with an introduction by Christopher Cahill,
preface by Seamus Heaney.
        p. cm. — (New York Review Books)
    ISBN 1-59017-106-3 (cloth)

  1. English literature—Irish authors—History and criticism. 2. American literature—
Irish American authors—History and criticism. 3. Irish Americans—Intellectual life.
4. Ireland—Intellectual life. 5. Irish Americans—History. 6. Ireland—History.
  I. Cahill, Christopher. II. Title. III. Series.
  PR8714.F58 2004
  820.9'9417—dc22

                                                                                2004017055

ISBN 1-59017-106-3
Printed in the United States of America on acid-free paper.
November 2004
1 3 5 7 9 10 8 6 4 2

For Jean Flanagan

Contents

Preface

"URBANITY FLUNG LIKE a careless cloak across a murderous sword":
Tom Flanagan's relish for what he is describing in his characterization
of the young James Joyce's style is unmistakable and understandable.
His own style had a definite urbanity and panache, and while it would
be wrong to ascribe murderousness to the blade he wielded, there
was nevertheless a Toledo steel spring and edge to it. He was more
like a fencer with a foil than a combatant with a weapon, but you
were always aware that he could make a rent if he had to. Nobody
was more capable of glee and happy, intuitive enjoyment in the company of friends, but his long familiarity with companies where the
knives were out meant that he knew how to take care of himself.
"I was proffered gossip, malice, and oblique, knife-edged anecdote,"
he says at one point, speaking of the Dublin where he came to be so
at home, but something tells you that in the circumstances the visitor
didn't exactly quail.

It was appropriate, therefore, that the last thing he published in his
lifetime should have been in *The Irish Times*, a review of a history of
St. Patrick's Day where he was identified by the paper's literary editor
as "a novelist and scholar...currently working on a book about
Irish-American writers." And given his own deeply felt and deeply
pondered Irish-American identity (I can just hear a faint rattle of the

foil as I use that hackneyed phrase), it was equally appropriate that when he died in Berkeley five days after the review appeared in Dublin, he had submitted to *The New York Review of Books* a piece (included here) on William Kennedy.

The Kennedy essay was the last in a series on Irish-Americans that he was hoping to publish as a separate book. As he continued to write with his usual mordant appreciation about the works and pomps and personalities of Scott Fitzgerald, Eugene O'Neill, John Ford, and others, there was a sense of a life's work being completed. His 1959 study *The Irish Novelists, 1800–1850* not only rescued the work of Maria Edgeworth, Lady Morgan, John Banim, Gerard Griffin, and William Carleton from critical neglect, it turned the novelists themselves into vividly imagined figures and created a country of the mind as well as a field of study. Fifty years ago, after all, what are now called "Irish Studies" did not have any institutional existence in American (or Irish) universities, but once the Flanagan book appeared, it showed what was needed and how it should be done.

In the age of the New Critic, Tom was a history and biography man. There was, moreover, a touch of the artist about him. At the same time as he was doing his academic research, he was writing crime mysteries and gaining Ellery Queen awards. Here, indeed, was somebody whose narrative gifts and feel for the social and cultural conditions of nineteenth-century Ireland made him the artistic heir to the writers in question, a role which he would fulfill ever more copiously and confidently in the ensuing years with the publication of *The Year of the French* (1979), *The Tenants of Time* (1988), and *The End of the Hunt* (1994). These novels, covering the history of Ireland from the 1798 rebellion to the War of Independence and Civil War, have earned Flanagan a place in Irish literature alongside the writer friends he knew and loved: Frank O'Connor, Benedict Kiely, and others about whom he writes in the following pages.

Yet the novelist who could imagine with total sympathy the mental and physical toils of an eighteenth-century Gaelic-speaking poet on the bog roads of Mayo began life with no great devotion to the old sod. Even though, as he tells us, "the words 'Ireland' and 'Irish'... had for me a special resonance, striking, somewhere within me, a faint clear bell," the pale shade of green which his father had retained from earlier immigrant Flanagans was paling "to the point of translucency" in his well-assimilated son. Graduating from "a most excellent college which had developed as a part of the New England Protestant tradition," he had gone on to study with Lionel Trilling at Columbia, and ended up teaching courses in the humanities program. And it was then that bells of Ireland, whose sound had once broken the hearts of the legendary children of Lir, began to ring in his ears with a new, commanding resonance.

Tom Flanagan amazed literary Dublin in the early Sixties by his encyclopedic knowledge of the history and topography of the country: the story goes that on his first taxi ride from the airport he was so immersed in Joyce that he could name the streets and buildings they passed en route to his hotel. He became something of a legend, so that when I eventually met him in Berkeley, where I taught for the year 1970–1971, I was ready to be in awe but found myself treated with great affection and would eventually feel like his literary foster child.

To begin with, the Flanagans took great care of us as a family when we landed. Jean was our chauffeur as we looked for an apartment and their house was a home away from home all that year. But as well as feeling total welcome on the domestic front, I was under the spell of Tom's strong Hibernocentric mind and imagination. It's no exaggeration to say that he reoriented my thinking. When I landed in California I was somebody who knew a certain amount of Irish literature and history, but my head was still basically wired up to Eng. Lit. terminals. I was still a creature of my undergraduate degree at Queen's University, Belfast. When I left, thanks mostly to Tom's brilliantly sardonic conversation, I was in the process of establishing new coordinates and had a far more conscious, far more charged-up sense of Yeats and Joyce, for example, and of their whole Irish consequence. I was starting to see my situation as a "Northern poet" more in relation to the wound and the work of Ireland as a whole, and for that I shall be ever in his debt.

In the end, however, as many of the pieces in this book attest, Tom was reckoning with the American side of his heritage. He had spent the last St. Patrick's weekend in New York where he met his agent, linked up with old friends from earlier days in Manhattan, with poets and diplomats in town from Dublin, and watched the parade from the balcony of the American Irish Historical Society's premises on Fifth Avenue. It was a lap of honor, and was probably understood as such by all concerned, since he had grown frailer in the previous year, after Jean's death, and in the words of Hopkins, "a heavenlier heart began."

Not that he ever lost any of his earthly powers. He was still the brilliant raconteur with a sense of humor as pungent as his sense of history. The great ironical intelligence never failed; he remained to the end as exhilaratingly capable of scorn as of merriment. He winced rather than winked at stupidity and generally kept us up to scratch by never himself falling below intellectual par. Whether you met him in the snug of Doheny & Nesbitt's civil public house among the conversational cutters and thrusters or in his home in the tonic company of Jean and his daughters, you came away the better for it.

In Ireland, we looked forward to his annual visits. For the best part of forty years, he and the family came to Dublin, and during those migrant weeks he took to the country and the country took to him. He was like a bard on his circuits. In fact, when *The Irish Times* called him a scholar, they could well have been using the word in the older Hiberno-English sense, meaning somebody not only learned but ringed around with a certain *draoícht*, or magical aura, at once a man of the people and a solitary spirit, a little separate but much beloved.

Since that first meeting in 1970 I felt, like the typical Irish son, closest at our times of greatest silence and remoteness: walking the fields of County Leitrim where the 1798 insurgents had been cut down in the Battle of Ballinamuck, climbing down a cliff path on the Antrim coast where Roger Casement would have wished to be buried, gazing out along the stony pier at Portland Bill on the south coast of England where the Fenian prisoners had done hard labor a century before. "And there was nothing between us there," as I once wrote of my own father, "That might not still be happily ever after."

— SEAMUS HEANEY

Introduction

THOMAS FLANAGAN, WHOSE *The Year of the French* is a great American novel set in the bogs of eighteenth-century Ireland, began his writing life as an academic critic, before that term had become wholly pejorative. Through the late Forties and much of the Fifties, Flanagan lingered in the Columbia University doctoral program, a student of Lionel Trilling and Mark Van Doren who wrote movie treatments and Ellery Queen mystery stories to pay the rent while avoiding completion of a poorly chosen dissertation on the novels of André Malraux. The best result of this prolonged deflection of attention from the task at hand was the gradual awakening of an enduring scholarly and personal passion for Irish literature and history, at that time a subject considerably aslant from the concerns of New York intellectual circles. This led to his first book, *The Irish Novelists, 1800–1850*, and eventually to the fiction of his middle career, a loose trilogy of novels that meditate upon Irish history and its discontents from the 1798 rebellion up to the Civil War of the 1920s. It also led to repeated and prolonged visits to Ireland, where he made lasting friendships with a number of writers, notably Conor Cruise O'Brien, Benedict Kiely, and Seamus Heaney. And so the pattern of his professional life was set: he became a transatlantic writer immersed in the culture of the land of his ancestors; an esteemed critic and professor, at Berkeley and later SUNY–Stony Brook, and one of the forerunners of Irish Studies as an academic discipline; and a critically and commercially successful novelist who rediscovered historical fiction as a mode of serious literature.

Throughout his career, Flanagan was also a reviewer and essayist whose witty, trenchant, and learned pieces were published regularly in journals, magazines, and newspapers in the US and in Ireland. Until now, though, there has been no volume of his critical writing published since that early study of nineteenth-century Irish novelists. *There You Are* collects both a great deal more and somewhat less of Flanagan's criticism than he had planned to include in the untitled book he was completing at the time of his death in the spring of 2002. This book was to have been based on the extended review essays, mostly on American and especially Irish-American literature and movies, that he wrote for *The New York Review of Books* in his last years. These pieces, which make up most of Part I of the present volume, represent at once a widening of his critical scope and a return to the core of his own nation's modern literature, his own precursors. They were written at a time when his last novel—set in Ireland during the period peculiarly known there as "The Emergency" (and elsewhere as World War II)—had stalled, and in the period just before and after the death of his beloved wife, Jean. Coming as they did in the midst of a great and in many ways disorienting grief, the late essays served their author as a refuge and a place of order. Their balance and mastery, as well as the undercurrent of sad, accomplished wisdom that moves beneath their lively surfaces, make of them a kind of corona, what Donne calls "the first last end, now zealously possess'd."

Though we will not have the exact book that Flanagan intended, we have a sense of the parts of it that will remain unwritten and of the shape it would have taken. A few months before his death, he discussed in a letter to Barbara Epstein, co-editor of *The New York Review of Books*, a second extended essay on Scott Fitzgerald that he was at work on for *Review*, and the remaining pieces he envisaged as filling out the book:

> I've finished the reading and thinking for the new Fitzgerald essay, and have started the rough draft. It will center on what he wrote during the four awful final years, but will look backward at what happened after 1926, after *Gatsby*. It happened to the creativity of one of America's finest writers of a certain kind of prose, and it wasn't just Zelda and the booze and Hemingway sticking pins in his Fitzgerald doll. It had more to do with a fatality built into that certain kind (ie. romantic, lyrical) and the sensibility that produces it. He writes of Gatsby's "heightened sensitivity to the promises of life, as if he were related to one of those intricate machines that register earthquakes ten thousand miles away." The machine was history and it blew up on him....
>
> The writers I'm writing about are all essentially of the Twenties, and I've thought of putting the first Fitzgerald essay early in the book and the second one late. And two critics I'd like to say something about. Mencken early on: we've forgotten how important he was and what a good critic; on *Gatsby* he's terrific except when he's swilling beer and giving teutonic belches. And, toward the end, something on Wilson. He was of course as much of the 30s and 40s as of the 20s, but his roots emotional and historical were in the Twenties. Or so it would be fun to argue.

And so it would have been.

In putting together the present volume, I have decided to include a much broader selection of essays, reviews, and introductions drawn from throughout Flanagan's career. It is organized around his central critical and creative preoccupations: American literature and film, Irish literature, Irish history, and the nature and possibilities of historical fiction. Considerations of space in a book already far longer than the one its author had in mind have led to the exclusion of a host of first-rate pieces on writers who fall somewhat outside of these given themes. It is to be hoped that this will be only the first of Flanagan's posthumous books. There is material in his archive for a full-length collection on nineteenth-century Irish literary and political writing—major essays on Wolfe Tone, John Mitchell, Thomas Moore, James Clarence Mangan, Somerville and Ross, George Moore, and others. A series of travel pieces that he wrote about Dublin, Cork, Connemara, and Mayo would make a fine companion still on a tour around that changing island. An early novel, set in China and entitled *The White Journey*, also exists in typescript, but Flanagan disavowed it years ago and I know of no one living who is likely to have read it. I never have.

٭ ٭ ٭

Tom Flanagan had a keen eye and strong gaze and a sharp tongue that he held in check until the exact moment, which was most often when his hapless, unwitting victim was safely out of earshot and harm's way. When the venom was delivered, it was always done with precision, grace, and a mending humor that spoke to both an abundant appreciation of his own "cleverality," to borrow a word from Myles na gCopaleen, and a resigned acknowledgement of his shared participation in the parade of human foolishness and self-deception. A controlled delight at the quizzical absurdity of everyday life strikes me as having been one of Tom's guiding characteristics, and it was applied alike to professorial trends and obscurantism, to students who thought that "Long Island was coterminous with the universe," to random snatches of conversation overheard, and to episodes of his own personal history.

After the attack on Pearl Harbor, Tom left Amherst College to enlist in the Navy and served in the Pacific Fleet. It was an act of considerable if ordinary bravery, but he never spoke of it, or of the time of combat that followed, in a heroic or self-aggrandizing light. He had a war story he liked to tell about standing beside a numskull in the gun tub of a destroyer who had just shot down an American plane with an antiaircraft gun. "No, no," Tom told him. "Don't shoot at the ones with the stars. Those are our guys. Shoot at the ones with the dots." It was the practice that every gun tub had a rising sun decal for each plane it shot down and Tom claimed to have bought and added a stars-and-stripes decal for the ill-fated American plane, but this may have been just an irresistible embellishment.

Much later in life, having found himself mentioned very oddly indeed in *The New York Times*, Tom filed a letter to the editor which began, "On a recent Sunday, I settled into a summer garden with iced tea and The Book Review, and found myself described as the possessor of someone else's penis." That someone else happened to be Napoleon Bonaparte (the imperial member, he wrote, was "a subject trifling even when animate"), and the process by which Tom found himself so described is too involved to repeat here, but the response it elicited is an apt illustration of his alert and supple style.

Apart from the months following Jean's death, when he was entirely bereft and adrift, this panache never abandoned him. It was good to see him regain his bearings, somewhat at least, in the months before his own sudden death. I shared a meal with Tom, and with the poet Derek Mahon, a few days before he died. It was the morning after St. Patrick's Day and he was in New York for the parade, which he had watched from the American Irish Historical Society. Derek and I met him at the apartment of his friend Andy Dupee on West 116th Street and we walked across the campus of Columbia University, where, when he was young, Tom had made himself into a teacher and a writer. He was in fine form, if moving a bit slowly, and I remember him telling the story of the handsome beatnik Lucien Carr's murder of a persistent gentleman admirer down the hill in Riverside Park, noting how Carr had assuaged his guilt afterward by going to Times Square for hot dogs with Jack Kerouac—this last detail a typical

Flanagan touch. He spoke about Gibbon's *Decline and Fall of the Roman Empire*, which he had gone back to for the first time in many years, and of his own theory that the parallel births of celebrity and of literary modernism in the 1920s were intertwined, a theory he was elaborating in that last essay on Fitzgerald, which he never completed. When I heard a few days later that he had died of a heart attack just after his return to California, it was good to think that he had been thinking and reading and working up to the end.

After Tom's death, I came across a postcard he had once sent me from Key West, "a curious and engaging part of the world" he had been visiting for the first time with Jean and his daughter Kate. "James Merrill died the other day," he had written, "and much of Key West is mourning him. It is difficult to think of places, outside Ireland, where the death of a poet makes a difference." Tom Flanagan was a writer who believed that prose should be at least as well written as poetry. He had a highly developed sensitivity and attentiveness to the formal and expressive properties of the medium across its full range, from the tensile, muscular cadences of Hemingway to the blossoming lyricism of Fitzgerald. His death has indeed made a difference, in Ireland, certainly, which he knew and loved and where he was known and loved, and no less here at home.

Tom often spoke of his intention to dedicate the book he was finishing to Jean, his wife of fifty-two years, a woman so resolutely upbeat and sociable that he once said she would have managed to have a good time at the Donner Pass. In his absence, the present book is likewise dedicated to her, as he would have wanted.

—CHRISTOPHER CAHILL

I

American Writers and Directors

I

JOHN FORD'S WEST

ONE FOURTH OF July, early in the twentieth century, young John Ford and his father stood in the main street of Portland, Maine, to watch the parade. The name in those days was not Ford but Feeney. "When the flag passes," the father said, "take off your cap." But the boy was not wearing one. "Then cross yourself, damn it!"

Like many of John Ford's stories, this one may even be true. True or false, it tells us that John Feeney, an emigrant from Galway's poverty-racked coast, held patriotic sentiments toward his new nation, and identified it, perhaps by a momentary slip, with his religion, which of course was Catholic. Some of his neighbors may have taken note of the slip. An intense dislike of the Irish, bred out of fear and detestation, was strong in New England and especially so in Maine. The fear was nourished by their violent and drunken ways and the detestation by their childish devotion to rosary beads, outlandish miracles, ritual, and superstition. Even their virtues—loyalty, courtesy, brute courage, a love of tradition and song—were those common among subordinate races. Dan Ford, the director's grandson, sums up the consequence with but slight exaggeration:

> The Yankees had their Protestant church, with its steeple pointing straight up to heaven; the Irish had their saloon, with its

swinging doors leading straight down to hell. The Yankees lived in the east end and ran the lumber industry, the shipping, and the counting houses, while the Irish huddled together in slums near the docks. There was little contact between the two cultures.

There was some, though. John Ford emerged from the public high school in 1914 with the football nickname of Bull Feeney, and may have briefly attended the state university. He claimed that he left the campus when a Yankee student shouted "Shanty!" at him, but students rarely shout at people named "Bull." He nurtured, though, a lifetime edge against Yankees and their straitlaced Puritan culture, as Eugene O'Neill did, and for similar reasons. He himself was to embody every single one of their anti-Irish stereotypes, as he well knew.

Joseph McBride, whose superb biography is rightly called *Searching for John Ford*,[1] has visited the time-battered cabin which John Feeney left in 1872, less than two decades after the great famine which swept his section of coast, near Spiddal. Himself of Irish descent, McBride knew as if by instinct to begin in the local pub, An Crúiscín Lán, "a smoky, stiflingly hot place by the sea," where assorted Feeneys and Currans guided him to the broken walls and hardened clay of what had once been the sort of dwelling that could be built in a day with the help of neighbors. Like the timber cabins which western pioneers threw together. It may well be the Irishness which McBride shares with Ford that gives his account a warmth and an understanding which are at once severe, witty, and admiring.

But there is more to it than this. He has been studying Ford for thirty years or so, and he writes of him with great skill and even, when appropriate, with eloquence. He deploys his wide knowledge of American social and film history with tact, wit, and imagination—

---

1. *Searching for John Ford: A Life* (St. Martin's, 2001).

rare virtues in the blighted acres of film studies, where often appear those diseased vocabularies which then spread to other fields.

Ford's father was summoned to America by an uncle, Mike Connolly, who, after various legendary wanderings in the New World, settled down into marriage to a prosperous Portland widow and set up shop as tavern keeper and bootlegger. Maine had outlawed hard liquor in 1851, partly as a stern gesture of Puritan virtue and partly to shield the incoming Irish from one of their most pernicious vices. Feeney followed his uncle into the family craft, and by the time his children were growing up he owned several taverns in the Irish quarter, in flagrant disregard of the law. He married a Galway girl, the prettiest girl in Portland, his son was to say, and smart enough to marry the most successful Irish saloonkeeper. The Connollys seem to have been a bit embarrassed by their connection with liquor, but the Feeneys took pride in theirs.

John Ford's call to the journey westward took a different form. His brother Francis, older by twelve years, handsome, clever, and ambitious in a lazy way, had drifted into the new but prospering world of motion pictures, first making two-reelers for Gaston Méliès in New Jersey and then for Thomas Ince and Universal in the streets and hills of Los Angeles. Now, after some pressure from the family, he promised John—who soon, like Frank, would be changing his surname to Ford—a job in what was still an engagingly improvised crapshoot, although one that was changing itself, year by year, into an industry.

Hollywood in 1914 was a small suburb with the scent of lemon trees and with bean patches and hayfields surrounding Sunset Boulevard. But Cecil B. DeMille had just made his first feature-length film, a western called *The Squaw Man*, in a barn at the corner of Selma and Vine, and D. W. Griffith was in the San Fernando Valley filming the battle scenes for the movie which he would later call *The Birth of a Nation*. Ford's brother was waiting for him in his yellow touring car, a cigarette propped in his mouth, dressed in the appropriate directorial breeches and jodhpurs. At his side was Grace Cunard, his mistress, codirector, and leading lady. As they drove toward Universal's new ranch for location shooting, Frank stopped so that his brother could admire the house he was building in the hills. At the ranch, though, Frank set him to humbler tasks, beginning with ditchdigging.

But John rose rapidly, a tough, quick-witted fellow. He was a handyman on Frank's serial *Lucille Love*, but assistant property man on the next, *The Mysterious Rose*. He was able, as McBride says, "to try his hand at just about every filmmaking job at Universal," which was pioneering the factory system of filmmaking. All the famous directors of the Twenties learned their craft this way, at one studio or another—Henry Hathaway, George Marshall, Raoul Walsh, Allan Dwan. It occurred to few of them that they were in at the birth of a new art.

Only Griffith, part genius, part ham, part medicine-show man, believed otherwise. One day, Ford played hooky and traveled down to open country where Griffith was filming. Later, he claimed that that morning he played one of the white-robed klansmen sweeping across a stream. McBride believes him, and prints a photograph which seems to bear him out. I am less sure. It seems to me an early instance of his insertions of self into history—the history of the Civil War (in one extreme version) and the history of the first great American film. Later, famous himself, he would say that "if it weren't for Griffith, we'd probably still be in the infantile stage of motion pictures.... Griffith was the one who made it an art—if you can call it an art—but at least he made it something worthwhile."

They all learned from Griffith, but Ford the most of all. Among other things, he knew, as did all Hollywood, of Griffith's uphill battle against his backers, with their money worries and fear of experiment. When he was making his own major films, he was ready from the first day on the set to do battle with the "front office" and the "people back East," and those hapless pawns known as associate producers.

He was stubborn and rough, and would earn more freedom than other directors then enjoyed. He was at Universal for seven years, three of them as a director, and earned a reputation for speed and reliability. He made about thirty films in those three years. Most of them were western two- or three-reelers, and all but a very few have disappeared, which says something about how film was then regarded. We know their titles—*Gun Law*, *The Gun Packer*, *Bare Fists*, *A Gun Fightin' Gentleman*.

He most enjoyed the ones he made with Harry Carey as his leading man. Carey, like Ford, was an easterner. So were many of the painters and writers and filmmakers who created our powerful and complex image of the West—Owen Wister, Zane Grey, William S. Hart, Frederic Remington. Much of what we know about the Carey of those years comes from Ford lore or from Ollie, Carey's salty, sardonic wife, a great debunker of Ford lore. "Jack said that? He's full of crap. God, how he romanced."

Carey possessed a style, a way of moving and walking, an attitude toward the characters he played, which Ford savored and, in the mysterious ways of cinema, passed on to his later leading men. Carey often played Cheyenne Harry, a badman who is compelled by circumstances or his own better nature to throw in with the other, weaker side. He makes the difference, and then he rides off into the sunset. Ford and Carey wanted to show working cowboys "as they really were"—and so they did, when it came to Harry's outfits. But they knew that in this figure, they were dealing with an image of considerable mythical power.

Carey, more singlemindedly devoted than Ford to the vanishing West, built a small ranch house in Newhall, north of Universal's acres, where the three of them at times shared quarters with a bunch of cowboys-turned-actors. Or Ford and Carey would sleep out in bedrolls, planning the next day's shooting. In theory, there was a hired writer, but these scenario men were not held in high regard, more important, perhaps, than property men but not to be compared with the fellows at the camera. It was a casual, condescending attitude which Ford would hold toward writers to the end, to the injured pride of Dudley Nichols, Frank Nugent, and Nunnally Johnson.

Ford moved quickly from setup to setup. "Occasionally the services of a carpenter or two was required to put up a rudimentary set suggesting the interior of a frontier home.... If a more elaborate set was needed, such as a saloon, a church, or a prison, Jack and Harry grudgingly returned to the back lot." Ford rarely looked at the rushes because, as Ollie says, "Ford didn't really need a cutter except for the mechanical works of it, because he shot just enough film that would be necessary for the picture. He never overshot." This too was a habit he carried with him, a useful guard against studio editing.

McBride is fine at creating for us the pioneer conditions under which Ford's early silents were made, but perhaps does not stress sufficiently the obvious fact that a pioneer was taking as subject the pioneer experience. He quotes Andrew Sarris, though: "Here we are at a time when the Western was still relatively new, and the Old West was virtually dead, and yet Ford was already casting a somber spell on the screen, his *mise-en-scène* already in mourning, his feelings of loss and displacement already fantasized through the genre." Sarris is on to something here, although it seems a heavy burden to rest upon the fact that Cheyenne Harry rides into the sunset at the end of *Straight Shooting*, the only Ford-Carey film to have survived intact, thanks to the film archive in Czechoslovakia.

But the tail end of the Old West did still survive. When the directors went down to Gower Gulch to recruit extras, they could find rodeo riders, kids who had worked on ranches, grizzled and bow-legged drunks who remembered the last days of the old cattle towns. From there or elsewhere, Ford was drawing the first generation of his stock company: Andy Devine and Chief John Big Tree, who had been one of the models for the Indian-head nickel, and "Pardner" Jones, who claimed to have killed the Apache Kid and who certainly was a dead shot with a rifle. Some of them had ridden the range; some of them had loud mouths, which didn't matter in silents; and a few of them affected the taciturnity of men familiar with guns. Only a few of them were old enough to have worked in the great cattle drives, but they knew the stories. The cattle drives were their *Iliad* and *Odyssey*, just as there were men back East whose uncles had been at Gettysburg and Shiloh, like Ford's Uncle Mike.

Emmet Dalton, sole survivor of the Dalton Gang, made western movies and so did Al Jennings, an inept but celebrated train robber. They did not look the part as impressively as did Harry Carey, Judge Carey's son, of Westchester County, and himself late of the New York University Law School. Wyatt Earp, the real Wyatt Earp, settled now in the Los Angeles area, would drift around the studios, not yet the iconic marshal of Tombstone, laconic and deadly, that he would become at the hands of, among others, John Ford. Ford claimed that when he staged the battle in the O.K. Corral in *My Darling Clementine*, he worked from a diagram drawn for him by Earp. Ollie Carey greeted this claim with derision.

There is indeed a strong tone of elegy in Ford's work. It seems to me that he later fantasized the Carey years into legend, when he was free to shoot movies as he wanted to, beyond the reach of studio accountants, provided he stayed within budget and within the boundaries of the genre. "The marvelous thing about Westerns," Jean Renoir told McBride, "is that they are all the same movie. That gives a director unlimited freedom."

"They adored each other," Ollie Carey would say about her husband and Ford, "they were just complete pals." "At night," she would remember for Ford's grandson Dan, "they would sit around this little tiny kitchen with a wood fire going in the stove and drink Mellowwood. They would talk, talk, talk until late in the night and Jack would take notes." They would plan every shot, every move almost. Ford modeled himself on Carey, the respect for traditional manners, the air of genial authority, the withering contempt for pretentiousness, especially on the part of people in the film industry. It was from Carey that he picked up his lifelong habit of referring to each of his films as "a job of work."

Then something happened that permanently blighted the friendship. *Desperate Trails* in 1921 ended their collaboration. Several decades later, "Dobe" Carey, a son whose birth Ford and Carey had celebrated on the ranch with Mellowwood whiskey, would become an important member of Ford's stock company, but the two friends would meet only once or twice a year, to tie one on or to exchange Christmas gifts, and never at the ranch.

Dan Ford suggests that Ford, who moved to Fox at about this time, was jealous of Carey's greater celebrity and his salary at Universal. Dobe, in his otherwise invaluable and candid memoirs,[2] scratches his head and shrugs. In later interviews with McBride, however, he and his mother were more forthcoming. One of the actors in the stock company, Joe Harris, later foreman of the Carey ranch, began making insinuations, as McBride puts it, about Ford's sexuality, and Carey seems to have found them amusing. "This may have been the first time, but it would not be the last, that such gossip was inspired by Ford's sensitivity, his diffidence around women, and his admiration for good-looking he-men."

Carey, McBride suggests, may have resented his replacement as leading man by "younger, brawnier, and more handsome actors." "That was Ford's dream," Dobe Carey says, paraphrasing his father, "to look like what he was directing. Ford was a frustrated athlete and wanted to be the Irish brawler, a big rough-and-tumble guy. He

---

2. Harry Carey Jr., *Company of Heroes: My Life as an Actor in the John Ford Stock Company* (Scarecrow Press, 1994).

wanted to be like Victor McLaglen, but he wasn't, so he created it on the screen."

"Ironically," says McBride, "the gossip about Jack's masculinity was spread only after he finally, and somewhat precipitously, took the plunge into marriage." That was in 1920, to a belle of the Southern gentry, Mary McBryde Smith, whose family plantation had been burned by Sherman, a circumstance which Ford would use to dramatic effect in *Rio Grande*. His own people, back in Portland, were doubtful about her: she was a Presbyterian and a divorced woman. Neither was she welcomed by Ollie and the fellows on the ranch, who recognized a snobbishness which she did little to conceal.

She never visited him on the set or on location, and her friends were not his. One Christmas, he gave her a Rolls-Royce, with a mink in the backseat carrying a note saying, "This ought to shut you up for twenty years." She hired a liveried chauffeur. They had two children, a boy and a girl, who did not grow up to lead happy lives. They shared a pleasant, deliberately unpretentious house in a respectable part of Los Angeles and kept it well stocked with books and bootleg liquor. In the 1930s he had a passionate and improbable affair with Katharine Hepburn. Hepburn, who seems to have had a weakness for mean Irish drunks, urged divorce, but he backed out—a bad case of Catholicism strengthened by cold feet. Mary found out about the affair, and it had the odd but common effect of stabilizing the marriage. She and Jack settled down into a lifelong union, fortified by books and booze.

At the marriage, Irving Thalberg, then an executive at Universal, was one of the witnesses. It was a portent. Thalberg and Ford were rising stars. Ford, in his first years at Fox, was marking time, but at least not all of his early films there were westerns; then, as later, he knew that directors who filmed *only* westerns were a bit déclassé; "shanty," as Mary put it. Then, in 1923, Ford was given his chance.

What he made was in fact a super-western, translated into national epic. *The Iron Horse* is a re-creation of what had truly been one of the heroic feats of America's westward expansion, the building of the Union Pacific Railroad, whose years of brutal and at times dangerous labor came to a triumphant close on May 10, 1869, when a golden spike was driven for the completion of a railroad which now linked the entire continent. Abraham Lincoln had signed the bill of authorization in 1862, in the middle of the Civil War, at the bidding of a group of farsighted and greedy Republicans. But Ford, rather to McBride's liberal regret, has no time for that side of the matter. His Lincoln, like the "Great Heart" in *The Birth of a Nation*, is an image of benign power, strengthened by that eerie gift of divination which permitted him to see through carnage to the future's powerful and united land.

The making of the film was itself an epic, parallel in ways to the story it was filming. It would pass down into cinema legend, as Ford intended that it should. Lefty Hough, one of the property men, would remember that "the Ford outfit was the roughest, goddamndest outfit you ever saw, from the director on downward." They were six weeks on location in Nevada in the dead of winter, very much, McBride reminds us, like the conditions at the time of the actual construction there. The men were well equipped with whiskey and whores. There were tough customers among the extras, but none tougher than Ford himself and they knew it. He displayed a cavalry major's ability to control masses of men by mixing jollity with discipline: there was music on squeeze-box and fiddle, the tunes which would later haunt his sound films—"Red River Valley" and "My Darling Clementine." He maintained a rigorous work schedule, although leaving himself room for improvisations, and he more or less threw away the script.

The building of the railroad is the real subject of the film, but custom—and perhaps commercial instinct—required that he throw in a subordinate, a more "human" story involving a handsome young scout, a heroine, and a white renegade who long before, disguised as an Indian, had killed the scout's father. It is the equivalent of the loves in *The Birth of a Nation* within the Cameron and Stoneman families, but less well integrated into the story. For Dave, the scout, he found a splendid replacement for Carey, a handsome athlete named George O'Brien. O'Brien became a star overnight, and was Ford's leading man well into the early years of talkies.

The Iron Horse was conceived as a national epic, and Ford lays stress upon the role of brawny Irish and Italian workers, many of them Civil War veterans. The Chinese are there as well, but chiefly as comic relief. The Indian tribes, sullenly hostile, are portrayed, as McBride says, "as childlike tools of an evil white man, a noble but simple people inevitably swept away by the forces of 'progress.'" Ford's developing, guilt-haunted feelings about Native Americans (to use a nicety at which he would have snorted) would become central to his internal drama of the West.

As would, of course, his feelings about his own people. There was always Great-Uncle Mike Connolly as an all-purpose ancestor. "I had four uncles in the Civil War," he told one interviewer. "I used to ask my Uncle Mike to tell me about the battle of Gettysburg. All Uncle Mike would say was: 'It was horrible. I went six whole days without a drink.'" Uncle Mike was a laborer on the Union Pacific Railroad when it was built. "By the last reel," as Kevin Brownlow says, "with the reconstruction of the wedding of the rails on 10 May 1869 at Promontory Point, Utah..., there is not the slightest doubt that the rails lie gleaming from sea to sea—and that the Ford company laid every inch of them."[3]

A still from the film offers eerie confirmation: the entire cast, the visiting politicians in their frock coats, the two locomotives, having their group photo taken by two nineteenth-century photographers

---

3. *The West, the War, and the Wilderness* (Knopf, 1979), p. 396.

with their cumbersome equipment. But behind those two, invisible to us of course, are the cameramen from the Fox studios. The past becomes eternally present, or as long as film lasts.

From the isolated triumph of *The Iron Horse*, Ford fell back into line as a director, by now a major one, at a studio which was bringing the factory system to the production of films. Ford's signature upon his was mostly limited to what he called his "grace notes." As the director and film critic Lindsay Anderson says, he was not the victim of commerce. "He seemed able to turn his hand to pretty well anything, and no doubt he was proud, as a practicing professional, to do so." They were jobs of work.

None of the surviving silent films, with the exception perhaps of *Hangman's House*, which happens to be his first film about Ireland, has a large claim on our attention, save as portent. Neither, it seems to me, although Anderson and McBride would disagree, do the early talkies. There are two films about the British army on the Northwest Frontier of India. *The Black Watch* (1929) gives us for the last time a magnificently unclad Myrna Loy, and *Wee Willie Winkie* (1937) offers Shirley Temple at her most depraved. These treats aside, these talkies display Ford's keen—it would become obsessive—fascination with the traditions, loyalties, reticences, and unspoken codes of fighting regiments, and of course their flags. There are three films made with Will Rogers—they got along wonderfully well—and photographed lovingly by the George Schneiderman of *The Iron Horse*. The middle one, *Judge Priest* (1934), sentimentally and craftily re-creates a turn-of-the-century Southern town, rich with oak trees, barber shops, folk wisdom, and a benign, unchallenged racism. In his final films, Ford would have debts to pay off to more minorities than the Cheyenne and the Apache.

Square in the middle of the Thirties, though, he made one extraordinary film, startling in its seeming lack of relationship to what preceded and what followed it. To make *The Informer* (1935), he had to fight against studio resistance both to its brutal and fierce subject and to the expressionist (read "arty") way in which he proposed to tell it. Most major studios had turned it down before he encountered Merian Cooper during his brief tenure at RKO. Taken from a Liam O'Flaherty novel, with O'Flaherty's eccentric politics smoothed out and with a cool, stripped-down shooting script by Dudley Nichols and Ford himself, it was filmed on the RKO lot by the brilliant cameraman Joe August. Victor McLaglen was lured by Ford (with the help of whiskey, legend has it) into a towering performance as Gypo Nolan, a brutish rebel gunman expelled from his "organization" and driven by fear and rage to betray a comrade. The nighttime Dublin through which he moves, created by Ford and August out of painted flats and moody lighting, becomes an exact equivalent of Nolan's guilty anguish. Everything is put to use, from a tattered wanted poster drifting along windy alleys to the hard-faced killer, a version of what Nolan had once been, who executes the sentence of the revolutionary court-martial.

The film should stir us to compassion for Gypo, but instead we are exhilarated by its sheer craftsmanship, its even flow of feeling joined to image. One critic summed up a common response: "Many consider it the greatest talking picture ever made in America. It is as much a landmark in the history of the sound film as *The Birth of a Nation*." But Griffith's film had pointed with certainty toward the future of American films, as Ford's did not. "It was above all," as Lindsay Anderson has written, "a film of precise and pre-determined style and the style was one that ran contrary to the predominantly naturalistic tradition of American conventional cinema." Ford went back to his more conventional jobs of work.

In the subterranean ways of art, though, *The Informer* would exert the power of its example on American films, including those which he himself would make. And it had its own prehistory. In 1926, Fox had imported the great German director F. W. Murnau, the creator of

Nosferatu and *Der Letzte Mann*, and given him free rein for his first American film. What he gave them in return was *Sunrise*, which one film historian called "one of the most beautiful and profoundly influential films ever made in Hollywood." It starred, of all people, Ford's George O'Brien, by now world-famous, and, as *Sunrise* would reveal, a silent-screen actor who was not merely handsome. After Ford had seen the rushes, he gave an interview: "Ford declared that he believed it to be the greatest picture that has been produced."

He was bowled over, as were all the Hollywood directors, by Murnau's way of telling his story, ways which McBride well summarizes: "the hypnotic rhythms of the director's sensuously moving camera, the subtly distorted use of both natural and artificial settings, the complex interplay of light and shade, the stylized acting that makes the characters seem like figures in a fable." He could be writing about *The Informer*, which Ford made eight years later. Ford's immediate reaction had been to apply some of Murnau's techniques boldly (McBride says "slavishly") to his next films, *Four Sons* (1928) and *Hangman's House* of the same year. After that, he lay low until he could for once, like Murnau, have something like total control.

But *Sunrise*, it seems to me, and McBride might not agree, taught Ford something more elemental than technique. It showed him ways in which an artist could use the camera to express his attitudes toward his subject, toward the world, perhaps even, obliquely, toward himself. Despite his wide reading and his cunningly concealed cultivation of spirit, he was all his life painfully unable to express himself in language. Those of his personal letters that have found their way into print might be those of George Babbitt describing the Grand Canyon, and his articles in magazines may have been dictated but surely were ghostwritten. He would always need writers to get his story ideas down in words, and would treat them as hacks. "I think John Ford almost dies because he can't write," said Nunnally Johnson, one of the best of them. "It just runs him nuts, that he has thoughts and ideas and has never trained himself to set them down on paper." It takes more than training.

What he had trained himself to use was a camera, beginning back in 1914, when he was his brother Frank's dogsbody, and all you needed was the camera, a bit of real estate, and a rudimentary sense of composition. As the tricks, as the technique developed, he developed along with them, but without seeing any reason to call the product other than a job of work. He and Harry Carey discovered together how a gesture, a stance, a way of walking, if the camera is allowed to rest quietly upon it, can express fairly complex feelings, even in a job of work. But films like those by Murnau showed him that the expression of feeling through light, shadow, cutting, and rhythm was what he had had in mind for the past few years. "Cinema," Erich Rohmer has written of Murnau, "organizes space as music organizes time, taking that total possession of space that music takes of time." By the time he saw those rushes of *Sunrise*, Ford knew that, although he would have called it "horseshit."

In 1934, he bought at a Depression price a 106-foot ketch which he rechristened the *Araner*. It would claim his life away from the camera and a major portion of his income. She took a professional skipper and a crew of six. "It was terribly expensive," Mary Ford said in her equable way, "but it was our life." So it was, at least as much as was their home in the hills, but when the family was ashore it served other needs. Occasionally, other women were allowed aboard: there is a photograph of Katharine Hepburn, sitting at Ford's feet, and smiling her Bryn Mawr smile. And occasionally, when he was planning a film, he would sail down the Mexican coast or out to sea, alone or with one of his writers.

But the *Araner* was basically a man's world. He only allowed on board men he trusted, and especially members of that stock company he had been building since the days of Cheyenne Harry Carey, slowly adding to it as the years accumulated them—Farrell MacDonald, the eternal bartender, and Joe Pennick, the eternal buck sergeant. George O'Brien would be asked aboard, but not too often, and a young cowboy star whom he had discovered as a prop boy and rechristened as John Wayne. Wayne had been a hit in his first film, Raoul Walsh's *The Big Trail* (1930), but during the Thirties he had been making B and C westerns on Poverty Row. Ford himself had not made a western since a silent with George O'Brien in 1926.

On the *Araner*, surrounded by raucous pals and toadies, Ford could afford to get slobbering, falling-down drunk. By the time he bought the *Araner*, he had become a drunk of legendary proportions and Hollywood knew it. Never on the set, of course, but as soon as a film was a wrap, he would be off on a bender, mean, abusive, and out of his skull. The meanness was by no means solely a function of his drinking. He had a second reputation for verbal cruelty, especially of inferiors, especially of actors, and for sly, humiliating practical jokes. Real actors like Thomas Mitchell and John Carradine wouldn't put up with it—nor would cowboy actors who had been real ranchhands, like Ben Johnson. Henry Fonda summed it up for them: "A son of a bitch who happens to be a genius."

But the members of the permanent cast, those whom he created and shaped, John Wayne and Ward Bond are instances, became, literally, his creatures, and he would kick their butts when the mood seized him. His uncritical admirers (McBride is not one) will claim that he was making them better actors. You can hear that argument in any night court.

Raoul Walsh's *The Big Trail* is a beautiful film, and the very young John Wayne looks great in it, like Fenimore Cooper's youthful hero, but the movie was a commercial failure. Shortly after that, Ford stopped talking to him, and no one knows why. He was exiled from the *Araner*. Perhaps Ford was angered that his discovery had played a lead for Walsh. Then one day Wayne was let back on board, but he continued to make C westerns, like *The Three Mesquiteer* series. "To this goddam day," Wayne told Ford's grandson, Dan, "I don't know why he wouldn't speak to me for years."

Ford's apologists claim that the young man needed seasoning, and certainly he got it. Wayne was more serious about his acting than is often realized. He had a strong cinematic presence, as he was well aware, but what he lacked as yet was the kind of personality that would carry him from one western to the next, and distinguish him from the innumerable Tim McCoys and Bob Steeles and Ken Maynards. He studied ways of walking, of holding himself, ways of generating his distinctive speech patterns with their broken rhythms. We still hear him calling someone "Pilgrim," or telling him, "That'll be the day." In the last scene of *The Searchers*, Wayne grasps hold of his forearm, in a gesture strongly reminiscent of Harry Carey, but he did not need Ford to coach him, as legend would have it. He had studied Harry Carey. Ford knew that Wayne "moved like a dancer," and so did Wayne. And, as Dan Ford says, his grandfather "knew that Wayne had the phenomenal, almost pathological drive that it took to survive in Hollywood."

Ford gave him his chance one day in 1937, as the *Araner* was under way. After a full day and night of cat-and-mouse, he told Wayne that he wanted him to play the Ringo Kid in a western called *Stagecoach*, his first in thirteen years. Wayne would be in for some ugly months of taunts and humiliations, but the film would make him a star, although it would take critics years to realize that he was a remarkable actor. As for Ford, he was ready to make the films by which he is remembered.

Frederick Jackson Turner's speech before the American Historical Association on "The Significance of the Frontier in American History" was delivered, as McBride reminds us, in 1893, the year before Ford was born. And he goes on to quote the key, familiar sentences. "American social development," Turner told his audience, "has been continually beginning over again on the frontier. This perpetual rebirth, this fluidity of American life, this expansion westward with its new opportunities, its continuous touch with the simplicity of primitive society, furnish the forces dominating American character. The true point of view in the history of this nation is not the Atlantic coast, it is the Great West." But "the frontier has gone, and with its going has closed the first period of American history."

Even effete easterners, on the Atlantic coast, knew not only that the frontier was closed, but that with its closing a dream had come hurtling against the actuality of that other ocean. The dream itself had not been closed but only its transient investiture in a movement across prairies and over mountains. Henceforth, it would exist in realms at once more hospitable and more treacherous, in the dreams of American writers.

For confirmation, we may look almost anywhere, into our most familiar texts, from *Huckleberry Finn* to *On the Road*, from Whit- man to Hart Crane and Scott Fitzgerald:

> Its vanished trees, the trees that had made way for Gatsby's house, had once pandered in whispers to the last and greatest of all human dreams; for a transitory enchanted moment man must have held his breath in the presence of this continent. . . .

Nick Carraway is wrong, though. Only the trees had vanished, not the dream, which has given him the very shape of his words. It is one of the largest of American themes, but we have learned to read and to accept it in our written literature. Perhaps, though, we have not learned to read it in our films, and specifically in the films of John Ford, his western films centrally, but also in other films which he has deliberately given continental resonances—*The Grapes of Wrath*, *They Were Expendable*.

"I knew the railroad was coming," Frederic Remington says in examining the purpose behind his western art. "I saw men already swarming into the land. I knew the derby hat, the smoking chimneys, the cord-binder and the thirty-day note were upon us in a restless surge. I knew the wild riders and vacant land were about to vanish forever." Remington is a specific and often-acknowledged influence on Ford: compare his version of Custer's stand with Ford's in *Fort Apache*. But his word "railroad" can conjure up a different image. There comes a moment in *The Iron Horse* in which Davy, the young scout, stands alone, looking along the completed track. Steel, money, and back-breaking labor have conquered the wilderness and soon Davy will be out of work. There will be no more need for scouts. One of Ford's last westerns, *The Man Who Shot Liberty Valance* (1962), opens with Tom Doniphon, once a celebrated gunfighter, quick as legend, lying dead in a pauper's coffin. It closes with a railway train moving eastward. The West was vanishing, even as dream, from Ford's vision and from ours.

Andrew Sarris, ever one for the *mot juste*, has called Ford "America's cinematic poet laureate," but we don't have poet laureates, thank God, not even Walt Whitman. Sure enough though, McBride speaks of Ford as having, as Whitman had, "a natural allegiance with the spirit of the American common people." McBride has written the best life of him we are likely to have, and his judgments of the films, his ways of telling us about them, are invariably intelligent and sensitive. Of the works of this astonishing artist, though, not enough can ever be said or written.

Ford, it seems to me, is a major American artist, using, as Mark Twain did, a popular form to express a private vision—a characteristically American circumstance. His westerns form an arc, beginning with *The Iron Horse* and passing through *Stagecoach*, the first of the great ones, "the ideal example," as André Bazin has said, "of the maturity of a style brought to classic perfection...like a wheel, so perfectly made that it remains in equilibrium on its axis in any position." The arc sets with *Liberty Valance*, darkened by time, almost at nightfall.

No image is more common in Ford's westerns than that of a wagon wheel, lost or abandoned, set upright against the horizon, or more emblematic.

He had been making westerns since his early days in silent films, so many one- and two-reelers that he could never remember them all. But as he established himself in his profession, his "trade" as he called it, he had moved on to other material. *Stagecoach* was the first western movie in thirteen years, and the first one in sound. From now on, though, his most significant films would be westerns. Taken together, they compose a profound, contradictory, troublesome image of America, of our history and our landscape. It becomes, in the final films, a melancholy image.

Stagecoach's classicism, its scrupulous adherence to tradition, is present everywhere—narrative, characters, and, especially, relationship of character to setting. Ford had discovered Monument Valley, on the Utah–Arizona border, and would use it for most of these westerns—thirty miles of mesa carved by winds into immense and foreboding towers of sandstone, abrupt and absolute. In their very density of effect they are not typical of the desert, but rather, as a prism does, they force together the desert's spacious and humbling cruelties. Monument Valley has been, as it were, premythicized. So closely are the valley and *Stagecoach* held together in memory that it comes as a shock to discover how little of the movie was shot there, and almost none of the scenes involving the principals were. Even the shot that brings John Wayne, the Ringo Kid, into the film, what Joseph McBride in his biography of Ford calls "one of the great star entrances in film history," was done in Hollywood.

You get what you see in *Stagecoach*, without the ironies, the sadnesses, the shadows of Ford's later westerns. A coachful of strangers sets out from one Arizona frontier town to another in New Mexico called Lordsburg—a whore named Dallas (Claire Trevor), who has been kicked out of town; Doc Boone (Thomas Mitchell), a rum-soaked Civil War veteran given to misquoting Shakespeare; a pregnant army wife, Lucy Mallory (Louise Platt), from the aristocratic but defeated South; a timid but not cowardly whiskey salesman (Donald Meek); Hatfield (John Carradine), once a Confederate officer but now a cardsharp; an absconding banker. Atop ride Andy Devine as the driver and George Bancroft as the sheriff, keeping an eye out for the Ringo Kid. The Kid has broken out of prison to confront his brother's murderers, the Plummers, who are holed up in Lordsburg. Driver and sheriff have a sneaking affection for Ringo and so will we.

Stagecoach rests upon the visual contrast of immensity and confinement—the vast, grotesque desert and the passengers locked within their separate pasts and their fear of an Apache war party. They are all stock characters, drawn from the warehouse of types which westerns had been accumulating. Hatfield has been lifted bodily from Bret Harte, but the voice and mannerisms, the air of deadly and self-assured hauteur, are all Carradine. God be with the days when the movies gave us supporting actors like Carradine and Mitchell: you knew where you were with those fellows. Ford rarely seeks to go beyond the stereotypes. Rather, he brightens and sharpens them, setting them against one another in ways that can pierce.

Quietly, seemingly casually, he establishes contrasts of gesture which bespeak differences of spirit. Hatfield pours water for the genteel Lucy Mallory from the shared canteen into a silver cup bearing the crest of his lost Virginia plantation, but "forgets" about the other "lady," as Ringo calls Dallas. The contrast in ways of being a gentleman is devastating.

Even Ringo had come originally from the property box of the genre—the good badman—but Ford was already at work transforming Wayne into one of his most important symbols, an image of one kind of American, and therefore, perhaps, of an aspect of America itself. But he simultaneously transformed the actor into something rather different from that. As Joseph McBride puts it, "The combination of gentleness and authority Wayne brought to the role of Ringo represented Ford's idealized image of himself, an image the director artfully created on-screen, but had trouble incarnating in reality."

During the filming, Ford had borne down hard on Wayne, subjecting him to a barrage of insults and taunts, and to every physical humiliation short of flensing. Claire Trevor offers the usual explanation: "He was trying to take away Duke's bad habits." At twenty-nine, Wayne was already too old for the part. Ten years earlier, when he was playing the part of the frontier scout in Raoul Walsh's *The Big Trail*, he would have been perfect—young, lithe, and, well, graceful. But here he does just fine, and he would go on to do much better. Back in the silent days, when he was making two-reel and four-reel westerns, Ford, an eloquent but inarticulate creator, had found ways of using a surrogate self so as to place himself within the narratives of his films—first Harry Carey as "Cheyenne Harry" and then George O'Brien. Over the years, as they aged together, Wayne would prove the perfect fit.

He would have been hopeless, though, as Tom Joad in *The Grapes of Wrath*, the film that Ford made a year later.

McBride remarks that *The Grapes of Wrath* is rare among Ford's films in confronting a major contemporary social issue:

> Ford's films had begun to turn increasingly to the past, to historical issues with more distant resonance for his audience. Ford's cinema was a cinema of memory and meditation rather than a meeting-hall for action.

That turning was already well under way. Certainly the plight of the Okies and their migration to the cruel orange groves of California offered the kind of material that was praised as "torn from today's headlines," and would call for a harsh, accusatory style, and that Ford's scriptwriter, Nunnally Johnson, liberated from the godawful cadences of John Steinbeck's prose and delivered as a lean, direct story. But the film is shaped visually by Ford's other collaborator, the great cameraman Gregg Toland, who a year later would be filming *Citizen Kane*. He and Ford were made for each other. Toland rarely employs here what McBride calls "the extreme, show-offy deep focus" for which he would soon be famous. Ford would say jubilantly that there was "absolutely nothing to photograph, not *one* beautiful thing in there—just sheer, good photography."

So good in fact that Ford was able to mythicize his story. It seems today not about wrongs that were still being suffered by close to a million migrants from the Southwest, but rather to be set in some realm of the imagination which is sensitive to history but indifferent to time. The early reels in which Tom Joad (Henry Fonda) returns from prison to the farm of his people is rich with the signifying detail of the Dust Bowl, but they reach back in time beyond themselves.

Ford was struck by the resemblances between the dispossessed Okies and the Irish evicted by their landlords—and by history itself—in the Great Famine, the subject of his friend Liam O'Flaherty's 1937 novel *Famine*. The ravaged landscape of Tom Joad's Oklahoma bears uncanny echoes of the abandoned famine villages of Connaught and Munster. So too does the migration to California resonate against memories of the coffin ships headed across the Atlantic.

The myths thicken the texture. Tom Joad, as I have written elsewhere, "is like the Irish rebel son—sweet-natured but quick-tempered and capable of murderous rages."[4] Casey, the wild, eloquent preacher, drunk on the language of the book, is modeled by Ford and John

---

4. "The Irish in John Ford's Films," in *The Irish in America*, edited by Michael Coffey and Terry Galway (Hyperion, 1997).

Carradine upon the hedge priests and prophecy men who tagged along with the Irish rebels. There were other shadowy people in the recesses of Ford's imagination. Not tough Irishmen alone, but also peasants from China and Italy who had built the Union Pacific. America itself had been built out of migrations, across the Alleghenies and the Missouri and over the Rockies into the promised land of orange groves and gold. In time, he would come to meditate upon those "trails of tears," the great countermigrations of cheated and harried Indian tribes of the mountains and plains, Cheyenne and Sioux and Apache.

Ford's own war was a distinguished and often dangerous one, beginning with a Purple Heart earned during the Battle of Midway. He and the photographic unit which he had created before Pearl Harbor held naval rank but reported directly to William Donovan's OSS. He went ashore on D-Day, and was reported as "a great inspiration in his total disregard of danger in order to get the job done"—an accidental echo of his lifelong description of his films as "jobs of work." He left the navy with the rank of captain and began campaigning for an admiral's stars.

During the war and because of strong navy insistence, he made only one commercial film, *They Were Expendable*, a fictionalized account of the torpedo boat squadron led by Lt. John Bulkeley (Robert Montgomery) in the disastrous first months of the Pacific war. Ford disliked it intensely, then and later. It is hard to see why. The mood of the film, battle sequences aside, is reflective and melancholy. A somewhat incredulous James Agee wrote that "visually and in detail, and in nearly everything that he does with people, it is John Ford's finest movie."

Throughout the filming, he had been in a state of disgust with Montgomery's costar, John Wayne. Wayne had turned out to be what in Ford's day was called a slacker. He allowed his employer, Republic, to wangle for him deferment after deferment, once murmuring that "I better go do some touring—I feel the draft breathing down my neck." Ford still needed him, though, and he still needed Ford. Ford had made him a star, but he craved superstardom, becoming in the cold war years an icon of proto-fascist politics. The relationship between the two men would become tragicomic, a fit subject for a treatise on the magic and mystery of film.

Ford's own swerve to the political right in later life, and at times what seemed like the fringe right, is a matter of far greater interest. Wayne and his Ford company buddy Ward Bond were products of Southern California's junk culture, a kind of muscle beach of the mind. Ford, on the other hand, came from other roots; he was a man of wide and various reading, whose tough-guy mannerisms concealed complex and, as he well knew, contradictory attitudes. To the end, he retained an admiration (he would have called it Irish) for the good badman, the reckless gunfighter with generous instincts. A childhood in one of New England's Irish ghettos had taught him to side with the poor against the rich. But that same background had given him a reverence for tradition, fierce loyalties, the sacramentalizing of flags, battles, styles of masculinity.

The proof rests in the films—his greatest, it seems to me—which he made during the dark years of the Fifties. Critics with high-powered lenses have, I am sure, discovered strands of rabid reaction—paternalism in particular. But the remarkable truth is that these films, bearing upon the "wars" between the army and the Indian tribes of the far West, are extraordinarily balanced in their presentation of a many-sided tragedy. And of none is this more true than the earliest of them, *Fort Apache*, which sets the tone for the ones that follow.

First, though, he had to make a film owed from before the war to Twentieth Century Fox. When *My Darling Clementine* was released in 1946, it was welcomed as a straightforward western, this time one about Wyatt Earp and the gunfight at the O.K. Corral.

Ford claimed to have known Earp, and he probably did. The old man had hung around the silent-film studios, a thin-haired, neatly dressed geezer who in the olden days had been a policeman in Dodge City and then a deputy marshal in Tombstone, Arizona, and had gone on to be a prospector in Alaska, a real estate speculator in California, a prize-fight referee. He had made a reputation throughout the West, faded now, because of thirty seconds of lethal gunfire in or near Tombstone's O.K. Corral on October 26, 1881. Before his death, he decided to "set the record straight" by telling his story to a western buff named Stuart Lake. Lake burnished the legend of the town-tamer who had civilized Wichita, Dodge, and finally Tombstone. After his death, two films were made about him, one with George O'Brien and one with Randolph Scott. "Shit," Ford said of them, "I can do better than that."

Ford knew that the battle at the O.K. Corral had not been one between good and evil. It was a gunfight between a bunch of rustlers and stagecoach robbers, the Clanton bunch, and a gang of gamblers, brothel keepers, and dance-hall enforcers, the Earp brothers and their murderous pal, Doc Holliday, a tubercular dentist with a reckless disregard for his own life and that of others. The Earps, known at times to fellow townsmen as "the fighting pimps," possessed a variety of town and territorial badges, behind which they intended to avenge a murdered brother. As a peace officer, Earp was well above the average, phlegmatic and sensible, but he was inclined to confuse the law with his code of personal honor. That, however, was not the movie Ford intended to make: the nation was not yet ready for the *noir* western, although it would be soon.

Toward the end of his life, in one of his final westerns, Ford has a newspaper editor say: "When the legend becomes fact, print the legend." It has the hollow ring of most pseudo-profundities. As both a creator and a celebrant of our folk imagination, he was at work in a time when he could draw upon the incalculable resources of our most powerful creative engine. It is the Earp created by Ford and Henry Fonda which lingers in the mind, laconic, self-possessed, courteous, sardonic, respectful of the law within limits, and a dead shot with a pistol or shotgun.

Fonda gives a superb performance. Ford seems to have thought of him as the image of a kind of American equal to Wayne in heroic qualities and yet strikingly different in tone, movement, attitude toward experience and self. It was a type common on our frontier, or at least in its literature, as far back as 1902, when Owen Wister wrote *The Virginian*. In Ford's *Young Mr. Lincoln* (1939), Fonda played Lincoln as a variant of the type, a prudent fellow for all his joshing ways, looking every gift horse in the mouth, ready to cheat a bit at the tug-of-war. Of course, there was something else about him: our knowledge of what he would become, a man almost sacred. Scoff if you will: it is *our* mythology, not Lincoln's.

In Ford's Tombstone, Earp and his brothers are heroes and Old Man Clanton and his slack-jawed sons are nearly motiveless dispensers of evil. Walter Brennan, who like other professionally trained actors came to loathe Ford, makes of Old Man Clanton a compact bundle of cunning and insane rages, who disciplines his sons with a bullwhip. "When you draw a gun," he tells one of them, "kill a man."

The movie, as everyone in the movie house knew, is moving inexorably toward the O.K. Corral, but Ford takes his time getting there. We get to know the town, its barber shop, its hotel and restaurant, a church under construction, a livery stable, a saloon. And a gentler Earp who remembers, as do his brothers, a childhood, churches, schools, and civility. There must be a jail but we never get to see it. Earp seems to conduct business while sitting lazily on the hotel's long porch, greeting town worthies, and telling crooked gamblers to be on the afternoon stage.

A second plot develops. Clementine Carter (Cathy Downs), a beautiful nurse from the East, comes looking for her fiancé, who is now a poker-table gunman, but had once been a brilliant young surgeon from Harvard or someplace like that, who has carried to the

West the corrosive knowledge of his own fatal illness and a mysterious self-loathing. Meanwhile, he has been consoling himself with Linda Darnell disguised as a Mexican Indian saloon entertainer named Chihuahua. Left to his own devices, he controls the gambling, kills disagreeable visitors, and impresses Earp by quoting Shakespeare from memory.

The easiness of pace allows for one of the loveliest sequences in Ford's cinema. There is a Sunday morning dance on the floor of what will one day be a church. Clementine and Earp walk to it from the hotel, down the long street of the barebones town in its Sunday light and quiet. Then, with the other dancers drawing back, Earp leads his "lady fair," as a church elder calls her, in a dance that (on his part) combines grace and awkwardness, one which Fonda had invented for *Young Mr. Lincoln*. It is an exquisite moment, hushed, tender, emotionally complete.

The central relationship, though, is that between Earp and Doc Holliday. As a perceptive critic noted, "Wyatt is one of the few Fordian heroes allowed a friendship with a man who is clearly his equal." Victor Mature plays Holliday with great effectiveness: he was an intelligent actor cursed by destiny with the face and muscles of a debauched lifeguard. Here he is a Holliday turned murderous and suicidal through self-contempt and self-pity. He answers to an aspect of Earp that only McBride seems to have caught, "signs of dandyism and cold fanaticism that Ford treats with some ambivalence."

The West existed spatially for Ford as Monument Valley, but there was also a temporal West, which can be placed with equal precision. It begins with the transcontinental railroad, which was planned during the Civil War and which simultaneously asserted the nation's ultimate union even as it spelled the ultimate end of the West as a wilderness Eden. Ford's first major film, *The Iron Horse* (1924), provided images of both aspects, the final, golden spike being driven in, and the scout Davy looking along the track which spells the end of his calling. The end of what once were called "the Indian wars," is nowadays taken to be the massacre at Wounded Knee in 1891, an event so late in the day as to seem anachronistic.

Ford, though, chooses to end his narrative of the West with *Cheyenne Autumn* (1964) and the astonishing march of the Cheyenne some 1,500 miles from their reservation to their ancestral home in the Dakotas. The Civil War was Ford's background, and the Indian wars both foreground and text. The notable exceptions are *My Darling Clementine* (1946) and *The Man Who Shot Liberty Valance* (1962), a sunset film, in which the admission of a territory to statehood completes the process begun by the railroad. Either the plots of these late westerns or else specific episodes and tones are drawn from the major events of those terrible years—the Sand Creek and Washita massacres by the army in 1864 and 1868, the destruction of Custer's cavalry at the Little Big Horn in 1876, the bad-faith negotiations with the Apache chief Cochise, the army's hunt for Geronimo, the final Apache raider. Ford liked to say, "I've killed more Indians than Custer, Beecher and Chivington put together," and he was taken at his word, the growling word of a Hollywood director stuck in the past and sharing its brutal prejudices. He was in fact an artist, although a deeply flawed one, with an instinct for the tragic even as he swerved away from it.

What is now called the cavalry trilogy—*Fort Apache* (1948), *She Wore a Yellow Ribbon* (1949), and *Rio Grande* (1950)—was never intended as such, but the three are held together by time, setting, characters, and theme. *She Wore a Yellow Ribbon* has a thinner narrative than the others, but it is a stunningly beautiful film. It is the only one in color, and it seems to radiate those colors so that in memory they touch the other two. For all three, Ford worked closely with the paintings and engravings of Frederic Remington and Charles Russell, and from their art, as McBride says, "and his own painterly eye for composition and movement, he developed a Western iconography distinctly his own, instantly identifiable in distant long shots of lines of riders outlined against the horizon, swift tracking shots of charging troopers arrayed in depth...."

"Who better than an Irishman," Ford asked, "could understand the Indians, while still being stirred by tales of the US Cavalry? We were on both sides of the epic." The crucial word here, however loosely it is being used, is "epic." He sees this historical conflict in terms that are essentially aesthetic, and thereby takes on the burdens as well as the strengths of that way of seeing.

All three films deal with the army's war against the Apaches, but spend much of their time, as we have come with him to expect, creating a thickly detailed sense of life in an isolated military outpost in the immediately post–Civil War years. They never spell out the historical truth, which is that the railroads, the various Homestead Acts, the greed of prospectors, and the safety of settlers required that the tribes be "pacified," removed from their vast hunting grounds, and herded onto reservations. There, they live at the mercy of corrupt agents and cynical politicians, cheated, swindled, and otherwise degraded. Occasionally, they will break out of the reservation. This will be termed "another Indian uprising" and the army will be called into the field.

In these films, it is once again a small, professional army, drastically cut back from Civil War days. Promotions will once again be slow. Even the dashing George Armstrong Custer, a general at twenty-three, has had to accept peacetime rank as lieutenant colonel. Similarly, *Fort Apache*'s Owen Thursday, during the war a distinguished major general, had had to accept the same rank, together with command of a sandy Arizona garrison. Custer had no intention of letting his career languish, and neither does Thursday. Their only hope would be through a splashy victory over the savages. Thursday is thought to be based on Custer, but there the resemblance ends. Custer came from solid Wisconsin farming stock, a self-infatuated show-off who finished at the bottom of his class. Thursday comes from genteel and scholarly Boston, and has studied the tactics of Caesar and Bonaparte.

It is an army rich in codes and rituals, traditions recently invented. Even in this outpost, tradition and a respect for hierarchy governs conduct. All three officers are veterans of the war—Thursday himself and his two captains, Kirby York (John Wayne) and Sam Collingwood (George O'Brien). The sergeants too are veterans, save for a Johnny Reb who had held a Confederate commission. O'Rourke (Ward Bond), the top sergeant, had been an officer himself, in the Irish 69th, an impressive man, sure of his worth whatever rank he holds. The buck sergeants, with Victor McLaglen as ringleader, drink to stupefaction, but sober up when duty calls. The wives on the post are held together in sisterly affection, while staying within the boundaries of caste. Ford tests these boundaries by bringing to the post Sergeant O'Rourke's son, a West Point lieutenant who falls in love with Thursday's daughter.

Thursday regards Apaches as half-naked barbarians: he had seen a handful of them while traveling to the post. "If you saw them," York says, "they weren't Apaches." York knows that they are formidable warriors, brave and sneaky. Thursday's inability to believe his subordinate brings disaster. Cochise has led his Mescaleroes off the reservation and has begun raiding. Thursday allows York to ride out, alone and unarmed, and to promise Cochise that the terms of an earlier treaty will be kept. But Thursday dismisses promises made to savages and breaks the treaty by planning a trap which will earn him a reputation as "The Man Who Brought Cochise Back." But it is Thursday and his regiment who are caught in a trap from which there are few survivors. He himself is killed, recognizing too late his arrogant folly.

There is a final sequence, set a few years later. York, who now holds the command and is about to lead the pursuit of Geronimo, says to visiting journalists about Thursday, who has become a national hero: "No man died more gallantly. No man brought more honor on his regiment." Then, with Lt. O'Rourke, his adjutant, he rides out of the fort. Young Mrs. O'Rourke, Thursday's daughter, takes her place on the balcony with the other women. The band plays "The Girl I Left Behind Me," as it had for Thursday.

In the context supplied by the scene, York's "noble lie" is being affirmed, by the film and probably by Ford himself. When questioned by Peter Bogdanovich on the point, years later, Ford replied, "Yes—because I think it's good for the country." Clearly, McBride argues, we should trust the tale here, though, and not the teller. In Ford's case, teller and tale knew all about each other.

The Indian stands at the center of Ford's West, enigmatic, mute, doomed. He was easier on Indians in earlier films, when they were trailing along behind Union Pacific tracklayers, or, as in *Stagecoach*, a silent line on a ridge. In towns, their dusty jackets and blankets mock a distant, flamboyant freedom. Wyatt Earp kicks a drunken Indian out of Tombstone and tells Chihuahua to get back to her reservation. But Ford knew that Indians were the best light cavalry and that within their unknowable world bravery was honored and rewarded with titles, insignia, distinctions; feats of skill under fire were applauded. Very much, in fact, as with the United States Cavalry. History, though, was on the white man's side, a pair of aces tucked up a blue-clothed sleeve. Ford's conservatism, a kind of fatalism, begins with his acceptance of such iron laws.

Eight years after *Fort Apache* he made a film about the races, white and red, which is unquestionably one of the greatest American films ever made. *The Searchers* (1956) begins with the return of Ethan Edwards (John Wayne) to a Texas farm in 1868. He is wearing a Confederate overcoat with sergeant's stripes and carrying a Confederate saber. He is greeted by his brother Aaron, Aaron's wife, Martha, and their children. He has presents for the children—a locket for Lucy, the saber for Ben, for little Debbie a medal which the quick-of-eye can recognize as earned by service in Mexico under Maximilian. But for the adopted boy, Martin, grown now, the one-eighth Cherokee survivor of a wagon attack, he has only the remark that he is "dark as a half-breed." Martha, as she tenderly brushes Ethan's cavalry coat, lets us know that secretly she loves him, and he her. In the long, star-crowded evening, Ethan sits alone on the step of the long veranda.

The next morning, the men of this and neighboring ranches are lured away, and in their absence Comanches raid the Edwards ranch. Aaron and Ben are slaughtered, Martha raped and killed, the girls abducted. Exhausted, a pursuing posse turns back, but Ethan and Martin set out on a journey which will take them years, in the course of which Martin discovers that Ethan's racial obsession has reached the point of madness.

A fair swatch of the film is shot in Monument Valley, but the search carries the camera from Canada to Mexico, following faint hints, false trails, the horses wading through the blizzards of Montana and riding the sun-baked deserts of the Southwest. Every year or so, a letter drifts home to their neighbors, the Jorgensons, to whose daughter, Laurie, Martin is somewhat engaged.

Once, in the snow country, the searchers encounter a herd of buffalo, and Ethan kills as many of them as he can, shot after shot into blundering, heavy-hided fur. Why that many? Martin asks. General Philip Sheridan, commander of the army's Department of the Southwest, could have explained to him that this was "destroying the Indians' commissary. Let them kill, skin, and sell until the buffalo are exterminated." Ethan's eyes give the same answer, but with the fierce, banked fires of savage hatred.

Now Martin knows all of the story. If Debbie has not been killed, as, we have learned, Lucy was years before, she is now the squaw of some Comanche brave and Ethan has been searching for her, not to rescue her but to kill her. Martin, a man of mixed blood, has two missions now, to save her from a Comanche and from a white man.

She is in fact the woman of the war chief Scar, and the two men briefly confront each other in a Comanche village somewhere in Mexico. Ethan and Martin are posing as traders, but Scar knows who they are. He is an adversary clever as Ethan and like him sardonic and relentless. Two of Scar's sons have been killed by white men, and now he takes many white scalps in vengeance. He shows Ethan some of them, strung out along a lance held by an impassive Debbie. Ethan and Scar are locked together, and as McBride wrote in 1974: "As the search progresses, it becomes increasingly difficult to appreciate the difference between Ethan's heroism and Scar's villainy." Despite a canyon-deep separation of cultures, the two are locked together by similar obsessions.[5]

Sometime later (months? years?), Ethan and Martin watch the cavalry riding down on a Comanche village, splashing through ice-flecked water, pennons flying, bugles sounding. And we witness the attack itself, the troopers riding past rows of tepees, slashing their sabers down on women and children, the bugles drowned now by screams of terror and pain. It becomes difficult to appreciate the differences between the two peoples.

At the cavalry post, they go one by one through a group of rescued white women—dazed, half-insane, one of them driven forever back into her childhood, clutching her doll and grinning lewdly. As Ethan, leaving, turns around for a last look, the camera twists suddenly toward him for a close-up. It is a shadowed, blood-chilling face, frozen beyond humanity.

But Ethan's madness, in his case fortified perhaps by his knowledge of his own adulterous love and by his discovery of her raped and tormented body in his brother's burned ranch house, is but an extension of emotions felt by most Americans. "Fetch *what* home?" Laurie

---

5. Joseph McBride and Michael Wilmington, *John Ford* (Secker and Warburg, 1974; Da Capo, 1975).

Jorgenson screams at Martin as he sets out on the final stretch of search. "The leavings of Comanche bucks, sold time and again to the highest bidder, with savage brats of their own.... Do you know what Ethan will do if he has a chance? He'll put a bullet in her brain. I tell you, Martha would want him to."

In the climax, Texas Rangers and US Cavalry ride together into Scar's village and Scar is killed. Not by Ethan, though, or by the Rangers, but by Martin in the course of rescuing Debbie. But when at last Ethan encounters them, seemingly bent upon Debbie's murder, he instead swings her high into the air, as he has in her childhood, and says, "Let's go home, Debbie." McBride finds this transformation "convincing and deeply satisfying." I wish I did.

Ethan's moment of transforming fulfillment had come minutes earlier when, finding that he had been robbed of his vengeance, he kneels beside Scar's body and takes out his scalping knife. When next we see him, very abruptly, he is outside the tepee, dazed, not fully aware of where he is or what he has been doing. His face is one that we have not seen before; unfocused, drained, transfigured. It is the face of orgasm.

Race and sex are lashed together in his mind, as in the mind of virginal young Laurie Jorgenson and perhaps in the mind of America. Perhaps, though, as McBride and most viewers feel, redemption has come through this memory of Debbie's gentle childhood. It is pretty to think so, as Jake tells Brett.

Finally, the door of the nurturing Jorgenson home stands open for Debbie and Laurie and Martin. But Ethan stands outside, somewhere south of nowhere, and the door mysteriously closes on him.

Ford said his goodbyes to the westerns, almost formally, in 1962's *The Man Who Shot Liberty Valance*, a shadowy, perverse, morally ambiguous film, which both reaffirms and questions the moral and aesthetic values of the genre. André Bazin would have called it a baroque western, and the old man would have agreed with him.

It opens with the arrival of a railroad train, somewhere around 1910, in the town of Shinbone in a southwestern state which a distinguished passenger had helped bring into being. Senator Ransom Stoddard (James Stewart) carries his fame and his importance easily, as he does his gray hair and the first beginnings of a paunch almost hidden by his white vest. He carries less easily his celebrity from years past, one on which all else has been built. He first became famous back in Shinbone's wild and woolly days as the man who shot down in a gunfight a mad-dog killer named Liberty Valance.

He and his wife Hallie (Vera Miles) have come back to town for the burial of an old friend, whom the town itself had forgotten. Tom Doniphon (John Wayne) had been a celebrity himself in those days, a horse dealer from down in Picketwire country, the sort of man with whom you didn't argue, fair-minded and courteous, but with six-gun skills learned in dangerous places. He hadn't worn that gun in recent decades, though, drifting downward to become one of the town's drunks. His pine-coffin funeral is to be charged to county expenses. The undertaker may not know it, but he is burying a man of honor and repute. And the man whom Hallie had loved in secret through the years.

Back in territorial days, Shinbone had been an ugly cluster of saloons, cantinas, eating-houses, and jails. Law had been replaced by lawlessness itself, in the person of Valance, a sadistic bully, duded up with silver doodads on his vest and wielding a steel-tipped quirt (Lee Marvin). Stoddard arrives in town, a fish-out-of-water young lawyer from the East, but on his way Valance robs him, horsewhips him, and shreds his law books. With the help of a quizzical Tom Doniphon, Stoddard tries to start a school and meanwhile earns his keep by washing dishes in the eating-house where Hallie, Doniphon's intended, waits on table.

All this, and most of what follows, we learn in a long flashback— an unusual device for Ford. Wayne and Stewart are men well into their fifties, Wayne with an already notorious hairpiece—and in the flashback Ford uses neither makeup nor lighting to compensate for this. And that is essential to the kind of film this is. It is a memory film about remembered youth and a youthful heroism. Wayne was by now fully established in his "real-life" role as an heroic icon of the political right, but the curious fact is that we don't see him doing anything heroic. We see him discover the horsewhipped Stoddard on the roadside. We see him face down Liberty in the eating-house, and we know he is the faster draw, but the gunfight we expect never takes place. Far from it. In the closing moments of the flashback (or rather, in the plural, flashbacks) it is a trembling Ransom Stoddard, wearing his long, absurd dishwasher's apron, who faces certain death from Liberty's gun. But it is Doniphon who kills Liberty, firing a rifle from night-time shadows. A well-timed shot, but not the stuff of which legends are made. Ironically, one is made: Stoddard will live in western legend as "the Man Who Shot Liberty Valance." As the crowd rushes out, drawn by the gunfire, someone shouts: "It's Liberty! Liberty is dead!"

We are deliberately kept away from Doniphon's interior life. We know only what he says and does. But we come to know him as a divided man, with a division which has run throughout Ford's films, helping to bring a civilization which runs as counter to his own wilderness life as it does to Valance's. And worst of all, civilization always comes in the form of some windbag like Stoddard who winds himself up and starts talking about schools and gardens and irrigation bills. "We want statehood," Stoddard tells the convention, "because statehood means the protection of our farms and our fences, and it means schools for our children and it means progress for the future."

And for this, Hallie gave up the fastest draw west of the Picketwire?

Wayne went on for years after Ford died in 1965, the American icon that Ford had created, beating his drum and scooting along like

the Energizer bunny. On Ford's coffin lay the flag that he had brought
back from Midway, a battle which Wayne somehow missed.

—The New York Review of Books,
November 29 and December 20, 2001

2

MASTER OF THE MISBEGOTTEN

THE LIFE OF Eugene O'Neill describes an arc which resembles the world of his plays with their atmosphere of fatality. The plays upon which his reputation rests most securely—*A Touch of the Poet, Long Day's Journey into Night, The Iceman Cometh, A Moon for the Misbegotten*—were drawn from his past or from his imagination of family, but they were written at the end of his career in such time as was spared to him by the devastating neurological disease which would first shackle and then destroy his physical ability to write. At the end, silent and eloquent, he would be locked in upon himself, like a character in Poe or in his own early plays. A dreadful end, but not beyond the range of an imagination which from the first had lived among extremities.

The plays were written in Tao House, which he and his wife Carlotta Monterey had built in 1937, in a coastal range east of San Francisco following their move from Sea Island off the Georgia coast. It is a pleasant house, now lovingly preserved, a blend of the Chinese and the Spanish, but a stiff one, despite Carlotta's striving for a studied informality. A *Life* photograph shows the Nobel laureate—"the Mah-ster" as she always referred to him—still remarkably handsome but looking ill-at-ease; Carlotta is grand, theatrically composed, faintly erotic. They are surrounded by books, and what she described as "all my beautiful, very delicate and graceful Chinese furniture."

One room, the smallest, still has a comfortable feel, as though it had been wafted there from the gimcrack and ramshackle house on the New London shore where O'Neill had spent the summers of his youth and where he would set *Long Day's Journey*. It is dominated by a gaudily painted player piano, rescued from a New Orleans whorehouse, on which he played rolls of vaudeville tunes, Tin Pan Alley hits. The wall behind it held photographs of friends, done with the dramatic backlighting of the Thirties—Carl Van Vechten, Sean O'Casey, George Jean Nathan, Alla Nazimova, who had taken the lead in *Mourning Becomes Electra* (1931).

The facing wall is thick with photographs from an earlier era of the American theater, that of his father, the actor James O'Neill, as celebrated in his day as the son was later, if differently. The son of famine-driven Irish peasants, he had risen by a combination of talent, need, and the looks of a matinee idol into the first tier of the stage, a possible successor to the great Booth, with whom he once played Othello and Iago on alternating nights. He had trained himself into the wide Shakespearean range, but, again like Booth, was fit for a variety of other roles. Then, on a star-crossed February night in 1883 (appropriately, in Booth's theater), he took the part of Edmond Dantès in *The Count of Monte Cristo*. For the next thirty years he was to play the part continually. It made him a rich man and destroyed him as an actor. The photographs show him in his prime, handsome and dashing, then gradually thickening.

O'Neill's study looked across the Las Trampas Hills toward Mount Diablo, the tallest peak in the range. Like his study on Sea Island, it was intended to suggest a sea captain's cabin. There were models of tall-masted schooners on the walls and his certificate of qualification as an able-bodied seaman, folded, refolded, fading. On good days, there would be a sliver's glimpse of bay, but the feeling is mountainous, not marine. This is strange, because from the first, water was his element. A skillful and powerful swimmer, often reckless in his distances, he now had only a swimming pool.

As a young man, he had had his memorable time aboard schooners and tramp steamers, had been an out-of-work sailor on the beach at Buenos Aires, had served his watches aloft. *Bound East for Cardiff*, the play which first attracted the Provincetown Players in 1916, had been based on an Atlantic crossing, and the best of the other early plays had come from his time at sea. *Anna Christie* came from his all-too-familiar knowledge of waterfront dives. Even Monte Cristo Cottage, as the family called its New London house, was close to water, where the river spills into Long Island Sound. Once New London had been a whaling town, second only to New Bedford, and it was still a port. His trilogy of plays, *Mourning Becomes Electra*, is set in the pillared mansion of a shipbuilder "on the outskirts of one of the smaller New England seaport towns," and aboard a clipper ship moored along a Boston wharf. Throughout the three plays runs the chanteyman's song "Shenandoah." His head was as full of sea chanteys as of Tin Pan Alley.

O'Neill brought with him to Tao House plans, notes, sketches, drafts, scenarios, for what had swelled, in his ambitions for it, into a cycle of eleven plays, to which he gave the title "A Tale of Possessors Self-Dispossessed." It would tell the story of the Harfords, well-born but grasping New Englanders, carriers across the land of that specifically American materialism which was the culture's fatal illness, a hybrid born of Calvinism and avarice. A fatal intermarriage had added to the blood "a touch of the poet," the wild and reckless spirit of the Irish.

The bulk of the preliminary material was in time destroyed by O'Neill, his physical tremor being now so severe that his wife had to assist, her eyes brimming with tears. Some inconclusive judgments have been formed. Travis Bogard, the dean of O'Neill scholars, expressed a widely held opinion: "That O'Neill could not complete the historical cycle as it was designed is one of the greatest losses the drama in any time has sustained."[1] Perhaps. What we do know from

---

1. *Contour in Time: The Plays of Eugene O'Neill* (Oxford University Press, 1972).

what survives is that the success of *Mourning Becomes Electra*'s three closely linked plays had shown him what had been missing from his earlier work, or at best only weakly present—a sense of history, of time at work on America.

Early on, he had sent a warning note to Lawrence Langner of the Theatre Guild: his cycle will be the history of a family, just that:

> What larger significance I can give my people as extraordinary examples and symbols in the drama of American possessiveness and materialism is something else again. But I don't want anyone to get the idea that this Cycle is much concerned with what is usually understood by American history, for it isn't.

Especially, he added, it will not be much concerned with economic history, "which so many seem to mistake for the *only* history just now."

By "just now" he meant the Thirties. His fellow Irishman, the cantankerous old Fenian John O'Leary, claimed that a gentleman could be an anarchist but not a socialist; O'Neill was instinctively on O'Leary's side. Profoundly nonpolitical, he retained a sentimental reverence for Greenwich Village's heady brew of anarchism and an affection for the disillusioned Wobblies who had battled against cops, hired guns, and Pinkerton spies. In the Village and on the waterfront, he had drunk with Dorothy Day and argued with Emma Goldman; in Provincetown, he had slept with Louise Bryant and moved scenery with John Reed. Shortly, he would summon up those years, their hopes and betrayals, in a play far outside the planned cycle.

By the time of *Mourning Becomes Electra*, O'Neill had become one of the world's most respected dramatists, although no one—least of all, American critics—seems to have known quite why. They— John Mason Brown, Richard Lockridge, Brooks Atkinson—had little in common beyond a tweeds-and-briar-pipe prose, but Joseph Wood Krutch, who should have known better, was the most unrestrained, reaching impatiently beyond Ibsen to Shakespeare as O'Neill's only equal. *Electra*, John Mason Brown wrote, "boasts the kind of radiant austerity which was part of the glory that was Greece." Difficult to refute. But when he was judged to have failed, as with *Dynamo*, *Mourning Becomes Electra*'s immediate predecessor, critical language flailed about as wildly: "It is sometimes ludicrous, frequently raving. . . ." *Dynamo* is, in truth, dreadful stuff, like *Marco Millions* and *Lazarus Laughed*. But other plays of his "middle" period, like *The Great God Brown*, fail, indeed risibly so, because of a wild, breathtaking, perhaps necessary ambition. It was not merely plays that he was trying to create, but a theater.

He had rejected in its entirety the theater, the theatrical style, the stage tradition which his father had not merely represented but embodied. But memory lasts longer than rejection, as of all people Robert Benchley reminds us in his shrewd and poised *New Yorker* review of *Mourning Becomes Electra*. Benchley, before he decided to fritter away his time in Hollywood's Garden of Allah, was a critic of taste and intelligence:

> Are we not forgetting one very important source of inspiration, without which he might perhaps just have been a builder of word-mountains? Was there not standing in the wings of the Guild Theatre, on that momentous opening night, the ghost of an old actor in a white wig, with drawn sword, who looked on proudly as the titanic drama unfolded itself, scene by scene, and who murmured, with perhaps just the suggestion of a chuckle: "That's good, son! Give em the old Theatre." The actor I refer to needs no introduction to the older boys and girls here tonight—Mr. James O'Neill, "The Count of Monte Cristo" and the father of our present hero. . . .

"In this tremendous play," Benchley goes on, "he gives us not one thing that is new, and he gives us nothing to think about (unless we are just beginning to think), but he does thrill the bejeezus out of us, just as his father used to...."[2]

Benchley had probably seen the endearing old melodrama more than once; *The Count of Monte Cristo* was a rite of passage, like seeing Joe Jefferson's *Rip van Winkle*. But for O'Neill it was a part of his past. He had been born into the production and spent his first seven years traveling with the company. Scattered parts of his early life had been spent selling tickets and acting as assistant manager, trying to get his older brother onstage sober, taking walk-on parts himself. According to an unfounded theater legend, the brothers had to crawl under blue canvas to suggest the raging sea through which the Count makes his spectacular escape. As a dropout from Princeton, he had stood beside his father in the bars of theatrical hotels as the father told of his days playing Shakespeare with Booth himself, the great Booth.

A sense of homelessness came to O'Neill quite naturally. Hotel bedrooms, rented houses, strict Catholic boarding schools, the bars of flophouses, the flimsy clapboards of Provincetown shacks, a "bastard Spanish peasant style" house off the coast of Georgia, a French château. Tao House, he said, would be his first real home.

The sense of homelessness had its roots in heritage and history, and so too perhaps his fascination with masks. James O'Neill the actor had been born in County Kilkenny in 1845, the first year of the Famine, and at the age of seven had been swept overseas with the rest of his family, victims of one of the worst calamities of the nineteenth century. By the time of their emigration, typhus, dysentery, and cholera had been added to starvation to cut Ireland's population and to drive survivors across the ocean on the notorious "famine ships."

Kilkenny, a beautiful and historied Norman town, had turned in

---

2. *The New Yorker*, November 7, 1931, p. 28.

those years into a charnel house, whose workhouse enjoyed a lurid reputation, filled to overflowing with the helplessly indigent. But James O'Neill, the celebrated and prosperous actor, chose to remember an imaginary Kilkenny, conjured up from Romantic travel guides: "Kilkenny, smiling Kilkenny, where I was born one opal-tinted day...." One almost hears the saloon-bar eloquence, the accents of W. C. Fields. He remembers, O'Neill says, "the romance of Kilkenny's mossy towers where walked the shadowy ghosts of Congreve and Bishop Berkeley, of Dean Swift and Farquhar—Irishmen all."

It was the father, self-educated but well-read in theatrical lore, who first taught the boy that theater in ancient Greece had begun with masks, depended upon them for effect. "One's outer life," Eugene O'Neill would one day write, "passes in a solitude haunted by the masks of others; one's inner life passes in a solitude haunted by the masks of oneself."

James O'Neill, onstage or in performance, was a skilled and disciplined professional, a coarse, unlettered immigrant who had combed from his speech "an Irish brogue you could cut with a knife," who had educated himself upon the plays of Shakespeare, the comedies of Sheridan and Farquhar (Irishmen all!), able to play an Italian bravo, a Regency fop, a wicked French marquis, even, fatally, the Count of Monte Cristo—"that God-damned play I bought for a song and made such a success—a great money success." Even the Count was a mask, hiding Edmond Dantès, a seaman hungry for revenge. Like all actors, he was a mask, many masks.

But he wore a different mask offstage, which was not really a mask at all, the Irishman of English and American stereotype—witty, gregarious, quick-tempered, patriotic, with a battery of Irish jigs and come-all-yous, ready to "drown the shamrock" on Saint Patrick's Day. That O'Neill, as a stage direction tells us about the James Tyrone of *Long Day's Journey*, "was by nature a simple, unpretentious man whose inclinations are still close to his humble beginnings and his

Irish farmer forebears. But the actor shows in all his unconscious habits of speech, movement, and gesture."

He never spoke in public of those beginnings, nor of the horrible poverty of the early years in America, first in Buffalo, then in the cities of Ohio. But in Monte Cristo Cottage, James Tyrone had much to say on the subject, in words which, the playwright told his wife, were copied almost verbatim from his father:

> Twice we were evicted from the miserable hovel we called home, with my mother's few sticks of furniture thrown out into the street, and my mother and sisters crying. I cried, too, though I tried hard not to, because I was the man of the family. At ten years old! There was no more school for me. I worked twelve hours a day in a machine shop, learning to make files. A dirty barn of a place where rain dripped through the roof, where you roasted in summer, and there was no stove in winter, and your hands got numb with cold, where the only light came through two small filthy windows, so on grey days I'd have to sit bent over with my eyes almost touching the files in order to see! . . . And my poor mother washed and scrubbed for the Yanks by the day, and my older sister sewed, and my two younger stayed at home to keep the house. We never had clothes enough to wear, nor enough food to eat.

Things were not quite that bleak, thanks to the determination and resilience of the older sister (so we are assured by Arthur and Barbara Gelb, in the first volume of the planned expansion of their earlier biography[3]), but they were bleak enough. "Well I remember

---

3. *O'Neill: Life with Monte Cristo* (Applause, 2000) is the first volume of an intended three-volume expansion and revision of their 1962 biography, *O'Neill*. There is also a two-volume biography which I highly recommend: Louis Sheaffer, *O'Neill, Son and Play-*

one Thanksgiving, or maybe it was Christmas, when some Yank in whose house Mother had been scrubbing gave her a dollar extra for a present, and on the way home she spent it all on food." For James O'Neill and most of his generation of immigrant Irish, their English overlords had been replaced by another superior class, drawn from the same blood and religious tradition. He nursed a quiet, settled hostility toward the English, but the Yanks were a palpable presence, silent assurances of social inferiority whatever his success onstage. He took care to confine his heavy drinking not to the second-rate local club which had accepted him, but to the taproom of the local hotel, blazing a path which his sons would follow.

And the sons, Eugene especially, shared his view of the matter, if they shared little else with him. Something of the power of Eugene O'Neill's portrayal of the American stock, whether rural as in *Desire Under the Elms* or patrician as in *Mourning Becomes Electra*, derives from his sense of a people with whom he is at home and yet alien. Certainly in those plays which place the two cultures in conflict, as in *A Touch of the Poet, A Moon for the Misbegotten, Long Day's Journey*, his sympathies are with the Irish, for all their bluster and mendacity.

The family of Ella Quinlan, O'Neill's mother, offered a variation on the theme, Irish immigrants settled in Cleveland, where Thomas Quinlan showed that indomitable stuff from which the bourgeoisie was shaped, transforming a newsdealer's shop into a general store, and that into an emporium dealing in "fancy goods" and wine, spirits, and tobacco. Emphasis should perhaps be placed on the word "spirits": Cleveland was more relaxed than eastern cities, but the liquor trade, wholesale or retail, was best left in the hands of the Irish, traditionally its most avid clients. Fate, in the form of the alcoholism

---

wright (Little, Brown, 1968), and *O'Neill, Son and Artist* (Little, Brown, 1973). All quotations from O'Neill's plays in this essay are from the three-volume Library of America edition.

which O'Neill learned early to regard as the special curse of his people, carried off Thomas Quinlan while his daughter was still at her convent school. He and James O'Neill had been pals in the old days: "It's true he never touched a drop till he was forty, but after that he made up for lost time. He became a steady champagne drinker, the worst kind. That was his grand pose, to drink only champagne."

His will bequeathed to Ella "One Piano Forte." In time, she had it moved to Monte Cristo Cottage. In the final minutes of *Long Day's Journey* she moves toward it, deeply gone into morphine, her enormous eyes glistening like black jewels, her face "a marble mask of girlish innocence." Her horrified husband and sons listen as she fumbles her way into a Chopin waltz.

Ella, who was thought to have musical gifts, was sent to Saint Mary's Academy, near the University of Notre Dame, where the piano instructor, Mother Elizabeth Lilly, encouraged her to think of a concert career. For a time though, and perhaps encouraged by the example of Mother Elizabeth, an English-born widow, she considered taking the veil, a common daydream of convent-bred girls. The play's final words are hers: "That was in the winter of senior year. Then in the spring something happened to me. Yes, I remember. I fell in love with James Tyrone and was so happy for a time."

Something, indeed. From the intense religiosity and the discreet, faintly romantic gentility of a convent school, rosaries, and the scent of roses, she was thrust into the life of a theatrical company, on the road with a husband who preferred bars to bungalows. And it was in a hotel room on New York's Great White Way, in 1888, that she gave birth to Eugene, in a delivery so painful that the hotel doctor—that "quack" in family history—administered the first shots of the morphine to which she quickly, perhaps voluptuously, surrendered. Her husband and sons would in time become persuaded that Eugene's birth was the proximate cause of what became a serious addiction. She had already persuaded Jamie, the older boy, that he was accidentally responsible for another child's death in infancy. Thus, within a few short years, she had sown various deep and abiding guilts throughout the entire family—her husband, the two surviving sons, and herself. A virtuoso performance, even by the exacting standards of Irish Catholic motherhood. And yet, in both life and the play, she was a woman capable of great charm and vulnerability.

O'Neill would one day say to his own son: "The thing that explains more than anything about me is the fact that I'm Irish. And strangely enough, it is something that all the writers who have attempted to explain me and my work have overlooked."[4] Arthur and Barbara Gelb are determined not to compound the oversight, but it is heavy going for them:

> Eugene fitted the somewhat mythologized designation of "black Irishman" that is vaguely based on looks, temperament and adherence to the church. The looks are dark (arguably the result of intermingling with Spaniards who reached the shores of Ireland after the defeat of the Armada in 1588), the temper is reputed to range from moody to morose (with alcohol often a factor); and the Faith has lapsed.[5]

O'Neill fits the description, although like most descriptions of ethnicity it is essentially circular. He possessed a fierce pride in ancestry and one which he often used to justify his excesses, and his "lapse from

---

4. Quoted by the Gelbs from Croswell Bowen, *PM* (1946).

5. The Gelbs rest their definition of "black Irish" "upon interviews with numerous American-Irish." Such interviews offer evidence only of the eagerness with which the American Irish seize upon whatever seems likely to glamorize them. As for the myth that dark-haired Irish are the product of intermingling with Spaniards who reached the Irish shores from the wrecked Armada, there were a few survivors, but they were promptly decapitated and their heads, packed in barrels, dark hair and all, shipped off to Dublin as proof by the Irish of their loyalty to the Crown. Or so I have heard, and I am black Irish myself.

the Faith" began early and never yielded. When the mood struck him, in Jimmy the Priest's or in the Hell Hole, he was given to reciting Francis Thompson's "The Hound of Heaven," a lachrymose and somewhat hysterical account of God's remorseless pursuit of a soul strayed from grace. It was the hypnotic versification and giddy imagery that drew him, though, and not any possible resemblance to his own circumstances. God may not have died for him, but the Church had, and with unwavering finality. He and Dorothy Day, at present a candidate for that Church's canonization, used to drink and recite the poem to each other: a subject for the pencil and pen of Max Beerbohm.

Sometime while a student at the Christian Brothers' De La Salle Institute in Manhattan, he declared "that he would no longer submit to the yoke of Catholic indoctrination." There, as earlier at Mount Saint Vincent, on the Hudson, he had shown himself a quiet, reflective boy, not inclined toward rebelliousness. All this changed with a dramatic and puzzling suddenness. The following summer, he decided that the time even for a pretense at religious conformity had ended, and his father's attempt to haul him off to Sunday Mass in New London resulted in an undignified scuffle which brought them both to the floor. His belated discovery of his mother's addiction to the needle was devastating for the young boy: it confirmed his growing quarrel with a supposedly benign Providence.

O'Neill completed the final years of his schooling at the academy in Stamford maintained by William Betts, an able and ferociously loyal alumnus of nearby Yale, with a handlebar mustache and a bulldog devotion to the classics. O'Neill was popular at Betts, despite a fondness for solitude, and was developing into a remarkably handsome young man, "tall, lean, with darkening brown hair and uncannily luminous eyes." He had become, as all his life he would remain, a prodigious reader, but of Nietzsche now, rather than the Baltimore Catechism. Billy Betts did not notice. Too slender for most sports, he was a strong and would become a daring swimmer. From the first, as readers of his plays know, the sea held a powerful attraction for him, life-giving and life-destroying.

It was in the summer of 1903, with Eugene home from Betts, that the event occurred which the speeches in *Long Day's Journey* evoke with hallucinatory intimacy. Ella (or Mary), her supply of morphine exhausted, ran down in her nightdress to their dock, apparently to throw herself in the river. The language and its voices evoke the hour —night, water, fog, the sound of the foghorn. It was "the spiritual turning point of his life": he said as much to his wife and to Elizabeth Sergeant, an early and sensitive biographer. Like most turning points, though, it was less discovery than crystallization, drawn from many sources.

A classmate would later say: "We had a few Roman Catholics at school besides Gene, but he never went to Mass with any of them." Billy Betts's muscular Protestantism, though, would have had far less appeal to him than the Church he was leaving. He would surely have said, as Joyce supposedly did, that it was his faith he had lost, not his mind. Like adventurous youths everywhere, he was turning to Nietzsche and Schopenhauer, Ibsen and Shaw. Every man, so it was coming to seem to him, existed within an arctic solitude of negation and self-doubt, a universe stripped bare of the consolations and certainties of all religions. There existed, but only for the brave, a specifically modern form of heroism, bleak yet exultant.

It was thus far only the posturing of a young iconoclast, swathed in Byronic melancholy and scorn, like young Richard Miller in *Ah Wilderness!* (1933), who awaits the day when "the people bring out the guillotine again and I see Pierpont Morgan being driven by in a tumbril." This play, his only comedy, in its abundant and nostalgic evocation of a long-gone 1906 Fourth of July, is of course, as he himself said, the tormented world of Monte Cristo Cottage turned inside out, down to the wallpaper with its "cheerful, ugly blue design." The older brother, home from Yale, with his football lineman's build and collegiate manner, has replaced Jamie O'Neill, sarcastic, self-destructive, the odor of whorehouse talcum clinging to him. Uncle Sid gets tipsy again and again proposes to prim, sweet-tempered Lily, but the family is understanding and protective. "Miller and his wife and the children are all roaring with laughter." At the play's close, Miller and his wife "move quietly out of the moonlight into the darkness of the front parlor." We will enter that front parlor in *Long Day's Journey*, but into a different kind of darkness.

In the back room of a doubtful hotel, Richard had had a bad quarter-hour with a prostitute, conjuring up, for those who know O'Neill's life, journeys from Princeton to New York's Tenderloin. In this play, though, Richard moves within a magic protection, although a stage direction offers us a dark ethnic messenger: "The bartender, a stocky young Irishman with a foxily cunning, stupid face and a cynically wise grin, stands just inside the entrance."

O'Neill's one college year was a disaster. Princeton had little to offer a young man who was bringing his explosive reading to bear on his own life. He would never regard universities with much respect, holding toward them the autodidact's derision flecked with fear. Instead, he would join that central American tradition which includes Melville, Whitman, Twain, Hemingway, Dreiser, solitary readers through the night. Like them, he was to become a man of wide, self-guided culture. Like them, he would create his own language.

In June of 1910, O'Neill shipped out from Boston aboard the *Charles Racine*, a Norwegian steel barque and one of the last of the square riggers, bound for Buenos Aires with a cargo of lumber. His later voyages, to his disappointment, were made under steam.

The powerful hold of the sea upon his emotions and his imagination is extraordinary. He tried often to put it into words, in *Bound East for Cardiff* and *The Moon of the Caribbees*, in *Anna Christie* and *The Hairy Ape*, and never with entire success. It went deeper than language and had been with him from the first. A small boy, he had watched ships making ready for sea in New London, and in his Catholic boarding school he could watch from the height as ships moved between New York and the river towns stretched along the Hudson. Part of him would always be the young fellow in the rigging of the *Charles Racine* or alone in its crow's nest fumbling for words remembered from Conrad's *Youth* about the glamour of the sea. Or Paddy, the old sailor in *The Hairy Ape*, remembering in a phony stage-brogue the days of sail:

> Or the full of the moon maybe. Then you'd see her driving through the gray night, her sails stretching aloft all silver and white, not a sound on the deck, the lot of us dreaming dreams till you'd believe 'twas no real ship at all you was on but a ghost ship like the *Flying Dutchman* they says does be roaming the seas forevermore without touching a port.

No sooner had O'Neill stepped on board the *Charles Racine* in Boston than he discovered his abiding image of human felicity— water, wind, and language.

He would always believe that long voyage to be the most intense of his experiences, and close behind it his eight months on the beach in Buenos Aires, where he had quickly run through his pay on booze and whores, so that he ended those days begging for money and his nights dodging the cops and the waterfront toughs. When he got back to New York, he holed up at Jimmy the Priest's, a Fulton Street flophouse which later served as one of the models for the setting of *The Iceman Cometh*. In July 1911, he shipped out for Southampton aboard the *New York*, and returned a month later aboard the *Philadelphia*, with able-bodied seaman papers.

That was the sum of his life at sea, considerably less than Melville had spent aboard the *Acushnet* and in the islands of the South Seas.

Less, for that matter, than Darwin, who would never have called himself a sailor, spent aboard the *Beagle*. Far longer, though, than the week or so which Hemingway spent under machine-gun fire on the Italian front. But calendar measurements are irrelevant in the creation of identity. For O'Neill, as for Hemingway, these were the weeks that shaped a core of being, with all its truths, lies, exaggerations, masks, mirrors.

But the years that followed his return to New York were enough to test that core, or anyone's, to the shattering point, years spent at Jimmy the Priest's or else the saloon in Greenwich Village nicknamed "the Hell Hole," where, as the Gelbs say, "he slid by degrees into a state of mindless alcoholism." Those who have experienced *The Iceman Cometh* may be excused for believing that he lived entirely inside, seeing sunlight only when the doors were swung briefly open. But there was a bit more than that going on. Thus in late 1911 he had to stage a "discovery" with a prostitute in a hotel room, in order to verify the adultery charges which would allow himself and a young woman named Kathleen Jenkins to dissolve an early and unfortunate marriage. And a few months later he would attempt suicide and almost succeed. (A child by that marriage would grow up, become a professor at Yale, and then, in his turn, commit suicide. Generation by generation, it would prove itself an unlucky family. Cursed might be a better word.)

There were a few affairs and romances; the Gelbs, nothing if not hardworking, have dug up the details. In the summer of 1912, O'Neill and Jamie were on tour with the father, playing bit parts in a cut-down vaudeville version of *Monte Cristo*. He was a newspaper reporter for a while. On the Christmas Eve of that year, having been diagnosed as tubercular, he entered Gaylord Farm, a sanitarium in Wallingford, Connecticut. He began writing plays and for a time was a student in George Pierce Baker's drama workshop at Harvard. His father, by no means the tightwad the son made him out to be, had the early, and pretty bad, plays published, in a volume called, with gruesome accidental appropriateness, *Thirst*.

Somehow in those years he contrived at the same time to educate himself as a dramatist and to drink himself almost to death in, to use his own words, a port of last call "for sailors on shore leave or stranded; longshoremen, waterfront riffraff, gangsters, down-and-outers, drifters from the ends of the earth." His instinct for the kind of theater he needed was faultless—Wedekind, Ibsen, Strindberg, Hauptmann. He went six times to see *The Weavers*—Hauptmann's five-act play about the revolt of Silesian weavers in 1844—and every performance by Dublin's Abbey Players during their New York engagement—Yeats's one-act plays, those by Lady Gregory and the gifted but now forgotten T. C. Murray, and, most to the point, Synge's *Playboy of the Western World* and *Riders to the Sea*. These were plays of atmosphere and their rhythms would linger in his mind. "They're all gone from me now," Maurya says at the close of *Riders*, "and there isn't anything more the sea can do to me." It was the language that created the atmosphere. Alice Brady, the Irish actress who played Lavinia in *Mourning Becomes Electra*, would one day say of it that it is "not like any ordinary play where if you drop a word you can substitute another. You must say every word exactly as it is written. Otherwise you throw the whole rhythm of the play out." It was a lesson O'Neill learned from Yeats and Synge and one which had never been taught on his father's stage.

The father's connections, of course, secured passes for him to the Irish and the other plays. Whether in the crow's nest of the *Charles Racine* or on the beach in Buenos Aires or in the back room of Jimmy the Priest's, and whether the son liked to admit it or not, he always had an ace to play—a middle-class father prepared, however grudgingly, to bail him out. Like many another young man, he was a gentleman-ranker out on a spree.

That 1912 attempt at suicide was a different matter though. The

Gelbs think it was "more like a macabre gesture than a sincere effort," but it looks pretty real to me. When you take a heavy overdose of Veronal and stretch out on a flophouse bed, you are likely to end up on a slab up the avenue at Bellevue. He was discovered, passed out, by a friend who would himself commit suicide a year later. At Jimmy the Priest's, that sort of thing was contagious. After he got seriously to work as a writer, though, we hear no more about suicide.

The Hell Hole, more formally the Golden Swan, was as disreputable, but, significantly, it was located not on the waterfront but in Greenwich Village, then in its first full flowering as the capital of America's Bohemia. It was still the watering hole of a peculiarly vicious gang of Irish toughs, the Hudson Dusters, still boasting of their youthful days as stickup men and bullies, but reduced now to ordinary thievery and the election-day destruction of Republican ballots. The other half of a severely segregated clientele was composed of the regulars and casuals who populated the Village and would stroll through every memoir—John Reed and Hippolyte Havel, George Bellows and Max Eastman, an assortment of anarchists and Wobblies, poets, scenery designers, heavy drinkers and hangers-on, novelists and fantasists. Beyond the doors lay the now legendary geography of the Village—the office of *The Masses*, Mabel Dodge's salon, little theater groups of which one, the Provincetown Players, would soon become famous thanks in part to O'Neill. That he was giving his patronage, these days, to the Hell Hole suggests a growing readiness for the stage.

O'Neill moved within the heady mix of art and political extremism, but without really being a part of it, although later legend would bestow full membership upon him. His deep sympathy for philosophical anarchism had begun years earlier on visits to Benjamin Tucker's bookshop, with its swaying shelves of Kropotkin, Tolstoy, Proudhon. Tucker, a sweet-tempered pacifist, was dedicated to nonviolence, but this could not be said of Emma Goldman and Big Bill Heywood, around whom clung wisps of cordite and dynamite, rendered romantic by time and distance. The radicalism of that time and place would one day be central to *The Iceman Cometh*, but ideas had real consequence for O'Neill only when they were embodied. They were embodied with bewildering diversity in the person of his closest friend, an Irishman named Terry Carlin—ex-Wobbly, Irish rebel, sometime syndicalist, poverty-stricken pal of hoodlums and poets, and a drinker of heroic capacity. Carlin's beliefs had passed beyond cynicism, then despair, to surface as hilarity: "Cheer up, Gene, the worst is yet to come." But it never came. Within a few years, O'Neill had established himself as a playwright, and was making a brutally painful but successful battle against the bottle.

In the summer of 1916, a few months after O'Neill and Carlin had drunk to the memories of the Irish rebels of Easter Week, they traveled to Provincetown and looked up the group of actors and writers whom George "Jig" Cook had gathered around him. Almost anyone who wanted to help was added to the company by Cook and his more talented, or at least more savvy, wife, Susan Glaspell. Jack Reed was in the company, of course, home after having ridden with Pancho Villa and helped to organize the silk strike in Paterson. He was sleeping with Louise Bryant, as O'Neill soon would be, a striking brunette whose theatricality was not limited to the stage. As for Jig Cook, he was one of those great-hearted, silly people who were creating a theater for America.

The group was reading plays toward a second season at the Wharf Theatre, and O'Neill asked them to look at a one-acter called *Bound East for Cardiff*. Too nervous to read it aloud himself he waited in another room, for an actor to read it. Everyone present had afterward an account of the evening: it was a foundational moment for the theater in this country. "Why," someone said, "it's like the Irish Players." And not by chance: he had studied the working of a noncommercial play, one which depended for effect upon silence, upon speeches which leaned against each other to form structure. Nor did it hurt that the play, set in a tramp steamer's forecastle, would soon be performed in a barn which had once been a fishhouse, with water moving beneath the floorboards. Susan Glaspell said it best: "Then we knew what we were for. We began in faith and perhaps it is true that 'all these things shall be added unto us.'"

He awoke to find himself famous, like Byron, whom he did not otherwise resemble. News has always traveled quickly between Provincetown and Broadway. "Who is Eugene O'Neill?" asked a *New York Times* headline, the perkiness of its theater section already established. Mencken and George Jean Nathan published the texts of *The Long Voyage Home* and *The Moon of the Caribbees* in the *Smart Set*, and in Nathan, O'Neill acquired a powerful interpreter, affected perhaps, but precise in his judgments. "In even the poorer of O'Neill's plays—and he has written poor plays as well as brilliant—one feels a trace of power and bravery. He may on occasion work weakly but he never works cheaply. Always there is perceptible an effort at something original and distinguished."

Would that the Gelbs had taken writing lessons from Nathan. When they roll up their sleeves to talk about the qualities of a particular play, there is just no holding them back. They close their first volume with the composition of *Beyond the Horizon* (1920) which earned him his first Pulitzer, and which "was perceived as a play of such tragic sweep and grandeur that it dwarfed the efforts of American playwrights who had come before." Like others who have written about him, they constantly seek to emulate his own frequent strivings toward some distant Something or Nothing, it seems not to matter which.

He was an artist of the first rank, whose very intensity of vision and willingness to risk allowed him to surmount a battery of verbal limitations. Mary McCarthy, reviewing *The Iceman Cometh* in 1946, nailed the central problem, which a universal respect for the Nobel Prize writer had kept under wraps: "To audiences accustomed to the oily virtuosity of George Kaufmann, George Abbott, Lillian Hellman, Odets, Saroyan, the return of a playwright who—to be frank—cannot write is a solemn and sentimental occasion." Or, she might have added, the leaden yet squishy pentameters of Maxwell Anderson. She places O'Neill in the unhappy company of Farrell and Dreiser, without quite acknowledging that all three were powerful writers despite this embarrassing impediment. "How is one to judge the great, logical symphony of a tone-deaf musician?" But her own words turn against her: "*The Iceman Cometh* is indeed made of ice or iron; it is full of will and fanatic determination; it appears to have been written at some extreme temperature of the mind." As backhanded praise, this is both felicitous and exact.

But it is unfair to measure the Gelbs against Nathan or McCarthy, show-offs of language. The Gelbs are journeymen, with uncertain control of their instruments. At times they are content with a careless flatness, as when they seek to evoke life within the O'Neill family: "Monte Cristo Cottage had become less a haven of togetherness than a pressure cooker in which the four O'Neills fed upon each other's neuroses." But at other times, they strive for the grand effect: "Now he had only to bleed and weep endless tears for the sake of his artist's dream." The trouble is not merely one of style: the more one reads about O'Neill, either here or in Louis Sheaffer's two-volume biography, the more impressed one is by the mysteriousness, the elusiveness, of our greatest—perhaps, with the exception of Tennessee Williams, our only great—playwright. Surely, though, the biographers cannot be faulted for lack of research: the list of those consulted would populate a city the size of Terre Haute.

—*The New York Review of Books*, October 5, 2000

3

FITZGERALD'S "RADIANT WORLD"

SCOTT FITZGERALD CONCEIVED of the story which would become *The Great Gatsby* on Long Island, where man, in the person of a crew of Dutch sailors, was placed "face to face for the last time in history with something commensurate to his capacity for wonder." That was in the spring of 1924. He wrote most of it, though, in a villa above St. Raphaël on the Riviera, with Roman and Romanesque aqueducts within sight, and beneath a skyline that reminded him of Shelley's Euganean Hills. There was a beach where he and Zelda swam daily, and came to know a group of young French naval aviators. Otherwise, he worked steadily at what he jokingly spoke of to friends as "a novel better than any novel written in America." By late October the manuscript was ready to be mailed to Maxwell Perkins, his editor at Scribner's.

He knew very well that the book in hand was far finer than anything he had attempted before. In April, on the eve of his departure for Europe, he told Perkins that "I cannot let it go out unless it has the very best I am capable of in it or even as I feel sometimes, something better than I am capable of." He would not be alone in that feeling; Perkins himself would say that the novel possessed the Fitzgerald glamour, but also "a kind of mystic atmosphere at times." He may have been remembering Fitzgerald's words in that April letter: "So in my new novel I'm thrown directly on purely creative work—not trashy imaginings as in my stories but the sustained imagination of a sincere yet radiant world."

He had first, however—and this would become a recurring problem—to clear himself of debt. He was at the beginning of a decade in which he would be one of America's best-paid writers of fiction, but money kept vanishing as though at the command of an evil sorcerer. Renting a mansion on Long Island Sound could not have helped, of course, nor could driving into Manhattan for parties and hotels, or living next door to his friend Ring Lardner, a notorious alcoholic. Or a staff that included a live-in couple, a nurse for the baby, and a laundress. When he had dug himself out of the hole, he wrote an insouciant account of the matter for *The Saturday Evening Post*, which he had come to think of as his guardian spirit. "Over our garage is a large bare room whither I now retired with pencil, paper and the oil stove, emerging the next afternoon at five o'clock with a 7,000 word story."

By April, he had sold enough commercial fiction to clear himself of debt, and to take himself and Zelda to France, where he would be free to write the novel. "I really worked hard as hell last winter— but it was all trash and it nearly broke my heart and my iron constitution." But they were going to the "Old World to find a new rhythm for our lives, with a true conviction that we had left our old selves behind forever—and with a capital of just over seven thousand dollars." Arthur Mizener, his second and perhaps most subtle biographer,[1] after quoting this passage, suggests that, like Gatsby, he "wanted to recover something, some idea of himself perhaps, that had gone into loving [Zelda]. His life had been confused and disordered since then, but if he could once return to a certain starting place and go over it all slowly, he could find out what that thing was." Mizener deliberately borrows Nick Carraway's

---

1. *The Far Side of Paradise: A Biography of F. Scott Fitzgerald* (Houghton Mifflin, 1951).

language to suggest similarities of circumstance between Gatsby and his creator.

The comparison was irresistible, if only because we keep looking for themes that connect Fitzgerald with his greatest work of fiction. Certainly Fitzgerald had reached a crossroads of sorts, but not one that had anything to do with Zelda. That, ironically, would be reached later that summer, when he was writing productively in France. It had much to do, however, with money and with "some idea of himself."

The sensational public success of *This Side of Paradise* in 1920, when he was twenty-three, had established him as a figure on the literary scene, and he had gone on to secure that reputation with enough commercial short fiction to fill two volumes—*Flappers and Philosophers* and *Tales of the Jazz Age.*[2] Those stories, even the slenderest of them, display with careless grace his uncanny ability to evoke atmospheres, moods, energies, through his deployment of sounds, colors, lights, shadows. But a few stories written later, and he knew which ones—"Winter Dreams," "Absolution," "The Sensible Thing," "The Diamond as Big as the Ritz"—had more than inborn grace and developing skill. Later, these would be the stories singled out by critics as signaling the tentative stirring of *The Great Gatsby* within his imagination. This may or may not be the case, but they may have reminded him that it had been his plan to become something more than the chronicler of flappers and playboys.

Fitzgerald himself had given currency to neither of those words; very few of his short-story women are flappers in the John Held sense of the word, and certainly not the young ladies, however liberated, in his novels. He did later admit ruefully to some responsibility for that phrase "the Jazz Age," and at one of Gatsby's parties a "Jazz History

---

2. *This Side of Paradise, Flappers and Philosophers,* and *Tales of the Jazz Age,* along with *The Beautiful and the Damned,* are reprinted in F. Scott Fitzgerald, *Novels and Stories, 1920–1922* (Library of America, 2000).

of the World" would be performed. He had shaped the literary image of that world, and it had been decided, in those quarters where such things are decided, that he was not merely the prophet of a new, reckless generation, with new songs to sing, but its living embodiment, with the looks of a movie star and a gift for outrageous public behavior. "The other evening at a dancing club," one of numberless journalists reported, "a young man in a gray suit, soft shirt, loosely tied scarf, shook his tousled yellow hair engagingly, introduced me to the beautiful lady with whom he was dancing and sat down." Mizener offers the familiar verbal snapshots: "They rode down Fifth Avenue on the tops of taxis because it was hot or dove into the fountain at Union Square or tried to undress at the *Scandals*, or, in sheer delight at the splendor of New York, jumped, dead sober, into the Pulitzer fountain in front of the Plaza. Fitzgerald got in fights with waiters and Zelda danced on people's dinner tables." They were already drinking far too much, especially Fitzgerald.

They were a well-known couple, Fitzgerald and his "barbarian princess from the South," creating a rotogravure legend which still exists, wavering, in our cultural memory, decorated with anachronistic stills of Astaire and Rogers dancing against a montage of top hats and champagne bottles. If they went broke every couple of years, there were always those fountains of eternal replenishment, *The Saturday Evening Post* and *Red Book* and *Liberty* and *Woman's Home Companion*. But that isn't how he had planned it. He had planned to become the best novelist of his generation, somehow or other.

This Side of Paradise had had a success which was almost freakish, capturing the aspirations of a generation and especially of those within that generation who, like its author, aspired to be great writers. Reading it today, one blanches at its emotional and rhetorical excesses, and yet, as Matthew Bruccoli says, it was received as "an iconoclastic social document—even as a testament of revolt. Surprisingly, it was regarded as an experimental or innovative narrative because of the mixture of styles and the inclusion of plays and verse." It was the autobiographical first novel of a very young writer who took himself very seriously, and who had not provided for his hero those escape hatches of irony which Joyce had built into *A Portrait of the Artist*. But it was not, by any stretch, the work of a man who planned a career as a writer of commercial fiction.

H. L. Mencken, who turns out, rather surprisingly, to have been the most perceptive of Fitzgerald's early critics, was the gentlest of them when writing of Fitzgerald's second novel, *The Beautiful and Damned*, when it appeared in 1922. For Edmund Wilson, the Princeton friend whom he would one day call his "literary conscience," Fitzgerald "has been given imagination without intellectual control of it; he has been given the desire for beauty without an aesthetic ideal; and he has been given a gift for expression without very many ideas to express." Wilson unkindly quoted Edna Millay as saying that he resembled "a stupid old woman with whom someone has left a diamond." But Mencken, who could wield a heavy saber when he wished, wrote differently. After the first novel, he wrote, Fitzgerald's future seemed uncertain and the "shabby stuff" collected in *Flappers and Philosophers* changed uncertainty into something worse, but the new novel has "a hundred signs in it of serious purpose and unquestionable skill. Even in its defects there is proof of hard striving."

Perhaps Mencken had been too easily impressed by the novel's pretentious chat about Spengler (who had not yet been translated), and perhaps Wilson had not placed proper value upon his friend's uncanny ability to evoke atmospheres, moods, emotional energies. Fitzgerald would never be an intellectual in the sense that Wilson already was, but he was beginning to learn that one uniquely novelistic gift which Wilson never quite mastered, the ability to translate ideas into art. It is at work, if falteringly and at times embarrassingly, in *The Beautiful and Damned*.

The sudden leap forward into the exquisite mastery of *The Great*

Gatsby is likely to remain one of art's abiding mysteries, but readers of Fitzgerald may be forgiven their speculations. The story called "Absolution," which Mencken published in the *American Mercury* in June of 1924, just as *Gatsby* was being finished, is a case in point. In a letter to a fan, Fitzgerald tells us that the character of Gatsby

> was perhaps created on the image of some forgotten farm type of Minnesota that I have known and forgotten, and associated at the same moment with some sense of romance. It might interest you to know that a story of mine, called "Absolution," in my book *All the Sad Young Men* was intended to be a picture of his early life, but that I cut it because I preferred to preserve the sense of mystery.

This surely cannot have been literally the case—there seems little connection between Jimmy Gatz, who, as we learn in the novel's final pages, had grown up a Lutheran, and Rudolph Miller, a Catholic boy who makes a boastful confession to a half-mad priest. There is, to be sure, a thematic connection: both boys live, dangerously, within the imagination, with the priest providing a creepy warning. As Fitzgerald explained to another reader, "The priest gives the boy a form of Absolution (not of course sacramental) by showing him that he (the priest) is in an even worse state of horror and despair."

The case with the story called "Winter Dreams" is stronger. Stylistically, it is fully on a level with *Gatsby*—well, almost—and it displays the same control of material. Young Dexter Green is a middle-class boy who works for pocket money each summer as a caddy on the local golf course, and each winter, in the fierce Minnesota cold, roams the frozen fields, imagining himself in scenes of local and imperial glory, swinging his arms to bring armies onto the field. He, or perhaps the authorial voice, has an ability to quicken both kinds of landscape into quiet, lyrical life. One day, this glory is entered by a girl, Judy Jones, a rich man's daughter, flirtatious, perhaps wanton, desirable, fickle, self-obsessed. And by a subtle alchemy, she comes at first to dwell with the glory of wealth, then to embody, at last to replace it in Dexter's increasingly eroticized imagination. He imagines the splendors of her mansion's floor of bedrooms, in words which Fitzgerald (ever a thrifty husbandman of his own prose) moved bodily into an equivalent scene in *Gatsby*.

As Dexter enters manhood, the complex dream of Judy and her world of social grandeur and illimitability remains with him, while he takes steps to transcend his own limited life, persuading his father to send him east to the Ivy League, where, with a subtle blend of dream and hardheadedness, he acquires the clothes and the mannerisms of Judy's class, while realizing that he can never himself fully enter it. "His mother's name had been Krimslich. She was a Bohemian of the peasant class and she had spoken broken English to the end of her days." As Fitzgerald tells us, Dexter was at bottom a practical man, and he becomes rich by a touchingly imaginative blend of dream and reality, building up a chain of dry-cleaning and laundry shops, specializing in the proper treatment of the imported tweeds of upper-class men and the delicate French lingerie of the wives. At last, years later and by chance, after he is established in a New York skyscraper, he learns that Judy is married now, with a thick and unfeeling husband, tied down with the children. And she has lost her looks.

"Winter Dreams" is a kind of rough sketch for the novel which Fitzgerald did not yet know he wanted to write. It is more rooted in social reality than *Gatsby* would be, and for that reason it has problems that *Gatsby* does not have, but also, as we shall see, it avoids problems that would in *Gatsby* loom formidably. We don't know what Dexter did in the war, beyond learning that, like Gatsby, he "went into the first officers' training camp." It is most doubtful though, if, like Major Jay Gatsby, he had held off the enemy for two nights with a hundred and thirty men and sixteen Lewis guns, winning a decoration from every government, even little Montenegro down on the Adriatic Sea. That sounds more like his adolescent imaginings on the frozen fairways. But then it is even harder to imagine Jay Gatsby as the proprietor of a dry-cleaning shop in Black Bear.

"Long ago," Dexter says at the story's close, "long ago, there was something in me, but now that thing is gone, that thing is gone. I cannot cry. I cannot care. That thing will come back no more." Like Gatsby, he has lived too long with a single dream, and when it shattered, he entered, as Gatsby would, a community of loss, "material without being real, where poor ghosts, breathing dreams like air, drifted fortuitously about."

Fitzgerald completed *The Great Gatsby* in the villa at St. Raphaël, had the typing completed, and sent it off to Perkins at the end of October. Soon after, Scott and Zelda drove to Rome, apparently because Zelda had been reading *Roderick Hudson* but perhaps also because the Riviera held complex and troubling memories for her. They settled into a hotel in the Piazza di Spagna, perhaps because it held associations with the dying Keats, whom Scott worshiped this side of idolatry, but came swiftly to loathe the city and its inhabitants. "Pope Siphilis the Sixth and his Morons," muttered the ex-Catholic, whom scholars tell us retained to the end something called "a Catholic sensibility." He got drunk and was beaten up by the police.

On December 6 and 30, the galley proofs arrived from New York, and he set to work on his revisions. This may seem an odd way of proceeding, but in those primitive days of publishing, Scribners was in the fortunate position of owning its own printing plant, on West 43rd Street, close to its Fifth Avenue editorial offices. Perkins's decision to have Fitzgerald's novel set immediately into type presumes that he did not expect extensive revisions, and he was in any case following his customary practice: Fitzgerald's earlier books were treated similarly, as Hemingway's would be. More astonishingly, he "had the novels of Thomas Wolfe typeset before he and Wolfe got down to serious work on them." Letterpress composition, back then, we are told, would not have cost much more than having a stenographer make a typescript.

We are now in the fortunate position of having available to us, and in two forms, the text as Perkins had it set into type, both of them bearing the word *Trimalchio* as title.[3] This is the title which Fitzgerald was insisting on at the time, and it is the running head on the galleys. The first is a facsimile publication of the proofs themselves, limited to five hundred numbered copies on laid paper, resting handsomely and snugly in a box of royal blue, with more or less the proportions, although of course not the size, of a coffin. There is an afterword by Professor Matthew Bruccoli, the dean of Fitzgerald scholars, to whose work on Fitzgerald and other writers of the period we are all of us in debt.[4] His is the one biography which can be said to supersede Mizener's, although its title, *Some Sort of Epic Grandeur*, may suggest that his admiration sometimes surges over the top.[5] We also have Professor James West's *Trimalchio*, described by Cambridge University Press as "An Early Version of *The Great Gatsby*."[6] It is a bound volume, one in the Cambridge Edition of the Works of F. Scott Fitzgerald, and it is therefore easier to use than the reproduced galleys, although much less fun.

Unless you are a scholar of bibliography, which is not a fun

3. In the *Satyricon* by Petronius, Trimalchio is a vulgar and rich ex-slave who gives gaudy banquets to derisive guests. *Gatsby* scholars who specialize in clocks (and there are some: Time and all that) should note Trimalchio's water-clock.

4. *Trimalchio by F. Scott Fitzgerald: A Facsimile Edition of the Original Galley Proofs*, edited by Matthew J. Bruccoli (University of South Carolina Press, 2000).

5. Harcourt Brace, 1981.

6. F. Scott Fitzgerald, *Trimalchio: An Early Version of The Great Gatsby*, edited by James L. W. West (Cambridge University Press, 2000).

profession, there are two reasons which make instructive a comparison of *Trimalchio* and *The Great Gatsby*. Cambridge tells us that
reading the "early and complete version is like listening to a familiar
musical composition—but played in a different key and with an alter-
nate bridge passage. It is the same work and yet a different work."
I myself am tone-deaf, unfortunately, but this seems fair enough:
maybe a bridge passage is like a transition, at which Fitzgerald, as we
shall see, was a master.

In the years that had followed his first publications, Fitzgerald
had become a thoroughgoing professional, and the way in which he
managed a major revision simply (!) by moving materials from various chapters to other chapters, on the galleys, is breathtaking, and he
did it without diminishing, but rather intensifying the required moods
and tonalities. He did it in two months, while turning out potboilers
to cover expenses—they were broke again—and getting into more
mischief with the Romans. Most of the revisions were addressed to a
specific problem, which Perkins had raised with him, but there was
another, more fundamental problem, which he could not quite define,
not even in a well-known letter to Wilson, who had written to con-
gratulate him:

> The worst fault in it I think is a BIG FAULT: I gave no account
> (and had no feeling about or knowledge of) the emotional rela-
> tions between Gatsby and Daisy from the time of their reunion
> to the catastrophe. However, the lack is so astutely concealed by
> the retrospect of Gatsby's past and by blankets of excellent
> prose that no one has noticed it—though everyone has felt the
> lack and called it by another name.

And that is what everyone did. Mencken "said that the only fault was
that the central story was trivial and a kind of anecdote (that is
because he has admiration for Conrad and adjusted himself to the

sprawling novel) and I felt that what he really missed was the lack of any emotional backbone at the height of it." As for the reviews, even the most enthusiastic, not one had the slightest idea what the book was about.

When Perkins read the typescript of—let us call it *Trimalchio*—he was shaken. "I think the novel is a wonder," he wrote back. "I'm taking it home to read again, and shall then write my impressions in full—but it has vitality to an extraordinary degree, and glamour and a great deal of underlying thought of unusual quality."

The novel has rarely had a better reader, so generous yet judicious as to restore what may be a waning awe for Perkins as a great editor. His remarks focus precisely upon the book's method and the scenes which are the most memorable and signifying. They deserve quotation at length:

> You adopted exactly the right method of telling it, that of employing a narrator who is more of a spectator than an actor: this puts the reader upon a point of observation on a higher level than that on which the characters stand and at a distance that gives perspective. In no other way could your irony have been so immensely effective, nor the reader have been enabled so strongly to feel at times the strangeness of human circumstances in a vast heedless universe. In the eyes of Dr. Eckleberg various readers will see different significances; but their presence gives a superb touch to the whole thing: great unblinking eyes, expressionless, looking down on the human scene. It's magnificent!
>
> ...I have only two actual criticisms:—
>
> One is that among a set of characters marvelously palpable and vital—I would know Tom Buchanan if I met him on the street and would avoid him—Gatsby is somewhat vague. The reader's eyes can never quite focus upon him, his outlines are

dim. Now everything about Gatsby is more or less a mystery i.e. more or less vague, and this may be somewhat of an artistic intention, but I think it is mistaken. Couldn't *he* be physically described as distinctly as the others, and couldn't you add one or two characteristics like the use of that phrase "old sport," not verbal, but physical ones perhaps.... The other point is also about Gatsby: his career must remain mysterious, of course. But at the end you make it clear that his wealth comes through his connection with Wolfsheim.... The total lack of an explanation through so large a part of the story does seem to me a defect;—or not of an explanation, but of the suggestion of an explanation.... There is one other point: in giving deliberately Gatsby's biography when he gives it to the narrator you do depart from the method of the narrative to some degree, for otherwise almost everything is told, and beautifully told, in the regular flow of it—in the succession of events or in accompaniment with them....

The presentation of Tom, his place, Daisy and Jordan, and the unfolding of their characters is unequalled so far as I know. The description of the valley of ashes adjacent to the lovely country, the conversation and the action in Myrtle's apartment, the marvellous catalogue of those who came to Gatsby's house, —these are such things as make a man famous. And all these things, the whole pathetic episode, you have given a place in time and space, for with the help of T. J. Eckleberg and by an occasional glance at the sky, or the sea, or the city, you have imparted a sort of sense of eternity. You once told me that you were not a *natural* writer—my God! You have plainly mastered the craft, of course; but you needed far more than craftsmanship for this.

All that Perkins singled out for praise—the narrative method, the individual scenes—are of course carried forward intact from

Trimalchio to *Gatsby* and so too is that light dusting upon existence for which Perkins could find no better word than "glamour" and neither can anyone else.

> The only completely stationary object in the room was an enormous couch on which two young women were buoyed up as though upon an anchored balloon. They were both in white and their dresses were rippling and fluttering as if they had just been blown back in after a short flight around the house. I must have stood for a few moments listening to the whip and snap of the curtains and the groan of a picture on the wall. There was a boom as Tom Buchanan shut the rear windows and the caught wind died out about the room and the curtains and the rugs and the two young women ballooned slowly to the floor.

There is no need, surely, to rehearse the plot of "probably the most widely read novel written by an American in the twentieth century." The opening chapters of *Trimalchio* and *The Great Gatsby* are pretty much the same, barring the kind of fussing every writer does with galleys. The chief changes come in Chapters Six and Seven of *Trimalchio*, and the long, late chapter, as Gatsby and Nick sit by the open French windows in Gatsby's house, the dawn after Myrtle's killing, when Gatsby breaks out "exuberantly": "I'll tell you everything. The whole story. I've never told it to anyone before—not even Daisy. But I haven't told many lies about it, either, only I've shifted things around a good deal to make people wonder." And shifting things about is what Fitzgerald, his creator—one of his surrogate fathers, like Cody and Wolfsheim—now proceeds to do. Perkins had surely been right: Gatsby's story comes to us much more persuasively measured out among chapters. And it has effects that could not have been anticipated. It is right, for example, that we should learn, much earlier, that "Jay Gatsby, of West Egg, Long Island, sprang from his Platonic conception of himself. He was a son of God—a phrase which, if it means anything, means just that."

In a jubilant, indeed cocksure letter to Perkins, Fitzgerald reported that he had brought Gatsby to life, accounted for his money, fixed up the second party scene and the climactic scene at the Plaza, and successfully broken up the long, autobiographical scene at Gatsby's French windows. In brief, by an act of stylistic legerdemain, he had addressed all of Perkins's concerns. What he had not addressed were his own misgivings about the novel's emotional center, or rather, its lack of one.

There is a moment in *Trimalchio* at one of the parties, when Daisy and Nick are dancing and Daisy, leaning backward to look into his face, tells him that she just wants to go, and not tell Tom anything. She is afraid of the riskiness of Gatsby's world, afraid of "some authentically radiant young girl who with one fresh glance at Gatsby, one moment of magical encounter, would blot out those five years of unwavering devotion." A few weeks later, the lights failed to go on one Saturday night, and "as obscurely as it had begun his career as Trimalchio suddenly ended." "I'm very sad old sport," he tells Nick a few days later. "Daisy wants us to run off together. She came over this afternoon with a suitcase all packed and ready in the car." In other words, Nick tells him, understandably if a bit brutally, you've got her—and now you don't want her. What Gatsby wants, as far as he had figured things out, is that he and Daisy should go back to Louisville and be married in her house and start life over. The bewilderment which this bizarre enterprise might cause in that conventional household seemed to him of no concern. As he walks frantically up and down, he seems to be in some fantastic communication with time and space. With a bit more experience, Nick could have pointed out to him that when you mess around with an excitable young married woman, you are buying yourself a peck of trouble.

It is at this point that there occurs the passage that, when carried over from *Trimalchio* into *Gatsby*, has caused much spilled ink. Gatsby remembers the time, five years earlier at the change of the year, when he kissed Daisy, and knew that now his mind would never romp again like the mind of God: "So he waited, listening for a moment longer to the tuning fork that had been struck upon a star. Then he kissed her. At his lips' touch she blossomed for him like a flower and the incarnation was complete."

The extremity of the language is necessary, though, if the relationship of these star-crossed lovers is to be grasped, and it is at least possible that Fitzgerald has conjured into being sets of feelings that run on different tracks. Daisy lives in the world we like to call real, in which women, real women, stuff their suitcases with real silks and drive real cars over to a lover. A bit headstrong, perhaps, but none the less real for that. But Gatsby lives in the world of romantic energies and colors, a world shaped as a conspiracy between himself and the writer who has been creating him. It is the world of Emma Bovary and Julien Sorel and Balzac's heroes. How it was wandered into by a cornball from the shores of Lake Superior must remain, no doubt, a mystery. But there you are.

As Fitzgerald wrote to his other literary friend from Princeton, John Peale Bishop, "You are right about Gatsby being blurred and patchy. I never at any one time saw him clear myself—for he started out as one man I knew and then changed into myself—the amalgam was never complete in my mind." But that would happen always with his central figures—Amory Blaine and Anthony Patch, Dexter Green, Dick Diver, Monroe Stahr. It is a common affliction of the romantic sensibility and still more of romantic aspiration. Small wonder that Keats was his favorite poet—perhaps his favorite writer—or that he wrote to his daughter that "The Eve of Saint Agnes" "has the richest, most sensuous imagery in English, not excepting Shakespeare." It would be somewhere within his mind when Gatsby begins throwing his London-made shirts before Daisy in multicolored disarray, "shirts

with stripes and scrolls and plaids in coral and apple green and laven-
der and faint orange with monograms of Indian blue." Small wonder
that when the single romantic dream shatters, the world disassembles
itself, uncreates itself, drains off its colors and names for things. "He
must have looked up at an unfamiliar sky through frightening leaves
and shivered as he found out what a grotesque thing a rose is and how
raw the sunlight was upon the scarcely created grass."

Fitzgerald—and Zelda too, in her different way—had received a
raven's wing of that terror of the suddenly unreal in that summer
when he was writing *Gatsby*, and Zelda either became infatuated
with or fell desperately in love with a young French naval aviator
named Édouard Jozan. He would appear, variously renamed, in *Tender Is the Night* and in Zelda's *Save Me the Waltz*. "Everybody knew
it but Scott," Sara Murphy said. But he found out. They always do.
Even Tom Buchanan did when he heard Daisy say to Gatsby: "You
always look so cool." Apparently the jury is still out on whether
Zelda went to bed with Jozan, but it might not have much mattered in
view of the enormous, the almost Gatsby-like investment which
Fitzgerald and Zelda had made in each other.

Back in 1920, a young woman friend of Fitzgerald's, bearing the
somewhat improbable name of Isabelle Amorous, heard that the
engagement had been broken off, and wrote to tell him that from all
she had heard he was well out of it. She got an earshot in reply, which
is what such people deserve:

> No personality as strong as Zelda's could go without getting
> criticisms and as you say she is not above reproach. I've always
> known that. Any girl who gets stewed in public, who frankly
> enjoys and tells shocking stories, who smokes constantly and
> makes the remark that she has "kissed thousands of men and
> intends to kiss thousands more," cannot be considered beyond
> reproach even if above it. But Isabelle I fell in love with her

courage, her sincerity and her flaming self respect and it's these things I'd believe in even if the whole world indulged in wild suspicions that she wasn't all that she should be.

But of course the real reason, Isabelle, is that I love her and that's the beginning and end of everything. You're still a Catholic but Zelda's the only God I have left now.

So much for this "lapsed Catholic sensibility" nonsense. He ends the letter with admirable restraint, perhaps because he is writing from Princeton's Cottage Club: "And don't reproach yourself for your letter. My friends are unanimous in frankly advising me not to marry a wild, pleasure-loving girl like Zelda so I'm quite used to it." To speak of Zelda, then at least, as what he has instead of God (which is eerily prophetic of something Brett says to Jake in *The Sun Also Rises*) is more than a lover's rhetoric; it is something closer to the fact.

Now, from the Riviera in August, a month after he has confronted Zelda, and as he is finishing the novel, he writes to another old friend, Ludlow Fowler, the model for Anson Hunter in "The Rich Boy": "That's the whole burden of this novel—the loss of those illusions that give such color to the world that you don't care whether things are true or false as long as they partake of the magical glory."

There remains now only the hygienic task of clearing up a misconception about this novel which has grown mushroomlike beside it, and threatens at times almost to replace it. This is the belief that *The Great Gatsby* is about something called "the American Dream." Scholars exchange their learned articles on the subject, and generations of college freshmen are told about it. If you whispered into a reader's sleeping ear the words "Scott Fitzgerald's *The Great Gatsby*," she would murmur drowsily "and the corruption of the American dream." By the time Mizener was at work on his biography, he was writing with confidence of "Gatsby's embodiment of the American dream." Subsequent libraries of Gatsby criticism are elaborations of the theme. There probably is an American dream, and it probably deserves some of the things that are said about it. (How else could we have wound up with Gore and Bush—such things are not accidents.) But this is not the subject of Fitzgerald's wonderful novel, which is "about" our entrance into the world "trailing clouds of glory" until

> *At length the Man perceives it die away,*
> *And fade into the light of common day.*

Wordsworth was not in a particularly American mood when he wrote the Immortality Ode. And he even went out of his way to tell us in a long note what he took his own poem to be about. Many times when going to school, he tells us, "have I grasped at a wall or tree to recall myself from this abyss of idealism to the reality." In his poem, he chooses to regard this "as presumptive evidence of a prior state of existence," an idea "not advanced in revelation" but with "nothing there to contradict it." And, if one would want some more recent speculations upon the subject, one might study what Nick feels after Gatsby's fear that his mind will not romp again like the mind of God:

> Through all that he said, even through his appalling sentimentality, I was reminded of something—an elusive rhythm, a fragment of lost words, that I had heard somewhere a long time ago. For a moment a phrase tried to take shape in my mouth and my lips parted like a dumb man's, as though there were more struggling on them than a wisp of startled air. But they made no sound, and what I had almost remembered was uncommunicable forever.

That memory came to a first European life in a Platonic dialogue, and since then we have been listening to fragmentary echoes from the

Cave. *Of course*, Fitzgerald has much to tell us about the life and the history of American culture, about the textures, the richnesses and thinnesses of our national life—because after all, as we've been told, poetry must have a local habitation and a name. And maybe we have persuaded ourselves that all American novels are really about America, and not about love and eros and death.

—*The New York Review of Books*, December 21, 2000

4

THE BEST HE COULD DO

> "We do not have great writers," I said. "Something happens to
> our good writers at a certain age. I can explain but it is quite
> long and may bore you."
> "Please explain," he said. "This is what I enjoy. This is the
> best part of life. The life of the mind. This is not killing kudu."
>
> —*Green Hills of Africa* (1935)

THE CONVERSATION HELD in the bush country of Kenya between
Ernest Hemingway and a stranded Austrian named Kandisky is the
only well-remembered part of *Green Hills of Africa*. It is otherwise
given over to the hunting of various beasts, especially the fleet though
luckless kudu, a sport for which the reader comes to share Kandisky's
puzzled distaste.

Kandisky, who had read Hemingway's early poetry in the *Quer-
schnitt*, implores him to tell how America destroys its writers:

> We destroy them in many ways. First, economically. They make
> money. It is only by hazard that a writer makes money although
> good books always make money eventually. Then our writers
> when they have made some money increase their standard of

living and they are caught. They have to write to keep up their establishments, their wives, and so on, and they write slop. It is slop not on purpose but because it is hurried. Because they write when there is nothing to say or no water in the well. Because they are ambitious.

Hemingway saw no need to inform either Kandisky or the reader that he himself had been moved up into a different world of money. The safari had been underwritten by a $25,000 check from his wife Pauline's generous uncle, who had also bought them, as a honeymoon gift, their handsome and spacious house in Key West. Some day soon, he would be associating his first wife, Hadley, with Paris and a benign poverty and, as Kandisky would say, the life of the mind, and the arduous and hard-purchased acquisition of a style. Pauline would then represent rich people and ease and artistic peril.

Instead, he tells Kandisky of the kind of writing that can be done. "How far prose can be carried if any one is serious enough and has luck. There is a fourth and fifth dimension that can be gotten" by a writer and "nothing else matters. It is more important than anything he can do." But you are speaking of poetry, Kandisky objects, and is answered: "It is a prose that has never been written. But it can be written, without tricks and without cheating. With nothing that will go bad afterwards." It is a prose, he says, much more difficult than poetry, which would have earned a wry smile from Pound and a sphinxlike one from Stein. Theirs was the Paris-based world of American writers in which Hemingway came into possession of his strength as a writer, and which he would come in the end to look backward to as to a lost Garden of Eden.

Every young writer is entitled to boast about the way he intends to write, but the young Hemingway actually got there. We keep saying that the Hemingway of those days was wonderful, but now we say it as ritual, as a stick to beat what he became, and our remembered wonder has faded a bit. Everyone has a favorite passage, though, in which nothing has gone bad:

> In the fall the war was always there, but we did not go to it any more. It was cold in the fall in Milan and the dark came very early. Then the electric lights came on, and it was pleasant along the streets looking in the windows. There was much game hanging outside the shops, and the snow powdered in the fur of the foxes and the wind blew their tails. The deer hung stiff and heavy and empty, and small birds blew in the wind and the wind turned their feathers. It was a cold fall and the wind came down from the mountains.

In freshman classes in the Fifties, when many of us were English instructors, we would tell our students that it was wonderful, the way that first paragraph of "In Another Country" prepares us for what follows. They don't go to the war because they report to a hospital where they are strapped into machines which promise to restore their shattered limbs, stretched out like the carcasses outside the shops. The narrator worries about how he will be if he is sent back to the front, and envies three soldiers with the predatory faces of hawks. That is symbolism, we would tell our students, God forgive us. One patient has no confidence in the machines, an idiotic idea, "a theory like another." Like theories of how to fight wars.

The experience of war, Lieutenant Henry learns in *A Farewell to Arms*, renders obscene its theories and abstractions:

> There were many words that you could not stand to hear and finally only the names of places had dignity. Certain numbers were the same way and certain dates and these with the names of the places were all you could say and have them mean anything. Abstract words such as glory, honor, courage, or hallow were

obscene beside the concrete names of villages, the numbers of roads, the names of rivers, the numbers of regiments and the dates.

Our memories make his point. The wartime rhetoric dried years ago into the mud of the sunken roads, and if today we remember Caporetto as a disastrous Italian retreat it is because of Hemingway's novel. We remember Lieutenant Henry on those roads as vividly as we remember Prince Andrei as he lies dying on the field of Borodino.

But as Henry tells us about war's lethal rhetoric, his creator is simultaneously announcing an aesthetic. It tells us that if what is actually there can be expressed *truly*, to use a word he would overuse, then the meanings packed within the prose will be released; meaning will draw upon silences and rhythms as well as words. A complicated aesthetic, and not without tricks and mystifications of its own: Hemingway himself had not been at Caporetto or anywhere near it. He did not arrive in Italy until June of 1918 and was wounded a month later at Fossalta. The retreat had taken place in the preceding autumn. Yet its veterans would speak of the astonishing accuracy and precision of the third book of *A Farewell to Arms*. As Hemingway would remind us, Stephen Crane had not been at Chancellorsville nor had Stendhal been at Waterloo. Art creates the truth of the trusting imagination— aided in this instance by a heavy reading of newspapers, memoirs, military histories. In his brief month, he had seen patriotic slogans peeling from walls and discouraged soldiers moving through mud.

He began the untruths about his own Italian war almost as soon as he got back to Oak Park, telling the local American Legion post that he had served as a lieutenant in the Brigata Ancona during the Monte Grappa offensive. He was a very young man who had displayed bravery under fire; by age-old tradition, returning veterans are not on oath. Unfortunately, the habit grew with the years—lies about himself and about what he was writing, lies of an almost certifiable grandeur. (Kenneth Lynn, in his biography, gathers many of them with the sardonic zeal of a prosecuting attorney.[1]) In *True at First Light* he tells his wife, "Miss Mary," who serves as the Kandisky of the second safari, that "all a writer of fiction is really is a congenital liar who invents from his own knowledge or that of other men."

We will come soon enough to that newly published "novel" or "memoir" or whatever its publishers choose to call it. Hemingway had been interested from early on in the interplay of form and imagination. *Green Hills of Africa*, he claimed, was an attempt "to write an absolutely true book to see whether the shape of a country and the pattern of a month's action can, if truly presented, compete with a work of the imagination." And in *Death in the Afternoon*, his book about bullfighting, he was exploring the shapes of discursive prose, and doing so, part of the time, with energy and wit. It is exasperating to read, passages of swaggering self-display and then pages of absolutely stunning prose, sequences of physical action in the bullring and passages which savor with equal delight Spanish food and the contemplation of death. At the very end of his life, he was hinting that *A Moveable Feast* should be read as fiction in the form of a memoir. Fictional memoirs are all the rage these days: the man has a lot to answer for.

But in that autumn of 1933, when he was on the first safari, he was at what proved to be the height of his achievement. He had behind him the triumphs of *The Sun Also Rises* and *A Farewell to Arms*, and two volumes of short stories, *In Our Time* and *Men Without Women*,

---

1. Carlos Baker's biography (Scribner, 1969) is the foundation stone on which later biographies rest (Martha Gellhorn called it "the Gospel according to Saint Carlos"). It was clear almost from the start that there would be a need for others. Those by Kenneth Lynn (Simon and Schuster, 1987) and Jeffrey Meyers (Harper and Row, 1985) are solidly written and display good literary judgment, but I prefer that by Meyers, which is unsentimental while lacking Lynn's curious dislike of his subject. Michael Reynolds has published *Hemingway: The Final Years* (Norton, 1999), the fourth in a biographical series. Oddly though, his most valuable contribution is *Hemingway's First War* (Princeton University Press, 1976), which is not part of the series, but began, soberly and quietly, the necessary demythologizing task.

which changed forever the ways in which American writers would imagine that form. A third volume, *Winner Take Nothing*, proved that the style remained little short of miraculous, but the title itself seemed to hint that he was expending it upon a world of losers which he had already explored beyond its worth. And yet, as he well knew, it contained some of his best work—"A Clean, Well-Lighted Place," "A Way You'll Never Be," "Fathers and Sons," "The Gambler, the Nun, and the Radio."

His reputation among other serious writers could not have been higher. As long ago as 1926 Allen Tate had written of "the recent prophecy that he will be 'the big man' in American letters," and the prophecy, despite Tate's ironical quotation marks, seemed to be coming true. Eighteen thousand copies of *Winner Take Nothing* were sold in the first accounting season, which was doing extraordinarily well for a book of short stories intended for the Christmas trade, in one of which a boy chooses that season to castrate himself. There now existed a market for any book written by "Ernest Hemingway." For already, by the early Thirties, there existed a Hemingway "legend"— a handsome, wounded soldier, boxer, and bullfighter, who was now off to Africa to shoot big game. That he should also be the great hope of American literature seemed too good to be true.

Nabokov says somewhere that the best part of a writer's biography is the biography of his style. In Hemingway's case, this presented unique problems. The Hemingway legend existed as a kind of penumbra surrounding the texts, easy enough for any intelligent reader to cut through, but with a slight, peculiar feeling of impropriety. He seemed beyond question a modernist writer, for whom impersonality was a treasured principle. But the stories hinted at a style, an attitude toward experience, which lay beneath the printed page and found affirmation in the public man. Eventually, of course, and in the final works, the legend, bloated beyond belief, would swallow up the words.

In *The Sun Also Rises*, someone asks Brett's friend Mike how he went bankrupt, and he says, "Two ways. Gradually and then suddenly." In the case of Hemingway's art, we will never know how it happened or how early. There is something heroic in his stubborn refusal to quit. It is chilling to read the accounts of the daily stint of pages, the words religiously counted up, and then, after lunch, because the sun was always below the yardarm somewhere in the world, the gargantuan drinking. But that "shit detector" which he said was essential to a writer was still working, and sooner or later a manuscript would be abandoned and a new one begun. Perhaps some day it might be fitted into the "big sea, air, and land novel" which he kept hinting about to editors and Broadway columnists. He was happily unaware of what would be the future of those unwieldy messes, thanks to the kindness of children and publishers.

First it went gradually, a slow erosion of his near-faultless control of material, and then, even more slowly, of his reputation as a writer whom it was essential to read. The irony—"the irony and the pity"— as Jake Barnes and Bill keep saying—is that as his serious readers came to realize that something was badly amiss, the popular legend swelled larger and larger. And so today he is a grizzled icon smiling and thinking deep thoughts behind sea-weathered eyes. An image of the writer as American hero, imperturbable, masterful, hard-drinking.

From time to time, in the final period, he would emerge from his Havana house to go on a second safari, to follow the bulls, to drink at Toots Shor's, or to shoot doves with Gary Cooper. Or, disastrously, to be interviewed in 1950 by Lillian Ross, who had mastered a technique, unknown to Boswell, by which anybody, talking unguardedly, can be shown to be pretty silly, especially if what he says is, in fact, pretty silly.

His reputation was seriously damaged not by Ross but by the appearance of *Across the River and into the Trees*. At the time of the interview he was carrying the galleys with him, like a cyanide pellet.

But the grave aesthetic lapses in the novel seemed to readers to find an explanation in the interview. It was there, amid the Injun Joe palaver, that he boasted that he had beat Mr. Turgenev, then "trained hard and I beat Mr. de Maupassant. I've fought two draws with Mr. Stendhal, and I think I had an edge in the last one." Time was, to continue his metaphor, when he would have had Ross on the canvas two minutes into the first round, but that time was gone.

What he had brought back from that first safari was the germ of two stories, written at the height of his powers, and one of them an impressive stretch of those powers. We read them differently now from the way we did then, now that we know so much more about his inner life, more perhaps than people need to know about other people. Today we read "The Short Happy Life of Francis Macomber" as a story of the divided self, with Hemingway as both the cool, tough white hunter and as Macomber, the man who comes to know his own cowardice and shame, masters them, and as reward is shot down by his wife. People used to argue about whether or not she had shot him entirely by accident, but there has never been any doubt that Margot Macomber is Exhibit A in any reading of Hemingway as misogynist. Beautiful, poised, lethal, mistress of her own abacus of sexual rewards and deprivations, she chilled at least one undergraduate with a conflict of feelings for which not even the Dragon Lady in *Terry and the Pirates* had prepared him. He was too unnerved to admire the story's technical perfection—the control of pace and the development of mood, the sparse, uncluttered dialogue that forces you to hear what is not being said.

Everyone knew, though, that in "The Snows of Kilimanjaro" Hemingway was writing about himself and his relationship to his art, in ways that at first seem direct but in fact are oblique and, perhaps, self-justifying. It is a crucial "perhaps." A writer named Harry lies dying of gangrene in the African bush country, waiting for a relief plane which, the reader intuits, will not arrive in time. His wife's cool sarcasm is difficult to criticize: Harry is a tough case, embittered, vengeful, full of hatred and self-loathing. The wife is society and rich, and he blames her for his corruption and the corruption of his art. He regrets the stories that he will have no time to write, remembering them as scenes, snatches of conversation, emotions which in the writing would have been buried beneath the words. They are memories from his life, and Hemingway's, shuffled like cards—the world war and its killing, a boyhood at his grandfather's house, skiing in Austria, things he witnessed as a correspondent in the Twenties. They are a bit like Joyce's epiphanies but far more like the interchapters of *In Our Time*:

> Now in his mind he saw a railway station at Karagatch and he was standing with his pack and that was the headlight of the Simplon-Orient cutting the dark now and he was leaving Thrace then after the retreat. That was one of the things he had saved to write, with, in the morning at breakfast, looking out the window and seeing snow on the mountains in Bulgaria and Nansen's Secretary asking the old man if it were snow and the old man looking at it and saying, No, that's not snow. It's too early for snow. And the Secretary repeating to the other girls, No, you see. It's not snow and them all saying, It's not snow we were mistaken. But it was the snow all right and he sent them on into it when he evolved exchange of populations. And it was snow they tramped along in until they died that winter.

Jeffrey Meyers, in his extremely helpful biography, dates the passage from October 18, 1922, when Hemingway left the Greek frontier for Sofia and then Paris. It is a mute accusation against Fridtjof Nansen for sending refugees to certain death in the Thracian snows. But the alternative, Meyers reminds us, would have been massacre by the Turkish forces. He doesn't comment upon the irony that Nansen, an Arctic explorer, should have known all about snow. Like all the flashbacks, it is intended to remind us that the Hemingway of *In Our Time* is alive and well in 1936.

And we are also intended to accept that Harry's corruption will not be Hemingway's, who is too tough, too disciplined. Unlike poor Julian—Scott, he was called in the *Esquire* version—whose romantic awe of wealth and its supposed grace "wrecked him just as much as any other thing that wrecked him." Hemingway usually attacked by going out on the battlefield the next day to pistol the wounded. He would wait until *A Moveable Feast* to do a complete job on Fitzgerald. But in this story, he allows Harry, his surrogate as victim, a dying measure of self-knowledge:

> She shot very well this good, this rich bitch, this kindly caretaker and destroyer of his talent. Nonsense. He had destroyed his talent himself. Why should he blame this woman because she kept him well? He had destroyed his talent by not using it, by betrayals of himself and what he believed in, by drinking so much that he blunted the edge of his perceptions, by laziness, by sloth, and by snobbery, by pride and by prejudice, by hook and by crook.

Serious readers of his work, Lionel Trilling, William Troy, and especially Edmund Wilson, who had been the earliest of his American supporters, worked out a formula to explain what was happening to him in the Thirties: there were two Hemingways, when he wrote as an artist and when he wrote as himself. It is a notion which could only have sustained itself in those high modernist days when the utter, Flaubertian inviolability of Art was taken as a given. Wilson gave it its most felicitous expression. When Hemingway writes in his own person, he is likely to become fatuous, maudlin, silly. But in his art, "his sense of what happens and the way it happens is...sunk deep below the surface and is not conveyed by argument or preaching but by directly transmitted emotion: it is turned into something as hard as crystal and as disturbing as a great lyric."[2]

In truth, though, art and "life" are not separated by impermeable membranes and each can begin leaking into the other. Not yet, though. *For Whom the Bell Tolls* is a successful novel, with marvelous scattered set pieces, but the relieved praise of critics as perceptive as Wilson and Trilling today seems excessive, shaded by pleasure at the author's recovery from his recent decline, and by complexities of feeling toward the Spanish Civil War. On his best days, Hemingway had a political as well as a literary shit detector, and he was one of the few novelists to be staunch in his defense of the Loyalist cause and wholeheartedly and eloquently shocked by the Stalinist manipulation. His portrait of Marty, the murderous Party functionary, is devastating, and so too are the sketches of Soviet journalists. Neither was it so easy, after his book, to think of La Pasionaria as an Iberian Joan of Arc. A disgust with all ideology runs through the book, a thick undercurrent. Simply, he supported the Loyalists because theirs was, for him, the Spanish cause.

But the book does not seem to me the triumph it once appeared to be, although Meyers argues that it is his best novel. It is a book that has faded, whereas *The Sun Also Rises*, despite unpleasant shadows, remains vivid and sunshot. It suggests despite itself that his was the art of the miniaturist. It tries to compensate by forcing a crowded narrative within the compass of three days, beginning and ending in the pine forest in the Sierra de Guadarrama, where Robert Jordan waits for his death. We carry away from it, though, not a sense of that imposed structure, but of isolated, discrete scenes of great power—the slaughter of the Fascists in Pilar's village, El Sordo's fight on his mountainside.

---

2. Edmund Wilson, *Letters on Literature and Politics, 1912–1972* (Farrar, Straus and Giroux, 1977).

The final word may be left to Scott Fitzgerald, Hemingway's improbable twin, their opposing selves now locked together forever. Hemingway had sent him a copy signed "To Scott with affection and esteem Ernest." Fitzgerald, replying, speaks of the massacre scene as "magnificent and also the fight on the mountain and the actual dynamiting scene." But to his notebook he confided: "It is so to speak Ernest's 'Tale of two Cities' though the comparison isn't apt. I mean that it is a thoroughly superficial book which has all the profundity of *Rebecca*."

It probably did even better in sales than *Rebecca*, with the Book-of-the-Month Club ordering 200,000 copies, and, within the first six months, 491,000 copies sold. After he had mailed in the galleys, he and Martha Gellhorn took off for Sun Valley, as Averell Harriman's guests, where Ernest organized a rabbit hunt with his sons and Merle Oberon and Gary Cooper. In December, on his way back to Havana, he learned of Fitzgerald's death of heart failure in Sheilah Graham's Hollywood living room.

In "The Snows of Kilimanjaro," Hemingway has an imaginary but famous conversation between himself and Fitzgerald. Fitzgerald— "Julian"—had begun a story, "The very rich are different from you and me." And "someone"—Hemingway—says, "Yes, they have more money." He was now and for the rest of his life would be in the world of the rich. In that world, once you have survived the rigors of the Membership Committee, you need not always have the money in a particular year. The coffers will be refilled by your next super-bestseller.

He never—to use a phrase just then coming into use—"sold out." He never, to borrow a word from his talk with Kandisky, wrote slop when he was writing seriously. It was always the very best he could do, and that, finally, became the problem. Curiously, that world of the rich, in which he was actually living and had identified as a source of corruption, hardly ever enters his work save for strokes of vulgar satire in *To Have and Have Not*. Harry, of "The Snows of Kiliman-jaro," had told himself "that you could write about these people; about the very rich; that you were really not of them but a spy in their country; that you could leave it and write of it and for once it would be written by some one who knew what he was writing of." In his final years, he became a serious reader of Proust, who had been a spy in several worlds, but it was a bit late to learn the lessons of that master.

The importance of the celebrity culture in the making and undoing of Ernest Hemingway should not be minimized. There is a fine, lively book on the subject, *Hemingway and His Conspirators: Hollywood, Scribners, and the Making of American Celebrity Culture*, by Leonard Leff,[3] although he ends with the 1932 film of *A Farewell to Arms*, when that culture was in its infancy. His villains are Hemingway himself, who presided over the process, the editors and publicists at Scribners, the gossip columnists who spread the news of the handsome war hero who just happened to be the best American writer, middleweight division.

He was the first writer of authentic stature to be caught in the crosshairs of that culture. Scott Fitzgerald had been even handsomer, but by the Thirties his Irish charm had faded and only after his approaching death would a deeper, darker legend surround him. To be sure, Mark Twain, Hemingway's spiritual father, had done his best for himself, with his cigar and his cornball white suit, but he had to work alone, without an infrastructure.

But from the first, Hemingway had been beset by demons with claws sharper than money or fame. Biographers have been telling us of the appalling mother and the suicidal father, of the mother dressing him up as a girl, of his fascination with women's hair—this last, I should have thought, a harmless caprice. They can appear in first

---

3. Rowman and Littlefield, 1997.

light, at a Havana worktable. To the annoyance of biographers, a writer's deepest problems often turn out to be those of language and structure, of a thwarted imagination.

His Second World War was of an idiosyncratic sort, organizing an amateur spy network in Cuba and transforming the *Pilar*, his cruiser, into a submarine hunter armed with rifles. Then, over in Europe, he had himself quite a war as an armed guerrilla disguised as a war correspondent. Martha Gellhorn, his leggy, ambitious, and breezy third wife, claimed that the submarine hunt was a dodge to get more gasoline for the *Pilar*, but Ernest took it seriously, and like his ragtag of young French gunmen it was woven into the legend. For at least one student of Hemingway, Gellhorn is the only one of his wives to earn respect and sympathy. She didn't hang around places to be abused, not by Hemingway, not by anybody. Great hair, too.

By the war's end, he had her replacement, a *Time* correspondent named Mary Welsh. We will encounter her in *True at First Light*, where he attempts by verbal chivalry to atone for a relationship in which he smothered her with abuse and scurrility. She seems to have been an ingenious, libidinous woman, and would require these qualities in her marriage to a husband given to the enactment of sexual fantasies.

Back in Havana, he settled down to "the big sea, land and air novel," which was to occupy him, in one form or another, until his death. It makes for a melancholy and knotted story, for which the reader is referred to Rose Marie Burwell's *Hemingway: The Postwar Years and the Posthumous Novels*.[4] This exemplary study of the texts of the various unfinished narratives is a brilliant piece of scholarship of the old school. Equally, she is a scholar of one of those new schools in which writers do not "write" but "inscribe"—a distinction I have never grasped—and I cannot accept her argument that Hemingway

---

4. Cambridge University Press, 1996.

intended *A Moveable Feast, Islands in the Stream*, and *The Garden of Eden* as an intricately intertwined "portrait of the artist as painter and writer, and as son, husband, and father." But the care and scrupulousness with which she argues entitle her to her theory.

In 1946, Michael Reynolds tells us in his *Hemingway: The Final Years*, Hemingway wrote "like a man possessed," an instance of his own lapidary prose. By late July, he had almost a thousand pages written although he had no set plan for the book, letting it develop as it would. Ominous words for an editor to read, but his letters to Charles Scribner exuded daiquiri-scented confidence. The day before, he once wrote, his word count had been 573 before breakfast, "after which I fucked three times, shot ten straight at pigeons (very fast ones) at the club, drank with five friends a case of Piper Heidsieck Brut and looked all the afternoon for fish." When you are a legend, publishers accept your lies without demurral, however unlikely they may be, however crudely expressed.

Another problem is that he was isolated, within no world of writers who could give him either dispute or the respect that he had earned. As he chose to put it: "I haven't known a writer who was a good guy since Jim Joyce died. And he was spotty sometimes." What about Scott Fitzgerald, who once had given him sound advice on the opening of *The Sun Also Rises*? "Then we have Scott borrowing on the outline of a thing he'd never, and never could, write, giving samples here and there like a mining prospector with a salted mine."

Or maybe he would do the war differently from what he had planned; maybe it would be only a noise offstage. This cycle of writing in the morning on narratives that rambled, as he always finally knew, down interminable and labyrinthine hedgerows, and then drinking and bullshitting in the afternoon, and facing his faceless demons in the night, went on for years until, in the fall of 1948, he took Mary to visit the Italian places that he remembered from his first war. He had not published a book, or anything of real worth, for nine years.

Venice, the lagoon, and Torcello yielded him a skyful of birds worth shooting and the atmosphere and feelings from which he created *Across the River and into the Trees*. His Colonel Cantwell is a professional who has been broken from general for obscure, unspecified errors, perhaps his own, perhaps his superiors'. He is embittered not by knowledge of his approaching death but by the degradation by modern warfare of the soldier's chivalric code. In Venice, he has fallen in love with an aristocratic beauty of nineteen named Renata (the Reborn), who is at once his muse, his love, and the embodiment of yet another code crumbling within the crumbling city. Cantwell is Hemingway, his noncombatant services as an ambulance driver and war correspondent transformed by the magic of self-love.

The opening chapters, of the duck shoot and the approach to the city, are superb:

> He watched the sky lightening beyond the long point of marsh, and turning in the sunken barrel, he looked out across the frozen lagoon, and the marsh, and saw the snow-covered mountains a long way off. Low as he was, no foothills showed, and the mountains rose abruptly from the plain. As he looked toward the mountains he could feel a breeze on his face and he knew, then, the wind would come from there, rising with the sun, and that some birds would surely come flying in from the sea when the wind disturbed them.

The trouble begins—and the novel is in deep trouble—when he walks through the doors of the Gritti Palace, and gets worse when he crosses over to Harry's Bar. He and the *maître d'hôtel* and the bartender belong to one of Hemingway's tiresome make-believe secret societies that exist for the sole purpose of keeping people out. Robert Cohn found out about them in *The Sun Also Rises*, although he did not find out enough. The novel gets still worse when we are given glimpses into that arcane society of two—Cantwell and his submissive muse—for whom everything from the buttering of toast to the arrangement of cushions in a gondola is part of an elegiac ritual.

Hemingway intends the book's secret to be buried within its structure. War is the book's true subject, and it is kept chastely offstage. Cantwell talks about it to his Desdemona in endless conversations held everywhere—at lunch, at dinner, in bed, in a gondola. And what we learn moves us deeper and deeper into a war fought without honor. Hemingway would not have felt offended had we thought of Dante, with Renata as his slightly soiled (by the colonel, in the gondola) muse. It is a marvelous notion, but Othello had more going for him. A novel cannot be saved by structure alone.

The book deserved its devastating reviews. But we know now that throughout those years of silence, or rather of not publishing, he had endured ever-deepening depressions and rages, had battled against temptations to suicide, against a waning creativity, and yet he had kept writing. As John O'Hara, his bellicose protégé, put it: "To use his own favorite metaphor, he may not be able to go the full distance, but he can still hurt you. Always dangerous."

It is an autumnal novel, and so is *The Old Man and the Sea*, but with a sad difference. He presented it as a segment of the "big novel." And so it is, burnished and hand-rubbed and as phony as a three-dollar bill. The mystery, as Kenneth Lynn says, is why this book with its lachrymose sentimentality and its "crucifixion symbolism of the most appalling crudity" should have "evoked such a storm of applause from highbrows and middlebrows alike—and in such overwhelming numbers." One half of the answer is that it is the perfect middlebrow work of art. *Life* published the entire text in an edition of 5,300,000, which sold out in days. Michael Reynolds speaks, alas, for posterity: "All the signs were positive; all the readers agreed. *The Old Man and the Sea* was a stunning book, a story told as simply as a fable, and as tenderly as a love letter." It is a perfect text for high schools.

❖ ❖ ❖

Three weeks after Hemingway's death in 1961, his widow traveled to Cuba for his literary remains, witnesses to creative struggle and defeat. Charles Scribner Jr. has described her arrival in the office, carrying a large shopping bag bulging with unpublished material—completed and uncompleted short stories and fragments, "and the typescripts of three major works, a novel set in Bimini and Cuba, later published under the title *Islands in the Stream*, the original transcript of Hemingway's bullfighting journal, *The Dangerous Summer*, and a major work of fiction, to which Hemingway had given the title, *The Garden of Eden*." The capacious shopping bag may also have contained the account of his second safari in 1953, which he abandoned after writing 200,000 words of a rough draft.

Maxwell Perkins, had he been alive, might have shaken his head in perplexity. These were not manuscripts in the ordinary sense, but attempts at coherence and thematic development, overlapping, entangled, repetitious, shifting beneath the author's pen. Editing Thomas Wolfe had been one thing: fierce slashes through an overgrown jungle of Spanish moss. These, on the other hand, were the pages of a major artist who had once possessed a dandy's finicking spareness of language.

But by the time of his death, Hemingway had become a superproperty. It was merely a matter of time and editorial ingenuity before the shopping bag was published. With the exception of the cameo which a skillful editor named Tom Jenks shaped out of *The Garden of Eden*, we do not turn to these "posthumous works" for any of the pleasures of art. That Hemingway abandoned them is not surprising.

Few readers would pick up *Islands in the Stream* for a second time save in the line of duty. A few landscapes rendered with his usual swift authenticity, long conversations that drift into verbal doodling, characters who are introduced abruptly and then are disappeared like so many Argentinian dissidents. The hero, a stalled painter named

Thomas Hudson, is deeply, suicidally embittered, a condition which he exhibits by acting grouchy. It is, as John Updike calls it, "a thoroughly ugly book, brutal and messy...."[5]

It was edited by Carlos Baker, Hemingway's first biographer, assisted by Charles Scribner and Mary: one cannot envy them their task. Hemingway's attitude toward the story he was telling and toward the plot itself fluctuated. Any writer's first draft can be a landscape of probes and emendations, and this places upon an editor a need to discover the text's developing life. But Mary Hemingway says, in a note as laconic as a Spartan epigraph: "Charles Scribner, Jr. and I worked together preparing this book for publication from Ernest's original manuscript. Beyond the routine chores of correcting spelling and punctuation, we made some cuts in the manuscript, I feeling that Ernest would surely have made them himself. The book is all Ernest's. We have added nothing to it." This is strictly true, in the negative sense that Willie Sutton never cracked a safe to make a deposit. The meaning of a work of fiction is shaped as much by what is cut away from it as by what is kept, especially in the case of a writer who worked through counterpoints of silence and language. The earthly Hemingway distrusted the judgments of editors and wives.

Of *The Garden of Eden* we know, although not from Scribner's, that it exists as some 2,400 pages, out of which Tom Jenks created a comely and absorbing novel of 247 pages. As we are told by a scholar who has examined the manuscript, it is "often more reiterative than cumulative, containing immense repetition that Hemingway seems to have been unable to control, and there is often little evidence among the variants that he privileged one text over another." *Seems to have been unable to control* is a chilling phrase.

But Jenks has performed a dazzling feat. The published text glows with language to bring to mind Hemingway at his best, tense with the

---

5. John Updike, *Odd Jobs: Essays and Criticism* (Knopf, 1991), p. 308.

excitement of narrative clarity yet hinting at mystery just below the skin of the prose. The Mediterranean is not there to be exploited but becomes part of the novel's texture:

> They were living at le Grau du Roi then and the hotel was on a canal that ran from the walled city of Aigues Mortes straight down to the sea. They could see the towers of Aigues Mortes across the low plain of the Camargue and they rode there on their bicycles at some time of nearly every day along the white road that bordered the canal. In the evenings and mornings when there was a rising tide the sea bass would come into it and they would see the mullet jumping wildly to escape from the bass and watch the swelling bulge of the water as the bass attacked.

The first paragraph has carried us into Hemingway country. David Bourne, a young writer, and Catharine, his venturesome bride, are on their honeymoon. Like most honeymoons, it is full of sex and sun and sensuous food and swimming. Catharine wants David to write about their honeymoon, and that is not all she has on her mind. She is eager to experiment with role reversal, and David goes along warily. But the reader knows (we are so clever nowadays) that she is deeply androgynous. Before long, a young and at first enigmatic lesbian named Marita drifts into their lives and first Catharine, then David, goes to bed with her.

There are both direct and hidden links between the story and the life of its creator. It opens on the stretch of the Mediterranean coast where Hemingway and Pauline spent their honeymoon, and it is set in the Twenties, for him, increasingly, a magical past time. He liked to fantasize a lesbian relationship between her and Hadley, his first wife. Both of his women here, like the two wives, have inherited money, which he liked to imagine a source of creative corruption. Bourne calls Marita "Heiress." Catharine turns out to be insanely jealous of his writing, and near the close of the story has become just plain crazy, with touches of Zelda. She douses Bourne's stories with gasoline, as Hadley once, by accident, lost Hemingway's. Throughout his life, he kept obsessively and unconvincingly forgiving her this, in print and out. What Catharine burns are "African stories," about a safari Bourne had once made with his father, in which an old elephant was killed. At the end, Marita and Bourne are deeply in love, and Bourne is writing steadily and well, like Ernest Hemingway. Whether or not this is an ending dictated by Jenks's wish to tidy things up is an open question.

Hemingway was dealing here with psychologically explosive material upon which he could never have imposed aesthetic closure. Behind the marlin-fighting bravado lay a different person, uneasily aware of the fragility of gender boundaries, sexually insecure, and aware of aspects of himself which created that insecurity. He had reached the edge of something dangerous and puzzling to him in this unfinishable manuscript.

True at First Light, which we are promised is the last unpublished text, is an account of his second African safari, in 1953, accompanied by "Miss Mary," as he cloyingly calls her, and financed in part by a photojournalism assignment from *Look*. His way was smoothed by the Kenyan government, anxious to demonstrate that the lucrative safari country was not threatened by Mau Mau activity farther to the east. Philip Percival, the model for the white hunter in "The Snows of Kilimanjaro," accompanied them to the Kamani Swamp, and, for the three weeks after he left, they were on their own, although the government kept a solicitous eye on them.

Those weeks form the substance of the unfinished manuscript of which one half is now published.[6] Hemingway had been appointed, with all due ceremony, as "honorary game warden," a position which

---

6. *True at First Light*, edited and with an introduction by Patrick Hemingway (Scribner, 2000).

in his judgment endowed him with great if unspecified powers, including the settlement of tribal disputes, protection of the shambas against attacks of rogue elephants, organization of defenses against armed Mau Mau infiltration, and whatever else appealed to an active, indeed inflamed imagination. The inhabitants seem to have endured all this with the courtesy extended by tribal societies toward the spiritually afflicted. He was also busy promulgating the doctrines and explaining the rituals of a new religion, and vigorously courting a young Wacumba woman named Debba, whom he intended to marry. Miss Mary may have given her approval, or so he says, but the young woman's family took a very dim view of the matter. This courtship and a tedious lion hunt form the twin centers of the narrative.

The stay in Africa was cut short by a ferocious air accident, in which Hemingway sustained severe injuries, which he bore with his customary stoicism. He appeared before journalists with his head swathed in bandages, and, according to a report carried globally, carrying a bottle of gin and a bunch of bananas. He later denied these particulars; he tended his legend with care and skill and it was not to be tampered with by some UPI stringer.

The writing in *True at First Light* is debased middle-Hemingway, put at the service of an autoeroticism which he scarcely bothers to translate from the raw material. From a letter to Harvey Breit: "My girl is completely impudent, her face is impudent in repose, but absolutely loving and delicate rough. I better quit writing about it because I want to write it really and I mustn't spoil it. Anyway it gives me too bad a hardon."[7] Here is what might be called a corresponding passage:

> When we rode together in the front seat she liked to feel the embossing on the old leather pistol. It was a flowered design

---

7. *Ernest Hemingway: Selected Letters, 1917–1961*, edited by Carlos Baker (Charles Scribner's Sons, 1981), p. 827.

and very old and worn and she would trace the design with her fingers and then take her hand away and press the pistol and its holster against her thigh.

Denis Zaphiro, the actual game warden, describes Debba as "a slovenly-looking brat" and none too clean. Miss Mary, although worldly in other ways, shared this hygienic reservation. To address such material with respect is impossible. I do not refer to the letter to Breit; we write the damnedest things to friends to enlarge their notion of what we think they think we are like. The publication of this book is a disservice to the reputation of a serious artist.

True at First Light is described by Scribner as "a fictional memoir" and by its editor, Hemingway's son Patrick, as "an ambiguous counterpoint between fiction and truth." Gussying up language that way is what the young Hemingway was fighting against. Now he himself is describing Africa as "a ruthless real world made of the unreality of the real." Send for Kandisky.

In an unpublished passage, Tom Jenks tells us, Hemingway, sleeping beside Miss Mary, dreams that the "wife I had loved first and best and who was the mother of my oldest son was with me and we were sleeping close together...." As Jenks rightly says, Hemingway never forgave himself for betraying Hadley, "whose memory he sentimentally held as an image of his lost innocence." In truth, so it seems to me, he held Hadley and innocence and the past and Paris and the company of his peers and his surest strengths and powers as a writer together in a congeries of sights and sounds, emotions and images. He had betrayed not merely Hadley but that entire constellation.

That is why *A Moveable Feast* is itself so moving a book, shot through with genuine (but perhaps not truthful) feelings and the fresh colors of a remembered youth. Small wonder that he turned to those memories after setting aside the tired theatricals of the African narrative. The plane which carried him out offered him a final glimpse of

Kilimanjaro, where, as a young writer, he had placed, "close to the western summit ... the dried and frozen carcass of a leopard. No one has explained what the leopard was seeking at that altitude."

Either by the impulse which now recalled him to Paris and his beginnings as a writer, or else by that grace in which all writers secretly believe (he always called it "luck"), he had regained, for one last time, that elegance and power which had once been at his command. Here, in these sketches, it is not a triumphant style, but rather an elegiac avowal of loyalty to a vanished past. He comes almost to the self-knowledge that the dying Harry achieves in "The Snows of Kilimanjaro," that the faults lay not in the stars—not in the celebrity, or the fat contracts, not in the money, not in the parish of rich women —but in himself.

It is evidence of true rather than public relations heroism that he was at work on these sketches right up to his admission to the Mayo Clinic, arranging and rearranging their order, as, in the Twenties, he had done with the brilliant interchapters of *In Our Time*. Down to the end, being a writer was at the core of his being, down to the hour when, outside the door of his hospital room, he taped up a sign saying FORMER WRITER, a message so plain that only psychiatrists could fail to understand it.

His brief capture of this late power does not mean that he became a nicer person. *A Moveable Feast* is the most mellow, but it is also the bitchiest of his books, part gin, part bitters. The capework and the swordwork are impressive: the respectful introduction of Gertrude Stein, the acknowledgment of what he learned from her, and then the seemingly casual: "The way it ended with Gertrude Stein was strange enough." Ernest Boyd, Wyndham Lewis, John Dos Passos, Gerald and Sara Murphy—down they go, like ducks flying over a frozen lagoon.

He is writing when we first meet him here, in a café on the Place St.-Michel, warm and clean and friendly. The story is "Up in Michigan," which was to shock some readers, and in the Paris streets outside, as in the story, it is a wild, cold, blowing day. Or he is in Lipp's, which he could not afford, thinking about his new theory "that you could omit anything if you knew that you omitted and the omitted part would strengthen the story and make people feel something more than they understood." You could hear that kind of talk all over Paris, from the old masters, Ford Madox Ford and Ezra Pound, and from countless two-bit phonies like Robert McAlmon. But he had brought his shit detector with him from Chicago, and he knew what to learn from and what to ignore. Mostly what you learned was to keep your own counsel.

When he couldn't get a story going, he "would sit in front of the fire and squeeze the peel of the little oranges into the edge of the flame," and then look out over the roofs of Paris and tell himself not to worry. "All you have to do is write that one true sentence." Everyone knows about Hemingway's "one true sentence," both mystification and manifesto, which is best remembered as attached to the peel of the little oranges and the sputter of blue flame.

Sylvia Beach from her bookshop lent him *A Sportsman's Sketches* and *The Charterhouse of Parma*, and the other texts from which Paris in the Twenties and Americans in that Paris were creating a tradition of the modern. Tolstoy showed him Prince Andrei dying at Borodino and Stendhal showed him Fabrizio bewildered at Waterloo.

Poverty was a requirement of that tradition, in a garret by preference, but Hadley and he were in the next best thing, rooms above a sawmill. He associates it not only with creativity but with domesticity and love, love of Hadley, love of little Bumby, love of the cat even. He gives Bumby a bottle and sets to work, with no one awake save Bumby and Puss the Cat and himself. "In those days you did not really need anything, not even the rabbit's foot, but it was good to feel it in your pocket." He does not get away with this particular bit of kitsch, and the failure reminds us that stylistically he has been walking the edge of a precipice. He sees the story in deeply sentimental terms, moving toward his corruption at the hands of the rich crowd at Cap d'Antibes, who have been led to him by Dos Passos, "the pilot fish."

> During our last year in the mountains new people came deep into our lives and nothing was ever the same again. The winter of the avalanches was like a happy and innocent winter in childhood compared to the next winter, a nightmare winter disguised as the greatest fun of all, and the murderous summer that was to follow. It was the year that the rich showed.

Right there, in that final chapter, the magic breaks into pieces and he becomes, almost but not quite, just another husband explaining how he fell in with a bad crowd and ditched his wife for a woman with more money. Satan made him do it. "When I saw my wife standing by the tracks as the train came in by the piled logs at the station, I wished I had died before I loved anyone but her." I hope he remembered to buy her flowers.

But before that last chapter, we forgive him everything for the sake of the words and the silences and the "luck." We even forgive him for what he does to poor Scott Fitzgerald, who didn't have enough malice in his heart to corrupt himself, let alone other people. "His chin was well built and he had good ears and a handsome, almost beautiful, unmarked nose. This should not have added up to a pretty face, but that came from the coloring, the very fair hair and the mouth. The mouth worried you until you knew him and then it worried you more." Nick Carraway describing Tom Buchanan didn't do better than that.

Before him, there had only been Mark Twain and Stephen Crane to show us what could be done with the American language, and not all that many after him.

—*The New York Review of Books*, October 21, 1999

5

JOHN O'HARA

IN JUNE 1933, John O'Hara, an unpublished writer of twenty-eight, wrote a fan letter to F. Scott Fitzgerald, who was then working on the final draft of *Tender Is the Night*. The occasion was one of Fitzgerald's *Saturday Evening Post* stories ("More Than Just a House"), in which a socially secure girl named Gunther snubs an Irish-American social climber named Lew Lowrie. O'Hara writes:

> And that easily we get to the second thing you've done so well: Lowrie, the climber; and I wonder why you do the climber so well. Is it the Irish in you? *Must* the Irish always have a lot of climber in them? Good God! I am the son of a black Irish doctor (gone to his eternal reward) and a mother who was a Sacred Heart girl, whose father was born Israel Delaney (Pennsylvania Quaker who turned Catholic to marry an immigrant girl, Liza Rourke). My old man was the first doctor in the U.S. to use oxygen in pneumonia, was recognized by Deaver as being one of the best trephiners and appendix men in the world. But do I have to tell you which side of the family impresses me most? I doubt it. You've guessed it: because Grandfather Delaney's connections included some Haarmons from Holland and a Gray who was an a.d.c. to Washington, and I have some remote

kinship with those N.Y. Pells, I go through some cheap shame when the O'Hara side gets too close for comfort. If you've had the same trouble, at least you've turned it into a gift, but I suspect that Al Smith is the only Irishman who isn't a climber at heart.[1]

Fitzgerald replied the following month:

> I am especially grateful for your letter. I am half black Irish and half old American stock with the usual exaggerated ancestral pretensions. The black Irish half of the family had the money and looked down upon the Maryland side of the family who had, and really had, that certain series of reticences and obligations that go under the poor old shattered word "breeding" (modern form "inhibitions"). So being born in that atmosphere of crack, wisecrack and countercrack I developed a two-cylinder inferiority complex. So if I were elected King of Scotland tomorrow after graduating from Eton, Magdalene, and the Guards, with an embryonic history which tied me to the Plantagenets, I would still be a parvenu. I spent my youth in alternately crawling in front of the kitchen maids and insulting the great.[2]

A discussion of the Irish-American as writer might well begin with this exchange of letters. A conviction of social inferiority is a powerful asset to a writer, and when it alternates with moments of social uncertainty it is likely to be especially potent. My present task is to suggest some of the ways in which O'Hara's background, or rather,

---

1. *Selected Letters of John O'Hara*, edited by Matthew J. Bruccoli (Random House, 1978), p. 76.

2. *The Letters of F. Scott Fitzgerald*, edited by Andrew Turnbull (Scribner, 1963), p. 503.

his sense of that background, which is not at all the same thing, entered his work.

The career of O'Hara's reputation has been a curious one. In his early creative years he was greatly admired, although for certain specific and severely limited virtues. His middle career was a puzzle for critics, although not one which exercised them strenuously. At the end, when he was writing enormous best sellers laced with brand names and kinky sex, he was viewed by critics, and not altogether unjustly, with a distant disdain. Thus Alfred Kazin seems to have reviewed *From the Terrace* (1958) as evidence that he can write about almost any book with derisiveness. Nevertheless, an O'Hara myth survives. His letters have been published, and he is the subject of at least two biographies.[3] The biographies set straight the facts—especially that by Frank MacShane, which is tactful, shrewd, respectful of O'Hara's large talent while making no eccentric claims for it.

The myth is somewhat, although not greatly, different from the biographical record, and myths have a particular power in the life of literary America. The myth goes something like this:

O'Hara was born around the turn of the century into a family of middle-class Pennsylvania Irish Catholics. In adolescence, his heart was set upon escaping upward by attending Yale, and through those mock-Gothic portals entering a social establishment dominated by Anglo-Saxon Protestants. But for whatever reason, he was unable to become a Yale man, a loss which he spent a lifetime brooding upon, a loss for which no future honor, save possibly the Nobel, could possibly have compensated. Instead, he became a reporter in the Manhattan newspaper world of the 1920s and 1930s, from which he drew the material for some of his early stories and novels. By the end of the 1930s, he had established himself as an impressively talented writer,

---

3. Matthew J. Bruccoli, *The O'Hara Concern: A Biography of John O'Hara* (Random House, 1975); and Frank MacShane, *The Life of John O'Hara* (Dutton, 1980).

influenced by Hemingway's laconic, understated style, but developing his own voice, his own sense of a story's shape.

This sense was to make him a master of the *New Yorker* short story as it then was, oblique, low-keyed, seemingly with a minimum of plot. The two novels which established his reputation, *Appointment in Samarra* (1934) and *Butterfield 8* (1935), scarcely lacked plot—they are hard, unsparing accounts of emptiness and catastrophe. They shared with his short stories, though, a fascination with actual and precise surfaces—how people really talk, how they dress and where they live, what brand of Scotch they drink, and, of course, where they went to college.

O'Hara, upon the plain evidence of these stories, was obsessed by the American class system, fascinated by its intricate, interlocking rituals and insignia. To some at least of his readers, he seemed also to be consumed by an envious hatred of a social Eden which had excluded him, but to others it seemed that the hatred was subdued, and the envy brilliant if faintly embarrassing. When these early novels and stories appeared, in the 1930s, they possessed an ability to shock which nothing, certainly not explicit sex, any longer possesses. They shocked because they took for granted, seemed indeed to relish, the existence in America of social classes, gradations, snobberies, cruelties. Our society, since at least the middle of the nineteenth century, has expended considerable spiritual energy upon the denial of this, in the very face of the facts. The role of snobbery, then and perhaps now, was denied and hidden by the snobs themselves, and exposed only to be excoriated by liberals in general and sentimental terms. (Snobs and liberals, to be sure, do not necessarily exist in separate categories, but that is another story.) A subject matter which was a commonplace of English and Continental fiction had been handed to O'Hara, and he seemed to have few competitors.

After the war, however, O'Hara, although maintaining his thematic concerns, turned to a very different kind of literary enterprise, embarking almost upon a second career, in which his accomplishments were more equivocal. In 1949 he published *A Rage to Live*, a very long novel set in Pennsylvania in the years between the turn of the century and the First World War. It was the first of a series of massive chronicles, of which the chief are *Ten North Frederick* (1955), *From the Terrace* (1958), *Ourselves to Know* (1960), and *The Lockwood Concern* (1965). All of them were long by conventional standards, and *From the Terrace* seemed positively obscene in length—and not in length alone. On the whole, and with the exception of *A Rage to Live*, they were not well received by serious critics. The length had a kind of corresponding massivity, an accumulation of social details, artifacts, gestures, patterns of speech and conduct. *From the Terrace* came to seem a species of tumor, spreading by metastasis through all his work. "Nine hundred pages!" Kazin complained.

Nine hundred pages of detail about rich men's stables, what workmen ate for lunch in a Pennsylvania steel mill in 1900, of careful notations about lemon phosphates and who was mad at whom and who slept with whom, and what people ate at prep school lunch in the 1920s. Nine hundred pages—to tell us that in the early 1920s it was still called "the Martini cocktail," not a martini, and that in this period collegians at a dance would tuck their black ties under their collars, that almost every young man thus attired wore a gold watch chain from which depended a collegiate charm, and that the majority parted their hair in the middle.

"The Great American Bore," Kazin titled his review.[4] But the people who read best sellers found O'Hara anything but a bore, and these blockbusters—they were almost the archetypal best sellers of the Fifties—made him a very rich writer indeed. The style of living which this wealth made possible changed the contours of the O'Hara myth. Something of the Thirties newspaper man had always been part of his

---

4. Reprinted in *Contemporaries* (Little, Brown, 1962), p. 167.

public personality—hard-drinking, quarrelsome, wisecracking, womanizing, cynical. This new O'Hara settled into the mold of the squire of "Linebrook," in Princeton. (He wanted to settle in an Ivy town, and New Haven, no doubt, was too close for comfort.) He was by now happily married to a woman of impeccable credentials, vacationed in the right resorts, adopted the proper political affiliations, belonged to the proper clubs, was attentive to the minutiae of dress shirts from Brooks, hats from Locke, shoes from Peale. His industry was immense, but somewhere, somehow, his true and rare talent had collapsed. At the end of his life, he seemed to serious readers not only a failed talent but one which had contrived to fail in a manner at once gigantic and uninteresting, an American phenomenon, a beached and gasping whale. Toward the end, he seemed a caricature of himself.

Thus the outline of O'Hara as it has passed into literary memory. It is substantially accurate. His desire for the proper—but only the proper —social recognition, the proper badges of acceptance, was so intense as to be, from a safe remove, touching. Once O'Hara brought to show to his publishers his Christmas gift from his wife—"a vast, glittering plaque, studded with shining emblems," each of them representing a club to which he belonged.[5] The special feeling for Yale is, once again, both touching and absurd. In his workroom, beside *Who's Who* and the *Social Register* and Baird's *Manual of American Fraternities*, stood the Yale Yearbook for 1924, which would have been his class.

There is a famous anecdote bearing upon this. Some writers found themselves with some funds left over from a Spanish Civil War fund, and Ernest Hemingway said, "Let's take the bloody money and start a bloody fund to send John O'Hara to Yale." O'Hara called it "a mean little story," which showed what his friends thought of him. Later, he decided that it was early evidence of Hemingway's envy of him.[6]

---

5. Hiram Haydn, *Words and Places* (Harcourt Brace Jovanovich, 1974), p. 104.

6. Bruccoli, *The O'Hara Concern*, p. 164.

The received notion of O'Hara as a talented, sharp, agreeably nasty observer of the social scene, working best in short forms, who turned unaccountably to the writing of enormous social catalogs, is at variance with fact, however. As a glance at his bibliography shows, he was writing short stories and short novels throughout his career. They vary, naturally, in merit, but the quality of the late stories seems to me quite as high as in the earlier ones, and some of these late stories are in fact extraordinarily fine. To read through the range of his short fiction is also to recall something often forgotten: that his range was a wide one. His stories about working-class people, waitresses, farmers, servants, are as sharply observed as any, and remarkably uncondescending, if only because he knew that all classes have their hierarchies.

Chiefly, though, a rereading of O'Hara reminds me of what a remarkably strange writer O'Hara was, and strange in ways which have not been sufficiently remarked upon. Harold Ross of *The New Yorker*, a shrewd if bizarre editor, once vowed, "I'll never print another O'Hara story I don't understand. I want to know what his characters are doing."[7] It is usually and no doubt rightly assumed that Ross suspected O'Hara of smuggling strong material past his prim screen of sexual taboos, but it is possible, at least, that Ross simply meant that O'Hara's stories, for all their limpid style, are often very strange indeed. So it seems to me, and so it seemed to Edmund Wilson, when in 1940 he wrote "The Boys in the Back Room."

Wilson's account of O'Hara is characteristically exact, balanced and just. Although it was written midway in O'Hara's career, it is almost definitive. O'Hara, he says,

> has explored for the first time from his peculiar semi-snobbish point of view a good deal of interesting territory: the relations between Catholics and Protestants, the relations between college

---

7. James Thurber, *The Years with Ross* (Little, Brown, 1959), p. 104.

men and non-college men, the relations between the underworld and "legitimate" business, the ratings of cafe society;
and to read him on a fashionable bar or the Gibbsville country
club is to be shown on the screen of a fluoroscope gradations of
social prestige of which one had not before been aware.

But these delicate and accurate analyses, Wilson says, exist on the
surface. Beneath it, O'Hara moves with far less certainty:

Julian English of *Appointment in Samarra* is apparently the victim of a bad heredity worked upon by demoralizing influences;
yet the emotions that drive him to suicide are never really
shown. The whole book is in the nature of an explanation of
why Julian threw the highball in the face of the Irish climber; yet
the explanation doesn't convince us that the inevitable end for
Julian would be the suicide to which his creator brings him. As
for Mr. O'Hara's latest novel, *Hope of Heaven*, I haven't been
able to fathom it at all—though here, too, there seems to be dis-
cernible a Freudian behavior-pattern.... What is the relevance
to the story, for example, of the newspaper woman in *Appointment in Samarra*, whose career is described on such a scale? The
account of her beginnings is amusing, but the part she plays in
the drama doesn't seem to warrant this full-scale introduction.
What is the point of the newspaper reporter who suddenly gets
into the picture, and more or less between us and it, at the end
of *Butterfield 8*? What on earth is the justification—aside from
establishing the atmosphere for a drama of general crooked-
ness—of the long story about the man who stole the travelers'
checks in *Hope of Heaven*?[8]

---

8. Reprinted in *Classics and Commercials* (Farrar, Straus, 1950). The discussion of O'Hara is
on pp. 22–26.

Wilson has asked the right questions, but he can no more answer them than I can. A novel in the naturalist mode in which both the crucial action and the suicide of the central character are left almost entirely without explanation! And there are similar puzzles in the long novels, although they lie buried beneath a warehouseful of social bric-a-brac. "We never know," Kazin says of *From the Terrace*, "why one leading character in the book turns homosexual, or why a big Texas oilman, after being sentimentally and almost fulsomely admired for his kindness to the hero, is shown up as a monster." We do know, though, that the unrelenting hostility toward the hero of another character is mysteriously bound up with his being an Irish Catholic. Irishmen in O'Hara, save for a few reporters, who are classless, and decent coachmen and chauffeurs, are a rum lot, gauche, flashy, coarse.

Wilson, in his remarks upon O'Hara's world, says shrewdly, and perhaps with a worldliness that O'Hara himself lacked, that "there is no longer any hierarchy here, of either cultivation or wealth: the people are all being shuffled about, hardly knowing what they are or where they are headed, but each is clutching some family tradition, some membership in a select organization, some personal association with the famous, from which he tries to derive distinction. But in the meantime, they mostly go under. They are snubbed, they are humiliated, they fail." O'Hara's main theme, Wilson says, is not snobbery, but the cruel side of snobbery.

A crucial distinction, and one which was missed by Lionel Trilling when in a 1945 *New York Times Book Review* account of *Pipe Night* he defined the terms upon which O'Hara was to be read and admired in the late 1940s, before the fall.[9] It was, as Professor Bruccoli says,

9. Lionel Trilling, "John O'Hara Observes Our Morals," *The New York Times Book Review*, March 18, 1945, p. 1; reprinted in Trilling's *The Liberal Imagination* (Viking, 1950), p. 213.

in a characteristic adjective, "the most prestige-giving" review that O'Hara had received, placing him in "the Howells-Wharton-James-Proust school."[10] A characteristic passage from Trilling's review:

> More than anyone now writing, O'Hara understands the complex, contradictory, asymetrical society in which we live. He has the most precise knowledge of the content of our subtlest snobberies, of pure points of social honor and idiosyncracies of personal prestige. He knows, and persuades us to believe, that life's deepest emotions may be expressed by the angle at which a hat is worn, the pattern of a necktie, the size of a monogram, the pitch of a voice, the turn of a phrase of slang, a gesture of courtesy and the way it is received. . . . For him customs and manners are morals.

O'Hara was overwhelmed, as well he might be. "The results began to come in on Sunday afternoon by telephone. Next day I went down to The Players and every man there, including some members I scarcely knew, congratulated me, and it has been that way ever since." He must have felt like the man in Molière who discovers that he has been speaking prose all his life without knowing it. In one of the stories in the book, a Hollywood actress says to a caller, "Cigarettes there, in that white pigskin box." Trilling calls this her "excess of specification." So much for Ross and Thurber and that crowd! O'Hara had been tapped by Morningside Heights.

Two years later, when Trilling delivered as a lecture his celebrated essay on "Manners, Morals, and the Novel," he did not mention O'Hara, although he could have been accommodated to one of the themes of the essay, which is that American novelists fail to touch "significantly on society, on manners." Had Trilling done so, he

---

10. MacShane, *The Life of John O'Hara*, p. 129.

would surely have modulated the terms of his praise. It is quite true that life's deepest emotions can be expressed through an act of courtesy, and the idea of courtesy has moral implications, but seldom if ever are they expressed by the pattern of a necktie or the size of a monogram. To assume otherwise, although one knows what Trilling means, is to assume a network of correspondences between the seen and the unseen so elaborate and so binding as to leave Baudelaire dumbfounded. Indeed, O'Hara himself might have knit his brows over the passage as he sat sipping his second martini in the Players Club. Indeed, his fiction may suggest that manners often distort morals and often betray true instincts. Wilson saw this: "The cruel side of social snobbery is really Mr. O'Hara's main theme." O'Hara, no doubt, would see in this the difference between Princeton and Columbia.

If Trilling defined the reasons why serious readers should read O'Hara, then Kazin, thirteen years later, explained why they need no longer keep on with the task, for in *From the Terrace* we are indeed "deluged, suffocated, drowned in facts, facts, facts." But Kazin seems to me unfair when he proposes a reason for this deluge of facts:

> What is all this information for? Why does O'Hara pour it on so? The answer is that "intensity" and "sincerity"—the cardinal American virtues when you are trying to sell something—take, when it comes to novels, the form of stampeding you with information. It is true, as Mr. O'Hara said in a recent interview, that the first half of this century was the most exciting time in the world's history. But what exactly do we learn of this period from his book that we did not know before?

It is even more unfair to assume that O'Hara was in the business of cynically constructing best sellers shaped for Hollywood and packed with sex both missionary and kinky. He clearly took a crude pleasure in his ability to make lots of money from what he wrote, but it is also clear, if less apparent, that he took seriously his responsibilities to his craft. The mountains of social detail and observation in O'Hara's novels are there, it seems to me, as ways, gigantic and eccentric ways, of avoiding confrontation with the meanings of the stories he tells. Even as the sudden, lurid, and unexpected eruptions of sexuality stem from his uncertainty as to the relationship between emotion and social texture. This, at any rate, is as close as I can come to answering the curious questions which are posed by his fiction.

"The truth is perhaps," Wilson concludes, "that O'Hara has never really had his bearings since he left Gibbsville, Pa." Gibbsville was the name that O'Hara gave to Pottsville, the setting for *Appointment in Samarra* and many of the stories. And he did in fact return to Gibbsville many times, for a setting and a social world. But Wilson's words have perhaps another resonance, that O'Hara had not had his bearings since he left the world of his early life.

Jimmy Malloy, the obviously autobiographical newspaper man whose presence in *Butterfield 8* puzzled Wilson, has this to say about himself:

> I want to tell you something about myself that will help to explain a lot of things about me. You might as well hear it now. First of all, I am a Mick. I wear Brooks clothes and I don't eat salad with a spoon and I probably could play five-goal polo in two years, but I am a Mick. Still a Mick. Now it's taken me a little time to find this out... for the present purpose I only mention it to show that I'm pretty God damn American, and therefore my brothers and sisters are, and yet we're not Americans. We've been here, at least some of my family, since before the Revolution—and we produce the perfect gangster type. At least it's you American Americans' idea of a perfect gangster type, and I suppose you're right. Yes, I guess you are. The first real gangsters in

this country were Irish. The Molly Maguires. Anyway, do you see what I mean about this non-assimilable stuff?[11]

Pottsville is in the very heart of Molly Maguire country. Which is to say that it is close to the center of the anthracite mining region then dominated by the Philadelphia and Reading Coal and Iron Company. The company had smashed the Mollies in the 1870s, but their legend, a lurid and bloody legend among the respectable, was still vivid. Much later, O'Hara was to tell his daughter that his own father had broken "a Kluxer's jaw for calling him a Molly Maguire." To a "Kluxer" this might have been a simple term of derogation, signifying Irish Catholic.

In "the Region," as it was called, the upper and much of the middle class was of English or Welsh or Pennsylvania Dutch descent, and the working class was Irish, Polish, Lithuanian. Most of the Irish worked in the mines or the railroad yards.

O'Hara's family, however, was solidly middle class and professional. His grandfather served as an officer in the Civil War, then settled in Shenandoah and established a successful business. He married well. His son Patrick studied medicine, took his degree at the University of Pennsylvania, and at least once went to Europe to study surgical practices. He established his practice in Pottsville, and married Katherine Delaney, whose father owned a wholesale grocery and hardware store in the area. She had been graduated from one of the Sacred Heart academies, and her letters display a vivid, graceful style, a sensitivity to language. John, their oldest child, was born in 1905.

At various times in later years, O'Hara attempted to correct the legends about his supposedly deprived background, citing the family's carriage horses, ponies, Buicks, Fords, and a five-gaited mare "that my father purchased from the Kirby Horse Farm in Bowling

---

11. John O'Hara, *Butterfield 8* (Harcourt, Brace, 1935), pp. 66–67.

Green, Kentucky."[12] At this remove, says Professor Bruccoli, "it is impossible to place the O'Haras accurately in the social hierarchy."[13] To know his work is to know that the problem is one to which he has given a devoted attention. The family, Professor MacShane says more crisply, "were quite plain middle class."[14]

They lived in Mahantongo Street, which was the best street in town, and Patrick O'Hara was known, for all his considerable professional distinction, as "the Irish doctor." Perhaps their "place" in the social hierarchy lies in the juncture of these two facts. Then and later, the social prejudice against middle-class Irish on the eastern seaboard was intense. Helen Howe, remembering family summers at Cotuit, near Hyannis, says: "As for any Irish-American family who played touch football, spent large sums of money that showed, belonged to some summer club or clubs, and went to a Catholic church —the Cotuit clan would have been no more likely to rub shoulders with them than with the few remaining Indians in the little village of nearby Mashpee."[15] Pottsville was probably a bit more easygoing, but the lines of division were firm.

Within the town's ruling class, many of the young men went off to prep school, most notably to Lawrenceville, and from there to Pennsylvania, or a bit farther afield to Princeton or Yale. O'Hara, from a very early age, was determined to join them at Yale, and his father, apparently, had no immediate objection. For his preparation, however, the family turned as though upon instinct to the Church. He was sent north to Fordham Prep, the popular name for St. John's College High School of Fordham University. It could have borne little

---

12. Bruccoli, *The O'Hara Concern*, p. 15.

13. Bruccoli, *The O'Hara Concern*, p. 16.

14. MacShane, *The Life of John O'Hara*, p. 5.

15. Helen Howe, *The Gentle Americans* (Harper and Row, 1965), p. 309.

resemblance to Lawrenceville: out of six hundred students, most of them Irish and Italians from the Bronx, he was one of fifteen boarders. He loathed the place, and after a year and a half dropped out. He spent a penitential year at Keystone State Normal School, a deplorably déclassé institution, and then was shipped up to Niagara, another Catholic institution. It seems to have been agreed that if he did well there, he would go on to Yale after graduation. And he did splendidly, the commencement program for 1924 listing him as valedictorian and class poet. On the night before graduation, he went into town, got drunk, and was brought home by the police. The O'Haras arrived from Pottsville to learn that he had been expelled without a diploma.

Back home, he drifted into work on the local newspaper. He continued to think about Yale as a possibility until the following spring, when his father died. By March of 1928, the year in which he would have been graduated, he was in Manhattan looking for work on a paper.

Patrick O'Hara's final months had been clouded by a professional dispute with sectarian overtones. A split separated the Catholic and Protestant doctors at the Pottsville Hospital, and although he was chief surgeon and chief of staff, he and the other Catholic doctors were forced to leave and organize a new hospital. The forces at work would clearly seem those of the nativist Protestant bigotry. John's relations with his father, in consequence of his academic scrapes, had been poor, but this crisis drew them together. He wanted to hunt out the Protestant doctors and beat them up. And on the night of his father's death, as he remembered it, he did knock down one of them. "The episode distressed him at a deeper level," MacShane thinks, "for it showed him how big a handicap his Catholic heritage was."[16]

Patrick O'Hara died intestate. Because Mrs. O'Hara had some money of her own, there was no immediate crisis, but the farm and

---

16. MacShane, *The Life of John O'Hara*, p. 32.

the summer place and the cars and the ponies vanished like fairy gold. There seems no reason why O'Hara could not have managed Yale. His two younger brothers went to Brown and Lafayette—not Yale perhaps, but good enough in a pinch. Perhaps, Bruccoli speculates, it wouldn't have been the real thing to be a "bursary boy who waited on tables while the gentlemen browsed at J. Press and danced at the Fence Club. It had to be the right way or not at all."[17] In Manhattan, he began to hang around the Yale Club.

Why did he hate Harry Reilly, Julian English thinks, as he sits in the Lantanengo Country Club, about to throw a glass of whiskey into Reilly's face. Edmund Wilson didn't know, and I don't know; Julian doesn't know, and certainly O'Hara didn't. It had something to do with Reilly being Irish and knowing the words to "Lord Jeffery Amherst" without being entitled to, and telling stories with a fake brogue. In one of the few studies of O'Hara as an Irish-American, a shallow and rather crude essay, the author says of Jimmy Malloy's speech that "behind Malloy's quasi-catharsis and semi-hysterical sociologizing lie were the facts of O'Hara's embarrassing class consciousness, his obsession with status, his disappointment that he had not been born in New York or Boston with a proper Wasp background and a congenital Phi Beta Kappa key from Yale."[18] (I can conceive, by a wild stretch, a symbolic Delta Kappa Epsilon pin, but a "congenital Phi Beta Kappa" key? This is the sort of thing that drove poor Julian to suicide.)

But this glib formulation turns away from consideration of precisely the sources of O'Hara's most complex and accurate social perceptions. He was torn between his deep attraction toward the Wasp establishment and his conviction that he had been sentenced to

17. Bruccoli, *The O'Hara Concern*, p. 42.

18. Joseph Browne, "John O'Hara and Tom McHale," in *Irish-American Fiction*, edited by Daniel J. Casey and Robert E. Rhodes (AMS, 1979).

exclusion from it. To be banished from Eden is to be presented with one of the oldest and most powerful of subjects.

He ceased in his adolescence to be a Catholic—"the Jesuits ruined it for me"—and was never tempted to turn to any other kind of belief in the supernatural. He was without religious convictions of any kind, and never felt their loss. Neither does there seem any evidence that the religious certainties of his childhood informed his imagination in some subterranean way. He lacked Fitzgerald's ambiguous faith in the power of illusion, and Hemingway's conception of a secular grace. Nor, after a youthful leftish fling, had he confidence in society's ability to transform itself.

For O'Hara, life was society, a complex, hierarchically ordered, mysterious organism. Total, that is, save for the instincts, and especially the sexual instinct, which is capable of erupting disastrously, smashing social identity. In *A Rage to Live*, Grace Tate has an affair with an Irish (dear God, not that!) contractor named Bannon. Her husband, coldly and bleakly ending the marriage, says that

> in this world you learn a set of rules, or you don't learn them. But assuming you learn them, you stick by them. They may be no damn good, but you're who you are and what you are because they're your rules and you stick by them.... I'm the first, God knows, to grant that you, with your beauty, you had opportunities and invitations. But you obeyed the rules, the same rules I obeyed. But then you said the hell with them. What it amounts to is you said the hell with my rules, and the hell with me. So, Grace—the hell with you. I love you, but if I have any luck, that'll pass in my new life.[19]

This is as close as O'Hara gets to the formulation of a code, and

---

19. John O'Hara, *A Rage to Live* (Grosset and Dunlap, 1949), p. 245.

even here one cannot be certain, because it is given to a chill, harsh, and imaginatively inadequate man. O'Hara wrote to a friend: "I must insist that sexually Grace had been preparing for a Bannon all her life and that it was merely circumstances that kept her from one earlier in her young womanhood, with either more disastrous results, or less." So much for rules.

Sidney Tate's "set of rules" has nothing in common with Jake Barnes's code of conduct in *The Sun Also Rises*, or Nick Carraway's judgments in *The Great Gatsby*. When Nick tells Gatsby that "you're worth the whole damned lot of them," he is not merely suggesting to us that the Buchanans and the Bakers may in fact be damned, he is expressing his recognition of Gatsby's essential innocence and nobility of being. Fitzgerald's "people" are O'Hara's—Tom Buchanan, after all, is a Yale man, or, as Fitzgerald and O'Hara would say, went to school in New Haven. But Fitzgerald's novel offers us a subtle confluence of social, aesthetic, and moral perceptions, where O'Hara gives us, instead, a meticulously constructed anatomy.

Fitzgerald and O'Hara came from rather similar backgrounds, middle-class and socially insecure Irishmen who early on left the Catholic Church. Neither of them believed in God. But as Professor Dan Piper has suggested, Fitzgerald carried forward into maturity and into his art the moral values which he had received with his faith, "the tree without the elements," the moral code without the sectarian dogma.[20] And he found the notion of a world without God intellectually compelling but imaginatively appalling. Piper calls the sign of Dr. T. J. Eckleberg, that huge, painted oculist's sign above the ash heap, "the symbol of a world without God, a kind of anti-God."

O'Hara did not avail himself of Fitzgerald's uneasy compromise. The mold of his vision was set by *Appointment in Samarra*, a bleak world of meaningless social ritual, incoherent passions, and suicide:

20. Henry Dan Piper, *F. Scott Fitzgerald: A Critical Portrait* (Holt, Rinehart and Winston, 1965).

Our story never ends.

You pull the pin out of a hand grenade, and in a few seconds it explodes and men in a small area get killed and wounded. That makes bodies to be buried, hurt men to be treated. It makes widows and fatherless children and bereaved parents. It means pension machinery, and it makes for pacifism in some and lasting hatred in others. Again, a man out of the danger area sees the carnage the grenade creates, and he shoots himself in the foot. Another man had been standing there two minutes before the thing went off, and thereafter he believes in God or a rabbit's foot. Another man sees human brains for the first time and locks up the picture until one night years later, when he finally comes out with a description of what he saw, and the horror of his description turns his wife away from him.[21]

That isn't a character speaking: it is O'Hara, summing things up, explaining, as it were, how a glass of whiskey tossed in Harry Reilly's face can lead to Julian English's suicide. In O'Hara's fiction, grenades go off, and the explosions set his world into motion. The explosions are uncaused, the consequences are meaningless. He sees the world through the eyes of Dr. T. J. Eckleberg.

When Dr. Patrick O'Hara was buried, the funeral was "as big as a politician's," with twenty priests present and forty cars in the cortege. "Dr. O'Hara Was a City Asset," the Pottsville *Republican* said. When his son died, in April of 1970, there was an Episcopalian service in the Princeton University Chapel. The chapel was not filled, although President Goheen was there and John Hay Whitney from the social establishment, and Bennett Cerf's wife and John Steinbeck's wife. He was buried in the old Princeton cemetery, where many of its graduates rest, including Aaron Burr. O'Hara's favorite car was parked outside

---

21. John O'Hara, *Appointment in Samarra* (Modern Library, 1953), p. 281.

the chapel, a green Rolls-Royce Silver Cloud III with the license plate JOH-1. The Bruccoli biography has a photograph of him showing it to his publishers in the Random House courtyard. Not in color, unfortunately. Cotuit and Hyannis might think it a bit showy.

Once, at an alumni function, President Kingman Brewster was asked why Yale had never given O'Hara an honorary degree. "Because he asked for it," Brewster said.[22] O'Hara should have known better. That is how things work in that world which he had studied with such close and elaborate attention. A world of intricate rituals, codes, gestures, tones of voice by which the elect are known to one another. That world, with its secret affirmations and rejections, its insignia, its badges of manner and dress, had become the substance of his fiction. But the substance had become all surface, frozen carapace-hard, and nothing beneath the carapace, nothing at all.

And in the end, it lets you down, that world does. Sooner or later, if you are a Mick from Pottsville and Fordham Prep, you make the one false step, you let them know that you want something, and so, even at the end, you never get to go to Yale.

—The Recorder, Winter 1985

---

22. Bruccoli, *The O'Hara Concern,* p. 273n.

6

MARY McCARTHY: LIVING AND READING

THE COMPANY THAT manufactures T-shirts and sweatshirts with pictures of famous writers—Jane Austen, Ernest Hemingway, Virginia Woolf—also has one with a quotation rather than a face, from Logan Pearsall Smith: "They say that living is the thing, but I prefer reading." I suspect that many writers, like myself, have wanted to send away for one, but have lacked the courage. It is shameful to admit how fully and how deeply one's reading has encroached upon one's living.

I was reminded of the T-shirt by a sentence in Carol Gelderman's biography of Mary McCarthy: "It was her reading, precocious for a fourteen-year-old, and her sexual experiments that really set her apart." There seems at first something a bit off about that sentence, as though the clause in apposition was modifying the wrong noun. But then one remembers passages in *Memories of a Catholic Girlhood* which place reading and living, living as sexual experiment, in curious juxtaposition.

The fifteen-year-old has been motoring through Yellowstone with girlfriends and with Bob Berdan, twenty-five and married, whose unexciting kisses have led only to more kisses. Then, in Great Falls, after another tepid night in a hotel, "I found a book store and while the others waited in the car I hurried in to make a purchase: the latest volume, in a boxed, de luxe edition, of James Branch Cabell. It is a disappointment: as it turns out, she has "outgrown" Cabell. (This was a common disappointment among bookish teenagers of her generation and my own. Cabell was a shameless tease: you took him home from the library, but he never really put out.)

Her excitement as she buys the book is real upon the page:

> I was tremendously excited by this act. It was the first expensive book I had ever bought with my own money. The whole trip to Montana for a moment seemed worthwhile, as I stood in the wide dull main street with the book, wrapped, in my hands. I was in love with Cabell and had written him many letters that I had not the courage to mail. Why, it would change my grandmother's whole life, I would tell her, if she would only let herself read a few pages of Cabell or listen to me recite them. Now, as the owner of a limited edition, I felt proudly close to him, far closer than to Bob Berden or to the girls, who were already honking the horn for me to get in and join the party.

Poor Bob Berdan, with his drugstore gin and unexciting kisses. But after making allowance for the affectionate self-mockery of reminiscence, there is a striking difference of tone as the prose moves from Bob to the deluxe edition. And in that avowal of belief that reading a book will somehow change one's life, every writer will guiltily, fondly, recognize one of his own former selves.

In McCarthy's explicit memoirs of education, *Memories of a Catholic Girlhood* and *How I Grew*, two intertwined subjects confront one another, each mocking yet affirming the other. They are the histories of two educations, an education into living and an education into reading. The contrasts provide dramatic and often comic differences of tonality.

This is largely a rhetorical strategy, a matter of decorum. The account of sexual education is offered in a manner deliberately dry, clinical, wryly self-observant, and deflationary. Here, as in the stories and novels, from the front seat of Forrest Crosby's Marmon to the Pullman sleeper in *The Company She Keeps* to Dolly and her diaphragm in *The Group*, sex is forever skidding on the banana peels of physiology and rubber goods.

But the account of the other education is written with an affection that is both romantic and nostalgic, as of entrance into a vocation. It is not simply an education into language. Language is for every writer an instrument of liberation, and she was to become one of the finest of American prose stylists. It is an education into books, of printed pages opening up an alternative existence, and she evokes their looks and weight, the smell of their bindings. And, especially, she commemorates the looks and bearings of the teachers who conducted that education, a series of women sternly or sweetly or primly dedicated to their task, beginning with "the tiny old whiskered nun" who read aloud to the girls from *Emma* or *A Tale of Two Cities*.

"'Charles Evremonde, called Darnay!'—the red-rimmed old black eye levelled and raked us all, summarily, with the grapeshot of the Terror." The scene, she tells us, is generic, occurring, for such was the universal and sweetly archaic rule of the Ladies of the Sacred Heart, at four each afternoon not only in Seattle but in Roscrea, Ireland, and Roehampton, England, a nun reading while the girls, heads bent, stitched French seams or embroidered bureau scarves with wreaths of flowers.

Nostalgia, no doubt, leads McCarthy herself to embroider this account, which joins reading with an aristocratic and obsolete regimen, but it is an instructive nostalgia. She was fresh from a parochial school, where little reading was done and where "grievous" was pronounced as "grievious." (My own upward progress was rather like hers, and I well remember that parochial school solecism—"Through my fault, through my fault, through my most grievious fault.") By a giddy feat of the historical imagination, she (not the girl, but rather the woman looking back upon girlhood) employs the rituals and traditions of her Seattle convent school to affiliate herself with France of the Restoration, "embalmed in the Sacred Heart atmosphere, like a period room in a museum with a silken cord drawn across it. The quarrels of the *philosophes* still echoed in the classrooms: the tumbrils had just ceased to creak. . . ." Byron's great star had arisen, and America beckoned in the romances of Chateaubriand and Fenimore Cooper. In the study hall, Madame McGillvra adjured the pupils against doubt, the sin of fine intellects, reminding them of the awful fate of Shelley, who came of good family, but had contracted atheism at Oxford.

They were indomitably bookish, these nuns, or at least so she makes them in retrospect. "Madame McGillvra, while she would have held it in bad taste to bow down, like Father Zossima, before the murder in Dimitri Karamazov's heart, would certainly have had him in for a series of long, intimate talks in her office." And, "like all truly intellectual women, these were in spirit romantic desperadoes." "The great atheists and sinners were the heroes of the costume picture they called history."

This soft-hued, romantically bookish retrospect is not corrected in those italicized afterpieces to *Memories of a Catholic Girlhood* in which she scrutinizes her memories for truthfulness, what her nuns would have called an examination of conscience. What she remembers is the power of books and their ability to make experience, to make life comely, powerful, and seductive. "You're just like Lord Byron," Madame Barclay, the French mistress tells her, "brilliant but unsound." "The reproof was a declaration of love as plain as the sentence on the blackboard, which shimmered slightly before my eyes. My happiness a confused exaltation in which the fact that I was Lord Byron and the fact that I was loved by Madame Barclay, the most puzzling nun in the convent, blended in a Don Juanish triumph."

So was it also to be, with appropriate changes of tonality and decor, at Annie Wright, the Episcopalian seminary at Tacoma, with mentors different in background, but equally bookish, equally genteel. Black-haired, Scottish Miss Gowrie, BA, MA, Girton and Edinburgh, "a genuine British Empire product, like the plaid woolen scarves you bore home from a steamer excursion to Victoria," who could turn the Gallic wars into a novel, "Caesar, master alike of warfare and prose, and noble, doomed Vercingetorix." And Miss Dorothy Atkinson, a Vassar woman, blond bun and pince-nez, who embodied "the critical spirit, will, cool learning, detachment, everything I suddenly wished to have and to become the moment I first heard her light, precise cutting voice score some pretentious, slatternly phrase of construction."

And from Annie Wright to Vassar, to Miss Kitchel and Miss Sandison, to the rules of English syntax and the reading of Tolstoy and Turgenev. There is a strong family likeness among these women— dry, precise, but decorously romantic and secretly rebellious, intellectually adventurous, but firmly anchored to caste and class, an aristocratic order of Catholic ladies, Vassar women, Girton College bluestockings. It was a training, or perhaps we should say that McCarthy, looking backward, liked to see it as a training in precisely those literary qualities, those traits of sensibility, which she was to bring down to the great world, meaning New York, as a portion of her personal and literary identity, and, if a portion only, then an important one.

No writer had a surer grasp than she of the signifying detail, but one detail, at least, I think carried a greater weight than she intended for it. She tells us in *Intellectual Memoirs* that her first New York apartment, hers and her husband's, at Beekman Place, was furnished with chairs and a small carved oak table and oriental rugs lent to them by Miss Sandison's sister, who taught Latin at Chapin, and with "a handsome card table with a cherrywood frame and legs and a blue suede top," which Miss Sandison had given them as a wedding present. These were offset by more contemporary details supplied by the newlyweds, a "'modernistic' Russel Wright cocktail shaker," and a chromium hors d'oeuvres tray. It seems to me fitting, if not downright portentous, that Miss Sandison should have followed her into Beekman Place, and with her those ghostly sisters, Miss Sandison's colleague Miss Kitchel and Miss Gowrie and Madame McGillvra and Madame Barclay. The aluminum cocktail shaker an insignificant echo of Bob Berdan and the front seat of Forrest Crosby's Marmon.

I have gone a long way around in order to suggest that Mary McCarthy was, as her writings make abundantly evident, a genuinely learned writer, erudite and in easy command of her erudition. She was a bookish writer, who never exhausted the energies, delights, enthusiasms both foolish and wise which reading first roused in her. Her Northcliffe lectures, for example, published later as *Ideas and the Novel*, which move easily among the novels of Balzac, Stendhal, Victor Hugo, Tolstoy, Dostoevsky, Dickens, George Eliot, and that (to me) incomprehensible enthusiasm of hers, Manzoni. Or a 1969 essay, which concerns itself with the disappearance from novels of descriptions of nature. "We have almost forgotten," she tells us, "that descriptions of sunsets, storms, rivers, lakes, mountains, valleys used to be one of the staple ingredients of fiction, not merely a painted backdrop for the action but a component evidently held to be necessary to the art.... We have come a long way from the time when the skill of an author was felt to be demonstrated by his descriptive prowess: Dickens' London fogs, Fenimore Cooper's waterfalls, forests, prairie, Emily Brontë's moors, Hardy's heath and milky vales, Melville's Pacific." And she reminds us of "the hunts of Turgenev and Tolstoy, the forest rides of Madame Bovary, Tolstoy's peasants reaping and threshing, the sawmill in Stendhal."

Here as elsewhere she makes her points by drawing not only upon what we used to call the "great novels" but also, with a careless exactitude, upon *Green Mansions, Typee, Moll Flanders, The Unfortunate Traveller, The Ordeal of Richard Feverel, The Blithedale Romance,*

Manon Lescaut. She nearly always remembered the right things from a novel: Julien Sorel at the sawmill, Vronsky's large, even teeth, Prince Andrei's small, white hands. The special world which had been opened to her by her reading, by the several disciplines which had guided her within it, which had been opened to her perhaps by—what was one of her favorite words and remains one of my own—History, was her particular terrain, her chosen landscape, the world of the novel, of reading.

Madame Bovary, she says in her marvelous essay on that novel, "is one of a series of novels—including *Don Quixote* and *Northanger Abbey*—that illustrate the evil effects of reading. *All* reading in the case of *Madame Bovary,* not simply the reading of romances. The books Emma fed on were not pure trash by any means: in the convent she had read Chateaubriand; as a girl on the farm she read *Paul et Virginie.*" So too is her lover Leon addicted to books, and the awful Monsieur Homais "is another illustration of the evil effects of reading." She reminds us of the exchange of platitudes between Leon and Emma, at dinner at the Lion d'Or: "'...is there anything better, really, than sitting by the fire with a book while the wind beats on your window panes and the lamp is burning?'" The central tension of *Madame Bovary,* her essay suggests, is between Flaubert's susceptibilities to the pleasures of reading and his recognition of their dangers.

This seems to me a not implausible nor indeed even an idiosyncratic reading of the book, and it could even be called, to what I'm sure must be her posthumous dismay, a currently fashionable notion of texts thriving upon themselves and each other, cannibalistically. She herself was forever, both with respect to her own art and that of others, watchful, busy with the pruning shears of wit, irony, and skepticism. But she was for all that certain, as earlier generations were, her generation and my own, that art opens out upon life, books upon experience. She saw the relationship between the two as endlessly dialectical.

To indulge the kind of closing sentimentality which she, like Miss Dorothy Atkinson of the Annie Wright School would have been swift to deride, a part of her remained in the wide dull main street of Great Falls, Montana, poised between Bob Berden and the girls in the touring car, and the boxed, deluxe edition of James Branch Cabell.

7

WILLIAM KENNEDY:
O ALBANY!

ROSCOE[1] IS THE seventh in William Kennedy's cycle of "Albany" novels, which began with *Legs* in 1975. This was followed by *Billy Phelan's Greatest Game* in 1978 and *Ironweed* in 1983. They were spoken of then as a trilogy, partly because they shared a setting and some characters and partly because the third of them, a harrowing narrative of pain and a possible redemption, seemed to bring certain shared themes to resolution.

But then came *Quinn's Book* in 1988, which reaches out from Albany to an impressionistic nineteenth-century America, a land of slavery and warfare and haunted rivers. There followed *Very Old Bones* in 1992 and *The Flaming Corsage* in 1996, set solidly in Albany, but bearing down not on the public scene but on erotic and creative energies within highly untypical (I trust) families in the city's Irish Catholic community. Now, with *Roscoe*, he returns to the larger city, a model, so he has persuaded us, of urban corruption.

Taken together, the cycle, which surely has not ended here, is one of the triumphs of recent fiction, uneven but audacious in its ambition and dazzling in its technical resources. Two Albanys exist within its pages, superimposed upon each other. The "actual" Albany is a

---

1. Viking, 2002.

middle-sized state capital on the Hudson River, with a patrician Dutch past. In the nineteenth century it glowed with the oyster-and-beefsteak opulence of the Gilded Age, its restaurants and music halls resting upon the shoulders of an exploited and chiefly Irish immigrant population. By the new century, though, it had become complacent, unguarded, and after World War I it came under the control of an Irish political machine almost comic in its organizational thoroughness. In the Twenties, it was in competition with the downstate gangsters who ran the distribution and sale of bootleg liquor, the Legs Diamonds and Dutch Schultzes who had moved northward from Manhattan.

Bookie operations, prostitution, poker parlors existed at the pleasure of the machine, whose decisions were enforced by the police. In this, Albany was probably no worse than Trenton or Philadelphia, and may even have been a bit better than Kansas City, but those cities have lacked chroniclers with Kennedy's voracious appetite for fact and local mythology, his journalist's strong net for detail. Like Crane and Hemingway, he is both reporter and artist, one of the central defining traditions of American fiction.

The Albany of his novels, though, is not one of those great cities which have given modern literature its characterizing images, not the London of Dickens and Eliot, nor the Dublin of Joyce, nor the Chicago of Dreiser and Bellow. It does not resemble the cameos carved by Runyon and Chandler out of New York and Los Angeles. These cities, in art as in life, overwhelm by their immensity, their unknowability. In Kennedy's Albany, everyone knows everyone else, even if they do not know themselves. They have been cheating and screwing one another for decades, one way or another. They know each other's bloodlines, alliances, vices, secret lyricisms, schemes for survival or success. The bosses and their lieutenants and goons know what buttons to press, what feudal loyalties to exploit. Ordinary people, the poor and the obscure and the homeless, can make themselves useful stuffing ballot boxes, or, like Francis Phelan of *Ironweed*, voting early and often. Their masters use power and triumph as counters to buy the best food and the gaudiest women. But they also cherish power for what in itself it is, a mysterious, self-justifying energy and delight.

Kennedy creates this setting with scrupulous accuracy, a Joycean reverence for street names, urban legends. It is quite possible that his knowledge of Albany's geography, its nooks and crannies and their histories, is wider than Joyce's knowledge of Dublin. It is displayed with flourishes not only in the novels but in *O Albany!*, the combined history, street guide, and memoir which he published in 1983, and which is based on wide reading, a childhood and youth lived there, and long experience as a reporter on the *Times-Union*. He speaks of himself, in the preface to that book, as "a person whose imagination has become fused with a single place, and in that place finds all the elements that a man ever needs for the life of the soul." He is not quite Dante and Albany is not quite Florence, but the principle is the same.

It is a city not without its detractors. "Misery, wretchedness, ennui and the devil," the architect H. H. Richardson wrote in 1870, "I've got to spend another evening in Albany." And Kennedy himself calls it "a pinnacle of porkhead bossism, Wasp and Irish." But is quick to add that he is fond of things "beyond the city's iniquity. I love its times of grace and greatness, its political secrets and its historical presence in every facet of the nation's life, including the unutterable, the unspeakable, and the ineffable."

Like Joyce, he employs his surface of precise naturalistic detail to move beyond it, to hint at shapes, destinies, states of being that are alien to naturalism if not hostile to it. His Albany of gravy-logged meals at Keeler's and Breughelesque hijinks in the whorehouses is also a city of spiritual mysteries and metaphysical illusions. The barrier between death and life is thin and permeable. *Roscoe* is restrained in this regard: on occasion, Roscoe's dead father sits in his familiar chair in the lobby of the Ten Eyck, and long-dead wraiths cling to a mountain resort. He creates his two Albanys and thrusts them against each other, balancing them with a zest that is out of fashion these days.

Kennedy plays for high stakes. *Ironweed*, a harrowing presentation of life in the hobo jungles and freight cars of the derelict, is at the same time an exploration of guilt and the tangles of loyalty, told entirely without condescension toward its battered characters. In *The Flaming Corsage*, a range of literary modes—prose narrative, drama, journalism, workbooks—disputes the meaning of the story's "facts." Its subjects are as extreme as its methods—lust, incest, paternity, sexual exploration. In that novel, he may have demanded more from fiction than the form can accommodate.

Like Joyce, Kennedy emerged from an Irish Catholic background and education with a skeptical, modern-day intellect and a strong residual sense of miracle, mystery, magic. And the social world which he creates is almost entirely Irish-American; that is to say, Catholic with trimmings of clan loyalty, deep-banked feelings of caste hostility unassuaged by good meals in the best restaurants. The most attractive of the novel's political figures, Elisha Fitzgibbon (clearly based on the "real-life" Erastus Corning), is a Protestant, but we do not enter his world. Otherwise, Protestants, rarely glimpsed, are like unicorns, comely but delicate of bone.

In the world of the novels, as in much of America in those years, religion set people apart from one another to an extent which is likely now to seem improbable. Not a hostile separation much of the time, but severe, weighable. Kennedy's world is that of the Knights of Columbus, the Legion of Decency, Father Coughlin's broadcasts from the Shrine of the Little Flower, parochial grade schools and high schools, and beyond that, for the lucky ones, colleges maintained by the Christian Brothers and the Jesuits.

Things were different for me, growing up in Greenwich, Connecticut. Kennedy has described Scott Fitzgerald as the first Irish yuppie, and like John O'Hara I was following in his footsteps. By the time

I was moving through the public high school, the very name of Father Coughlin's shrine evoked sickeningly the odor of Easter lilies and candle wax which I remembered (still remember!) from my days as an altar boy. Soon I would be off to my minor Ivy League college in Massachusetts, where I would join my peers in denouncing Boston's Irish boss, James Curley, whose counterpart in Albany was Dan O'Connell, Kennedy's Patsy McCall.

Kennedy takes a far more complex view of that world than I did in those years, though, a view touched with ethnic loyalty and affection, while he does not fail to dramatize the brutality and hypocrisy on which the political machine rested or the parochial narrowness which it expressed. But then back in those years, as he tells us in O *Albany!*, he had believed that "the enemies of the world were the goddamn Irish-Catholic Albany Democrats." He was detained though, as I eventually would be, by "the Irishness, which was the only element in my history that wasn't organized, the only one I couldn't resign from, and, further, the only one that hadn't been shoved down my throat." Me too. In *Quinn's Book*, his foundation myth of the nineteenth century, young Daniel Quinn carries with him from famine-ridden Ireland a grime- and dirt-encrusted plate said to possess magical powers, and which when scraped down and cleaned proves to be an antique Celtic disc, its power enigmatic and undeniable.

The more immediate foundation myth, its power pervading all of the novels, is the use by the political boss Patsy McCall of the assessor's office in 1919 to pry open the oyster of Albany's political power. From that all else flowed. By the end of the Twenties, the Irish were in full possession, Patsy controlling the patronage and his brother Binty controlling Nighttown, which meant the speakeasies, the poker parlors, the whorehouses, the police. This night world is most vividly and thickly present for us in *Billy Phelan's Greatest Game*, a world in which Billy moves as a skillful denizen, not of champion class, but able to make a living at poker, billiards, keeping a small book. But when the McCalls put out the word, he is cut off from that world as absolutely as if he had been exiled to Alaska, unable to buy a drink, place a bet. And he knows better than to challenge his fate.

In that novel, as in *Ironweed*, the novel about Billy's father, Kennedy displays a truly impressive ability to write on a level with his characters, to share the way in which Billy, a gambler on the margins, thinks and moves, but he is equally resourceful when it comes to portraying the world of Billy's masters, the masters of city life who pull the strings and jerk the puppets. Kennedy has no master when it comes to the juicy and horrifying story of city and state politics.

Politics is present in all the novels, but it holds center stage in *Legs* and *Billy Phelan's Greatest Game*, and now in *Roscoe*. It is 1945, and the machine is still in power, with the same bosses and the same henchmen carrying out their dark instructions. Times change, though, and as the novel suggests by indirection, it will soon be time for the machine to be taken over by young lions back from Normandy and the Pacific. Not better men, so the novel hints; indeed a bit more sinister perhaps but different in style.

Roscoe Conway, the machine's chief fixer, is already ready to step aside. He is painfully aware that he is overweight, overeducated for the slippery skills he has perfected, and, for a man in his mid-fifties, oversexed. He spends his days at party headquarters, sweeping rolls of tribute money into a desk drawer, dining on oysters and chablis at Keeler's or the Ten Eyck, and polishing the curious prose in which his perceptions are expressed, a kind of Henry Adams gravitas jazzed up with a hail-fellow breeziness. "Righteousness doesn't stand a chance against the imagination." Lately, though, these and other pleasures have begun to lose their savor. Roscoe's soul, though he himself does not yet know it, has been preparing him for death.

In *Legs* there is a rough sketch of what Roscoe may have been like as a young man. Marcus Gorman, the narrator, might have had a bright political future, but threw it away to become the upstate attorney for Jack "Legs" Diamond, the notorious bootlegger and gangland killer. Gorman is a student of Rabelais and a knockout speaker at Knights of Columbus communion breakfasts. For him too, as for the aging Roscoe, if for different reasons, life has something lacking, some essential cocktail sauce of danger. Diamond supplies it, for reasons made clear to us by the story, "pieced painfully together from Joe, Jack and a half-dozen others," of how Jack Diamond had dealt with a couple of noisy troublemakers at Manhattan's Hotsy Totsy club one night in 1929, after the fights:

> Standing then, Jack fired into Tim's forehead. The head gave a sudden twist and Jack fired two more bullets into it. He fired his last two shots into Tim's groin, pulling the trigger three times on empty chambers. Then he stood looking down at Tim Reagen.
>
> Billy opened his eyes to see his bleeding brother beside him on the floor. Billy shook Tim's arm and grunted "Timbo" but his brother stayed limp. Jack cracked Billy on the head with the butt of his empty pistol and Billy went flat.
>
> "Let's go, Jack, let's move," Charlie Filetti said.
>
> Jack looked up and saw Elaine's terrified face peering at him from the checkroom. The bartenders' faces were as white as their aprons. All faces look at Jack as Filetti grabbed his arm and pulled. Jack tossed his pistol onto Billy's chest and it bounced off onto the floor.

A fine piece of Hammett pastiche, but the credit goes not to Kennedy but to Gorman, our narrator. It is Gorman who has pulled the facts painfully together and shaped them into a narrative which impresses us with its studied lack of affect. Like much hard-boiled prose, though, it is really not neutral but expresses a covert admiration. "Tossed," for example, would not be the word chosen by Joe Vignola, who is one of the Hotsy Totsy witnesses. Rather, it expresses

Gorman's sense of a man who can kill in blind fury and then not give a damn. Dumbfounding, but rather stylish.

Poor Joe, a family man with children, winds up in the Tombs prison, a material witness. At night he begins to see Jack Diamond, disguised as a Boy Scout, coming through the bars of the cell window, sometimes accompanied by another underworld figure, Herman Zuckman. "The night the dead fish jumped out of Herman's tuxedo Joe finally won his straitjacket." For Joe, Legs was now a figure out of legend, out of nightmare, and Gorman sees the comedy of telling it to us this way. And so, God help us, do we.

Jack Diamond was a real person, of course, a tough kid out of Philadelphia who had somehow acquired the nickname Legs, although never called that by his friends, but only by the tabloids and the columnists and eventually by the general public. He got very famous very fast, a hijacker of trucks and distilleries, ready to use torture and to leave henchmen in the lurch, a dispenser of random, casual favors and brutalities. He worked with the most powerful of the New York bosses, Owney Madden and Arnold Rothstein, and at the time of his death was in a volatile competition with Dutch Schultz and Lucky Luciano. Luciano did not share Jack's love of the limelight, which allowed him to live into old age. He was a creature of the Thirties and Forties.

Crime and celebrity fed upon each other in the Twenties. Their common theater was nightclubs like the Hotsy Totsy—all of them mob-owned, and peopled by the types that form our cultural memory of the decade: reporters and racketeers, showpeople, chorus girls, shysters, boys down from Harvard and Princeton, enforcers. Every reader of Winchell knew that Diamond's wife was named Alice and that his latest girlfriend was Kiki Roberts, a showgirl with the tawdry good looks then in vogue. The posters for the movie *Public Enemy*, which opened shortly before Diamond was suddenly killed in 1931, hinted at the resemblance between the Jimmy Cagney character and a certain celebrated desperado. Cagney played a highly specific type—violent, trigger-tempered, impudent, swaggering, with the charm and magic of a young roughneck on the way to riches but not breaking into a sweat about it. And very Irish. Diamond too had a certain charm and also good looks, especially when the competition was Dutch Schultz and a psychopath named Mad Dog Coll. Not even Jimmy could boast of having limped away from four murder attempts. But Legs, like the Cagney character, was doomed to die young: everyone knew that. Unless, of course, he was immortal.

This was also the celebrity decade in the world of letters, stars of the columns and the rotogravure, Hemingway and Fitzgerald. Fitzgerald met Arnold Rothstein and used him as the model for Meyer Wolfshiem in *The Great Gatsby*, the man with cuff links made of human molars. The brilliant economy with which he creates Wolfshiem is made possible because everyone had heard about bosses like Rothstein.

Critics have seen a resemblance between the two narrators, Nick Carraway and Marcus Gorman, but as Kennedy himself has remarked, Nick, like his creator, is too much the yuppie. At critical moments he breaks into purest yuppiespeak. "Gatsby who represented everything for which I have an unaffected scorn," nevertheless "turned out all right at the end." There is, though, a more profound difference between the two characters. For Gorman the foul dust that trails in Diamond's wake is part of his glamour—the violence, the swift rages, even the vulgarity. They beckon Gorman toward his exciting new life. Like Jack Burden, the narrator of *All the King's Men*, he shares his leader's corruption.

On Gorman's first visit to Diamond's Catskill hideout, Legs and Alice offer a trial of a new machine gun, their equivalent, perhaps, of a fast set of tennis. "I smiled at Alice to imply I was her friend, and Jack's too. And I was then, yes I was. I was intuitively in sympathy with this man and woman who had just introduced me to the rattling, stammering splatter of violent death. Gee, ain't it swell." He's a goner. Like every true New Yorker, though, he uses slang and self-mockery to let us know he realizes what is happening to him.

Diamond spent his final months in Albany. On the night of December 18, 1931, after celebrating a courtroom victory which Gorman had won for him, he was shot to death, alone, in a back-street rooming house. "Who shot Legs Diamond?" is still a lively subject of discussion in Albany's better bars, or so Kennedy assures us. With *Legs*, he himself had made certain that this would be the case. But the novel asks a second question, which holds more interest for Gorman and for Kennedy. Diamond, Gorman tells us, has passed from life into legend and from legend into myth. And as myth, he has been granted immortality, hasn't he?

Parts of the Legs Diamond legend had begun to accumulate even while Jack was alive. He was aware of the process and tickled by it, if puzzled. Birds fall silent at his approach, it was said, and the story goes that he could tie both his shoes at once. Years after his death, an old whore swears that he could turn on the lights by snapping his fingers. Gorman has an explanation out of popular science for that one, as Leopold Bloom would. "He had a luminous quality at certain moments, when he stood in shadow: the luminosity is pure energy."

One time the tabloid headlines had read: JACK DIAMOND SHOT FIVE TIMES BY GUNMEN IN 64TH STREET HOTEL. Lew Edwards the impresario visits him in the hospital and promises him a publicity campaign that could make him the biggest thing since Billy Sunday and Aimee Semple MacPherson, with the help of speech coaches. He could found a new religion. Only in America. The reader remembers that in the same years, Zelda Fitzgerald was telling friends that Al Jolson was greater than Jesus. She may have been onto something. The transformation of celebrity into legend into myth in specifically American terms is the real subject of *Legs*. The final, surreal image is a bit like the Ascension in a Renaissance painting, Gorman and

Arnold Rothstein helping Jack out of his body through his bullet-shattered skull. "'Honest to God, Marcus,' he said going away, 'I really don't think I'm dead.'"

Jack Diamond makes his final appearance in *Roscoe* in one of its flashback chapters. The real Legs, out of luck and out of money, unprotected by goons or crooked cops, is sitting in his underwear on the side of his bed, pleading for his life. His killers, of course, are the cops themselves, O. B. and Mac. O. B., the chief of police, is Roscoe Conway's compliant brother, and Mac is a thick-witted brute. Jack's fate, though, had been decided at the highest Albany level.

In the spring of the year, Governor Franklin Roosevelt was preparing his run for the White House, and people like Legs Diamond operating on his doorstep did not look good, especially now that Legs had added kidnapping and torture to his repertoire. Roosevelt sent his troopers over to "rip Jack's empire up the middle and sideways." Jack, though, had never been one to listen to reason, and instead he proposed to Roscoe, the machine fixer, a scheme to make Albany his headquarters in exchange for cheap beer. Roscoe agreed to pass the question along to Patsy and Binty McCall, out of politeness, but he never doubted their reaction. Diamond, Coll, and Schultz had been leaving corpses all over Manhattan in the beer wars, and newsmen reckoned that Diamond was ahead in the corpse count. "Did Albany need beer that came in coffins?" Patsy's response was mild, as words go: "That fella's going to be a serious nuisance if they don't put him in jail."

"Roscoe *at that moment*," so the narrative tells us, making a rare use of italics,

> became the outsider in future Jack talk: Patsy trusting him like nobody else apart from certain cosmic decisions. You run the party, Roscoe, I'll run the nighttown—as if they could be separated. But Patsy believed in separate realms of power, pitted

even his closest allies against one another when it suited him. Like pitting chickens. Competitive truculence. See who survives.

But of course Roscoe understands Patsy's decision as clearly as his murderous knights understood the words with which Henry II ordered the death of Becket. "Probably we'll never know the truth," the narrator tells us. "So many out there who wanted vengeance on the man. Whoever did it give him a medal, one cop said." Kennedy's use of third-person narrative in *Roscoe* is deliberately disingenuous. At times it seems to be recording Roscoe's thoughts—shrewd, artful, cynical, yet often and fundamentally large-minded and chivalrous, especially in matters of the heart. But at other times, as here, it is the wised-up voice of wised-up Albany itself talking *at that moment* off the record. Kennedy's deepest allegiance is to language, and in return it lets him say just about whatever he wants to say.

It may be that Kennedy takes it a bit too easy on Roscoe in this account of his twilight years, giving him as problems to solve the suicide of his aristocratic friend Elisha Fitzgibbon, his unconsummated love for Elisha's wife, and a deadly feud between the chief bosses of the city, Patsy and Binty McCall, a feud over their fighting chickens. The first and third of these problems seem unworthy of the worldly wisdom and skill with which we are asked to credit him. These are tasks better left to Scattergood Baines in the old *Saturday Evening Post* stories or David Harum in the old Will Rogers movie. But theirs, come to think of it, is the world in which Roscoe has grown up and which one day soon, rueful and reflective, he will join.

The plot earns its keep though. Kennedy has never written a more vivid and sanguinary chapter than his description of a cockfight at a pit in neighboring South Troy, "in the opinion of cockers east and west, north and south, the most famous cockpit in the Northeast, maybe in all of America." That chapter captures it all—the birds themselves, their owners and handlers, the circular dirt pit with its three-foot-high canvas wall, the surrounding crowd of gamblers and lovers of bloody murder. Here is Kennedy describing how to rig a fight with the help of a little anticoagulant:

> His neck will swell with blood and he'll be cyanotic, presumed dead. The savvy handler will quickly massage the blood out of his neck in the ring and revive him before he goes into irreversible shock, then will do it again at the first-aid bench, and the bird will recover, but now be known as a loser. Take him off the coumadin and fight him again, with long odds against him now as the loser; but this time he'll be wearing proper-length spurs to kill, he will have fought and lived, and he will think with the serrated edge of a survivor.

"To Roscoe," we are told by that eerie, unstable (to use a word in vogue) narrative voice, "spectating at cockfights was a lifelong education in tension, cowardice, unpredictable reversals, and courage. The birds, bred for battle, fought for neither God nor glory, neither to eat nor for love. They fought to conquer the other, to impose death before it was imposed. Just like politics, Roscoe decided, but without the blood. 'Well, sometimes there's blood.'"

Ask Legs. *Neither to eat nor for love.* Now the unstable voice can quote Shakespeare, as Roscoe can. Whose voice it is now is beyond me.

The richest sections of *Roscoe* are the ones that move backward in time to the machine's seizure of power and to its full, flowering existence ten years later, when the book deals with Jack Diamond. But that story pauses with a shadow of the future on it, with the Democratic gubernatorial convention in the autumn of 1932. It is then that the boys learn that Jimmy Walker, the pride of Tammany Hall and the Albany machine, will be thrown to the wolves by FDR and Al Smith himself, the prince of Irish Catholic pols, himself denied the presidency in 1928 by a nation of Protestant bigots. Not only that, but

FDR and Smith, unlikely allies, are throwing the governorship not to Elisha Fitzgibbon but to Herbert Lehman, partly for political reasons and partly because the country is experiencing one of its recurring morality epidemics, as Roscoe calls them. Roscoe has consoling words for Patsy. "Pat, we are Democrats, remember? And we are steeped in Democracy. We own the city, the county, the state, and the nation. Things could be worse."

Kennedy's art is an eccentric triumph, a quirky, risk-taking imagination at play upon the solid paving stones, the breweries, the politicos and pool sharks of an all-too-actual city. The collisions of setting and stance, if nothing more, bring Yoknapatawpha County to mind, despite the vast distances, geographical and cultural, which separate the Mississippi and the Hudson. But Faulkner and Kennedy also share old-fashioned themes like honor, betrayal, the foreverness of the past.

—*The New York Review of Books*, April 25, 2002

II

Irish Literature

8

ANGLO-IRISHRY

IN 1171, MAURICE FITZGERALD, a Norman fighting man who had come over to Ireland with Strongbow and who at the moment was being besieged in Dublin, said to his fellow barons: "Such in truth is our lot that while we are English to the Irish, we are Irish to the English. For the one nation does not detest us more than the other." Thus, at the very outset, the core of the Anglo-Irish plight was given lapidary formulation. There is even the requisite aspect of the linguistic bizarre, because Fitzgerald, like most of the early Normans, could speak neither English nor Irish. And Fitzgerald has even contrived to sound what would prove in time to be the distinctive Anglo-Irish note, that curious marriage of sturdiness and self-pity. It might even be argued that he foreshadows the Anglo-Irish overtones of elegy and lament.

Julian Moynahan, in *Anglo-Irish: The Literary Imagination in a Hyphenated Culture*,[1] this brilliant, quirky, and indispensable book —adjectives which define the Anglo-Irish themselves—addresses not so much the history of the Anglo-Irish as the history of their imagination of themselves and of their culture. Early on, he quotes from John Fitzgibbon's famous speech to the entirely Protestant Parliament in Dublin, at the time (1800) when the self-destruction of the "Nation

---

1. Princeton University Press, 1994.

of Ireland" and its absorption into Great Britain was being debated. Fitzgibbon was cautioning the members against any giddy trafficking with patriotism or liberality, and was reminding them that they held power by the sword alone. "Confiscation," he said, "is their common title; and from their first coming they have been hemmed in on every side by the old inhabitants of the island, brooding on their discontents in sullen indignation.... And what is their security to this day? The powerful and commanding protection of Great Britain. If by any fatality it fails, you are at the mercy of the old inhabitants of the Island."

Moynahan does well to quote that speech early on, marked as Elizabeth Bowen says by its "superb detestable realism," and it would have served his design had he gone on to point out that it is a speech possessing a rhetorical glitter which is more Irish than English in its lurid imaginings. It was matched by the speech of Grattan, the patriot, after Fitzgibbon had succeeded: "Yet I do not give up my country. I see her in a swoon but she is not dead; though in her tomb she lies helpless and motionless, still on her lips is the spirit of life and on her cheeks the glow of beauty." What with Fitzgibbon's sullen and angry malcontents brooding in the shadows and Grattan's image of Ireland lying in her tomb rosy of lip and cheek, it is small wonder that at the century's end the Anglo-Irish imagination brought forth the vampires of Le Fanu and Bram Stoker. Nor, and this is more to the point, is it any wonder that when the Irish began to attend the Parliament in London they were noted and mocked for their oratorical ornaments and rhetorical excesses.

The last great speech in that tradition was the one delivered in 1925 by William Butler Yeats to the largely Catholic Senate. His subject was the proposed divorce bill. "We against whom you have done this thing are no petty people. We are one of the great stocks in Europe. We are the people of Burke; we are the people of Grattan; we are the people of Swift, the people of Emmet, the people of Parnell. We have created the most of the modern literature of this country. We have created the best of its political intelligence." He does not say that they are also the people of Fitzgibbon, perhaps upon eugenic grounds: Fitzgibbon, if not descended from the very oldest inhabitants of the island, came close to it. His father was a Catholic who, back in penal days, had turned Protestant in order to become a barrister.

By Yeats's day, of course, the social order in whose name he claimed to speak had had the sentence of history well and truly passed upon it, although scarcely the sentence of the literary imagination. Indeed, it was the genius of the writers of the Literary Revival to give a new, lustrous life to the Anglo-Irish Ascendancy precisely at its point of farthest decline. A paradox of that literature, Moynahan says, "is that it flowers just when the social formation producing it enters a phase of contraction and decline. As Anglo-Irish literature 'arises,' the Anglo-Irish begin to go down in the world."

But when, in social fact, *did* the Anglo-Irish begin to go down in the world? Various dates have been offered—the 1800 Act of Union, the Famine, the rise of the Land League, the rise of O'Connell, the rise of Parnell, the disestablishment of the Church of Ireland, the various ameliorative Land Acts. Mark Bence-Jones, whose plangent threnody for a "doomed aristocracy" is announced in its title, *Twilight of the Ascendancy* (1989), suggests: "The Lords and other landowners of Ireland, known, together with their relations, as the Ascendancy long after they had ceased to be in the ascendant, entered a twilight period just over a century ago when they lost most of their political power at the same time as their economic foundations were eroded by economic depression and agrarian disturbances." Which is a good baseline for some purposes, although Moynahan, for other and perhaps more useful purposes, uses the Act of Union. Myself, I would choose Maurice Fitzgerald's plaintive and truculent cry of 1171.

I have called Moynahan's book brilliant and quirky, and it is appropriate that *Castle Rackrent*, the literary work with which he opens his discussion, should have as its narrator a servant named Thady Quirk.

And equally appropriate, in a different way, that Maria Edgeworth's novel was published in the year that saw the passage of the Act of Union. In my own day, some thirty-five years ago, I praised this novel to the skies, or thought I had, not knowing until Moynahan how high the heavens are. *Castle Rackrent* traces the decline of one family of the gentry, and does so in a way intended to suggest the decay of a social order. It does so in large part through the ventriloquial skill with which Edgeworth deploys the voice of the quirky Thady—a devious, wheedling, deceiving, self-deceiving, naive, shrewd voice. Moynahan explores the social and linguistic resources which went into the making of the voice, and suggests persuasively that this is indeed an Anglo-Irish, perhaps even an Irish, and certainly not an English voice. The voice, that is, of Edgeworth herself, shaping and controlling Thady's voice.

The discussion of Edgeworth concludes by oblique allusion to a moment in 1798 when the Edgeworths fled before the invading French and then returned, expecting that their house had been destroyed but instead finding it untouched: "Maria Edgeworth, the great Maria who founded the line of literature this book investigates, had imagined her home to be doomed, but she discovered it had been spared. Actually, it had only been reprieved. This she may have understood in her deepest imagination, where Thady, her Mask and Daimon, spoke old family scandal and prophecy too, as fast as she could write it down." Moynahan deplores the tendency to read historical allegory into works of the Anglo-Irish literary imagination, but he does a pretty good job of it himself.

And it was perhaps inevitable: to believe oneself to be Anglo-Irish was to see oneself positioned within history. And thus, to write in fiction or even to write of oneself, was to traffic in portent. Nor was the Anglo-Irish situation unique: "The great writers of nineteenth-century Russia, from Lermontov and Pushkin to Turgenev, Dostoevsky, and Tolstoy, were all products of a class—the landed gentry and nobility of the provinces—which steadily declined in political and social consequence...." So too the fiction of Faulkner and O'Connor, the poetry of the Fugitives, emerged from the socially and culturally shattered American South. And so too of individuals: "Charles Dickens, James Joyce, and F. Scott Fitzgerald are just three of the many writers whose literary imaginations received powerful stimulus from their early discovery that their families were headed downward on the scales of economic security and social standing. It appears that the relation between accomplishment in literary pursuits and in the world is often inverse. The literary muse, at least in certain periods, dearly loves a loser."

But not merely the literary muse. Lost causes have always had their sentimental and often maudlin adherents. George IV, the Hanoverian dynasty being by his time secure, fancied himself a bit of a Jacobite, wearing kilts and passing along some money and a small pension to the last of the Stuarts in Rome. The Southern Lost Cause produced not only *The Sound and the Fury* and Flannery O'Connor, but *Gone With the Wind* and hundreds of even worse historical novels of the moonlight-and-magnolia school. Not to mention wretched statues of proud, somber Confederate soldiers in every courthouse square from Charleston to Galveston.

Roy Foster, in an appreciative and perceptive *TLS* review of Moynahan's book, asks, as well, whether it is relevant to liken writers inspired by their declining families to those produced by a declining culture. But in fact, it is relevant when the writers themselves, in the largeness of their mythic imaginations, make the connections. Thus Joyce, finding his family's downward slope toward bankruptcy linked to Parnell's progress toward betrayal and downfall. And buried somewhere within *The Great Gatsby* lies Fitzgerald's lament for his genteel Maryland forebears, dragged westward to the bleak snows of Minnesota and then downward into a Jazz Age of bootlegging and shady stock transactions. And surely, above all other instances, the connection between declining family and declining culture is one of the powerful engines driving

Faulkner's imagination. Noting the uncanny resemblance between Jason Compson and Jason Quirk, Moynahan, in one of his giddier moments, suggests that *Castle Rackrent* was "probably mined" by Faulkner for *The Sound and the Fury*. The point is well made, but goes a bit far.

Perhaps, though, all writers are inclined to see themselves as ruined aristocrats, suffering, stoic but eloquent, in an indifferent and philistine world—versions, every last one of them, of Jacobite swordsmen, claimants to rich lands of the imagination, their mansions burned down by Sherman's bummers or the IRA. And happy indeed, those writers whose actual circumstances in history conform, or can be made to conform, to the needs of their imagination.

Roy Foster complains, and rightly, that Moynahan has left out Bram Stoker, "a vital link in the chain of Ascendancy occultism." That subject has also been addressed by Foster in "Protestant Magic," one of the essays in his *Paddy and Mr. Punch*. Neither Foster nor Moynahan, it seems to me, comes close to exhausting the subject. From Maturin onward, Le Fanu, Stoker, Wilde, Somerville and Ross, Elizabeth Bowen, Yeats—there is something spooky about the Irish Protestant fascination with spooks. And most of these writers (notably not Somerville and Ross) are not merely Protestant, but Protestants from a particular subculture—middle-class Dublin professional class, doctors, solicitors, clergymen, magazine editors. It is almost as though they felt the dying world of the eighteenth-century Ascendancy city in the gaunt, claret-brick houses of the squares—Mountjoy and Merrion and Fitzwilliam. But not the city only, of course: the West Cork of Somerville and Ross was mad for spiritualism and ouija boards and table-rapping and ghosts howling in the smugglers' inlets, and the narrow mountain roads. Edith Somerville, of course, believed that Violet Martin ("Martin Ross") lived on in spirit after her mortal death, still her active collaborator, her name appearing on the title page of each new book, including *The Big House of Inver*, that frightening tale of bloodlines and miscegenation and crime. Very curious, all that.

One of the great triumphs of Moynahan's book is that he manages marvelous set pieces. The discussions of Charles Lever, William Carleton, Somerville and Ross and Elizabeth Bowen are superb, not merely as stages in his argument, but as careful, shrewd, and sensitive responses to remarkable writers. Best of all, though, it seems to me, is his account of Charles Robert Maturin's *Melmoth the Wanderer* (1820), that "marvellous baroque machine for generating (and detonating) narratives, for transforming, reversing and inverting, undermining and confounding relationships among narrators, characters, and readers...." It is certainly, as Moynahan says, "Anglo-Irish Gothic's greatest prose romance." But it is much more than this, both as a feat of narrative legerdemain and as an exfoliation of the complex, constricted world in which Maturin lived. If Moynahan's account sends readers back to it, it will have earned its price, but that is only one virtue of this witty, humane, and learned study.

Some years ago, at a Christmas party in what were then the offices of the Irish Consulate in New York, a mildly intoxicated Irish-American asked me if I could identify the series of portraits which stretched along one wall. Yes, I told him, they are the great writers of the Irish Literary Renaissance, and I identified those closest at hand—Yeats, Synge, Lady Gregory, Douglas Hyde, Wilde, Sean O'Casey. "Well," he said, pleased and proud. "And yet you'll still find people who say that Catholics can't write." "In fact," I said, "those particular Irish writers were Protestants." "All of them?" he asked, looking a bit unnerved. "All of them," I said firmly, although O'Casey didn't really look Protestant. "Well, how about that?" he asked gamely, adding, "Of course, I knew that James Joyce was a Protestant." After I had instructed him on that point, he headed off to the bar. I had not the heart to call after him that the Guinesses and the Jamesons were also Protestants. All in all, it would seem "we" owe "them" quite a lot.

—*The Recorder*, Fall 1995

9

THE LITERATURE OF RESISTANCE

THE PROGRAM NOTE at the opening night of Sean O'Casey's play *The Shadow of a Gunman* in 1923 informed the audience: "Any gunshots heard during the performance are part of the script." It was a sensible precaution. As Declan Kiberd reminds us in *Inventing Ireland*,[1] a critical study laced with wit, energy, and an unrelenting adroitness of discourse, on that April night the civil war between the Free State and the Republic—between the "moderates" who had signed a treaty with the British and the "die-hards" who rejected the compromise—had another week to run, and sporadic rifle fire peppered the streets outside the Abbey Theatre.

The second play in O'Casey's Dublin trilogy, *Juno and the Paycock* (1924), is concerned with the civil war itself, as though his art fed on history as it was being enacted in the streets. But with the third play, *The Plough and the Stars*, in 1926, history moved into the aisles and onto the stage. It dramatized the Easter Rebellion of 1916, which had ignited a decade of revolutionary violence, bloodshed, and, in the end, fratricide. Now it earned for itself an outburst that far surpassed the celebrated "riots" caused by J. M. Synge's *Playboy of the Western World* in 1907. In the audience were veterans of that rebellion,

---

1. Harvard University Press, 1995.

mothers and widows of others, and a new generation of rebels. They came prepared to battle O'Casey's brutal yet hilarious demythologizing of what had become sacred—the blood sacrifice by Patrick Pearse and the other martyrs of Easter Week.

The only wonder is that the reaction was so slow in coming. Seamus Shields, the disillusioned and far from heroic former patriot in *The Shadow of a Gunman*, had clearly been speaking for O'Casey himself: "I believe in the freedom of Ireland and that England has no right to be here, but I draw the line when I hear the gunmen blowin' about dyin' for the people, when it's the people that are dyin' for the gunmen! With all due respects for the gunmen, I don't want them to die for me!" "With all due respects" is authentic O'Casey, at once droll and deadly.

To O'Casey, a militant socialist, the Rising was suicidal and befuddled, and a betrayal of the working class. But in Ireland, as the matter is put by Kiberd, who has a weakness for aphorism, "'socialism' never stood for much more than a fundamental goodness of heart," and O'Casey was a cardinal case in point. He thought with his heart rather than his head, and thinking with the more conventional organ, Kiberd suggests with delicacy, was not his forte. The powers of his art were of a different order.

Kiberd, a lecturer in English at University College, Dublin, and a distinguished critic, possesses a special gift for patient exploration of works of art in relationship to their surroundings. For example, he locates with precision the source of a powerful feeling we experience when we watch O'Casey plays. They are set in the Dublin slums, where in the early twentieth century the death rate was higher than in Calcutta, and where the poor were crowded to overbursting in rotting slum houses that had once been the mansions of a vanished aristocracy. "Such a setting dictated the controlling mood of the Dublin plays, each of which is a study in claustrophobia, in the helpless availability of persons, denied any right to privacy and doomed to live in

THE LITERATURE OF RESISTANCE

one another's pockets," Kiberd writes. "Many of O'Casey's poetic speeches are attempts by characters to create a more spacious world in the imagination than the drab, constricted place in which they are expected to live. In that respect, O'Casey is an heir to Synge, who had found in the rich idiom of the peasantry an implicit critique of a monochromatic world."

A joining of O'Casey's boisterously vulgar imagination with that of the oblique, private, and often enigmatic Synge is made possible by one of Kiberd's unifying themes—the variousness with which Irish writers have used language, including the particularities of dialect, to explore cultural identities. Through language, every Irish writer has conducted a dialogue between the often warring parts of his own being, and other dialogues with other Irishmen separated from him by class or religion, and above all else he has maintained a dialogue with that enormous colonizing empire that hovers, as fact or memory, over every Irishman's shoulder.

For Kiberd, the generating energy in Irish culture in recent centuries has been British imperialism (at first military, political, and economic, but ultimately cultural) and the protean native resistance to that process. He is concerned with Ireland's literature as that of a postcolonial culture, but he gives that term a most elastic definition. A literature does not become postcolonial only after the occupier has withdrawn: "Rather it is initiated at that very moment when a native writer formulates a text committed to cultural resistance."

Thus Edmund Burke, writing in the eighteenth century, is a postcolonial, a defender of Ireland's necessary connection with England who was at the same time a mordant critic of Ireland's Protestant rulers as little better than "a junto of robbers," brutal and craven. This works well enough with Burke, but in its more universal application by Kiberd it may best be described as highly convenient. He delights in paradox, and to speak of the Gaelic historian Seathrun Ceitinn (in English, Geoffrey Keating) as postcolonial, although he wrote at the very height of England's military triumph, must surely appeal to that delight, setting at defiance as it does the common meanings of words.

At times he stretches too thin his all-embracing formula, as with overly ingenious discussions of Wilde and Shaw. Wilde was very conscious of his Irishness, which afforded him occasions for wit. As when he declared that he had no religion: he was an Irish Protestant. Nevertheless the adroit attempt to make of him a kind of stylistic freedom fighter is one that not even the broad shoulders of his genius can support.

But the mention of Wilde and Shaw reminds us that wit, paradox, and an almost indecent delight in verbal jugglery place Kiberd himself in a central Irish literary tradition, a tradition that also includes Swift, Joyce, and Beckett. He resembles that stereotype of the Irish writer "invented" by Ireland's imperial masters—impudent, eloquent, full of jokes and irreverence, by turns sardonic and conciliatory, blithely subversive but, without warning, turning to display wide and serious reading, generosity of spirit, a fierce and authentic concern for social and political justice. Rather like Wilde and Shaw.

In so headlong and many-branched a discourse, there are the inevitable slips, some of which the solemn and pedantic reviewer sets forth as his revenge upon wit. Of the two government officials murdered by extremists in Dublin's Phoenix Park in 1882, Lord Frederick Cavendish was the Chief Secretary and Thomas Burke the Under Secretary—not, as Kiberd has it, the other way round. And no allegations of homosexuality were made at the trial for treason of Sir Roger Casement in 1916. The British government circulated such stories, supported by entries from his diaries, outside the courtroom and surreptitiously, with the intention of blackening his reputation.

In both instances, the facts could have served Kiberd's elaborate anti-imperial design. Lord Frederick Cavendish, an amiable and mild-mannered Englishman, was recently arrived with a mission of conciliation. But the actual tough work of evictions and political repression had been entrusted years before to Burke, his subordinate, who of course was a native Irishman serving the empire. And the whispering campaign against Casement, conducted with Cabinet knowledge, seemed almost to imply that transgression of the Victorian moral code was an offense more grievous than high treason.

Kiberd's remarkable achievement may seem to fall within the modish academic enterprise "cultural studies," which too often seems a kind of safe house where theorists with tin ears can give solace to one another. But his own ear is splendid, and he is careful to place a distance between himself and fashionable cultural theorists in words that a few years ago would have been unnecessary, but in the present climate are almost flamboyant: "It is wise to recognize—despite current critical fashions—that certain masterpieces do float free of their enabling conditions to make their home in the world. Ireland, precisely because its writers have been fiercely loyal to their own localities, has produced a large number of these masterpieces, and in an extraordinarily concentrated phase of expression."

It is heartening to find an academic critic talking about masterpieces and writing in celebration of them.

—*The New York Times Book Review*, March 17, 1996

10

A COLDER EYE

NO CRITIC NOW writing has an eye and ear more alert to language than Hugh Kenner's. Perhaps this is because he is himself a fine if idiosyncratic writer, quirky, witty, mischievous, precise.

Influential critics who also write well are becoming rarer and rarer. The work of the fashionable poststructuralists is exciting, indispensable, far-reaching in its assumptions and its consequences, but only disciples can find it pleasurable. Often the reader pauses over a paragraph of ensnarled opacity, puzzled as to whether he is baffled by the profundity of the methodology or by the needless tortuosity of the syntax.

Kenner, on the other hand, is quite capable of laying traps for the reader, but they are intended to jolt us out of our literary complacencies, to sharpen dulled eyes and sensibilities. He is both the scholar and the celebrant of the modernist movement, and has written well and instructively about its masters—Ford, Pound, Joyce, Eliot, Wyndham Lewis. Pound, above all the others. *The Pound Era* (1971), his massive and deliberately eccentric study of the entire movement, defines its thesis in its title.

His own literary manners and strategies have been formed upon those of his master. Like Pound, he knows how to argue by juxtaposition and surprise, how to use wit as a form of logic. He knows the value of the exact image and the resonant anecdote. And like Pound, he is a skilled swordsman: reading Kenner is a lively and illuminating experience, but it is best to keep one's guard up.

His present book, *A Colder Eye: The Modern Irish Writers*,[1] seeks to explain the emergence, beginning in the 1890s, of a large and spectacular series of writers in a country as small as Ireland, and a country which at the time had no firm identity and was regarded, even by itself, as a provincial backwater. He attempts to establish for the literature of modern Ireland a central line of development, which begins with Yeats and closes with Beckett. As he says, it might have taken, as subtitle, *Yeats and His Shadow*. Therefore, he does not consider Ireland's living poets, Heaney, Kinsella, Montague. They do not work beneath that shadow, and are "the beginning of a new story entirely." They themselves, I suspect, would say that this is both true and not true, and I suspect, even more strongly, that they would be uneasy about the line of reasoning which carries him to this conclusion.

At first glance, the subject would seem ideally suited to his talents. In the past, he has touched it in tangents: in tracing Yeats's evolution from dreamy Celtic Pre-Raphaelite to monumental modern, in exploring Joyce's extraordinary appearance, while in his twenties, as a fully hatched modernist. But something seems to have fallen athwart his enterprise, separating intention from execution. And that something, I suspect, was Ireland. Sooner or later, the various commanders sent out by Elizabeth to conquer Ireland sent back reports cursing the place as "a quaking bog." Later, academic explorers (myself included) have had similar experiences. Kenner joins a long procession. He has written a wonderfully witty and perceptive book, but it does not answer the questions it engages.

He begins with an assumption which is as sensible as it is bold. English literature in our century exists in one or another of three

---

1. Knopf, 1983.

major dialects—the British (Woolf, Auden, et al.), the Irish (Yeats, Beckett, et al.), and the American (Frost, Stevens, et al.). This falls pleasingly upon the ears of us American and Irish ex-colonials: a linguistic liberation from the English imperium. England's literature, as he says, has become a special case, "the literature of one province among several." And indeed, Seamus Heaney has in his prose, most notably in an essay called "Englands of the Mind," developed a similar argument in a characteristically congenial and subversive manner. Characteristic, that is, of Heaney: Kenner, I fear, would say, characteristically Irish.

The assumption is a genuinely liberating one, allowing the critical intelligence to move among the works of modern literature with a freedom not permitted by the straitjacket of conventional classification by nationality. Kenner's difficulty issues from his further and more polemical assumption that all three literatures, British, Irish, American, are "dialects in the light of a fourth phenomenon, *International Modernism*," which happens, apparently because of Joyce, to have elected English as its language. International modernism, however, while it is a term quite properly employed when speaking of Joyce and Beckett, is largely irrelevant to the tale which Kenner's book unfolds. Were it relevant, then one would expect to discover Flann O'Brien and Patrick Kavanagh, two of the three recent writers discussed, to be international modernists in full flower. In fact, however, they were nothing of the kind. Indeed, in their very different ways they directed toward it the scorn of which they were vituperative masters.

There is a famous and pertinent passage in Joyce's *Portrait of the Artist*, which Kenner quotes, as well he might. Stephen Dedalus listens to his English-born dean of studies, and thinks:

> The language in which we are speaking is his before it is mine.
> How different are the words *home*, *Christ*, *ale*, *master*, on his

lips and on mine! I cannot speak or write these words without unrest of spirit. His language, so familiar and so foreign, will always be for me an acquired speech. I have not made or accepted its words. My voice holds them at bay. My soul frets in the shadow of his language.

This locates with precision the situation of the Irish writer with respect to the language in which he thinks and feels. Or rather, to make a crucial distinction, of those writers who came, like Joyce, from the Catholic side of Ireland's divided culture. That other great Irish writer, Yeats, came to English as to his native inheritance, with no sense of it as either acquisition or imposition. "My ancestors," Stephen says bitterly to a friend, "threw off their language and took another." But Yeats's ancestors, English colonists, did not.

It is quite possible to see Ireland's great Literary Revival in comic terms, and Kenner is alert to that possibility. Yeats, luxuriantly at ease within the English language, sought to create within it a specifically Irish variant. He did so by turning, subtly and warily, toward those legends, traditions, habits of thought which were most firmly embedded in Gaelic, the older language. At the time, the turn of the century, it was a language which history had relegated to the peasants of the western seacoasts, although it was being revived by enthusiastic nationalists.

Yeats himself took no part in this revival. For one thing, he was, notoriously, a monoglot. More importantly, he was wedded to English as the very syntax of his imagination. Nevertheless, he was glad that it was there, somewhere, influencing Irish speech much as underground lodes of magnetic ore affect compass needles. He encouraged colleagues and one playwright of genius, Synge, to draw from the resources of Gaelic a kind of English which would be redolent of the verbal odors of Irish life. He himself employed this Synge-song sparingly and with indifferent results, but it served as a resonating-board for his own language. For some twenty years, from Synge's *Playboy of the Western World* to O'Casey's *Plough and the Stars*, it gave to Irish literature, and thence to the world, a beguiling and richly expressive language.

The Irish themselves were less impressed by Yeats's gift to them. Both Synge's play and O'Casey's provoked celebrated riots at the Abbey Theatre. The provocations, to be sure, were cultural and political rather than linguistic, but in Ireland such matters are not easily separated. Yeats, Synge, and Lady Gregory were Protestant members of the British Ascendancy. (O'Casey was also a Protestant, but he was poor, which took the curse off it.) And the "plain people of Ireland," as they were forever calling themselves, had for long been schooled to look upon gifts from that source with a suspicion which, upon the whole, was justified by historical experience.

The great irony of the revival is that Joyce was equally suspicious, if for quite different reasons. The aboriginal Gaelic and the peasant English which had been formed upon it were alike to him the speech of serfs, patronized for the moment by such summer visitors as Yeats and Synge. "Shakespeare," says a character in *Ulysses*, satirizing the revivalists, "the chap that writes like Synge." Aside from being other, and perhaps greater, things, *Ulysses* is Ireland's declaration of linguistic independence. It was begun, in a Swiss exile, at about the time that other young Irishmen launched in the streets of Dublin a political rebellion to which Joyce was, on the whole, indifferent.

Kenner is attentive to such ironies. And he is right to assume that contemporary Irish literature, being post-Yeatsian, lies outside his subject. Ireland has found its voice, or rather its voices, and they come from within their culture. But the tension within those voices generated by the knowledge that English is an "acquired speech" persists. As we know from the poetry of Kavanagh and Heaney and Montague, it is a complex, subtle, muscular, and enriching tension, divisions of the soul and of the culture expressing themselves in the syntax of lines and the roots of verbs. And these tensions are too local—Kavanagh would say, too parochial—to be explored as aspects of internationalism.

Kenner began his book during a Dublin residence, and his opening chapter, entitled "Warning," cautions the reader that in Ireland a fact does not have the same specific gravity that it has in more sedate countries. An "Irish Fact," he says, "is definable as anything they will tell you in Ireland, where they tell you a great deal and you had best assume a demeanor of wary appreciation." He can explain no better than I can why this "maddening ostentation of the pseudo-fact should seem an Irish specialty." My suspicion, though, is that Ireland acquired its Anglo-Saxon respect for "facts" from the same source which gave it the language of the Anglo-Saxon—that is, without its consent. And Irishmen therefore feel entitled to use facts as they use the English language, creatively, resourcefully, and with a conjoined wish to deceive and to give pleasure. Kenner is Anglo-Saxon in his fidelity to fact, but Hibernian in his resourceful use of English. He and his Irish friends must have delighted and exasperated each other.

I I

THE QUAKING BOG

DENIS DONOGHUE, WHO is among the most lucid and intellectually powerful of modern critics and literary theorists, does not tell us directly what he means by "We Irish."[1] Certainly this is because the various occasions that have elicited these essays and reviews collected under the title would have made so personal a statement intrusive, and he is a writer of immense tact and grace, rarely moving between his subject and the scrutiny that he is instructing us to bring to bear upon it.

But he also knows that the phrase "we Irish" rests upon a quaking bog. It refers at once to a social and historical certainty and to a great many ideological and aesthetic viewpoints. Derek Mahon, a poet of Northern Protestant "stock" (to use a Yeatsian noun), is not alone in looking forward to the day when the question "Is so and so really an Irish poet?" will clear the room. But the day is not yet upon us, and occasional protests to the contrary carry the chill of Quentin Compson saying quickly, panting in the iron New England dark, that he does not hate the South.

Donoghue's title essay traces the vicissitudes of the very phrase, "we Irish," from its appearance in a journal of Bishop Berkeley through

---

1. *We Irish: Essays on Irish Literature and Society* (Knopf, 1986).

its transformations in the imagination of William Butler Yeats to its final appearance in Yeats's late, swaggering poem, "The Statues" (1938):

> *We Irish, born into that ancient sect*
> *But thrown upon this filthy modern tide....*

Confronting so lurid a precedent, Donoghue sensibly eschews avowals of identity, rightly trusting that the various attitudes, judgments, and occasional prejudices which inform his essays will assert, implicitly and without fuss, that he writes as a critic and an Irishman. His book is divided into four sections, "Yeats," "Joyce," "Contexts" (pieces that bring politics and literature more closely together than elsewhere in the book), and "Occasions" (a category reserved for reviews).

I must here declare an interest, because I am, so to speak, an "occasion." Donoghue reprints his review of my first Irish historical novel, *The Year of the French*. Clearly he liked the book: it was a handsome and generous review. And as clearly, he had some reservations, but they were expressed with a courtliness that made them seem, at first reading, almost like compliments.

On less cordial occasions, the courtliness remains but can be lethal. He reviews the 1981 autobiography of a man named Patrick Shea, a Catholic, Irish-speaking Kerryman who served in the Royal Irish Constabulary until it was disbanded following the Anglo-Irish treaty of 1921, when he moved to the new statelet of Northern Ireland. To this point, his background and career were identical with those of Donoghue's father, who took the option of joining the Royal Ulster Constabulary, eventually becoming sergeant of the Warrenpoint barracks. Shea became a clerk of the Petty Sessions in Newry.

But it was made clear to Donoghue's father that as a Roman Catholic he could not expect promotion, and he retired as he began, a sergeant. Shea, a far more adaptable man, became the second Catholic ever to attain to the rank of permanent secretary of a department. Partly this is because he encountered "decent" sympathetic superiors: "I am ready to believe," Donoghue says, "that his masters were fine fellows: so were they all, all honourable men. It was easy for them to be fine, when every Papist knew his lowly place." But partly also because Shea survived into those final days when Stormont Castle was frantically and fruitlessly dressing up the shop by putting a few Catholics on display in conspicuous windows.

Donoghue quotes from Shea, with grave detachment, such pearls of wisdom as that "the influence of Orangeism was, I believe, considerable." Then it is as though an Elizabethan headsman, solicitous of his client's comfort, were delicately to unlace the doublet, draw down the lawn shirt, part the long, impeding hair, accommodate the neck gently to the block, and raise the ax:

> His autobiography, after all, is justified chiefly as a success story: how a Catholic won the keys to a Protestant kingdom. It is a good story, vigorously told, but there is nothing in it to interest either Patsy O'Hara or Bobby Sands. Besides, if Shea's judgment had obtained, there would have been no Easter Rising, no Irish Free State, Ireland would have been united, but as a colony, John Bull's other island. My children and I would now live under a government we could not accept as legitimate. When I think of that, as Yeats said, "my tongue's a stone." Violence is an appalling thing, but Mr. Shea's comfortable judgment is merely a function of his success in accommodating himself to a government many Catholics found intolerable and illegitimate.

The reference to O'Hara and Sands, both IRA men who were to die on hunger strike, should not permit the assumption that Donoghue's sympathies lie with the present Irish Republican Army. "The Literature of Trouble," which addresses literary responses to

the violence in the North and, more generally, violence as the pro-
vocation of much of modern Irish literature, opens with a fact of history presented with an objectivity that does not leave Donoghue's
attitude in doubt. On February 17, 1978, a bomb was exploded by
the IRA in the La Mon Hotel in County Down. Twelve people were
killed out of five hundred who were in the hotel, "most of them
attending the annual dinner of the Northern Ireland Junior Motor
Cycle Club; these included several boys who attended to receive their
prizes. Other people were in the hotel as members of the Irish Collie
Dog Club." Donoghue does not specify the denomination of the
dead. Most were probably Protestant, but that doesn't matter. Nowadays, the IRA and their Loyalist paramilitary equivalents are fairly
precise in their targeting, but in 1978 they were equal-opportunity
murderers.

Donoghue properly specifies in his introduction that his professional concern is not with politics but with literature. Yet his subtitle,
"Essays on Irish Literature and Society," suggests that in Ireland
at least, to look no farther, the two are not to be kept unentangled. As
he says:

> It is well known that much of modern Irish literature has been
> provoked by violence, and that images of war soon acquire a
> symbolic aura in this country. Our traditions are histrionic and
> oratorical. The themes of Irish literature are few: if we list child-
> hood, isolation, religion, and politics, we come nearly to the end
> of them.

One of Donoghue's central strengths as a critic derives, quite simply, from a literary intelligence so confident of its powers that he can
move with ease among Bakhtin and Foucault and Kristeva while
remaining intellectually loyal toward those writers who helped to
shape his sensibility—Ransom, Tate, Blackmur, and, above the others

perhaps, Kenneth Burke.[2] In some of the present essays—in, for example, his astonishing and bravura application of Bakhtin to *Finnegans Wake*—the subject and occasion allow him to function as a "pure" critic. For the most part, and for the reason he has himself set forth, Irish literature draws him, of necessity, to the politics of Irish culture and even, in some of the shorter pieces ("Drums under the Window," "De Valera's Day," "Castle Catholic"), to "pure" politics—how people live from day to day in his divided island—their strategies and resources of spirit.

But the book is dominated by its first two sections, on Yeats, the contriver and heroic embodiment of "Romantic Ireland," and on Joyce, whose work can be seen as the equally heroic deconstruction of that myth. Donoghue cautions us, though, that

> a full account of Joyce's work in the deconstruction of Romantic Ireland...would eventually begin to deconstruct itself, and would find Joyce baptised by desire, as deeply as by revulsion, in the naivete he would officially expose.

"We Irish, born into that ancient sect." The sect, which of course existed only in Yeats's imagination, as Donoghue reminds us in the essay called "Romantic Ireland," extended backward to an abyss of time where dwelt the heroes of pagan Ireland: Finn, Oscar, Oisin, and above all others Cuchulain. Unlike most historical narratives, that of the "sect" grows more hazy as it moves into later centuries. It is peopled by an unnamed host of swordsmen, monks, lechers, porter drinkers, shepherds, "renowned generations," lords and ladies who were beaten into the clay "through seven heroic centuries." Then, suddenly, as we approach our own day, the members of the sect become named, vivid—Yeats's father, John O'Leary, Parnell, John Shawe

---

2. See his essay on Burke in *The New York Review of Books*, September 26, 1985.

Taylor, Standish O'Grady, John Millington Synge, the "indomitable Irishry."

A curious list, whether measured as being indomitable or as being Irish: all suffered some form of defeat, and all, save O'Leary, were Protestant. Presumably, O'Leary's long imprisonment and exile atoned for the fact that "his ancestors probably kept little shops." A second Catholic, Kevin O'Higgins, the Free State minister assassinated in 1927, was later added to the list. Apparently his ruthless measures against Republicans during the Civil War helped to encourage in Yeats the eugenic belief, expressed in *On the Boiler* (1939), that Catholic military families of the future would produce men with a Protestant-resembling strength of intellect and will. They would be refutations of those Catholic hucksters, the "Paudeens," who "fumble in a greasy till and add the halfpence to the pence."

Little shops seemed to enrage Yeats, not big ones. At the time he wrote the words just quoted, 1913, most of the great Dublin shops, except those owned by pals of the odious William Martin Murphy, were in Protestant hands: they boasted staffs and mechanical cash registers, thus eliminating greasy-till fumbling. Yeats's own blood, as we are reminded in the dedicatory poem to *Responsibilities*, was "merchant" blood "that has not passed through any huckster's loin." And this, as Conor Cruise O'Brien has said, is quite true: his mother's people, the Pollexfens and the Middletons, were strictly wholesale.

But it is easy to make fun of Yeats's pretensions. George Moore and Gogarty and of course Joyce did so in their day, and Dublin is not yet tired of doing so. But Donoghue reminds us that there are serious issues behind the jokes and real stakes on the table:

> In Ireland, it is fair to say, Yeats is resented; not for his snobbery, his outlandish claim to the possession of Norman blood, or even for his evasion of history by his appeal to two classes of people who existed only as shades—Gaelic-Irish and Anglo-

Irish—but because he claimed to speak in the name of the "indomitable Irishry."

Now this resentment is in effect, as Donoghue says, "a political judgment imposed upon poetry," and he is therefore bound both by principle and by temperament to resist it. But it would be equally fair to say that the resentment has been provoked by the political attitudes struck by Yeats in his late poetry. Central among these is a claim not merely to speak for the "Irishry"—a word that can no longer be used in that country without a blush—but to define them as a spiritual and social community, and to prescribe for them. Thus, in the very section of "Under Ben Bulben" which contains the notorious phrase, he bids Irish poets to learn their trade, generously providing them with themes upon which (jointly with Synge and Lady Gregory) he held the copyright—peasants, horsemen, and the other anachronistic members of the Irish Literary Revival repertory company.

"Resentment" may in fact be too mild a term. Donoghue writes:

> In the past few years, Yeats's dealings in the rhetoric of "We Irish" have been much resented. Seamus Deane is not alone in arguing—I'm thinking of his *Field Day* pamphlets and other essays—that the wretched state of the North is at least partly due to the fact that its two communities have inherited stereotyped images of themselves which, subconsciously, they live and die to resemble. These images, in turn, are based upon a presumed spirit or essence which is to be identified with the very soul of Ireland, the special privilege of being Irish. Yeats, according to Deane's argument, did much to present the question of Irishness as a moral criterion.

Deane—like Donoghue a Northerner and as it happens his successor as professor of modern English literature at University College

Dublin—does indeed seem persuaded that a fearsome specter called "essentialism" has been stalking Europe since the days of Hegel at the latest, and is at present squatting among the chimney pots of Derry. It can only be exorcised, he thinks, by deconstructive and decentering incantations. It is a persuasion shared by the other Field Day writers, and as my tone suggests, I share Donoghue's reservations.[3] But Deane, as he would surely agree, is too serious and resourceful a critic to be dealt with so summarily. Thus *Celtic Revivals: Essays in Modern Irish Literature*[4] is more revisionist and far more ideological than is Donoghue on that subject, but its shrewd and challenging essay "Yeats and the Idea of Revolution" closes upon words that might have been Donoghue's: "He was a revolutionary whose wars took place primarily within himself, and he knew that in the end, struggle as he might, it was a losing battle. Not even art could quite compensate for that."

My only other reservation offers a curious counterpart. Conor Cruise O'Brien floats into a number of these essays, lingers in them for a sentence or two, and then floats out again, wraithlike, blighting, almost "un-Irish." O'Brien is faulted, because although Irish nationalism plainly stands in need of a certain amount of demythologizing, this should not go beyond a certain line and O'Brien has crossed it.

But his subordinate sin, displayed most elaborately in his 1965

---

3. Since 1983 the Field Day Theatre Company, in Derry, Northern Ireland, has been publishing a series of pamphlets on Irish culture, politics, and literature, with particular reference to the "problem" of the North. Its most significant essayists, besides Deane, are Declan Kiberd and Tom Paulin. Six of the pamphlets have been published as a book, with the title *Ireland's Field Day*. The English edition (Hutchinson, 1985) carries an introduction written by Donoghue. The American edition (University of Notre Dame Press, 1986) carries, instead, an afterword written by me. The reasons for this variance are at once too baffling and too tedious to justify explanation. It may suffice to say that both introduction and afterword display an enthusiastic wariness uncommon in these genres.

4. London: Faber and Faber, 1985.

essay "Passion and Cunning: An Essay on the Politics of W. B. Yeats," is a readiness to treat literally the political violence, expressed at moments by a deliberate savagery, of Yeats's final poems and of such prose as *On the Boiler*. O'Brien, Donoghue argues, "can't imagine what it would mean for a poet near the end of his tether to recite such promises and threats." But I cannot accept a charge of imaginative failure on such a point against a critic who can write as movingly as does O'Brien (in *The Suspecting Glance*[5]) about Yeats's hero Edmund Burke, when Burke was at tether's end:

> During his very last period, the tragic last two years—after the death of his beloved son and just before his own death—when his sense of a gap between reality and prevailing conventions swelled to the dimensions of nightmare, the irony which is his way of responding to this gap becomes copious, furious, almost feverish, especially in the *Letters on a Regicide Peace* which are the most reckless and unbalanced of his political writings, but the finest of his prose.

Donoghue, O'Brien, and Deane are in agreement that poems are written by real people, in what Donoghue elsewhere and winningly calls the "ordinary universe," that they are addressed to real audiences, and that they handle real passions and emotions. In the critical mood of the moment, one has to thank God for that. But on all else, it is likely that they disagree: as political animals, as the particular kind of political animal called an Irishman, and as critics they differ in particular on the ways in which literature and politics are situated toward each other.

O'Brien, in his essay on "Nietzsche and the Machiavellian Schism" (in *The Suspecting Glance*):

---

5. London: Faber and Faber, 1972.

But the real creative and destructive process of communication goes on in jumps, and criss-cross jumps at that. Each mind, and each age, takes from the messages what it can absorb and feels it needs, and in this process it is irrelevant whether the signaller or the receiver is classified as politician, poet or philosophical writer. Machiavelli is more important for Nietzsche than were the "purer" men of letters of the sixteenth century. Nietzsche, and later Burke, and an idealized picture of Renaissance Italy, were more important in the development of Yeats's imagination than were any of the poets of those places and times. A few lines of poetry, the selected aphorisms of a retired man of letters, may liberate the daemon of a charismatic political leader. The whole imaginative and intellectual life of a culture is one interacting field of force.

And now Donoghue, in the introduction to *We Irish*:

I find it hard to maintain an appropriate voice when political issues are in question. In retrospect, my few political interventions now strike me as respectable, but erratic in tone. But in any case my concern is with literature. I don't disavow an occasional inclination to set statesmen right; their being so regularly wrong is a sufficient excuse. Professionally, I am concerned with politics only when it invades literature and prescribes the gross conditions under which poems, plays, stories, and novels are written. The fact that the same conditions impede the general work of the intelligence hardly needs to be emphasised.

There is no formal disagreement between these passages, save that of tone. But there is an implicit disagreement over the relationship between literature and politics, the two being taken in their broadest sense. This disagreement, though, may be less extreme than either writer would admit.

One of the finest and most illuminating essays in *We Irish* is "Yeats, Ancestral Houses, and Anglo-Ireland." It illuminates not only its subject but Donoghue's procedures as a critic and his literary conscience. He traces, with a subtlety that joins literary taste with historical and specifically political shrewdness, Yeats's complicated relationship with what the poet took to be Ireland's surviving tradition of gentility, centering upon Lady Gregory's Coole Park. He begins with the entry in Yeats's journal for August 7, 1909, which later that day would turn into a draft of the poem "Upon a House Shaken by the Land Agitation," but he turns then not to an immediate consideration of the poem, but rather to the specifics of the agitation, the pieces of legislation that it effected, and the immediate consequences of these for Coole Park—a 20 percent reduction of rents secured by fifteen tenants of the Gregory estate of July 30, 1909, in consequence of their application to the Land Court.

This may seem, in my summary, a scholar's dutiful provision of "background." Instead, it opens the dialectic which Donoghue establishes between Yeats's imagination and the richly circumstantial world upon which it played, moving forward through those days (evoked in "Ancestral Houses," the first poem in "Meditations in Time of Civil War") when he "gave up thinking of 'the Big House' as an emblem of intelligence in active relation to power. He saw it now as an aesthetic image of defeat, the enslavement of the strong to the weak." And so forward, to the remaining poems of the sequence, in which Yeats seeks "to escape from 'Ancestral Houses' by Nietzschean devices and tones." And finally (another formulation of his disagreement with O'Brien) those last poems that "embody, with two or three exceptions, a certain hysteria of the imagination, and display a Nietzschean will at the end of its tether."

Tether's end has always seemed to me the normal location for Nietzschean wills. But that is not my point, which is that Donoghue's real quarrel is not with O'Brien, but rather with writers such as the

Marxist critic Fredric Jameson, who does indeed, as Donoghue puts it toward the close of this essay,

> make readers feel that the political issue, the nature of political attitudes, takes priority over every other consideration, and especially over those which would be represented as formal or aesthetic.

Jameson, it is true, genially allows on the opening page of *The Political Unconscious* that

> traditional literary history has, of course, never prohibited the investigation of such topics as the Florentine political background in Dante, Milton's relationship to the schismatics, or Irish historical allusions in Joyce.

But he says that such information remains just that, and anyway is usually recontained by "an idealistic conception of the history of ideas."[6]

Maybe so, but for Machiavelli and the Florentine background to Machiavelli I commend the reader to O'Brien, and for Joyce's dialectic with history—and with Yeats—I commend the reader to Donoghue and *We Irish*. About Milton and the schismatics, I know little and care less.

—*The New York Review of Books*, March 31, 1988

---

6. *The Political Unconscious: Narrative as a Socially Symbolic Act* (Cornell University Press, 1981), p. 17.

12

RICHARD BRINSLEY SHERIDAN

STEPHEN DEDALUS, James Joyce's surrogate in *A Portrait of the Artist as a Young Man*, tells his snobbish classmates at fashionable Clongowes Wood that his father is a gentleman. In Victorian Ireland, gentility was still a crucial mark of social identity. In the mid-eighteenth century, when another small Irish boy, Richard Brinsley Sheridan, left for Harrow, the barriers that hived off gentlemen from ordinary people were even taller and more formidable, being guarded, literally, by swords. Gentlemen dueled only with other gentlemen.

In Joyce's day, it was possible for a Roman Catholic to be accounted a gentleman, but just barely. In Sheridan's boyhood, legislation against Catholics denied them entry into the learned professions or into the army as officers. Among other defects of character, they were thought to be disloyal to the Crown. These were disabilities that Sheridan himself, in the London Parliament, would strive to lift, displaying in the effort a zeal and a consistency rare in his sinuous and slippery political career.

Sheridan had the good fortune, socially speaking, to be a Protestant, but for him there was a different barrier. His grandfather, Thomas Sheridan, had been a clergyman and the literary crony of the great Jonathan Swift. But his father, also Thomas, was not only manager of a Dublin theater but had trod its boards as an actor. He was a man of scholarly attainments, but this did not remove the stain of being a commercial actor. Once he had to fight off the stage rowdy Trinity College students, crying, as he did so, "I am as good a gentleman as you are." Sheridan himself would later describe, with tears, how at Harrow he was "slighted by the master and the boys, as a poor player's son." Part of his problem, as he discovered when he reached manhood, was that gentility, especially if dubious, required not only a sword but money and servants. The only way to acquire them was through the family's theatrical trade.

He addressed himself to the task with an energy and skill that Balzac would have envied, although disguising it behind a gentleman's mask of indolence and mild dissipation. Within a few years, he had become manager and part owner of London's Drury Lane theater, had written two of the most brilliant comedies in the language, *The Rivals* (1774) and *The School for Scandal* (1777), and had created Mrs. Malaprop and other immortals of the English drama. For most of his later career, he would be involved with Drury Lane but not as a writer. He ceased entirely to write plays and, although his masterpieces were often revived, he refused to have them published. Instead, he turned to politics.

First, however, the awkward "gentleman" business had to be settled once and for all. He settled it in a manner that joined sensibility and shrewdness: by fighting a duel with a cad who had impugned the honor of the beautiful young singer with whom Sheridan had eloped and by conducting himself on the field of honor with courage if not great skill. It was more an armed scuffle than a duel, but at its close, Sheridan demanded and received his opponent's sword. Sheridan was now a gentleman. His wife, Elizabeth, apparently one of the great sopranos of the day, never again performed commercially. Ladies did not. It reads like a comedy by Sheridan, and in a sense it was.

Sheridan's career in politics was to stretch across forty years, beginning with a blaze of rhetorical glory in his two speeches denouncing Warren Hastings, the corrupt administrator of British

India. Sheridan was a member of Charles James Fox's wing of the Whig Party, which held advanced, indeed radical, views toward Irish independence and toward the revolution in France. As Fox himself did, he became an adviser to the Prince of Wales, the future George IV, from whom much was to be expected once the old king, George III, either died or went permanently insane. It is a mark either of Sheridan's essential innocence or of his gambler's recklessness that he relied upon the promises of this royal buffoon, to whom gratitude was an alien concept. When the King once again plunged into looniness, the prince became prince regent and celebrated by abandoning his friends. Sheridan ended his days a drunkard and a bankrupt, his mind at times badly astray, in and out of debtor's prison. Being a gentleman is hard on the liver. In his final years, he spent his time regaling the young Lord Byron with tales of the old days.

Fintan O'Toole is one of the very ablest of Ireland's new generation of critics and essayists. Equally at home in narrative and theory, in the nineteenth century and the twentieth, and especially in matters Irish, he commands a wide historical and literary range. (A selection of his essays, The Lie of the Land: Irish Identities, has been published by Verso.) In A Traitor's Kiss,[1] he conducts us with skill through Sheridan's dramatic and literary careers, seldom condescending to his subject, who was a strange compound of brilliance, melancholy, and thwarted ambition. O'Toole argues that Sheridan's imagination was shaped by Ireland's divided inheritance and that his life looks contradictory because it was "lived in two different places—a real England and a passionately imagined Ireland." This presumably is what literary critic and biographer (and herself an Anglo Irishwoman) Victoria Glendinning means when she says in an early review that "his book is more than a biography; it is a history of one aspect of Irish genius."

---

1. A Traitor's Kiss: The Life of Richard Brinsley Sheridan, 1751–1816 (Farrar, Straus and Giroux, 1998).

O'Toole rightly and generously acknowledges his indebtedness to Conor Cruise O'Brien, whose book on Edmund Burke, *The Great Melody*, suggested the way "an Irish life could affect English politics in the eighteenth century." The comparison is tempting but risky: two young Irishmen with careers to make in London, both possessed of literary style bordering on genius, both members of the loose-knit Whig Party. They were allies in the campaign against Hastings but never personal friends. In England's public debate over the meaning of the French Revolution, they became bitter antagonists. If they were both "Irish," then that word can mean very different things. And indeed it does.

Burke, as Cruise O'Brien has demonstrated, was a conservative whose sense of political and social life was deeply affected by his Irish origins. He came from a family of the middling gentry who had turned Protestant only a generation earlier and who remained thickly webbed within the Catholic and nominally Protestant families of County Cork, although Burke was himself a sincere Anglican. He attended school in rural Ireland and went on to Dublin's Trinity College, in his day an entirely Protestant institution. Today, the college flourishes proudly on its front lawn a splendid statue of one of its greatest sons. From the London Parliament, he kept up his varied Irish contacts. His passionate protests against the anti-Catholic laws came from intimate knowledge of their retrograde effect upon Irish lives.

Sheridan, by contrast, left Ireland for Harrow as a small boy and never returned, not even when he stood for an Irish parliamentary seat. If, somewhere within his chameleonlike nature, he nourished "a passionately imagined Ireland," he kept it well concealed. Burke's passionate denunciations of the revolution in France, at once prophetic and unmeasured—his accurate fears of a Terror that had not yet begun—were nourished by roots sunk deep into a culture that had known civil war and anarchy. Sheridan, it is true, argued strenuously for Catholic rights and, as Ireland moved closer to its 1798 rebellion, expressed his sympathies for the United Irishmen, by now an underground organization moving toward revolution. He was on friendly terms with the aristocratic rebels Arthur O'Connor and Lord Edward Fitzgerald. (The friendship with Fitzgerald cooled a bit after he seduced Sheridan's wife. Sheridan seems to have regarded this as retribution for his own notorious philandering. In any event, gentlemen were expected not to fuss about such matters.) But such pro-Irish sentiments were shared by, among many others, Fox and Tom Paine, in neither of whose veins was lodged a single globule of Irish blood, either literally or culturally. They were the common store of the radical Whigs, springing from the hopes and fears of the Enlightenment.

In making his case for Sheridan's "Irishness," O'Toole is at his best, that is to say his cleverest, when he is at his most literary. He traces, generation by generation, the curious matter of the family's fascination with language. It begins in the 1640s. "Sheridan" looks like one of those sturdy English names brought over by conquerors—like "Burke," for example. In fact, it is the Anglicization of the Gaelic name "O Sioradain." In that decade, three O Sioradains who had been converted to Protestantism were given holy orders by William Bedell, the Anglican bishop of Dromore, and set to work on his grand project of translating the Bible into Gaelic. In the turmoil of Ireland's seventeenth century, this was less quixotic a project than might appear. Bedell, a man whose wide human sympathies were respected even by his enemies, was engaged in what O'Toole, whose style cheerfully courts overstatement, calls "the bravest, oddest, and potentially most far-reaching enterprise in Irish history: the attempt to found, in the drumlins of Cavan, a Gaelic Protestantism, to escape the identification of Catholic and Irish, Protestant and British, that would bedevil that history for centuries." In the great rebellion of 1641, the Catholic rebels spared Bedell, whose honesty of purpose they respected, and they spared his Sheridan disciples. It is a rare, poignant moment in that bloody century.

From that time forward, however, the destiny of the Sheridans would be bound up with Protestantism, with the exploitation of the English language, and with what O'Toole regards as a provisional and slippery loyalty to the British Crown. Donnchadh O Sioradain, now Dennis Sheridan, would produce in the seventeenth century five clergyman-sons. Their Gaelic fell, inevitably but slowly, into disuse. One son, William, a bishop, was deposed by the victorious William-ites as a "traitor"; he died "exceeding poor and crazy." In a final let-ter, to his doctor, he wrote that "I shall no longer be a false prophet." As O'Toole puts it: "Even as they made their way in the world, the shadow of madness, poverty, and treason would always follow the descendants of Dennis Sheridan."

What did follow, generation by generation down to the playwright, was an extraordinary interest in language, its equivocations and eva-sions and especially its political instability and potential ambiguity. The letters between Thomas Sheridan and his friend Jonathan Swift are exchanges of puns, word games, anagrams, riddles, with occa-sional advice upon matters of rhetoric and casuistry. Language and its boundaries were the very soul of the relationship. And especially the multiple uses of irony, a mode by which the literal is rendered subver-sive. "It was an inheritance of linguistic attitudes, of ways to use words to keep afloat in the dangerous cross-currents of loyalty and betrayal that swept the shores of Irish Protestant radicals."

The playwright's father, Thomas, aside from those theatrical per-formances that had placed his gentility in question, was a teacher of elocution and rhetoric engaged in a longer struggle to reform English society by reforming English speech. An Irishman from County Cavan, who himself either had a thick brogue or, more likely, had painfully eradicated it, was offering instruction in the pronunciation of polite English to the Englishmen themselves. As O'Toole puts it: Thomas's obstinate belief in the spoken rather than the written word "was itself a legacy of his family's complex relation to language, pulled between Gaelic and English, between an oral literature and a written one."

And so we come to Richard Brinsley Sheridan, whose arts were precisely those of the spoken rather than the written word: the dazzling playwright, whose Mrs. Malaprop is forever stumbling into verbal errors which make their own surreal sense, and the superb parliamentary creator of the speeches against Warren Hastings, unmatched in his century. It strengthens O'Toole's argument about Sheridan's preference for the spoken rather than the written word that only at the end of his life, broken and impoverished, would Sheridan allow his plays and speeches to be published.

But this argument, tracing through the generations a specific linguistic propensity, is more allusive and suggestive than it is persuasive. Attitudes toward language are not passed along in the genes, like left-handedness or color blindness. What has really captured O'Toole's imagination is the way in which for all Irish writers, there lurks behind the English they use the ghosts of another language—Gaelic, maimed and defeated. It has given many Irish writers, including O'Toole himself, an awareness of language as both presence and absence, an awareness of its duplicities and treasons and loyalties. O'Toole proves his own "Irishness" in this learned, witty, and adroit book.

—*Los Angeles Times*, January 3, 1999

13

THE APPRENTICE MAGE

A BIOGRAPHER OF William Butler Yeats places himself in dangerous competition with Yeats himself, an artist with a dazzling ability to shape a series of shifting, compelling public images. He turned into poetry his family and his past, his friendships and alliances, his enmities, his quarrels with Ireland, that "blind bitter land," his storm-wracked love for Maud Gonne. And in published extracts from journals and several volumes of prose, most notably *Reveries Over Childhood and Youth* (1914) and *The Trembling of the Veil* (1922), he shaped through narrative structure, arrangement of events, and carefully deployed rhetoric the version of his early life which his readers have inherited.

Roy Foster, a distinguished Irish historian, handsomely survives the implicit competition, not by seeking to supplant that hypnotically seductive version, but rather by situating it firmly within its contexts of social and political history. *The Apprentice Mage,*[1] the first of two volumes, carries Yeats forward from his birth in 1865 to the 1914 publication of *Responsibilities*, the book in which he emerged from the protecting shadows of the Celtic Twilight and fin-de-siècle

---

1. *W. B. Yeats: A Life, Volume I: The Apprentice Mage, 1865–1914* (Oxford University Press, 1997).

aestheticism into the challenging sunlight of modern poetry. It gives us "a man involved in life and history: notably in the history of his country, at a time of exceptional flux and achievement." It leaves us with a strengthened respect for Yeats's emotional and political resilience, as he moves within Ireland's webs of classes, creeds, hatreds, and loyalties.

He was born into a family of clergymen on his father's side, with the vivid exception of the father himself, John Butler Yeats, a willful, improvident, charming portrait painter. And on his mother's side, Pollexfens and Middletons, mill owners and shippers settled in Sligo, a market town on Ireland's western coast, set between ocean and mountains rich in heroic and supernatural lore. These were distinct branches of that extended family of Irish Protestantism which had already begun its long slide toward first political and then social marginalization. It was to be replaced, as Foster puts it, "by the new world of self-confident Catholic democracy." This century-long historical process is one by which Yeats's life was bordered, and this biography keeps it before our eyes.

His youthful years were divided between the Pollexfens in Sligo, and Dublin and London, where his father pursued his career. There wasn't much money. Most of it came from some tenanted farmlands and was steadily whittled away by the agrarian wars against the landlords. These were wars associated with the political leadership of Charles Stewart Parnell, like Yeats an Irish Protestant who espoused a nationalism which, increasingly, became a Catholic preserve. Indeed, Parnell's fall from power following an adulterous scandal would be regarded by Yeats—as later by the Catholic Joyce—as a signal instance of Irish ingratitude.

Yeats developed his craft in the London of William Morris, Wilde, Shaw, and the "decadent" poets of the 1890s. By the time he published *The Wind Among the Reeds* in 1899 he was recognized as the most gifted of the symbolist poets writing in English. Equally, he was the chief artist within the Celtic Twilight, a movement which sought to create a literature in English which would be contemporary and yet rooted in traditional Irish culture and beliefs. The phrase was his coinage and he came to detest it. His literary situation embodied many of the complexities confronting a writer seeking to achieve personal and national identity within what had become, over the centuries, both a cultural and a political colony.

And it was in youth that he began his lifelong study of magic and the occult. Foster rightly insists here upon the centrality of the magical to Yeats's thought and imagination, although elsewhere he has rather unfeelingly described this "Protestant magic" as the product of "an insecure middle class, with a race memory of elitism seeking refuge in the occult."

Ireland was represented for the young Yeats with special vividness by John O'Leary, the old Fenian rebel, who had returned after prison and exile, haughty, impenitent, and by now harmless. Through him, Yeats met his great love, Maud Gonne, an eccentric English beauty who had persuaded herself and others that she was the very soul of an unconquered Ireland—romantic, dangerous, unattainable. He would remember his first sight of her, standing with her great height, luminous as "apple blossoms through which the light falls...by a great heap of such blossoms by the window." The setting was suburban London and the month was January: heaps of such blossoms would have been in short supply.

In the new century, he was involved with Lady Gregory and John Millington Synge in the creation of what would become the famous Abbey Theatre. With it came quarrels, increasingly intense, with Irish culture itself. He had liberated himself, or so he thought, from the confines of Irish Protestantism, only to encounter a corresponding Catholic intolerance and the fierce political sectarianism of Sinn Fein, by which older and more genial forms of patriotism were being replaced by a harsh, exclusivist ideology. The conflict was crystallized by the disturbances which in 1907 greeted the appearance of Synge's masterpiece, *The Playboy of the Western World*, believed by its detractors to be a libel on the purity of peasant and Catholic Ireland. (One of Foster's revelations is that Lady Gregory, although she staunchly supported the play, did not share Yeats's passionate admiration for it, nor, indeed, Synge himself. The rifts in that celebrated trinity—"John Synge, I, and Augusta Gregory"—have been concealed by the capework of Yeats's marvelous rhetoric.)

There were other shocks. Maud Gonne, far from being a vestal whose virginity was pledged to Ireland, had for years been the mistress of a right-wing French politician named Millevoye, by whom she had two children. One, a boy, died in infancy; the other, a daughter, was, on a medium's advice, conceived on the boy's tomb. A lesser man than Yeats might have found this last detail off-putting. Finally free of Millevoye, she turned for a husband not to Yeats but rather to a soldier of Ireland, John MacBride, whom Yeats was later to describe, with understatement, as "a drunken, vainglorious lout." In 1908, the year which saw the publication of his *Collected Works*, she admitted Yeats to her bed, but very briefly because of her "dread of physical love." Some of Yeats's most magnificent poetry was inspired by this addlepated zealot:

> *Why should I blame her that she filled my days*
> *With misery, or that she would of late*
> *Have taught to ignorant men most violent ways...?*

The Yeats of 1914 at times wrote as if his life had been rounded out. In verses prefixed to *Responsibilities*, he asks pardon of his "old fathers," Yeatses and Butlers and Middletons and Pollexfens,

> *...that for a barren passion's sake,*
> *Although I have come close on forty-nine,*

I have no child, I have nothing but a book,
Nothing but that to prove your blood and mine.

But Yeats is at his most dangerous when he affects to disparage his books of poetry. In a review of this one, Joseph Hone, who was to be an early and shrewd biographer, and who like Yeats was a rooted Dublin Protestant, would write: "We watch him in these controversial poems of his building up a legend around himself, a stirring legend that will, I believe, hit the fancy of the young men of Ireland as the Celtic Twilight never did." One way in which he shaped the legend (with some journalistic help from Hone) was by turning to those roots, by celebrating the Ireland of the "old fathers"—the Protestant Ireland of the Ascendancy.

It was a daring wager. Despite a thin, vivid line of heroic Irish nationalists, running from Wolfe Tone to Parnell, Protestant land-owning Ireland, battered by the land wars and affronted by a triumphalist Catholicism, was solidly antinationalist, save for a few exotics like himself. Neither did his aristocratic airs sit well with those who, like his father, knew how thoroughly middle class were his immediate origins. His erstwhile Irish friend George Moore, described by Foster with lapidary exactness as "devious, uncontrollable, unable to resist the temptations of a demonic sense of humor," would in his memoirs describe, alas unforgettably, the new Yeats rising from his chair at a public meeting, expensively dressed and disdainful of his audience, to rebuke the middle class because it would not properly support the arts. "And we asked ourselves why Willie Yeats should feel himself called upon to denounce the class to which he himself belonged essentially: on one side excellent mercantile millers and shipowners, and on the other a portrait painter of rare talent...." It was the publication of this infernally inspired caricature that prompted Yeats to write his own memoirs.

But some of the bitter, rancorous poems of these years are among his most splendid. "September 1913," with its defiant opening stanza, is, as Foster says, one of the great polemics of literature:

> *What need you, being come to sense,*
> *But fumble in a greasy till*
> *And add the halfpence to the pence*
> *And prayer to shivering prayer, until*
> *You have dried the marrow from the bone;*
> *For men were born to pray and save:*
> *Romantic Ireland's dead and gone,*
> *It's with O'Leary in the grave.*

In thus summoning up the shade of the fierce old rebel who had been the hero of his youth, Yeats may seem to have moved full circle, but this is, imaginatively speaking, an O'Leary deployed for other purposes. The poem was first printed in *The Irish Times*, then the newspaper of the Protestant loyalists. And although the poem is discreetly nonsectarian, "prayer to shivering prayer" was widely taken in Dublin's malice to refer to Catholics. The phrase which once had followed, "by the light of a holy candle," would have settled the matter.

When O'Leary was lowered into his grave in March 1907, Yeats was not among the mourners, "in Irish society, a notable and deliberate gesture." In later years this would make him uneasy. But O'Leary and Maud Gonne had quarreled over her marital separation from John MacBride. By 1913, the austere patriotism of O'Leary had been taken over by new leaders whom Yeats did not especially like, but whom he was fated to commemorate three years later in one of his most famous poems. In "Easter, 1916," written in enigmatic tribute to the men executed for their roles in the rebellion of that year, John MacBride, the "drunken, vainglorious lout," took his place beside the others:

I write it out in a verse—
MacDonagh and MacBride
and Connolly and Pearse
Now and in time to be,
Wherever green is worn,
Are changed, changed utterly:
A terrible beauty is born.

Rich as Yeats's achievements had been, Foster says in his final paragraph, what lay ahead would be more astonishing. The old magician, apprentice no longer, has found in Foster a worthy biographer. He would be relieved to know, as readers of Irish writing have known for some years, that the biographer is himself a fine writer, bearing with grace his knowledge of Irish history, and writing with wit, authority, and, when appropriate, considerable eloquence.

—*The New York Times Book Review*, April 6, 1997

14

BEAUTY AND THE BARD

IN 1889, WHEN the Irish poet William Butler Yeats first met Maud Gonne, he was twenty-three—romantic, passionate, inexperienced, and ready to be overwhelmed by beauty. Nothing, however, could have prepared him for the extraordinary woman who presented herself at his door with a letter from John O'Leary, the old rebel and patriot. In his *Memoirs*, he describes the effect upon him of their first meetings:

> I had never thought to see in a living woman so great beauty. It belonged to famous pictures, to poetry, to some legendary past. A complexion like the beauty of apples, and yet face and body had the beauty of lineaments which Blake calls the highest beauty because it changes least from youth to age, and a stature so great that she seemed of a divine race.

The course of their relationship, a decisive one in Yeats's life and art, is shadowed forth in their first meetings. Of the first, he remembered only that she spoke in praise of war. At dinner in her rooms that evening, "she spoke of her desire for power, apparently for its own sake."

The twenty-two-year-old Maud, daughter of an English army officer with remote Irish connections, had become an impassioned Irish nationalist, active on behalf of the evicted peasants of the west and making anti-English speeches of shrill, sincere intensity. This would have accorded well with Yeats's own nationalism, but she had also a second life of which he was not aware for several years. Maud was the mistress of Lucien Millevoye, a reactionary and anti-Semitic French politician by whom she was to have a son who died in infancy and a daughter, who was named Iseult. Iseult may have been conceived in the burial vault of the dead boy, whither Maud and Millevoye had repaired for spiritualist reasons.

She liked to think that her relationship with Millevoye was on the astral plane, she fighting for Ireland and he for the lost French province of Alsace-Lorraine. Millevoye may have viewed it differently. Their relationship cooled, and he took up with a singer from a café chantant, whose political views, so the editors of *The Gonne–Yeats Letters* tell us, "appealed to him more than those of Maud's 'absurd Irish revolutionaries'."[1] As she was to assure Yeats, repeatedly and convincingly, "I have a horror and terror of physical love." (It may be remarked that copulation in a funeral vault does not seem a likely cure for frigidity.)

Yeats's love for Maud had burned for eight years before ever she kissed him "with the physical mouth." By then, he had written to her some of the loveliest and most desolate love poems in our language, and their love had passed, still living, into Irish legend. Ella Young saw them in a Dublin library: "No one else is consulting a book. Everyone is conscious of those two as the denizens of a woodland lake might be conscious of a flamingo, or of a Japanese heron, if it had suddenly descended among them."

Yeats came to feel that her legendary past was that of Helen of Troy, whose beauty brought a city to destruction. In a famous poem he asks:

---

1. *The Gonne–Yeats Letters, 1893–1938*, edited by Anna MacBride White and A. Norman Jeffares (Norton, 1993).

Why should I blame her that she filled my days
With misery, or that she would of late
Have taught to ignorant men most violent ways,
Or hurled the little streets upon the great,
Had they but courage equal to desire?

And answers himself with another question:

Why, what could she have done, being what she is?
Was there another Troy for her to burn?

But what she could and did do was to destroy her own well-being by acting out of the extremity of her impulses toward heroism. In 1903, she married a hard-drinking, boastful swaggerer who had earned easy Irish fame by fighting against the British in South Africa. Their Paris life became a nightmare until, a little more than a year later and after the birth of their son, Sean, the marriage broke up. John MacBride had the ear of Dublin, and she became a woman abused in print and scorned in public by the nationalists. Through all this, Yeats stood resolutely at her side.

In 1916, when the Easter Rebellion broke out in Dublin, Yeats was in England and Maud in France, but MacBride, still hard-drinking and now obscure, joined the rebels and, as one of its leaders, was executed by firing squad. From France, Maud wrote to Yeats of the executed rebels: "I am overwhelmed by the tragedy & the greatness of the sacrifice our country men & women have made. They have raised the Irish cause again to a position of tragic dignity." Of the man who had bullied her and mistreated her daughter, she said only that "Major MacBride by his Death has left a name for [Sean] to be proud of. Those who die for Ireland are sacred." It may well have been with those words in his imagination that Yeats wrote his stunning memorial poem to the slain, "Easter, 1916," which names the leaders, one by one, among them "a drunken, vain-glorious lout":

> *I write it out in a verse—*
> *MacDonagh and MacBride*
> *And Connolly and Pearse...*
> *Are changed, changed utterly....*

He sent her an early copy of the poem, and of course she did not like it. The poem takes a complicated attitude toward the Rising, and Maud detested political complexity. She had hoped for a poem "which would have avenged our material failure with its spiritual beauty." This had long been a point of contention. For Maud, as for many other nationalists, poetry and art were important only if they offered practical service to Ireland. She lacked an ear for poetry, at any event, as these letters make clear, as they also make clear that she was entirely without either humor or wit.

Although the present volume is properly called *The Gonne–Yeats Letters*, it contains only a handful from Yeats. She had saved his to her, as he had hers to him, but his were apparently destroyed when her house was ransacked by government soldiers in 1922. All here published have been scrupulously edited by her granddaughter, Anna MacBride White, and the distinguished Irish literary scholar A. Norman Jeffares.

In 1919, Maud Gonne returned to Ireland and lived there until her death in 1953. She remained an unrepentant and fiery apostle of the Irish Republican Movement, supporting it first against the British, and then, after 1922, against the Irish Free State. The young Yeats had been wrong to think her beauty the kind which changes little from youth to age. Age transformed her to a gaunt, black-robed figure out of some desolate Celtic mythology, demonstrating outside prison walls or at platforms on street corners. Most painful to Yeats was that her appearance, that of a time-ravaged beauty, seemed the shadow of her mind, enslaved, as he put it in a poem, "to fanaticism and hate." As for Yeats, he accepted the compromises of the Irish Free State, became one of its senators and in his words, "a sixty-year-old smiling public man," plump, sleek, honored.

It is the material of either tragedy or comedy, according to one's inclinations. In an earlyish poem, "Words," he laments that

> *My darling cannot understand*
> *What I have done, or what would do*
> *In this blind, bitter land.*

But then decides that if he had been able to make her understand,

> *I might have thrown poor words away*
> *And been content to live.*

It is curious to reflect upon the fact that Maud Gonne served the cause of Irish poetry by not returning his love and by being unable to understand what he was doing. And it is a final irony that his poor words, in his letters to her, should have been destroyed. Yeats might have seen the grim joke of this, and Maud might not have cared.

—*The Washington Post Book World*, February 14, 1993

15

THE HERITAGE OF YEATS

HE IS "a gargoyle," Ford Madox Ford reminded Ezra Pound, "a great poet but a gargoyle." A weighty and a complex inheritance for any culture, but especially so for one which has as its physical boundaries the shores of a small island. As literary historians know, there are certain specific ways in which William Butler Yeats may be said to have created the possibilities of modern Irish literature. But there are also ways, as Irish writers have long known, in which that literature has also developed out of a resistance to Yeats, out of debate, secret or strident but always one-sided, with his lengthening shadow. A long shadow indeed, one cast by a great poet, but, caught against some lights, involuted and grotesque, the shadow of a gargoyle, a magnificent mistake.

"When a poet so great as Yeats is born into a country as small as Ireland," Donald Davie has written, "that is a wonderful windfall for everyone in that country *except the poets*. For them it is a disaster." A recent survey of the last two decades of Irish writing raises the issue on the first page of its introductory essay: "Difficulties raised by the wide acceptance of Yeats by the Irish public have been kicked against at least since the 1930s. Pitiful as it is that Yeats's blend of melody, magic, politics, and the spirit of Irishness should have become a burden upon the creativity of his contemporaries and successors, there is no denying that his purchase on Irish expectations is as severe as ever. Thomas MacGreevy, Brian Coffey, and Denis Devlin were, like Beckett, and like Austin Clarke, cramped by the almost embarrassing presence of Yeats." This is loosely and inaccurately formulated. The creativity of Thomas MacGreevy, for example, may have had constraints upon it more cramping than those provided by the example of Yeats. Recent efforts have been made to establish him as the first considerable poet to emerge from within the shadow of the then living Yeats, but these are dashing Jacobite raids upon the territory of the old Williamite gargoyle, and in the manner traditional for such enterprises, they look in vain for help from France. In fact, the present situation in Irish poetry with respect to the authority exerted by Yeats is far too complex to admit of easy formulation. There have intervened, for example, such natural and ferocious elements as history and Patrick Kavanagh, to name but two, but each of them a power capable of breaking ground toward old yet unanticipated promises and energies.

"Wide acceptance of Yeats by the Irish public" is a phrase which would rightly have aroused Yeats's laughter, a sound once described by George Moore as one of the most melancholy in nature. He has been honored with a postage stamp. Ballylee has again been restored and has been equipped with a linguaphone device whereby visitors may listen to recitations of his verses by a gifted poet from Kerry, a county whose fecund contributions to poetry he had in life approached with a characteristically complex wariness. The Irish universities, although unsparing in their amusement at the American Yeats industry, have not been slow to join that common market. The Irish newspapers dutifully summarize the lectures delivered each year in what is known during the summer months as "the Yeats country," although a more strict attention to social history might call it "the Pollexfen country." A number of educated Irishmen know that a terrible beauty was once born, and are prepared to believe that all was somehow changed utterly by that birth. Some will assent in piety and some few in violence to the declaration that only blood can make a right rose tree. Others, many more others I believe, know also that too long a sacrifice can make a stone of the heart, and that hearts fed upon fantasies grow brutal. In short, certain passages from Yeats have taken deep and lasting root in Ireland, for the most part those which express, with whatever reserves of irony, an intense and heroic nationalism. But this merely declares him a part of Ireland's official culture, a culture sustained by an increasingly threadbare rhetoric, and his views on rhetoric are well known. All this is far removed from an acceptance of either the man or his poetry in any sense which would have gratified him.

Of the language I have quoted, however, the words which seem to me the most dangerously imprecise are those which characterize his poetry as a "blend of melody, magic, politics, and the spirit of Irishness." It could be argued that many of his poems which we honor as great are ones which have successfully avoided that blend. But this would be an evasive argument, because the ingredients specified for the blend are all among those which we characterize as Yeatsian. And one phrase, "the spirit of Irishness," brings us close to the issue that I wish here to consider. If Donald Davie is right in describing a great poet as a disaster for the other poets of a small country, then Yeats must be accounted a double disaster, for the country itself was a chief theme and object of his poetry, and he was greatly concerned to define the proper relationship between an Irish artist and the world around him.

Yeats's career spanned the decades between the 1880s and his death in 1939. There is a gulf, more deep than wide, between the poet of the 1890s, who "sang, to sweeten Ireland's wrong," and the poet of the 1930s, who urged his fellow poets to cast their eyes on other days, "That we in coming days may be / Still the indomitable Irishry." But in each instance, the poet has set himself slightly apart from the company which he has declared as his. In the earlier poem, the claim is direct, managing to be at once proud and faintly apologetic: "Nor may I less be counted one / With Davis, Mangan, Ferguson...." In the later and more notorious poem, all is pride rather than apology, and the claim to a special wisdom and autonomy, if no longer direct, is far stronger. I would assume, that is, that anyone who knew what the Witch of Atlas knew and what the sages spoke round the Mereotic lake would find something better to do with his time than to sing of hard-riding country gentlemen and the randy laughter of porter drinkers. And Yeats did have something better to do with his time, else we should not attend to him today. However remote from each other "To Ireland in the Coming Times" and "Under Ben Bulben" may be in time and in feeling, Yeats is in each instance placing a delicate, crucial distance between his own poetry and his more general hopes for the poetry of Ireland. The latter is to be intensely "Irish," the intensity deriving in part from a severe limitation upon subject matter and form. The former is to be Irish as well, but as part of a more vast and intricate design. It was precisely in the space between the two that Yeats established the necessary dialectic between his own autonomy as an artist and the Irish literary culture which he sought to foster.

From the outset of his career, he was in a paradoxical situation. He aspired to write as a traditional poet within a tradition which did not exist, to assimilate and then transform the national literature of a country which possessed neither nationality nor a literature. The lack of present nationality was rather a benefit than a handicap, for this provided both a subject and a variety of unsweetened wrongs. But all else was wasteland. In the 1880s and 1890s, Ireland did not possess a poetry in English worthy of the name, and it seems to have been accepted by everyone that any future literature would be the creation of writers shaped by that language. The representative poetry of the preceding half-century was the verse of the *Nation*, facile yet sincere, most dreadful when most sincere, a kind of rhymed patriotism. It was barbarous stuff, and not in the antique and heroic sense of that word. Otherwise, there existed a few isolated translations from the Irish, chiefly by Jeremiah Callanan and Edward Walsh, which suggested, faintly, a road back to the older language and then forward from it. The example of William Allingham could suggest to Yeats that a poet, trained in the traditions of English poetry and without any pretense of national feeling, might make a true and passionate response to local setting. "He was no national poet," as Yeats wrote of him, "but loved the hills about him and the land under his feet." Confronted by a thin and scattered inheritance, Yeats's earliest strategy as a "Celtic" propagandist was an audacious one. He asserted a tradition where in fact there was none, and then urged Irish writers to develop their talents within it. He made do brilliantly with what existed, recklessly praising Samuel Ferguson as "the greatest poet Ireland has produced, because the most central and the most Celtic," and discovering the heroic epic world in the overwrought Carlylean prose of Standish James O'Grady.

It was upon the foundations of that ancient literature that Yeats intended to raise up a modern one, and he seems, then and later, to have been extraordinarily sanguine with respect to what would now appear the most pressing of issues—that of language. The magnificent traditional literature of Ireland, ancient, complex, and glittering, was locked within the older language, accessible only in stiff and inaccurate translations or as it existed, unwritten, within the memory of the Irish-speaking countrypeople of the western and southern fringes. In 1885, when Yeats was publishing in the *Dublin University Review* his Spenserian and very "un-Irish" *Island of Statues*, Douglas Hyde published there a plea on behalf of what he described as a humble form of literature:

> This field consists of the songs and folklore of our peasantry
> as preserved in the Gaedheilg tongue, which form a kind of

literature in themselves, none the less real for never having been committed to writing, and which owing to the inexorable connection between thought and language, will last as long as the tongue of Oisin lasts, and will die when it dies.

"The inexorable connection between thought and language"—it is from Yeats, the poet, that one might have expected such words, the Yeats who at the close of his career rightly declared that "I owe my soul to Shakespeare, to Spenser, and to Blake, perhaps to William Morris, and to the English language in which I think, speak, and write, that everything I love has come to me through English...." And yet, despite the naked power and truth of those words, he did not share Hyde's belief that literary traditions are inextricably bound up with the language in which they are preserved. In 1892, when Hyde delivered his consequential lecture on "The De-Anglicising of Ireland," Yeats was quick to reply:

> Let us by all means prevent the decay of that tongue where we can, and preserve it always among us as a learned language to be a fount of nationality in our midst, but do not let us base upon it our hope of nationhood. When we remember the majesty of Cucullin and the beauty of sorrowing Deirdre, we should not forget that it is that majesty and that beauty which are immortal, and not the perishing tongue which first told of them.

A fair and an eloquent reply, but it remains the case that he was curiously indifferent to the problems created by the appropriation by one language of what he liked to call the "traditions" of an older one, conquered by now and servile. These traditions might be termed the objects of a final act of appropriation, which, like all such acts, had its historical sources, and would have, in history, its consequences.

Yeats's understanding of tradition was a special one, and lies close to the power with which, almost from the first, he asserted his identity, as an Irish writer. This was, of course, given the circumstances of the times, an act of choice. Conor Cruise O'Brien suspects a slight element of calculation in the matter, quoting from an 1889 letter in which he advises a young Irishwoman to "make verses on Irish legends and places and so forth. It helps originality and makes one's verses intense, and gives one less numerous competition." But he does not quote the sentence which follows: "Besides, one should love best what is nearest and most interwoven in the heart's affections." That "besides" does carry the faint embarrassment of afterthought, but there can be no question but that Yeats goes forward from it to express the deepest of his literary and personal convictions. His love of Ireland began not as an abstraction but as a Virgilian piety of place, an abiding affection of the heart, resting beneath those concerns to which literary criticism carries us. The letter to Miss White carries a postscript: "I see that your letter dates from Banbridge. My grandfather was rector there years ago." And on the envelope he has written: "My grandfather was rector of *Tullylish* near Banbridge." Grandfathers had not yet been elevated into ancestors. He expected more from poetry, however, than love of legend or place. William Allingham had loved the hills about him and the land under his feet, but had failed, as Yeats reminded the readers of *United Ireland*, to become what then was called "a national poet." But for Yeats himself there was a more radical failure. Allingham was "a poet of the accidental and fleeting—of passing artistic moments"; "he had no sense of the great unities—the relations of man to man, and all to the serious business of the world." In this judgment passed upon Allingham there echoes Yeats's sense of a more general poetic situation, and there echoes also, faint yet persistent, a sense of his own ambitions and standards.

The words "national" and "nation" came easily to Yeats in the 1890s, and for the most part he gives them what were then their accepted meanings in Ireland. As he uses them, however, we are constantly aware that he and his readers have very different values in mind. Yeats knew, for example, that the current political sentiment of nationalism was a modern contrivance, at most no older than a century or two. He was even a bit suspicious of it, as he was of all things modern. He was especially wary of the copybook version of history upon which conventional nationalism grounded much of its rhetoric and most of its verse. He preferred what may be termed a mythological nationalism, and was solicitous of his audience's sensibilities in the matter:

> There is a distinct school of Irish literature which we must foster and protect, and its foundation is sunk in the legend and lore of the people and in National history. The literature of Greece and India had just such a foundation, and as we, like the Greeks and Indians, are an idealistic people, this foundation is fixed in legend rather than in history.

All nations like to be reminded that they are idealistic, and impoverished ones tend to feel that they have special claims upon the honor, but Yeats had much more at stake in such pronouncements than patriotic feeling. John P. Frayne, the editor of Yeats's uncollected prose, characterizes the 1893 lecture from which I have quoted as "the most candid and developed expression of Yeats's hopes for Irish literature in the early nineties." It is the most developed, probably, but "candid"? In his imaginative dealings with Ireland, complementary but quite distinct aspects of his temperament drew him away from history and toward mythology, or, to be more precise, toward a mythologized history. In the 1890s, however, his special concern for mythology also arose, in part, from his own special literary needs. He was arguing, in the early Nineties, for a verse which, because somehow national, would be somehow public, but the direction of his own verse was, increasingly, toward the allusive, the personal, almost, at times, the private. The resolution, upon which he had a grip which then was but half-secure and fully intuitive, was the assimilation into his verses of the dim, tradition-haunted, and tradition-sanctioned figures of the ancient mythology. By the end of the decade, this resolution had flourished forth into a theory of tradition and a theory of the social imagination.

Five years later, the issue of the relationship of modern Irish literature to the older tradition was again joined in a controversy conducted through the autumn and winter columns of the Dublin *Daily Express*. The question, as first posed by John Eglinton, bore upon the appropriateness of the ancient legends as subjects for a modern Irish drama. The question was timely, for the dramatic movement was just then being organized by Yeats, Lady Gregory, and Edward Martyn. But the issues swiftly broadened and deepened. Yeats had by then published most of the poems which make up *The Wind Among the Reeds*, and he had them very much in mind. So too did Eglinton. Where, asks Eglinton, would an Irish dramatist, but by implication any writer, look for his subject? "Would he look for it in the Irish legends, or in the life of the peasantry and folk-lore, or in Irish history and patriotism, or in life at large as it is reflected in his own consciousness?" In the latter, so the question implies. Eglinton was not a nationalist: he was a disciple of Emerson and Arnold, a feat which he managed by misunderstanding Transcendentalism. "In short," he concludes his first article, "we need to realize in Ireland that a national literature or drama must spring from a native interest in life and its problems and a strong capacity for life among the people." By his second article, it is clear that his specific target is Yeats and the Yeatsian poetics:

> There are two conceptions of poetry, mutually antagonistic so far, and not to be reconciled except in the life of another great

poet, of which one may be called Wordsworthian, which regards the poetic consciousness as acting from within outward and able to confer on even common things the radiance of the imagination; the other, to which those who are rather in sympathy with art than with philosophy are inclined, regards the poet as passive to elect influences and endowing old material with new forms. The first regards the poet as a seer and a spiritual force; the second as an aristocratic craftsman. The first looks to man himself as the source of imagination; the second to tradition, to the forms and images in which old conceptions have been embodied—old faiths, dreams, myths.

Yeats made two immediate responses, of which the second, "The Autumn of the Body," was reprinted in *Ideas of Good and Evil.* It serves with great elegance its purpose in that artfully ordered book, and without a hint of the controversy that had occasioned it, a shimmering and appropriately oblique defense of the presence "in the arts of every country" of "those faint lights and faint colours and faint outlines and faint energies which many call 'the decadence,' but which I, because I believe that the arts lie dreaming of things to come, prefer to call the autumn of the body." But the more pertinent of the questions which Eglinton had raised—he did not quite formulate them—were not answered until 1901, when Yeats published "What Is 'Popular Poetry'?" which now appears as the first essay in *Ideas of Good and Evil.* He had perhaps not been greatly offended by the implied description of himself as an "aristocratic craftsman"—he had begun his visits to Coole—but a variety of circumstances were pressing him toward a definition of the relationship between modern art and traditional culture.

"What Is 'Popular Poetry'?" is a defense of his own practice which enlarges to become, and was to remain, the center of his Irish aesthetic. Its audacious and imaginative thesis begins with his self-acceptance as a poet of "the coteries," the author of allusive, obscure, "unpopular" verses which, while they draw upon materials from the antique world of Celtic tradition, do so in a deliberately oblique and shadowy manner. But he then proposes, or rather he defines, not a separation but an alliance and an identity: "There is only one good kind of poetry, for the poetry of the coteries, which presupposes the written tradition, does not differ in kind from the true poetry of the people, which presupposes the unwritten tradition. Both are alike strange and obscure, and unreal to all who have not understanding, and both, instead of that manifest logic, that clear rhetoric of the 'popular' poetry, glimmer with thoughts and images whose 'ancestors were stout and wise,' 'anigh to Paradise,' 'ere yet men knew the gift of corn.'" He proceeds then to the elaboration of a historical myth which was to prove itself one of great power both for himself and for the ideology of the Literary Revival: "Indeed, it is certain that before the counting house had created a new class and a new art without breeding and without ancestry, and set this art and this class between the hut and the castle, and between the hut and the cloister, the art of the people was as closely mingled with the art of the coteries as was the speech of the people that delighted in rhythmical animation, in idiom, in images, in words full of far-off suggestion, with the unchanging speech of the poet."

This alliance of the written and the unwritten tradition, an alliance with clear political and social implications, however pastoral its initial formulation, remained central to Yeats's thought, despite severe modifications, and despite changes wrought by its association with new feelings and ideas. Thus, by 1907, when circumstance and passion had readied him to confront rather than to conciliate the middle-class world of rhetoric and counting house, he changed not the elements but their relationship in his formula: "Three types of men have all made beautiful things. Aristocracies have made beautiful manners, because their place in the world puts them above the fear of life, and the countrymen have made beautiful stories and beliefs, because they have nothing to lose and so do not fear, and the artists have made all the rest, because Providence has filled them with reck-lessness. All these look backward to a long tradition, for, being with-out fear, they have held to whatever pleased them." This essay, although it bears "Poetry and Tradition" as its title, opens and then closes with an evocation of John O'Leary, the old Fenian who had just died, and whose austere, sacrificing, implacable life had made of him, for Yeats, an emblem of an ennobling and reckless defeat. Of O'Leary and his pupil John Taylor, Yeats says that "that ideal Ireland, perhaps from this out an imaginary Ireland, in whose service I labour, will always be in many essentials their Ireland." It was phrased in pre-cise terms: an Ireland ideal and perhaps imaginary.

The spiritual descendant of these assumptions, but expressed now in the willful and, at last, genuinely reckless manner of his late prose, appears in the "General Introduction for My Work" (1937):

> Our mythology, our legends, differ from those of other Euro-pean countries because down to the end of the seventeenth cen-tury they had the attention, perhaps the unquestioned belief, of peasant and noble alike; Homer belongs to sedentary men, even to-day our ancient queens, our mediaeval soldiers and lovers, can make a pedlar shudder. I can put my own thought, despair perhaps from the study of present circumstance in the light of ancient philosophy, into the mouth of rambling poets of the seventeenth century, or even of some imagined ballad singer of to-day, and the deeper my thought the more credible, the more peasant-like, are ballad singer and rambling poet. Some modern poets contend that jazz and music-hall songs are the folk art of our time, that we should mould our art upon them; we Irish poets, modern men also, reject every folk art that does not go back to Olympus. Give me time and a little youth, and I will prove that even "Johnny, I hardly knew ye" goes back.

As an old man's expression of poetic faith, of vigorous fidelity to the principles of his youth, of pride in all that he and others have accomplished, this is splendid. It echoes the verse. He has this, with much else, in mind when, in "Coole Park and Ballylee, 1931," he speaks of "Whatever's written in what poets name / The book of the people." And again in "The Municipal Gallery Revisited," when he speaks of his belief, and that of John Synge and Augusta Gregory, that "all must come from contact with the soil." But in considering not Yeats himself but his heritage, difficulties begin with that casual, confident reference to "we Irish poets," who apparently, like Bishop Berkeley, "think otherwise." A similar phrase in "The Statues," "we Irish," has troubled Conor Cruise O'Brien, who describes the Yeatsian "we" as "a mass-executioner, a 'we' of the Samurai." Fortunately, nothing so drastic or so lurid is involved in our present instance, although there may be a mild analogy. What I have chiefly in mind is that Yeats, as we have seen, displays a striking and one might almost say an "un-Irish" disinclination to consider the actual stuff of the Irish past, or to consider present Ireland as it has been shaped by the actual processes of history.

His concern in his poetry is with ancient, mythological Ireland, with his own relationship toward certain severely selected and highly stylized aspects of contemporary Ireland, and with an abstract Ireland which I have elsewhere described as "totally autonomous, a Platonic form of which the actual island is but a smudged and imperfect copy."[1] On occasion, and usually indeed for certain famous occasional poems, he will evoke shadowy, heroic figures from an actual historical past, but nearly always for the purpose of reproving the present, and with the emphasis upon the present and the reproof. Disconsolate, the shade of Parnell revisits Dublin. The names of Emmet, Tone, Fitzgerald reprove those who, being come to sense, but fumble in a greasy till. (At times, this required skillful management. "Yet they were of a different

---

1. See page 228.

kind," he says of the '98 rebels: "The names that stilled your child-hood play." "Stilled" is a word of masterly neutrality from a poet whose childhood play it had been to imagine himself fighting against a Fenian rebellion on the seashore near Rosses Point.) At the very close of his career, Irish poets are bid to "Sing the lords and ladies gay / That were beaten into the clay / Through seven heroic centuries." But Yeats himself, to our great good fortune, had had other songs to sing than those which he prescribed for his successors, "we Irish poets."

The Ireland created by Yeats's intense and heroic imagination excluded much of the actual Ireland, and most of Ireland's actual experience in historical time, and these were to be exclusions of moment to his successors, for Ireland is a history-haunted land. History is a part of the textures of lives lived; it finds expression in cadence and diction, in memory and feeling. Stephen Dedalus had good cause to struggle against its nightmare, but the nightmare itself is given new definition by that struggle and by the work of which it is a part. And as for the actualities which lay beyond the Yeatsian terri-tory, it is by a telling, accidental irony that one later Irish poem was to begin where Yeats's last poem ended, with clay, although clay without heroism: "Clay is the word and clay is the flesh. . . . "

> *And what rough beast, its hour come round at last*
> *Slouches towards Bethlehem to be born?*

There is a genuine magic in Yeats's poetry, and it may be that the question posed in "The Second Coming" received, in Irish terms, an actual answer, for it was in 1939, the year of Yeats's death, that Patrick Kavanagh left Monaghan for Dublin. A few months earlier, Yeats, leaving Ireland forever, had spent the night before his depar-ture with a younger poet. They did not part until after midnight, and the poet was to remember Yeats, his figure erect and challenging, gleaming through the darkness, chanting with slow, powerful accents the section of "Under Ben Bulben" which begins, "Irish poets, learn your trade." The younger poet was F. R. Higgins, who followed the Yeatsian prescription, as opposed to the Yeatsian practice, with a kind of hideous fidelity: the randy laughter of porter drinkers echoes hollowly through his verses. Kavanagh was to call him "the gallivanting poet," and to excuse him after a fashion by remarking that he after all "grew up in an Ireland which had only recently been invented."

Yeats was a great poet and Kavanagh was not, but he was a true poet and a very important one. He liberated us, as one contemporary Irish poet has splendidly said of him, "but he liberated us into ignorance." When he is contrasted to Yeats and the other writers of the Literary Revival, the possibilities for comedy are strong but fatal: the dream of every revivalist come true at last, a ploughboy poet, race of the soil, and, as in a nightmare, he rejects, with a disconcerting mixture of oafishness and dignity, every cherished value of the revival. No one has written of him with greater accuracy of feeling and judgment than Seamus Heaney, who points to that aspect of "The Great Hunger" which is a conscious rejection of the Yeatsian "dream of the noble and the beggarman," answering it with a vision of "the peasant ploughman who is half a vegetable," "a sick horse nosing around the meadow for a clean place to die." Kavanagh's rejection was not of Yeats, whom he excepted with a gruff genuine warmth: "Alone among modern Irish writers Yeats got there merely by being himself, by being a sincere poet. He dug deep beneath the variegated surface to where the Spirit of Poetry is one with Truth. I say this with reservations, but none the less it is largely true." What, rather, he rejected, out of the actualities of his own experience and imagination, was that "Ireland the poets have imagined, terrible and gay."

Kavanagh, when taxed by the editors of his 1947 piece on Higgins with the charge that he seemed to be saying that a Protestant cannot be an Irish writer, responded with an adroitness, though scarcely an urbanity, worthy of Yeats: "Who wants to be an Irish writer! A man is what he is, and if there is some mystical quality in the Nation or the race it will ooze through his skin." This is fine in what it says, less so in what it evades, for passages in that article are, to say the least, outrageously nonecumenical. So too are there such passages in Yeats's prose, although managed more discreetly. Thus, we are indebted to Denis Donoghue's edition of the full 1909 journal for the discovery of the last Irish Catholic capable of direct thought. It was Owen Roe O'Neill, who died in 1649. (Although Yeats does not remark the coincidence, Cromwell had landed just two days earlier; fortunately, therefore, the chain of reasoning in Ireland remained unbroken.) Such loyalties, sentiments, suspicions, judgments, casual and fierce as winds, are parts of the Irish experience. When deepest and most ungovernable, they can become sources of that hatred which Yeats rightly calls great but leaves carefully unspecified.

If, as I have suggested, Yeats dealt at best obliquely with Ireland as it has been shaped by time, this is not the case with contemporary poets. Seamus Heaney, especially in *Wintering Out* and *North*, Richard Murphy in *The Battle of Aughrim*, John Montague in *The Rough Field*, are all concerned, though in very different ways, with history as a felt pressure upon their lives and imaginations, as it has shaped their cultures, as it acts upon their communities. The specific kinds of historical concern present in their work imply imaginative, personal, and social imperatives different in kind from those which inform Yeats's poetry. To say this, however, is not to imply discontinuity, nor to ignore what doubtless must be the large task before every Irish writer of coming to his own kind of terms with his great predecessor. He must be for all of them, I would suppose, a formidable presence, a great poet who was also something quite different but in his case obscurely and powerfully allied, a man of noble character, willful, generous, obsessed, and passionate.

Ultimately, Yeats's heritage may be that which all great poets pass on to their successors: the example of a powerful imagination intensely at work upon the self and the world. The "General Introduction" opens with this sentence: "A poet writes always of his personal life, in his finest work out of its tragedy, whatever it may be, remorse, lost love, or mere loneliness; he never speaks directly as to someone at the breakfast table, there is always a phantasmagoria." The Ireland of his poetry, because it was a portion of his phantasmagoria, was personal to him, and therefore was, and has remained, unavailable to other poets. But it is equally true to say that his poetry has become a portion of the spiritual history of his nation, and indeed of Irish history in other meanings of that term. The courses of his influence are free-flowing, subterranean, and beyond need for acknowledgment. It can be said of him, as he once said of Parnell, that he is kept in mind by every man that sings a song.

16

YEATS, JOYCE, AND
THE MATTER OF IRELAND

IRELAND IS AN island of towers: its history is inscribed upon their stones. The tall, sturdy keeps of the Norman settlers stand upon rich, wide pasturelands, byres for cattle now as often as not, but retaining the trim, soldierly bearing of the Normans. Derelict manor houses of the Tudor times stand upon lonely headlands, half fortress, half dwelling. Unexpectedly, at the end of a twisting, weed-choked avenue, ancient carriage ruts faint beneath thick grasses, the gutted carcass of a Palladian mansion leaps into view, burned during the troubles, great blocks of Portland stone streaked black from the fires of great hatreds released within little room. Older than these and more mysterious, round towers stand sentinel beside the ruined ecclesiastical cities of Cashel and Clonmacnoise. Most ancient of all, the dolmens and cromlechs, the cairns and subterranean tombs of a vanished and unrecoverable culture. Dwelling places, Yeats was to tell us, of the Sidhe, the gods of the old religion.

We are concerned here with two towers. One is a Norman keep in the Galway barony of Kiltartan, some twenty miles from the western seacoast. The second, one of a chain constructed by the British to withstand a Napoleonic invasion, stands facing eastward toward the Irish sea at the village of Sandycove, a few miles south of Dublin. Yeats's tower at Ballylee—Ballylee Castle as once it was grandly termed—and the Martello tower in which Joyce lived for a few weeks in 1904, the setting upon which *Ulysses* opens, take on central and symbolic roles in the art of each man, and enter also those shorthands of symbols by which we, in our turn, hold the two writers in our imagination.

I propose to consider the very different manner in which each man came to accept his identity as an Irish writer. And this in its turn involves some consideration of what for convenience we may term the "matter of Ireland," the body of oral and written Irish literature, and the accumulated symbolic powers of the word "Ireland" itself. If I place their two towers, Ballylee and Martello, as twin emblems at our entrance way, it will at last appear, I trust, that I do so for substantial rather than decorative purposes.

When Yeats purchased Ballylee Castle from the Congested Districts Board in April 1917, for the princely sum of £35, he was a very famous poet indeed and the central figure of a literary movement which had attracted the attention of the world. But he had first visited the small barony of Kiltartan in August of 1896, when he had just turned thirty-one, and it is with this younger Yeats, the Yeats of the Nineties and of the decade which followed, that we shall be concerned. He was already a distinguished writer: Arthur Symons, the friend who accompanied him on this visit, was to dedicate to him an influential study of symbolist poetry.[1] He had published several volumes of verse, and was now at work upon the complex, perfectly controlled lyrics which he gathered together three years later in *The Wind Among the Reeds*. He had produced an impressive quantity of essays, reviews, journalism of various kinds, had edited volumes of Irish folklore and of tales by Irish writers. In 1893, he had published *The Celtic Twilight*, a work of extraordinary prose which was to lend its name, in a faintly ambiguous and reluctant manner, to a movement.

---

1. Arthur Symons, *The Symbolist Movement in Literature* (London: W. Heinemann, 1899).

Much of his prose was directed, openly or by insinuation, toward the establishment of that movement.[2]

Almost, though not quite, from the outset of his career, he regarded himself as an Irish poet, and he wished to be so regarded, both in London and in Dublin. He wished, moreover, to be one of a company of writers. His work was to be a part of the literature of Ireland. And this placed him in a delicate and peculiar situation, for it could be argued, and in fact was argued, that Ireland, in 1896, possessed neither a literature nor a coherent cultural identity. Sullen hostilities divided the social classes, the political parties, the social creeds. In the recent past lay the violent and at times savage Land War. A powerful political movement, upon which the national and in part the social aspirations of the Catholic population had centered, was shattered by the destruction of Charles Parnell. The immediate social atmosphere was one of torpor, broken by brief, sudden flashes of venomous ill will. But Yeats had predicted, in the introduction to his collection of stories from the Irish novelists, that an intellectual movement would begin to gather strength at the first lull in politics.[3] Writing of this period long afterward, in *The Trembling of the Veil*, he preferred the more arrogant and flamboyant language of his later years. Ireland after the fall of Parnell, he says, was like soft wax.[4]

There is little in his early prose which contradicts the ambition implied by that image. But the prose also demonstrates his tireless resourcefulness as a politician of culture: a willingness to accept battle, with allies more often than with opponents, but a far greater readiness to ingratiate, to flatter, to praise, and, especially, to "put a skin" on his criticism. Young James Joyce, a decade later, was to

---

2. W. B. Yeats, *The Wind Among the Reeds* (London: E. Matthews, 1899); *The Celtic Twilight: Men and Women, Ghouls and Faeries* (London: Lawrence and Bullen, 1893).

3. W. B. Yeats, *Representative Irish Tales* (G. P. Putnam and Sons, 1891), pp. 15–16.

4. W. B. Yeats, *Autobiography* (Doubleday, 1958), p. 133.

criticize Yeats's "fatal instinct for adaptibility," and the judgment was one which Yeats had brought upon himself. For Yeats, in his efforts to create an Irish literature, played at times a devious game, and with no weapon at hand save that extraordinary style, borrowed from Walter Pater and then transformed—elusive, insinuating, concessive, an urbanity of utterance conjoined, perhaps, to an outrageous thesis, the burden of argument carried by cadence and image, illusionary webs of cold, tempered gossamer. He had proposed for himself a politics of the imagination far different from Parnell's, but, like his, at once absolute and adroit.

Yeats's sense of identity with Ireland began at a psychic level deeper than those to which criticism carries us: it began with a profound, Virgilian piety of place, an attachment to native scene which is nourished by all of the heart's affections. But it soon became his central, compelling, and complex image, wrought from inchoate and fragmentary materials and yet more pure than a candle's flame, at once object and source of creative energy. Indeed, in certain of his poems, this image of Ireland is totally autonomous, a Platonic form of which the actual island is but a smudged and imperfect copy. "Races and individuals," he was to write much later, "are unified by an image, or bundle of related images."[5] The epigram implies the interrelationship of his personal and his public concerns. "Ireland" was an image powerful enough to draw into focus, as in a burning glass, his scattered impulses and preoccupations. But he also held, as a belief almost reciprocal to this, that Ireland itself, that incoherent, shattered, and bitter land, might be brought to a unity by the powerful images of art. Of all the poets who have used our language, only William Blake, Yeats's great mentor, held so literal and so immense a confidence in the boundless powers of the imagination. And not even Blake—for Blake's sanity was ultimately and paradoxically preserved by his very

---

5. Yeats, *Autobiography*, p. 132.

dottiness—addressed with the directness of the young Yeats the task of shaping by means of art the soft wax of a society.

It was an ancient land. Gods and warriors, dimly perceived, moved beyond its mists. Aengus, Finn, Cuchulain, Usheen, Maeve—they people his early poetry, creating deep temporal recesses stretching backward toward a past almost unimaginably remote. This vast repository of heroic and magical shapes was the imaginative birthright of the Irish writer. But how was a modern writer to gain access to that potent, vanished world? By what strategies of spirit and art could it be made to serve his own concerns? *Ideas of Good and Evil,* with its subtle arrangements of theme, explores in a high and delicate fashion this question, which is central to both his private and his public conception of poetry. The myths of ancient Ireland were "popular" in his special meaning of the term: they had been shaped by the imagination of a people and were therefore a part of that great memory within which lie stored those symbols upon which power depends for both its reality and its efficacy.

But in the more general meaning of the word, these myths had not been truly popular in Ireland for better than two centuries. They had once been embodied in a vast literature, written and oral, of which the nineteenth century possessed but a small portion, the random manuscripts which had somehow survived the pillages of time, war, neglect, and senseless destruction. An oral literature indeed survived, but it was the possession, almost entirely, of the peasantry, who had shaped it to the particularities of their own existence, endowing heroes and gods alike with form and meaning far different from that bestowed by the aristocratic, prefeudal society which had given them birth. In an early book review, Yeats acknowledges his difficulties with a candor not always present in his more polished essays. Of that ancient literature, he writes, "there remains but a wild anarchy of legends—a vast pell-mell of monstrous shapes: huge demons driving swine on the hill-tops; beautiful shadows whose hair has a peculiar life and moves responsive to their thought; and here and there some great hero like Cuchulain, some epic needing only deliberate craft to be scarce less than Homer. There behind the Ireland of today, lost in the ages, this chaos murmurs like a dark and stormy sea full of the sounds of lamentation."[6] And yet, he writes elsewhere: "Of the many things the past bequeaths to the future, the greatest are great legends; they are the mothers of nations. I hold it the duty of every Irish reader to study those of his own country till they are as familiar as his own hands, for in them is the Celtic heart."[7]

But almost impenetrable barriers separated both Yeats and his audience from that legendary world. To pause upon one large and embarrassing circumstance: only a small portion of the surviving material had been translated into English, and these translations, by John O'Donovan, Eugene O'Curry, and other self-trained scholars, were inaccurate and inexact, and were set forth in a stiff and clumsy English prose. Only one of the nineteenth-century scholars possessed both erudition and a graceful, though elaborate style. But even Standish Hayes O'Grady, in his great *Silva Gadelica*, renders thus a passage which concerns one of Saint Kieran's pupils: "He...and a virgin fell immoderately in love with each other and conceived a contaminated intention of sinning."[8] Expressive, perhaps, of an Irish attitude toward sexuality, but in no other respect a felicitous formulation.

And of Yeats's predecessors, only one, Samuel Ferguson, had possessed knowledge and talent sufficient to put this body of material to the uses of English poetry. He was a fine, solid craftsman, and Yeats,

---

6. W. B. Yeats, "Bardic Ireland," in *Scots Observer* (January 4, 1890); reprinted in *Uncollected Prose by W. B. Yeats*, edited by John P. Frayne (London: Macmillan, 1970), p. 166.

7. W. B. Yeats, "The Poetry of Sir Samuel Ferguson," in *Dublin University Review* (November, 1886); reprinted in *Uncollected Prose*, pp. 103–104.

8. Standish Hayes O'Grady, *Silva Gadelica*, 2 vols. (London: Williams and Norgate, 1892), Vol. 2, p. 11.

being desperately in need of ancestors, praised him recklessly and evasively. He was "the greatest poet Ireland has produced, being the most central and most Celtic," and Yeats imagines him "like some aged sea-king sitting among the inland wheat and poppies—the savour of the sea about him, and its strength."[9] It is disappointing to turn from this image of a Hibernian Neptune to a photograph of Ferguson, a mild, portly, and bespectacled attorney, the camera suggesting with harsh, accidental accuracy an antiquarian with literary interests. Ferguson offered a particular embarrassment, for although he shared Yeats's hope for a distinctly Irish literature, he was in politics a staunch loyalist and a devoted servant of the queen. This did not trouble Yeats, for whom love of land was a passion which has its being far below party badges and slogans, but as a politician of culture he found himself working with associates accustomed to apply, with inquisitional rigor, precisely those tests.

For an Irish literature of sorts had been in existence since the Young Ireland movement of the 1840s. Its patriotic purpose was irreproachable, and it had schooled a generation of Irishmen to judge poems and writers by that purpose alone. In Dublin, the disciples of Young Ireland formed a majority in those literary societies with whom Yeats hoped to work, and it was therefore necessary for him to put forward with great delicacy his settled and quite accurate conviction that the poetry of Young Ireland was sorry stuff, the will, as he was to say in a later context, doing the work of the imagination. On one occasion, when weariness had perhaps overcome discretion, he was to write of Thomas Davis, the school's founder: "Of his political poetry I cannot speak; suffice it to say that it still goes on, whether for good or ill, serving its purposes, making converts."[10] There is

---

9. W. B. Yeats, "The Poetry of Sir Samuel Ferguson"; *Uncollected Prose*, pp. 103–104.

10. W. B. Yeats, "Popular Ballad Poetry of Ireland," *Leisure Hour* (November 1889); reprinted in *Uncollected Prose*, p. 159.

something touching and faintly ludicrous in the spectacle of the author of *The Wind Among the Reeds* avoiding criticism of verses upon which their creator had set no great store. For Davis had sought only to create a popular and patriotic balladry for a demoralized people, and had brought into being a literature as mechanical as the looms of Manchester.

Yeats's devotion to Ireland had, as its reverse, a detestation of urban, industrial civilization, a civilization which fettered the imagination and denied it access to those traditional modes of feeling by which it is nourished. England was for him at once the nearest and the most powerful embodiment of such values, and it is nearly always upon these grounds, rather than those of conventional Irish nationalism, that he condemns the culture of modern England. But he was well aware that Dublin, at least, shared that culture, inhibited from full membership only by its poverty and its sentiment of patriotism. The literature of Young Ireland, and for that matter most of what was written in English in nineteenth-century Ireland, was shaped upon principles which he considered hostile to those of both art and genuine community. It might indeed be argued, although Yeats never quite did so, that nationalism is less a principle counter to modernity than one of its specific manifestations. Young Ireland, expressing patriotic feeling through metrical forms borrowed from, of all people, Lord Macaulay, offers impressive supporting evidence. And yet even such verse was touched and ennobled by the pathos of defeat, of poverty, of spoliation at the hands of a more powerful neighbor. Ireland had at least been spared the indignity of success.

At the heart of Yeats's problem lay an issue which he addressed in a complex and subtle manner, in part because the issue was in itself complex, in part because it touched directly upon his own social identity: the issue of language. Instinct and logic alike suggested to him that the strong nourishing root of Irish culture was its Gaelic traditions, but he was reluctant to accept that these traditions were vested in the Irish language. That language had endured, in a most precise fashion, the fortunes of those who spoke it. By the end of the seventeenth century, the native aristocracy had been destroyed, and Irish remained as the language of the peasant population, which is to say, a language of the majority of the inhabitants. The aristocracy, those who had not fled or had not been slain, were forced down by dispossession into the ranks of the peasantry, and their traditions of a written literature were forced down with them. A most extraordinary situation thereby developed in which the literature of an aristocracy had passed into the keeping of a peasantry. The consequences can be traced, decade by decade, across the course of the eighteenth century, from the poems of an Egan O'Rahilly, courtly, sardonic, and austere, his patrons Gaelic gentry who had stood beside King James at the Boyne, to those of an Eoghan Ruagh O'Sullivan, at the close of the century, day laborer, press-ganged sailor, hedge schoolmaster.

But by the close of the nineteenth century, Irish had come close to vanishing as the language of the peasantry. Connaught and Munster, the western and southern provinces in which its use had been almost universal, were those most heavily devastated by the Great Famine of the 1840s, and, at about the same time, the system of national schools was introduced, and with it a deliberate policy of replacing Irish with English. By the 1890s, therefore, Irish lingered only in scattered and impoverished regions, and the bulk of the peasantry had come to speak an English heavily affected in diction, syntax, and modes of thought by the language of their parents and grandparents. And so successful had been the system of educational propaganda that Irish had become, even to English-speaking peasants, a stigmatized tongue, the possession of barbarous herdsmen and fisherfolk.

In their journey from the old tongue to the new, they had carried with them more than syntax: they had carried into English, in however attenuated a form, the habits and beliefs of a traditional culture which had once expressed itself in Irish. Their English, savory with unexpected idiom, had received literary transcription only at the hands of novelists who employed inaccurate versions of it for comic effect, and their traditional beliefs had not fared much better. But theirs was the language, and theirs the beliefs, upon which Yeats hoped to found a literature, the popular subsoil which would nourish his own imagination and those of other writers. But why, it may be asked, did he not turn to Irish itself, as his fellow workers, Douglas Hyde and Lady Gregory, and J. M. Synge, were to do? The caustic answer is that he could not: he was never able to read or to speak Irish. All things, perhaps, are possible to a poet capable of receiving the formidable influence of Mallarmé and Verlaine despite an ignorance of French. A more comprehensive answer, however, is apt to prove more rewarding.

In 1892, Douglas Hyde, who in the following year was to found the powerful Gaelic League, delivered a consequential lecture on "The DeAnglicisation of Ireland,"[11] in which he proposed that the Irish language be nourished to the point where it could first rival and then supplant English. Hyde had seized upon a truth, that language is the most certain instrument for the preservation and transmission of cultural values. Yeats replied within the month, asserting what he believed to be the sorrowful truth, "that the Gaelic language will soon be no more heard, except here and there in remote villages, and on the wind-beaten shores of Connaught." He then put a question which was to have a longer existence than he could ever have anticipated: "Can we not keep the continuity of the nation's life by transplanting or re-telling in English, which shall have an indefinable Irish quality of rhythm and style, all that is best of the ancient literature...? Let us by all means prevent the decay of that tongue where we can, and preserve it always among us as a learned language to be a fountain of nationality in our midst, but do not let us base upon it our

11. Reprinted in *The Revival of Irish Literature* (London: T. Fisher Unwin, 1894).

hopes of nationhood. When we remember the majesty of Cuchullin and the beauty of sorrowing Deirdre we should not forget that it is that majesty and that beauty which are immortal, and not the perishing tongue that first told of them."[12]

This may well be termed special pleading by a poet who had turned for subject matter to the ancient literature, but whose own verbal resources were entirely English. Indeed, at this point Yeats's knowledge of Cuchulain depended entirely upon the overwrought Carlylean prose of Standish James O'Grady,[13] who was also (unlike his learned cousin) unable to read Irish, but had, in his turn, depended upon the faulty translations of O'Curry and others. The true Cuchulain, the Cuchulain of the *Tain bo Cuailnge*, possesses a heroic magnificence, but could not be called majestic. And again, Yeats's own Paterian style was singularly unsuited to convey the particular rhythms of peasant English.

The Celtic Twilight, at once the most ambitious and the most successful of his early prose works, is a triumph of allusive style, in which the beliefs of the western peasants are expressed by a narrator who neither affirms nor denies the world which he is creating, maintaining what Joyce was to call, with a slight imprecision, a "delicate scepticism." But the actual social texture of that represented world is quite thin. Many of the stories, Yeats tells us, were given to him by a little man named Paddy Flynn, whom he once encountered huddled over a can of mushrooms, and then asleep under a hedge. It is difficult to resist the suspicion that the narrator has gone from one Sligo village to the next seeking out in each its resident idiot and listening with a sympathetic but defective ear.

---

12. W. B. Yeats, in a letter to *United Ireland* (December 17, 1892); *Uncollected Prose*, pp. 255–256.

13. Standish James O'Grady, *Cuculain: An Epic* (London: Sampson, Low, Searle, Marston and Rivington, 1882).

Precisely the strength and integrity of Yeats's vision, his scrupulous attention to a language which might evoke it, prevented him from shaping for literary purposes the English vernacular of the peasantry. And yet, as though he had summoned them from the deep, writers were now to appear who addressed themselves to that task—Douglas Hyde himself, Lady Gregory, John Millington Synge. Lady Gregory was to work directly under Yeats's inspiration, while Hyde and Synge wrote from impulses specific to their own talents and needs, but their work was to form a loose unity, creating a speech, a spoken world of colors and textures which registered what Yeats took to be the actualities of Irish experience. Long afterward, in "The Municipal Gallery Revisited," he was to write:

> *(An image out of Spenser and the common tongue).*
> *John Synge, I and Augusta Gregory, thought*
> *All that we did, all that we said or sang*
> *Must come from contact with the soil, from that*
> *Contact everything Antaeus-like grew strong.*
> *We three alone in modern times had brought*
> *Everything down to that sole test again,*
> *Dream of the noble and the beggar-man.*

The language formed by that extraordinary collaboration, and the poetic and social assumptions by which it was sustained, is the essential circumstance of what is termed the Irish Literary Revival. It was an extraordinary movement, and it produced also an extraordinary countermovement. W. B. Yeats was the chief architect of that movement, and James Joyce the chief rebel against it, his aesthetic principles being shaped in part by his resistance to its assumptions and its modes of expression.

It was at almost exactly the turn of the century, on one of his earliest visits to Lady Gregory at Coole Park, that Yeats first saw Ballylee, at that time a part of the Coole estate, "a little group of houses," as he says, "not many enough to be called a village." He described it in an essay called "Dust Hath Closed Helen's Eye," which he added to the 1902 edition of *The Celtic Twilight*: "There is the old square castle, Ballylee, inhabited by a farmer and his wife, and a cottage where their daughter and son-in-law live, and a little mill with an old miller, and old ash trees throwing green shadows upon a little river and great stepping-stones."[14] The square castle, which Yeats was later to own and to claim as a central symbol in his art, was at that time occupied by a family named Carrick. Yeats had recently been advised by "a certain symbolic personality" who called herself Megarithma that he must live near water and avoid woods "because they concentrate the solar ray."[15] Patrick Carrick had received roughly the same advice: the castle stands on the east bank of the tiny Cloone River, and bailiffs from Galway were forbidden by law from crossing it to serve the notices of his numerous creditors. But the castle itself is barely mentioned in Yeats's 1902 essay, and a different purpose had taken him with Lady Gregory to the village. Ballylee was famous throughout Irish-speaking Connaught because of a peasant poet and a peasant beauty.

Nearly lost in brambles and sloe bushes stood the foundations of a cabin in which, sixty years before, had lived a girl named Mary Hynes. And Mary Hynes had been made immortal in a song, which is still sung in Ireland, by Anthony Raftery, the last of the Gaelic poets—or so Yeats chose to regard him:

> *Going to Mass by the will of God,*
> *The day came wet and the wind rose;*

---

14. W. B. Yeats, *The Celtic Twilight* (London: A. H. Bullen, 1902); reprinted in *Mythologies* (London: Macmillan, 1959), p. 22.

15. Yeats, *Autobiography*, p. 247.

> *I met Mary Hynes at the cross of Kiltartan,*
> *And I fell in love with her then and there.*[16]

So it begins. Old people in Ballylee still remembered Mary Hynes: "They say she was the handsomest girl in Ireland, her skin was like dribbled snow, and she had blushes in her cheeks. She had five handsome brothers, but all are gone now." And they remembered Raftery: "He was the greatest poet in Ireland, and he'd make a song about that bush if he chanced to stand under it. There was a bush he stood under from the rain, and he made verses praising it, and then when the water came through he made verses dispraising it."[17] Joyce was later to comment with murderous equanimity upon Raftery's ability to draw inspiration from a leaky bush. But Raftery's song about Mary Hynes—the girl's beauty and a poet's words were remembered with equal affection—made a powerful impression upon Yeats, a collocation of emotions and images. "It may be that in a few years Fable, who changes mortalities to immortalities in her cauldron, will have changed Mary Hynes and Raftery to perfect symbols of the sorrow of beauty and of the magnificence and penury of dreams."[18]

In 1903, Douglas Hyde was to publish a volume of *Songs Ascribed to Raftery*, the fifth of a series in which he collected the songs of Connaught. His method was to print the poems with connecting narrative and notes in Irish on one side of the page, and an English translation on the page facing. For the English both of the poetic and the prose passages, he employed a language which endeavored to maintain the simplicities and idiosyncrasies of the peasantry, and in that endeavor may be discovered the basic language of the Irish Literary Revival. Here is a passage, chosen quite at random:

---

16. Yeats, *Mythologies*, p. 24.

17. Yeats, *Mythologies*, p. 23.

18. Yeats, *Mythologies*, p. 30.

When Raftery was once in Cappaghtagle, a place which is half-way between Loughrea and Ballinasloe, and about four miles north of Aughrim, he got good material for a song out of a wedding which took place there. There was a very poor couple in that place, but as poor as they were, they determined that they would marry one another. It was not usual at that time for the people to be married in the churches, but the priest used to go to the sick man's house to marry him, and the poor man used to come to the priest's house. The youths of the village thought to make fun for themselves out of the wedding, and they gathered together and came in company, with the couple, to the priest's house. When the pair was there, waiting for the priest, the lads went into a tavern that was near them and began drinking. There were a couple of bacachs, or sturdy beggarmen, there, before them, asking for alms, and the boys gave them plenty to drink that they might pick fun out of them. It was not long until the two were drunk, and they began fighting and beating one another. When the newly-married couple came out of the priest's house after being married, the company gathered round them and left them at home; but alas! the poor couple when they came home had only boiled potatoes and a salt herring for their supper. When Raftery heard an account of this the next day he was laughing until the water ran from his eyes, and he never stopped till he made this poem about the wedding.[19]

Raftery's sense of humor may strike the modern reader as a bit unfeeling, but it is due to his memory to add that the song itself is impressive, both in its metrics and in his command of a satirical, mock-heroic spirit. He came at the very tag end of a great tradition, and his poems cannot stand comparison with those of an O'Rahilly

---

19. Douglas Hyde, *Songs Ascribed to Raftery* (Dublin, 1903), pp. 241–243.

or an O'Sullivan, but precisely because he was himself a peasant his songs seem to arise naturally from his people. This was a quality which Yeats found also in Hyde himself, the son of a country rector and a university scholar. "He had the folk mind as no modern man has had it," he was to write of him, and was to praise "that dialect which gets from Gaelic its syntax and keeps its still partly Tudor vocabulary." Yeats's volume *Dramatis Personae* offers a charming picture of Hyde and himself at work at Coole Park, Yeats writing five or six lines a day, and Hyde scribbling away hour after hour, his mind, as Yeats puts it, unfettered by "our modern preoccupation with the mystery of life." He had no need, as has "the writer of some language exhausted by modern civilization," to "reject word after word, cadence after cadence."[20] Yeats's words hold admiration and irony in a delicate balance, perceiving in Hyde a simplicity which he had no wish to share.

Hyde suggested to Yeats the ways in which peasant idiom could become accessible, but the true intermediary between Yeats and the peasantry was Lady Gregory, whose relationship to Yeats was from the outset complex. Yeats and Hyde were her literary mentors even before she met them, and at the bidding of Yeats's prose she had already taken up the task of setting down into English the legends and folk tales of Ireland. And she had forged precisely the instrument of which he stood most in need: a language grounded firmly upon the syntax and diction of peasant Ireland, but flexible enough to encompass other and subtler purposes. The authenticity of that language—"Kiltartanese" as it has been termed by numerous well-informed detractors—must lie open to question. In my own judgment, it would be difficult to find in her work very many individual phrases or turns of speech which did not have actual existence in the English of County Galway, and yet the language, taken as a whole, seems a concoction,

20. Yeats, *Autobiography*, pp. 294–295.

and partly for reasons which are social in their source. She was a gentlewoman, setting down the words of her peasants or of old country people in the Galway workhouse, and she lacked Hyde's uncanny ability to enter without condescension a world of experience far removed from her own. But by the same measure, her mind possessed a complexity and toughness which placed it closer to that of Yeats. And unlike Hyde, she shared with Yeats a wish to create an Irish literature in English.

In 1902, in the first flowering of their collaboration, she produced one of the crucial texts of the Literary Revival, *Cuchulain of Muirthemne*, which draws together into a coherent narrative the fragmentary accounts of the hero's life, battles, and death. Her version of the *Tain*, the epic which is the center of the legend, is more paraphrase than translation, but a paraphrase at once brilliant and scholarly and one which has won the praise of Thomas Kinsella, the poet whose own translation is perhaps the finest we have. Her intention, and Yeats's, was that she should make the *Tain* available to her countrymen, and she at least succeeded in making it available to Yeats. In selecting a language, however, she made a curious and significant decision: she recast the versions she used, modern translations of the twelfth-century text found in the *Book of Leinster*, into the modern language of Kiltartan, to whose people the book is dedicated: "I have told the whole story in plain and simple words, in the same way my old nurse Mary Sheridan used to be telling stories from the Irish long ago, and I a child at Roxborough."[21] That is to say, she wedded an epic which arose within a prefeudal and intensely hierarchical culture to the language of a modern peasantry.

Yeats was to call it a language beautiful and powerful, and in his introduction to her book he writes: "I knew of no language to write about Ireland in but raw modern English; but now Lady Gregory has

---

21. Lady Gregory, *Cuchulain of Muirthemne* (Oxford University Press, 1970), p. 5.

discovered a speech as beautiful as that of Morris, and a living speech into the bargain. As she moved about among her people she learned to love the beautiful speech of those who think in Irish, and to understand that it is as true a dialect of English as the dialect that Burns wrote in. It is some hundreds of years old, and age gives a language authority. We find in it the vocabulary of the translators of the Bible, joined to an idiom which makes it tender, compassionate, and complaisant, like the Irish language."[22] It would be difficult to sort out the number of cultural generalizations which are compacted within that statement. The peasants themselves would, I think, plead piously that they and their fathers before them had had little contact with the King James version of the Bible. But Lady Gregory, who was raised in a family of strict evangelical Protestants, had indeed had such contact, and Yeats is correct in detecting biblical contributions to the vocabulary of Kiltartanese. Her family was in fact notorious among the peasantry through its efforts to proselytize with the aid of that very Bible. In Ireland, such facts are known, remembered, and are sooner or later put to malicious account.

The great figures of the Irish Literary Revival, virtually without exception, were Protestant, and either members of the landlord class or else, as in Yeats's case, allied with it by sentiment. In point of fact, the two supreme artists of the movement, Yeats and Synge, were not Christian at all but pagan; in Ireland, however, religion is a mark of cultural identity, not to be washed away by mere disbelief. Almost from the first, therefore, in clerical and in certain nationalist circles, suspicions were harbored as to the movement which now was in the process of formation. They were suspicions lacking equally in generosity and in perceptiveness, for nothing could be more certain than that the architects of the revival, and Yeats above all the others, had in view the creation of a community. But neither had

---

22. Lady Gregory, *Cuchulain of Muirthemne*, p. 12.

Yeats rightly gauged the depth of those fissures by which Irish life was fragmented.

The most vivid but not the earliest manifestation of these suspicions occurred in 1899, when the Irish Literary Theatre, a collaborative enterprise by Yeats, Lady Gregory, and Edward Martyn, presented Yeats's play *The Countess Cathleen* at the Ancient Concert Rooms. It is a simple play: Yeats, unfortunately, as matters developed, called it "a miracle play." Starving peasants in a time of famine sell their souls to demons disguised as merchants, but the souls are purchased back, at the expense of her own, by the countess. It had not occurred to Yeats that his play at once vilified the peasantry and outraged Catholic sensibilities, but such was apparently the case. Cardinal Logue condemned it, without having either read or seen it, thereby setting a precedent which was not lost upon later generations, and at the opening performance there were organized disturbances which rose at last to "a storm of booing and hissing." On the following day, students at the Royal University composed a letter of denunciation and set about getting signatures. But one signature which they did not get was that of young James Joyce, who had been an admiring spectator the night before, and who now made a dramatic event of his refusal to join the protest.

"We feel it our duty," says the letter, "in the name and for the honor of Dublin Catholic students at the Royal University, to protest against an art, even a dispassionate art, which offers as a type of our people a loathsome brood of apostates."[23] "Even a dispassionate art..."; Joyce himself could not have contrived a better phrase. His refusal to sign was of course remembered against him, as doubtless he intended, and upon a later occasion he was publicly reproved by a leading article in the university magazine: "If Mr. Joyce thinks that the artist must stand apart from the multitude, and means he must

23. Quoted in Richard Ellmann, *James Joyce* (Oxford University Press, 1959, 1965), p. 69.

also sever himself from the moral and religious teachings which, under Divine guidance, moulded its spiritual character, we join issue with him, and we prophesy but ill-success for any school which offers the Irish public art based upon such a principle."[24]

In a letter to a Dublin newspaper, published three days after the letter by the Catholic students, Yeats asserted, with a seeming indifference to their protest, that Cardinal Logue "represents in no way the opinion of the younger and more intellectual Catholics, who have read his letter with astonishment."[25] He does not provide, wisely no doubt, the names of these broad-minded young gentlemen. He would have been unable to offer Joyce's name, for at that time Joyce was entirely unknown to him, a situation which was shortly to be remedied. Joyce was well-known in circles of literary undergraduates, but not beyond them, although a year later, in his own twentieth year, his essay on Ibsen would appear in the *Fortnightly Review*. At this time, as his paper on "Drama and Life" makes clear, he regarded drama as a higher form of art than literature, a communal art of widespread domain, in which "the artist forgoes his very self and stands a mediator in awful truth before the veiled face of God."[26]

It is appropriate, perhaps inevitable, that this first conjunction of Yeats and Joyce should rest upon an irony. Yeats believed, at least as strongly as did Joyce, that drama is a communal art. He had founded the Literary Theatre for precisely that reason. But he had a more complex and a less intransigent sense of the necessary relationships between artist and community. The rough reception which had been accorded to *The Countess Cathleen* had a curious and entangled effect

24. Ellmann, *James Joyce*, p. 94.

25. W. B. Yeats, in a letter to *The Morning Leader* (May 13, 1899); reprinted in *The Letters of W. B. Yeats*, edited by Allan Wade (Macmillan, 1955), p. 319.

26. *The Critical Writings of James Joyce*, edited by Ellsworth Mason and Richard Ellmann (Viking, 1959), p. 42.

upon him. His confrontation with the Catholic and nationalist establishments he found oddly exhilarating: his long warfare with his society had now begun. But he also decided that the disturbances were in part his own fault: "In using what I considered traditional symbols I forgot that in Ireland they are not symbols but realities."[27] They were, in fact, the chief symbols of Christian belief, and his forgetfulness is therefore impressive in its proportions. He had a strategist's awareness of the community with which he was involved, a fiercely partisan, culturally defensive, and aesthetically unsophisticated audience which required delicate and tactful handling. But this society was the series of constricting nets which Joyce was determined to fly above on the strong wings of an uncompromising art. These conflicting ambitions established firmly the ground of a coming misunderstanding.

> *Who will go drive with Fergus now,*
> *And pierce the deep wood's woven shade,*
> *And dance upon the level shore?*

Aleel's lovely lyric from *The Countess Cathleen* runs, a leitmotiv, through *Ulysses*, a touchstone, for Stephen Dedalus as for James Joyce, of a clear and unconstrained beauty. And Joyce's response toward its author was complex and powerful. In 1918, after Yeats had purchased Ballylee's old square tower, he wrote to a friend: "I am making a setting for my old age, a place to influence lawless youth, with its security and antiquity. If I had had this tower of mine when Joyce began to write, I daresay I might have been of use to him, have got him to meet those who might have helped him."[28] Imagination falters, unable to form a picture of young Joyce, long-jawed and sardonic, stalking grimly beside Yeats as they went from cabin to cabin, gathering fireside tales

---

27. Yeats, *Autobiography*, p. 279.

28. *The Letters of W. B. Yeats*, p. 651.

of Raftery and Mary Hynes, or standing, rigid with taciturn hilarity, upon the battlements, as Yeats pointed out to him the seven woods which sheltered Coole Park and Lady Gregory from the Atlantic winds.

> *And no more turn aside and brood*
> *Upon love's bitter mystery;*
> *For Fergus rules the brazen cars.*

As Stephen Dedalus stands atop a different tower, the Martello tower at Sandycove, lines from *The Countess Cathleen* drift through his mind, and prompt a delicate, wonderfully exact evocation of the world created by Yeats's early verse:

> Wood shadows floated silently by through the morning peace from the stairhead seaward where he gazed. Inshore and farther out the mirror of water whitened, spurned by lightshod hurrying feet. White breast of the dim sea. The twining stresses, two by two. A hand plucking the harp-strings merging their twining chords. Wavewhite wedded words shimmering on the dim tide.[29]

The world evoked is that of *The Wind Among the Reeds* and *The Shadowy Waters*, a self-contained world of murmuring voices, dim, luminous colors, intricate and haunting cadences, a poetry half in love with an unimaginable beauty, half in love with its own loveliness. Yeats's early poetry and the poetry of his early prose existed for Joyce as a strong web of delicate symbols, sheltering within its gossamer sheen a subtle and austere rebelliousness. He committed to memory the words of two of the early stories, and like Stephen, like the unnamed narrator of "Araby," carried them through the raw, damp chill of Dublin autumns. They created a lovely and coherent world,

---

29. James Joyce, *Ulysses* (Random House, 1961), p. 9.

which by its very coherence offered an unspoken rebuke to the world in which he found himself—the rancorous, squalid, and repressive world of Dublin and Ireland.

That Yeats, whom Joyce honored as a symbolist poet, aloof from society and indifferent to its clamors, should at that very moment be finding ways of coming to terms with the society was an irony which Joyce was as yet unprepared to savor. The spectacle of his classmates denouncing *The Countess Cathleen* fortified his suspicions as to the populace and its attitudes toward art, and confirmed his belief that nationalism and the Church were powerful twin opponents of imaginative freedom. Yeats would not have lacked sympathy with this harsh and uncompromising judgment, but he was concerned for the moment with establishing a movement and a theater.

Two years later, in 1901, that theater was preparing its third season, and Yeats astutely smoothed its way by issuing the first number of *Samhain*, a journal in which he hoped to set forth the aspirations and the national character of the dramatic movement, and thus, perhaps, forestall riots. The theater would that season present Douglas Hyde's version in Irish of one of Yeats's Red Hanrahan stories, and Yeats's play based upon the ancient legend of Diarmuid and Grania. The choices could not have offended anyone, but Yeats was taking no chances, and *Samhain* fairly oozes with goodwill. The names of priests are invoked with that special deference heard in Ireland only when a Protestant is addressing an audience of Catholics, and Yeats goes to considerable length to express his popular sympathies: "All Irish writers have to choose whether they will write as the upper classes have done, not to express but to exploit this country; or join the intellectual movement which has raised the cry that was heard in Russia in the seventies, the cry, 'To the people.'"[30] Having seen this conciliatory message through the press, he returned to his rehearsals.

---

30. W. B. Yeats, *Samhain* (1901); reprinted in *Explorations* (Macmillan, 1962), p. 83.

Joyce read it with cold fury, and with cold fury wrote and published his response. The measure of anger may be taken by the fact that he paid for the publication of his pamphlet with his own money, an experiment which he was never tempted to repeat. *The Day of the Rabblement* opens upon a note which is sustained throughout: "No man, said the Nolan, can be a lover of the true or the good unless he abhors the multitude, and the artist, though he may employ the crowd, is very careful to isolate himself." He disposes of Edward Martyn and George Moore, collaborators in the project, with a few implacable words (Martyn, he says with uncharitable accuracy, is disabled by an incorrigible style), but gives close attention to Yeats: "It is equally unsafe at present to say of Mr. Yeats that he has or has not genius. In aim and form *The Wind among the Reeds* is poetry of the highest order, and *The Adoration of the Magi* (a story which one of the great Russians might have written) shows what Mr. Yeats can do when he breaks with the half-gods. But an aesthete has a floating will, and Mr. Yeats's treacherous instinct of adaptability must be blamed for his recent association with a platform from which even self-respect should have urged him to refrain." The Irish Literary Theatre, he concludes, has surrendered to the trolls, and must now be considered the property of "the rabblement of the most belated race in Europe."[31]

Like all of Joyce's early prose, the pamphlet rings with a steely authority, urbanity flung like a careless cloak across a murderous sword. But the phrase which I have just quoted suggests a depth of feeling not fully accounted for by his apparent objective. It was to this most belated of races that Yeats had turned for inspiration, and Joyce regarded as infernal the collaboration between an artist and "a nation which never advanced so far as a miracle play," as he says in malicious reference to Yeats's claim for *The Countess Cathleen*. Nor

---

31. James Joyce, *The Day of the Rabblement* (Dublin: Gerrard Bros., 1901); reprinted in *Critical Writings*.

would he have been heartened by the news that Douglas Hyde had dramatized, and in Irish, Yeats's story of "The Twisting of the Rope and Hanrahan the Red." The center of Joyce's attack is what he takes to be Yeats's instinct of "adaptability," but at the buried heart of that center is his half-uncomprehending detestation of Yeats's involvement with peasant and primitive Ireland. The "folk" whom Yeats celebrated, the "people" to whom his art was dedicated, were for Joyce the dark, bitter bog of the past. In 1901, he believed that he had discovered in the forms and energies of modern European art the courage and liberality of spirit which he required to liberate himself from that past. Yeats, London aesthete, Rhymers Club poet, symbolist, had turned by conscious and willing choice to precisely that past from which Joyce was struggling to free himself. He was poised between two modes of transcendence—the harsh moral and social realism of Ibsenite drama, and the aestheticism of the early Yeats. And he now saw Yeats surrendering to the half-gods and the trolls.

Yeats and Joyce met on only a few occasions, but the first of these meetings has passed into legend. It was in October 1902, exactly a year after *The Day of the Rabblement*, and through the offices of Yeats's friend George Russell (AE), who had written to him: "The first spectre of the new generation has appeared. His name is Joyce. I have suffered from him and I would like you to suffer."[32] Yeats was thirty-seven at the time, and Joyce barely twenty. By Joyce's artful design, they met not at AE's but on Nassau Street, near the National Library, and walked to the smoking room of a café. Several versions of the legendary encounter exist, the most circumstantial and probably the most accurate being a manuscript which Yeats intended as a preface to *Ideas of Good and Evil*. All the versions dwell upon Joyce's arrogance, which is beyond dispute: at twenty he was insufferable. But it is worth mentioning that when Herbert Gorman summarized

---

32. Quoted by Ellmann, *James Joyce*, p. 104.

several of them in his biography, Joyce remarked on the galley proof: "J. J. had at this time an immense admiration for Yeats as a poet."[33]

It is a pity that Yeats did not publish his account with *Ideas of Good and Evil*. Although the form of Yeats's account is loosely narrative, it is the clearest and most suggestive statement of what he took to be the necessary relationship between the modern artist and traditional folk culture, enlivened by his amused, slightly exasperated sympathy toward the extraordinary creature who had come before him. He was now drawing his plots from folklore, he explained to Joyce; a proof, Joyce suggested, that he was deteriorating. The plots came to him easily, he said; Joyce remarked that this made matters certain. Impatient, Yeats picked up the manuscript volume of stories which Joyce had brought with him, pointed to a page, and said, "You got that from somebody else who got it from the folk." No, Joyce replied equably, his book owed nothing to anything but his own mind, which was nearer to God than to folklore. At this point, Yeats arose and walked up and down in his vexation, delivering a lengthy lecture which explained the dependence of all true art upon popular tradition—an unusual occurrence within the decent confines of a Dublin café but well within his capacity for exalted obliviousness. He closed upon resounding references to the art of Homer, of Shakespeare, and of Chartres Cathedral. Joyce said, "Generalizations aren't made by poets; they are made by men of letters." And thence the encounter moved toward its celebrated conclusion:

> Presently he got up to go, and, as he was going out, he said, "I am twenty. How old are you?" I told him, but I am afraid I said I was a year younger than I am. He said with a sigh, "I thought as much. I have met you too late. You are too old."[34]

33. Ellmann, *James Joyce*, p. 105.

34. Ellmann, *James Joyce*, p. 108.

Joyce left his manuscripts with Yeats, who returned them with a long and sympathetic letter, which includes this passage: "The qualities which make a man succeed do not show in his verse, often, for quite a long time. They are much less qualities of talent than qualities of character—faith (of this you have probably enough), patience, adaptability (without this one learns nothing), and a gift for growing by experience and this is perhaps the rarest of all."[35] Clearly, Joyce's reference to his "treacherous instinct of adaptability" had lodged somewhere in his mind, perhaps because it had struck a nerve. A month later, by Yeats's introduction, Joyce was dining with Lady Gregory. "The members of the Irish literary movement," as Richard Ellmann says, "were doing their best for Joyce, but all were to discover that he was not a man to be helped with impunity."[36]

"*6 April, later:*" Stephen Dedalus writes in his journal, on the eve of his flight from Ireland to Europe. "Michael Robartes remembers forgotten beauty and, when his arms wrap her round, he presses in his arms the loveliness which has long faded from the world. Not this. Not at all. I desire to press in my arms the loveliness which has not yet come into the world."[37] The reference is to the lyric in *The Wind Among the Reeds* which first was called "O'Sullivan Rua to Mary Lavell," and finally, "He Remembers Forgotten Beauty." The meanings, as of all Stephen's cryptic journal entries, are multiple, but among them is his rejection of an artistic passion which draws its fires from traditional objects of veneration, or from traditional modes of feeling. And this may be taken, if in a loose way, to define Joyce's own resistance to the Celtic aesthetic which Yeats was formulating. But the resistance was as much psychological as it was aesthetic, and it had also its distinct social and even political overtones. The Anglo-Irish

---

35. Ellmann, *James Joyce*, p. 108.

36. Ellmann, *James Joyce*, pp. 108–109.

37. James Joyce, *A Portrait of the Artist as a Young Man* (Viking, 1964), p. 251.

Yeats had chosen Ireland, exercising an option, making use of that dual-citizenship passport with which every Anglo-Irishman was born. But Ireland was Joyce's fate, a condition of his being with which he could come to terms only through rebellion.

In *A Portrait of the Artist*, Stephen finds himself involved in a verbal misunderstanding with the English-born dean of studies, and thinks: "The language in which we are speaking is his before it is mine. How different are the words *home*, *Christ*, *ale*, *master*, on his lips and on mine! I cannot speak or write these words without unrest of spirit. His language, so familiar and so foreign, will always be for me an acquired speech. I have not made or accepted its words. My voice holds them at bay. My soul frets in the shadow of his language."[38] At the heart of this may rest Stephen's arrogant refusal to accept any language save that which he can himself freshly remint, but the surface is shaped by his perception that he speaks the language of his masters, imposed upon the enslaved people of whom he is a part. "My ancestors threw off their language and took another," he tells Davin, the country-bred Gaelic enthusiast. "They allowed a handful of foreigners to subject them."[39] And James Joyce, shaped equally by the native Irish community and by his rebellion against it, prisoner struggling against its tangled chains of memory and feeling, viewed the Irish past through somber eyes. Peasant Ireland was the dark soil of his past, offering to him neither light nor liberation, its emblem not seabird or hawk, but bat, blindly circling cabin and bogside. An entry in Stephen's journal offers his, but not Joyce's, final view of the matter:

14 April: John Alphonsus Mulrennan has just returned from the west of Ireland. (European and Asiatic papers please copy.) He

38. Joyce, *A Portrait of the Artist as a Young Man*, p. 189.

39. Joyce, *A Portrait of the Artist as a Young Man*, p. 203.

told us he met an old man there in a mountain cabin. Old man had red eyes and short pipe. Old man spoke Irish. Mulrennan spoke Irish. Then old man and Mulrennan spoke English. Mulrennan spoke to him about universe and stars. Old man sat, listened, smoked, spat. Then said:

—Ah, there must be terrible queer creatures at the latter end of the world.[40]

This bleakly comic exchange between peasant and language enthusiast had been anticipated in the review which Joyce wrote in 1903 of Lady Gregory's *Poets and Dreamers*, which gathers together some essays on peasant poetry, translations of Douglas Hyde's little plays (including the one which had helped to provoke *The Day of the Rabblement*), and an extended account of conversations which Lady Gregory had conducted with old men and old women in the cabins and workhouses of Galway. Lady Gregory had herself arranged that the *Daily Express* should send Joyce books for review, and Longworth, its editor, naturally but quite mistakenly believed that he was placing *Poets and Dreamers* in friendly hands. Joyce spends little time with Hyde's plays, which he dismisses as dwarf drama: Ibsen was still furnishing his vocabulary with dwarfs and trolls. And Raftery fares little better: "He took shelter one day from the rain under a bush: at first the bush kept out the rain, and he made verses praising it, but after a while it let the rain through, and he made verses dispraising it."[41] Joyce had already gone far toward mastering that murderous neutrality by which an object is allowed to reveal its own absurdity. But it is the folk, and that imaginative habit by which the folk is celebrated, which stands at the center of his wintry prose:

---

40. Joyce, *A Portrait of the Artist as a Young Man*, p. 251.

41. Joyce, *Critical Writings*, p. 104.

In her new book she has left legends and heroic youth far behind, and has explored in a land almost fabulous in its sorrow and senility. Half of her book is an account of old men and old women in the West of Ireland. These old people are full of stories about giants and witches, and dogs and black-handled knives, and they tell their stories one after another at great length and with many repetitions (for they are people of leisure) by the fire or in the yard of a workhouse. It is difficult to judge well of their charms and herb-healing, for that is the province of those who are learned in these matters and can compare the customs of countries, and, indeed, it is well not to know these magical-sciences, for if the wind changes while you are cutting wild camomile you will lose your mind.

"In fine," he concludes, her book, wherever it treats of the "folk," sets forth "in the fulness of its senility a class of mind which Mr. Yeats has set forth with such delicate scepticism in his happiest book, 'The Celtic Twilight.'"[42] The compliment is barbed: Yeats had recently published an essay praising William Morris as "the happiest of poets," but implying that happiness was not the condition most appropriate for high art. But these gnarled and crabbed old people of the west exercised a power over Joyce which his prose, the stiff urbanity of a provincial cosmopolitan, strives to conceal. "I fear him," Stephen writes of Mulrennan's cabin dweller. "I fear his redrimmed horny eyes. It is with him I must struggle all through this night till day come, till he or I lie dead, gripping him by the sinewy throat till...Till what? Till he yield to me? No. I mean him no harm."[43] Joyce's struggle with that weighty past made emblematic in the figure of the old Irish-speaking peasant was resolved in his art only when he came to

42. Joyce, *Critical Writings*, pp. 104–105.

43. Joyce, *A Portrait of the Artist as a Young Man*, p. 252.

write "The Dead," that story of lovely and intertwined resolutions in which the constricting bonds of self fall away from Gabriel Conroy, as he stands by his window in the Gresham Hotel, watching a snow which falls "on every part of the dark, central plain, on the treeless hills, falling softly upon the Bog of Allen and, farther westward, softly falling into the dark mutinous Shannon waves." And for Gabriel, the messenger of that resolution is not an old man, but one who died young, Michael Furey of Oughterard, who died in Galway, and about whose memory in Gretta Conroy's mind is entwined a folk song, "The Lass of Aughrim."

Joyce left the Irish literary movement much as he had entered it, stiff, hostile, suspicious. "That mumming company," as he calls it in "The Holy Office," his farewell broadside of departure.

> But I must not accounted be
> One of that mumming company—

The lines echo satirically Yeats's poem, "To Ireland in the Coming Times":

> Know, that I would accounted be
> True brother of a company
> That sang, to sweeten Ireland's wrong.

And the litany of mummers begins, of course, with Yeats:

> With him who hies him to appease
> His giddy dames' frivolities
> While they console him when he whinges
> With gold-embroidered Celtic fringes— [44]

---

44. Joyce, *Critical Writings*, pp. 150.

And in "Gas from a Burner," his publisher boasts:

> *Though (asking your pardon) as for the verse*
> *'Twould give you a heartburn on your arse.*
> *I printed folklore from North and South*
> *By Gregory of the Golden Mouth:*
> *I printed poets, sad, silly and solemn:*
> *I printed Patrick What-do-you-Colm:*
> *I printed the great John Milicent Synge*
> *Who soars above on an angel's wing*
> *In the playboy shift that he pinched as swag....*[45]

Buck Mulligan, in *Ulysses*, shouts to Stephen in mock reproach: "Longworth is awfully sick, after what you wrote about that old hake Gregory. O you inquisitional drunken jew jesuit! She gets you a job on the paper and then you go and slate her drivel to Jaysus. Couldn't you do the Yeats touch? The most beautiful book that has come of our country in my time. One thinks of Homer."[46] He misquotes. Yeats had in fact written: "I think this book is the best that has come out of Ireland in my time. Perhaps I should say that it is the best book that has ever come out of Ireland; for the stories which it tells are a chief part of Ireland's gift to the imagination of the world—and it tells them perfectly for the first time."[47] But the misquotation is correct in spirit, for Yeats was writing of Lady Gregory's *Cuchulain of Muirthemne*, the translation which seemed to him to answer the claim of his youth that the story of Cuchulain was an epic "needing only deliberate craft to be scarce less than Homer." But of course it is *Ulysses* itself, the book within which Stephen and Mulligan walk, that bids

---

45. Joyce, *Critical Writings*, p. 244.

46. Joyce, *Ulysses*, p. 216.

47. Lady Gregory, *Cuchulain of Muirthemne*, preface by W. B. Yeats, p. 11.

us think of Homer. When, in the 1880s and 1890s, Yeats called for a heroic literature, he had not any book like Joyce's *Ulysses* in mind, but heroic spirits, when they answer Glendower's call, are likely to emerge from the vasty deep in unexpected forms. Defending *Ulysses* on the floor of the Irish Senate in 1927, he was hampered by his own uncertain feelings; it is far from clear that he ever read it through in its entirety. "It has our Irish cruelty," he had written to Olivia Shakespeare, "and also our kind of strength and the Martello Tower pages are full of beauty—a cruel playful mind—like a great soft tiger cat."[48] But to the senators he said, in words which measure the largeness of his own nature: "I do not know whether Joyce's *Ulysses* is a great work of literature. I have puzzled a great deal over that question. All I will say is that it is the work of an heroic mind."[49]

The Martello tower is an ugly graceless building, thrown up hastily at the instructions of an alien Ministry of War, its history recent and accidental, and the only past which speaks to us from its stones is that of the young man who lived there for a few weeks, and the surrogate self whom he placed there for the few early-morning hours of June 16, 1904. That surrogate self is a man doubly dispossessed—by Mulligan, the gay and mocking Irish betrayer, and Haines, the visiting Englishman who affects an interest in things Irish. "It is a symbol of Irish art," Stephen thinks, looking into Mulligan's shaving mirror; "The cracked lookingglass of a servant." "Cracked lookingglass of a servant," Mulligan cries. "Tell that to the oxy chap downstairs and touch him for a guinea."[50] Beneath his eyes, the old woman bringing milk for morning tea becomes the *shan van vocht*,

---

48. *The Letters of W. B. Yeats*, p. 679 (March 8, 1923).

49. *The Senate Speeches of W. B. Yeats*, edited by Donald R. Pearce (Indiana University Press, 1960), p. 148.

50. Joyce, *Ulysses*, pp. 6–7.

the personification of Ireland in the verses of the eighteenth-century poets and in Yeats's *Cathleen Ni Houlihan*: "A wandering crone, lowly form of an immortal serving her conqueror and her gay betrayer, their common cuckquean, a messenger from the secret morning. To serve or to upbraid, whether he could not tell: but scorned to beg her favour."[51] "I am the servant of two masters," he tells Haines, "an English and an Italian.... And a third there is, who wants me for odd jobs." "I can quite understand that," Haines tells him with the inane benevolence of the conqueror, as deadly as earlier tyranny. "An Irishman must think like that, I daresay. We feel in England that we have treated you rather unfairly. It seems history is to blame."[52]

But history, that particular history, is the nightmare from which Stephen is trying to escape. "This race and this country and this life produced me," he had told Davin. "I shall express myself as I am."[53] "You suspect," he tells Bloom in the cabman's shelter off Butt Bridge, where they have just encountered a wandering, mythomaniacal sailor named W. B. Murphy, "that I may be important because I belong to the *faubourg Saint Patrice* called Ireland for short.... But I suspect that Ireland may be important because it belongs to me." "What belongs?" Bloom asks, puzzled. "Excuse me. Unfortunately I didn't catch the latter portion. What was it you...." "We can't change the country," Stephen says. "Let us change the subject."[54] Ireland, or Dublin to be more exact, had indeed become a part of Joyce's imagination: he had liberated himself from it by taking possession of it. "The whole ugliness of the modern world," Yeats had told him in 1902, "has come from the spread of the towns and their ways of

---

51. Joyce, *Ulysses*, p. 14.

52. Joyce, *Ulysses*, p. 20.

53. Joyce, *A Portrait of the Artist as a Young Man*, p. 203.

54. Joyce, *Ulysses*, p. 645.

thought and to bring back beauty we must marry the spirit and nature again."[55] But Joyce recognized the town as the countryside which is precisely ours, and he discovered his folk upon its crowded streets, catching their speech in public houses thick with gossip, song, profanity, and the smell of spilled porter.

"It's what I'm telling you, mister honey," Mulligan says to Stephen in a fair imitation of Kiltartanese laced with Synge-song, "it's queer and sick we were, Haines and myself, the time himself brought it in. 'Twas murmer we did for a gallus potion would rouse a friar, I'm thinking, and he limp with letching."[56] But Joyce's ear caught a different folk speech: "The bloody mongrel let a growl out of him that would give you the creeps. Be a corporal work of mercy if someone would take the life of that bloody dog. I'm told for a fact he ate a good part off the breeches of a constabulary man in Santry that came round one time with a blue paper about a license."[57] *Ulysses* is many kinds of book: one thinks of Homer. Among them, it contains a culture, the many-tongued voice of a culture. Stephen struggles to throw off that society, Bloom intrudes upon it: exile and alien, they define its contours.

The two towers, Ballylee and Martello, are separated by the full width of the small island they share. "An ancient bridge and a more ancient tower, / A farmhouse that is sheltered by its wall, / An acre of stony ground, / Where the symbolic rose can break in flower, / Old ragged elms, old thorns innumerable...." "There is no obstacle / But Gregory's wood and one bare hill / Whereby the haystack- and roof-levelling wind, / Bred on the Atlantic can be stayed." "I pace upon the battlements and stare / On the foundations of a house; or where / Tree, like a sooty finger, starts from the earth." For us, as first for him,

55. Quoted by Ellmann, *James Joyce*, p. 101.

56. Joyce, *Ulysses*, p. 199.

57. Joyce, *Ulysses*, p. 295.

Yeats's tower is a symbol of his art and self; imagination, the intricately conjoined powers of sun and moon, have established his claim to tower, stair, and bridge. From the battlements of Joyce's tower, one looks across the dull gray waters of Dublin Bay toward the Hill of Howth, remembered by Molly Bloom in images which were a portion of Joyce's memory. Dublin lies stretched along the crotch of curving shore between hill and tower, the sleeping giant of *Finnegans Wake*, the improbable, extravagant answer to Yeats's demand for a literature founded upon the ancient heroic epics. Between the two towers, nets of words cross and recross, uttered at cross-purposes; glittering and shadowed, they fill the capacious air.

"The poets of Ireland," a manuscript of the ninth century tells us, "were one day gathered around Senchan Torpeist, to see if they could recall the *Tain Bo Cuailnge*[58] in its entirety. But they all said they only knew parts of it."

—*Critical Inquiry*, Autumn 1975

---

58. *The Tain*, translated by Thomas Kinsella (Dublin: Dolmen Press, 1969), p. 1.

17

JAMES JOYCE AND THE
IMAGINATION OF IRISH HISTORY

AN ESSAY WITH such a title would seem to have its epigraph chosen in advance: it is one of the most famous sentences in *Ulysses*, perhaps the most famous, with the exception of "yes I said yes I will Yes." "History," Stephen Dedalus says to Mr. Deasy, the schoolmaster who employs him, "is a nightmare from which I am trying to awake." Stephen, as we know, is thinking of history in its largest terms, the chain of inexorable events by which the individual soul is bound and circumscribed. History is the "art" which Joyce assigns to that episode in his scheme for the novel, which is suffused with Stephen's reflections upon it. But the context of this utterance makes it clear that at the moment he has Irish history most immediately in mind. Mr. Deasy, in his querulous, hectoring way, has been lecturing Stephen on the rights and wrongs of the quarrels between loyalists and "fenians," Irish Catholics and Irish Protestants, his facts a garble of historical half-truths. Thus, because he assumes that Stephen is a Catholic, he assumes that he is also a "fenian." The error is so egregious that Stephen, for all his sardonic alertness, makes not a flicker of internal response: egregious, but also, within the context of Irish life, habitual. Mr. Deasy, Protestant, loyalist, uncertain as to whether to call himself English or Irish, is the counterpart of Stephen's university friend Davin, in *A Portrait of the Artist*, and of the bellicose and hyper-Irish Citizen, whom we are to meet later in the "Cyclops" episode, although Joyce spares Stephen that encounter. Stephen, in his flinty way, feels a certain affection for Davin, a warmhearted, ingenuous fellow, but he thinks of him as "the peasant student," as "the rude Firbolg," and remembers that Davin had sat at the feet of "Michael Cusack, the Gael," who was to become the original of the Citizen.

Davin, the "young peasant," worships "the sorrowful legend of Ireland," his "rude imagination" shaped by "the broken lights of Irish myth," his attitude toward the Catholic religion that of a "dull-witted serf," his mind armed against "whatsoever of thought or of feeling came to him from England or by way of English culture." It is Davin who tells him of the peasant woman he had encountered one night in the Ballyhoura hills, half undressed, hair unbound, standing at her cottage door, furtively sexual, and who becomes for Stephen "a type of her race and his own, a batlike soul waking to the consciousness of itself in darkness and secrecy and loneliness." (History, incidentally, was later to come upon Davin with a vengeance: he was based upon a university friend of Joyce's named George Clancy, who was to become an officer of the IRA, and was murdered by the Black and Tans.) It is to Davin that Stephen utters the most comprehensive of his rejections. Davin has been urging him to join the national cause, and Stephen, famously, answers him, "You talk to me of nationality, language, religion. I shall try to fly by those nets." "But a man's country comes first," Davin says. "Ireland first, Stevie." And Stephen answers, with cold violence, "Do you know what Ireland is? Ireland is the old sow that eats her farrow."

Davin has been shaped with affection for his actual virtues, but Michael Cusack, his mentor, appears in *Ulysses* as a grotesque, a foul-mouthed and mean-spirited chauvinist, his mind nurtured upon a stale version of history which is as mangy and ill-smelling as his repellent dog Garryowen, that travesty of the traditional Irish wolfhound, itself a cliché of nationalist iconography, one with the harp and the round tower:

> We'll put force against force. We have our greater Ireland beyond the sea. They were driven out of house and home in the black 47. Their mudcabins and their sheilings by the roadside were laid low by the batteringram and the *Times* rubbed its hands and told the whitelivered Saxons there would soon be as few Irish in Ireland as redskins in America. Even the grand Turk sent us his piastres. But the Sassenach tried to starve the nation at home while the land was full of crops that the British hyenas bought and sold in Rio de Janeiro. Ay, they drove out the peasants in hordes. Twenty thousand of them died in the coffinships. But those that came to the land of the free remember the land of bondage. And they will come again with a vengeance, no cravens, the sons of Granuaile, the champions of Kathleen ni Houlihan.

And the theme is taken up, if less stridently, by Ned Lambert: "We are a long time waiting for that day, citizen. Since the poor old woman told us that the French were on the sea and landed at Killala." And by John Wyse Nolan: "Ay. We fought for the royal Stuarts that reneged us against the Williamites and they betrayed us. Remember Limerick and the broken treatystone." The exhortation is rhetorical, for no one in Barney Kiernan's pub, save perhaps Bloom, certainly not the cur Garryowen, need be told to remember Limerick and the broken treaty stone: they are parts of the nationalist version of Irish history.

The bellicosity of Lambert and Nolan might be dismissed as public-house patriotism which fuels itself upon Guinness and Jameson, but the Citizen's is a different matter, even though he shares their fondness for the national beverages. For all that he is shaped as a comic grotesque, cut down and ridiculed by the episode's two narrators—both the unnamed, scurrilous Dubliner and that voice of windy mock-heroics which is his counterfoil—there is an actual distant thunder of violence behind his speech and his being. The nameless narrator may mock him, but never to his face, never in the presence of his mastiff and his blackthorn cudgel. Men did indeed die for Ireland, and George Clancy was not the only one yet to die, and they killed and were killed within the rhythms set by the Citizen's speech, the seamless garment of Ireland's sad, bloody history. The gravity of Joyce's theme is not established by language; the tone of presentation in this episode is broadly comic; even Bloom's words on behalf of love and gentleness are mocked, made to seem not merely ineffectual but silly. "But it's no use, says he. Force, hatred, history, all that. That's not life for men and women, insult and hatred. And everybody knows that its the very opposite of that that is really life." What, Alf Bergan asks, and "Love, says Bloom. I mean the opposite of hatred." And the voice of the episode picks up the word. "Love loves to love love. Nurse loves the new chemist. Constable 14A loves Mary Kelly. Gerty MacDowell loves the boy that has the bicycle. M. B. loves a fair gentleman. Li Chi Han lovey up kissy Cha Pu Chow. Jumbo, the elephant, loves Alice, the elephant...." The gravity, rather, is established by juxtaposition.

Ireland's wrongs and her hoped-for vengeance are not the only subjects under discussion in Barney Kiernan's. Bergan, who is a Dublin subsheriff, has been advertising in England for a hangman, and he has brought some of the replies to hand around, including one from "H. Rumbold, Master Barber." This brings the conversation around to hangings, killings, stabbings—and, in *Ulysses*, the murderous knife is the symbol of that violence which lies at the heart of history. It is the razor which lays upon the shavingbowl in the opening sentence. It is the lancet of Buck Mulligan, healer and betrayer. Stephen Dedalus, pondering the paradoxes of history, the actual as the destroyer of the possible, finds a knife for his image: "Had Pyrrus not been felled by a beldam's hand in Argos or Julius Caesar not been knifed to death?" More immediately, the knife is the image of Irish history. Remembering the past of his people, Stephen sees in "the starving cagework city a horde of jerkined dwarfs, my people, with flayers' knifes, running, scaling, hacking in green blubbery whalemeat. Famine, plague and slaughters. Their blood is in me, their lusts my waves." Kevin Egan, the Fenian conspirator with whom Stephen drinks in Paris, with his stories of conspiracies, vengeance, bomb plots, and deaths, who reminds Stephen that "You're your father's son," sings the fragment of a street ballad: "O, O, the boys of Kilkenny..." and there breaks off, but what the boys of Kilkenny were, the ballad tells us, were "stout roaring blades." But the knives which are *Ulysses*'s central image of Irish history are the knives which had been wielded in the Phoenix Park on the 6th of May 1882, the year of Joyce's birth, when the Invincibles hacked to death Lord Frederick Cavendish, the newly appointed Chief Secretary for Ireland, and Thomas Burke, the Under Secretary. Allusions to the Phoenix Park butchery flicker throughout *Ulysses*, until, at last, at night, Stephen and Bloom visit the Butt Bridge cabman's shelter, whose manager may be "Skin-the-Goat" Fitzharris, one of the Invincibles. The same event resonates through *Finnegans Wake*.

Irish history has, for Joyce, the configuration of a knife blade, with the Phoenix Park killings as its defining event—senseless butchery committed at the behest of Kathleen ni Houlihan, which is to say, at the bidding of a gnarled and narrow vision of history. (The actual killings, incidentally, were the quintessence of meaninglessness and sordidness. Only Burke was an intended victim. Cavendish, a well-meaning young man from whom moderate nationalists hoped much, was slain almost by accident. Most Irishmen were at the time revolted by the deed, and Parnell considered abandoning politics when he learned of it. The killers were ill-educated laboring men, with the exception of their leader, James Carey, and Carey, in a breathtaking example of perfidy, won his freedom by turning Crown witness and testifying against those who had followed his order. His freedom, but not his life: within weeks, he had been shot dead by a Fenian, who, in his turn, was tried and hanged. Bloom, as he sits in Hallows Church in Westland Row, remembers that Carey had reputedly been a daily communicant there: "And plotting murder all the time. Those crawthumpers, now that's a good name for them, there's always something shifty looking about them." But, and this is Joyce's point, it was a revulsion of the moment only. By 1904, the year in which *Ulysses* is set, the picture of the Invincibles had faded and mellowed; they had become part of the tapestry of Irish history, the gore which had stained the park faded away. What was remembered was the courage of Joe Brady, one of those hanged, inarticulate and unrepentant. Soon after the executions there was a street ballad so apt to his purposes that it is surprising that Joyce does not weave it in. It begins, "My name it is Joe Brady, and I'm called the Fenian blade." W. B. Murphy, the wandering seaman who joins Stephen and Bloom in Skin-the-Goat's, says, "And I seen a man killed in Trieste by an Italian chap. Knife in his back. Knife like that." And he draws what the narrator of that episode calls "a dangerous looking clasp-knife." "That's a good bit of steel," he adds, meditatively. Then he snaps it to, and stows it, says the narrator, "in his chamber of horrors, otherwise his pocket." One of the cabmen glosses: "They're great for the cold steel.... That was why they thought the park murder of the Invincibles was done by foreigners on account of them using knives." Skin-the-Goat, during this exchange, maintains an "inscrutable face, which was really a work of art, a perfect study in itself." "Oblige me," Stephen says to Bloom, who has been plying him with food, "by taking away that knife. I can't see the point of it. It reminds me of Roman history."

History, for Joyce, was universal. The knife lies at the root of all history, poised against it. But Irish history was, for him, its most urgent and most passionately felt manifestation. Felt urgently and felt passionately for several intertwined reasons. The history of Ireland, measured against those of other cultures, was a particularly somber one, and as squalid, almost, as it was somber. But it was a history which, as he recognized, was specifically his. Stephen thinks of Simon Dedalus as "the man with my eyes": he would cast off father, culture, race, but he knows that he cannot. "This race and this country and this life produced me," he tells Davin; "I shall express myself as I am." History to Stephen, taken in the full context of his thought and feeling, is the contingent universe which presses against his wish for a full and unconditional autonomy of being, but it is the history of his country which presses against his skin, and in part, as all three of Joyce's novels make clear, because in Ireland history is a part of the atmosphere, a density of the air men breathe. "We feel in England," Haines tells Stephen, "that we have treated you rather unfairly. It seems history is to blame."

Ulysses is a novel so richly and so abundantly full of its present, so fully crammed with the odors and sounds of June 16, 1904, that it is easy to miss the fact that it is a book saturated in history. And the explanation of that paradox is not far to seek. History is present, as it is in a culture dominated by it, in the modes of thought and consciousness of the novel's characters. A fully annotated *Ulysses* would require many hundreds of notes upon Irish history, although it is unlikely that this was one of Joyce's many fields of special knowledge. Quite to the contrary, his references, most of them, are drawn from the store of knowledge which would have been shared by most university-educated men of his generation, and especially by those from his Catholic and nationalist background. Thus, for example, in the "Aeolus" episode, set in the editorial office of the *Freeman's Journal*, the designated art is rhetoric, and the talk, turning to oratory, dwells upon two instances familiar to everyone in the room, Kendal Bushe's defense of the murderer Childe, and A. E. Taylor's defense of the Irish language, a defense which W. B. Yeats remembered as vividly as did Joyce. Neither of them in fact had heard Taylor's brilliant and elaborate speech, and, apparently, no exact copy of it was made at the time, but as a part of Dublin's popular culture, it became a mental landscape. In the "Sirens" episode, where the art is "music," Ben Dollard sings "The Croppy Boy" and summons up remembered patriotic emotions from the men gathered around him. In the "Wandering Rocks" episode, Ned Lambert and J. J. O'Malloy remember the great Norman family of the Fitzgeralds. "God," Lambert cries, "I forgot to tell him that one about the earl of Kildare after he set fire to Cashel Cathedral. You know that one? *I'm bloody sorry I did it,* says he, *but I declare to God I thought the archbishop was inside.* He mightn't like it, though. What? God, I'll tell him anyhow. That was the great earl, the Fitzgerald Mor. Hot members they were all of them, the Geraldines." The Dublin of 1904 possessed a rich oral culture, and Joyce was attentive to its tonalities, its turns of phrase, its allusions. Living within that culture, men knew that a wink was as good as a nod, and a phrase, from a corner of the mouth, as good as a sentence. Better, in fact, for the speaker could count upon his listeners to fill out the sentence, thus reaffirming community. "Who fears to speak of nineteen four?" Bloom thinks at one point: any Dubliner would have known that he was parodying the patriotic ballad "Who fears to speak of '98?"

We are accustomed, and with good reason, to remember *Ulysses* as a novel which presents a broad panorama of urban life, and yet this is in part a carefully created illusion. Most of the characters are drawn from a very specific social stratum—most of its characters are middle class, Catholic, decently educated, and working at occupations whose middling salaries are compensated for by the leisure time which is available to them, time to attend a funeral, time to meet on the street for a leisurely chat, to while away an afternoon in a hotel bar or a public house, to discuss oratory in a newspaper office and Shakespeare in a library. And most of them have a sense of living within history, within Irish history. They remember, or rather they misre-member the past, and they know that they have been shaped by their memories.

The novel's attitude toward this absorption within history is com-plex, elusive, and ambiguous. History has given to these characters a measure of their savor and tang, it is constituent of their particular humanness. But at the same time, the novel's massive and elaborate ironies are enrolled against it, mock it, place bleak and withering lights upon it. Stephen in his way and Bloom in his stand apart from the historical illusions which sustain the other characters. "Profes-sor" MacHugh, in the *Freeman's Journal* office, recites J. F. Taylor's speech to the Historical Society, and tells his listeners, who share his emotions, "That is oratory." But Stephen thinks: "Gone with the wind. Hosts at Mullaghmast and Tara of the kings. Miles of ears of porches. The tribune's words howled and scattered to the four winds. A people sheltered within his voice. Dead noise." Stephen, that is (here another footnote of annotation may be in order), is remember-ing a more powerful, more mythological orator than J. F. Taylor (whom Yeats, incidentally, in a withering phrase was to describe as "an obscure great orator"): he is remembering Daniel O'Connell, the great nineteenth-century tribune of Catholic Ireland, whose power was in part a power of the voice, whose "monster rallies" at, among other places, Mullaghmast and Tara, had drawn crowds numbering in the hundreds of thousands, a voice speaking to a submerged peo-ple, arousing them, enspiriting them. And he is remembering also, without need to formulate words for the memory, that the shelter was flimsy, that O'Connell's movement collapsed amidst the desolation of the Great Famine. Oratory is but dead noise, blown away upon the wind. Similarly, though in a very different key, that afternoon, in the Ormond Hotel, Bloom listens to Ben Dollard, bass barreltone, sing "The Croppy Boy." The tribal feelings which it evokes from his other listeners leave Bloom unmoved. "Chords dark. Lugugugubrious.

Low. In a cave of the dark middle earth. Embedded ore. Lump music. The voice of dark age, of unlove, earth's fatigue made grave approach, and painful, come from afar, from hoary mountains, called on good men and true." As Bloom is leaving the Ormond, Ben Dollard is singing another patriotic ballad of '98, "The Memory of the Dead," which can serve equally as a drinking song: "True men like you men, / Will lift your glass with us." (It is appropriate that many of the centenary '98 songs should have been written by P. J. McCall, who kept a public house in North Dublin.) And indeed, the men in the Ormond do lift a glass to the dead martyrs of '98—Tom Rochford and Bob Cowley and the others. But not Bloom, who has hurried outside because of a pressing attack of flatulence. Standing outside Lionel Marks's shop, viewing a print of the gallant, martyred Robert Emmet, his flatulence releases itself, intertwined with Emmet's speech from the dock, that his epitaph should not be written until his nation had taken its place among the nations of the world. Bloom's visceral response has, as its counterpoise, the narrative voice of the episode, that measured, remote voice which speaks of embedded ore, lump music, in a cave of dark middle earth. The Sirens of Homeric myth lured sailors to their deaths. Here, a song of death, the croppy boy, archetypal Irish rebel, father and brothers slain in battle, is deceived and captured by the yeoman captain in fiery red, is hanged in Geneva barracks, and the Dubliners in the Ormond die with him, drown their transient, pleasurable grief in whiskey. Music, like oratory, like patriotism, binds them to history. In the phantasmagoria of "Circe," "Rombold, Demon Barber," hangs the croppy boy, who protests that he bears "no hate to a living thing," while the Citizen calls out for "a cove with teeth as sharp as razors to slit the throats of the English dogs."

The Dublin of *Ulysses*, like the Dublin of *Dubliners* and *A Portrait of the Artist*, is a paralyzed city, the heart of a paralyzed culture. The sources and the manifestations of that paralysis are manifold, but it is palpable upon the page. In other countries, as Hugh Kenner has written, rivers, flowing through cities, bear away "all the past that floats," but Dublin has "kept its past above the waters," choosing "to preserve its form rather than its life." The past, in that context, is history, a shell, like the bowl of shells in Mr. Deasy's study, "an old pilgrim's hoard," Stephen thinks, "dead treasure, hollow shells," like the shells beneath his feet as he walks along Sandymount strand. But the novel's two protagonists, Stephen and Bloom, do not accommodate themselves to this patterned paralysis, although, as might be expected, this is so for quite different reasons. Stephen is engaged, quite consciously and deliberately, in a quarrel with history, in resistance to its crushing power, and however he fares with this quarrel— which is one of the questions upon which readings of the novel hinge —its existence sets him apart from the other Dubliners. Bloom too, though otherwise, is shielded from history's powerful narcotics. To be sure, he is bound by history in the immediate sense, bound by his own past, a father's suicide, a son's death, a wife's infidelity. But in the larger, though ultimately perhaps the less important sense of the word, the social sense, he is not bound. His race, his ancestral religion, the attitudes toward him of the other citizens of his city, separate and shield him. Oration, song, gesture lack resonance for him, and his reveries make it clear, by their absence of such linked allusions, that his sense of the Irish past is thin. What is his surest shield, however, is that his mind and his imagination are profoundly ahistorical. Not only is he rooted in the present, alert to its sights and odors —it is Bloom, rather than Stephen, the artist, who does the novel's *seeing*: it is through Bloom rather than Stephen that we learn how people look, how their voices sound—but the very atmosphere of his mind, his modes of thinking, are scientific, or at least quasi-scientific, and the scientific mind, curious as to how things work rather than how they came into being, fascinated by relationships rather than genealogies, is the antitype of the historical. This is by no means all gain. Bloom's defining loneliness runs deeper than the circumstances of his domestic situation. He is cut off from the life of this city which breathes history. Because of this spiritual isolation, he stands apart from its communal rituals and traditions, its invocations both of God and of the household gods of the tribe. At Mass in All Hollows, he watches the communicants: "The priest bent down to put it in her mouth, murmuring all the time. Latin. The next one. Shut your eyes and open your mouth. What? *Corpus*. Body. Corpse. Good idea the Latin. Stupefies them first. Hospice for the dying. They don't seem to chew it; only swallow it down. Rum idea eating bits of a corpse why the cannibals cotton to it." But, as he concedes idly the next moment: "There's a big idea behind it, kind of kingdom of God within you feel. First communicants. Hoky-poky penny a lump. They feel all like one family party, same in the theatre, all in the same swim." As with the large God, so with the local gods of history, tradition, shared legend. Bloom is inaccessible to their narcotic seductiveness, but by the same token he is inaccessible to the community which they have shaped.

The powerful impulse among the Irish to shape history into myth, and to serve that myth, is one from which Joyce himself was not immune. There is scarcely a hero in the pantheon of Irish nationalism who does not receive from *Ulysses* the same odorous wind with which Bloom favors Robert Emmet, with a single striking exception. In Joyce's imagination, and in his own imaginative reconstruction of Irish history, Charles Stewart Parnell bears a charmed life. His admiration of Parnell was intense and lifelong, and his first composition, lost to literary history, at the age of nine, was a poem which, presumably, joined grief at Parnell's death to angry scorn of his political Judas. "Et Tu, Healy," it was called, and though it is lost, it was long remembered, at least within his family. "Remember it?" his father long afterward said to a bookseller. "Why shouldn't I remember it? Didn't I pay for the printing of it, and didn't I send a copy to the Pope?" (This leaves hope that some day a devoted Joycean will discover it in the Vatican Library.) "At the end of the piece," Stanislaus Joyce recalled, "the dead Chief is liked to an eagle, looking down on the grovelling mass of Irish politicians from 'His quaint-perched aerie on the crags of Time.'" In the Roman allusion of its title, it is a precocious prefiguring of history's murderous knife. It is also a conception of Parnell which Joyce was to retain. The ghost of Parnell, silent, reproving, austere, is present in "Ivy Day in the Committee Room." He is present at the Christmas dinner in *A Portrait of the Artist*, and although, in that scene, Parnellite and anti-Parnellite strike Stephen with terror, so savage is their language, our feelings move in sympathy, at its close, toward Mr. Casey, his head bowed on his hands. "'Poor Parnell!' he cried loudly. 'My dead king!'" The ghost of Parnell moves through *Ulysses*, in conversation, memory, a glimpse of his Glasnevin grave in the "Hades" episode, in "Wandering Rocks," his living ghost, his brother John Howard Parnell, bearded, long-faced, his eyes "ghostbright."

The Parnell of Joyce's imagination was the Parnell who had passed into mythology—heroic, austere, passionate, destroyed by his own people at the behest of the English enemy. The fullness with which he accepted it is best revealed in the essay which he wrote in Trieste in 1912 for *Il Piccolo della Sera*, and is called "L'ombra di Parnell"—the shade of Parnell. In that year, it seemed as though the Irish nationalist and the English Liberal politicians had achieved Home Rule for Ireland, and it is Joyce's point that the shadow of the betrayed leader will fall upon their success, "mild and proud, silent and disconsolate." The ghost of that "uncrowned king" will weigh heavily on his countrymen. "In his final desperate appeal to his countrymen, he begged them not to throw him as a sop to the English wolves howling around them. It redounds to their honor that they did not fail that appeal. They did not throw him to the English wolves; they tore him to pieces themselves."

The strong attractions for Joyce of this Parnell have obvious explanations. In the matter of historical figures with whom he could identify, he was highly selective: only Parnell and Jesus Christ quali-fied. In "Et Tu, Healy," he joined Parnell to the betrayed and mur-dered Caesar, but in the Trieste article, he raises the stakes. "The melancholy which invaded his mind was perhaps the profound con-viction that, in his hour of need, one of the disciples who dipped his hand in the same bowl with him would betray him. That he fought to the very end with this desolate certainty in mind is his greatest claim to nobility." That he should have granted to Parnell the rare, high quality of spiritual nobility is in itself evidence of the privileged posi-tion which he held in Joyce's imagination. In 1902, reviewing the works of the patriotic versifier William Rooney, he had spoken, in delicate scorn, of "those big words which make us so unhappy," and "nobility" is one such word. Discussing the Irish with Mr. Deasy, Stephen echoes Joyce's words: "'I fear those big words,' Stephen said, 'that make us so unhappy.'"

But this Parnell was not a creation of Joyce's imagination. Rather, his imagination moved toward and appropriated that Parnell which had been shaped by the Irish popular imagination, a Parnell accepted in retrospect even by those who had, at the time, betrayed him. It is the Parnell of the *United Irishman* funeral editorial: "They have killed him. Under God today we do solemnly believe that they have killed him.... Murdered he has been as certainly as if the gang of con-spirators had surrounded him and hacked him to pieces...." And of Yeats's "Parnell's Funeral" and "Come Gather Round me, Parnellites." And of Frank O'Connor and Sean O'Faolain. The "Uncrowned King" of Dublin street ballads. There is no need of revisionist biography and history to know that the historical Parnell was a more complex figure, or that the circumstances of his fall were tangled and ensnarled by circumstance. My point, rather, is that here, at this point, Joyce is responding to the past, to history, with a characteristically Irish mode of emotional shaping and apprehension. (How Irish may be measured by attempting to imagine Gladstone in such terms, let us say, or

Clemenceau, or Grover Cleveland.) "Try to be one of us," Davin urges Stephen in *A Portrait of the Artist*. "In your heart you are an Irishman but your pride is too powerful." "No honourable and sincere man," Stephen replies, "has given up to you his life and his youth and his affections from the days of Tone to those of Parnell but you sold him to the enemy or failed him in need or reviled him and left him for another. And you invite me to be one of you. I'd see you damned first." It seems the utterance of an unqualified rejection; in truth, it is the articulation of a particular mythic view of Irish history, the myth of the betrayed leader. Stephen rejects a myth by espousing one of its variants.

The habit of thought to which he—and behind him, Joyce—has here turned is one which establishes a special relationship to the historical past. The novel, *Ulysses*, is, with this one privileged exception, suspicious of such relationships. In the opening episode, Stephen tells Haines, the silly and humorless English visitor to the Martello tower, that he is the servant of two masters, an English and an Italian. "And a third there is," he adds a moment later, "who wants me for odd jobs." He explains the first two to the puzzled Haines—the imperial British state and the holy Roman Catholic and apostolic church—but not the third, although he sees, in his mind, "a crazy queen, old and jealous." The old, jealous queen, of course, is Kathleen ni Houlihan, the personification of Ireland. Earlier, he had seen her embodied in the woman who brings milk to the tower:

> Crouching by a patient cow at daybreak in the lush field, a witch on her toadstool, her wrinkled fingers quick at the squirting dugs. They lowed about her whom they knew, dewsilky cattle. Silk of the kine and poor old woman, names given her in old times. A wandering crone, lowly form of an immortal serving her conqueror and her gay betrayer, their common cuckquean, a messenger from the secret morning.

And that night, in "Circe," in Bella Cohen's brothel she will appear to him as "Old Gummy Granny," the "deathflower" of the potato blight in her breast, thrusting toward Stephen a dagger with which to kill an English soldier: "Remove him, acushla. At 8:35 a.m. you will be in heaven and Ireland will be free."

In W. B. Yeats's play of 1902, Cathleen ni Houlihan had been given a more conventional and a more romantic embodiment, as the poor old woman wandering the roads near Killala in 1798, on the eve of the French invasion, who lures away the peasant bridegroom, Michael Gillane, to go off to a hopeless rebellion: "Many a man has died for love of me.... There was a red man of the O'Donnells from the north, and a man of the O'Sullivans from the south, and there was one Brian that lost his life at Clontarf by the sea, and there were a great many in the west, some that died hundreds of years ago, and there are some that will die tomorrow." Joyce's reduction of Cathleen ni Houlihan to Old Gummy Granny is more than burlesque blasphemy; it is one of the strategies by which he has his—and our—defenses against her seductions.

"Stately, plump Buck Mulligan came from the stairhead, bearing a bowl of lather on which a mirror and a razor lay crossed." That razor, polished and murderous, becomes, as I have suggested, one of Joyce's images of history, undergoing many changes before its appearance as Old Gummy Granny's dagger. The meaning of the mirror, or at any rate one of its meanings, is more quickly revealed. It has been pinched by Mulligan from the skivvy's room at home, and it has a crack in it. Stephen, peering into it, says with bitterness, "It is a symbol of Irish art. The cracked lookingglass of a servant." His sense—which was also Joyce's—of the inferiority of Irish art has been a constant one. "My ancestors," Stephen tells Davin, "threw off their language and took another." The bitterness which flavors this is explained by that earlier scene in which Stephen, talking with the English-born dean of studies at the university, thinks:

The language in which we are speaking is his before it is mine. How different are the words *home*, *Christ*, *ale*, *master*, on his lips and on mine! I cannot speak or write these words without unrest of spirit. His language, so familiar and so foreign, will always be for me an acquired speech. I have not made or accepted its words. My voice holds them at bay. My soul frets in the shadow of his language.

Language lies at the root of Joyce's sense of reality, his sense of self. Inevitably, therefore, language is the point at which he feels most bitterly the subservience of their people. His ancestors—and Davin's, and Stephen's—had left him, as his inheritance, a borrowed tongue. And, by extension, a borrowed literature. One of the extraordinary facts about *Ulysses*—it may well be the most extraordinary fact of all—is its seeming emergence from a void. If we turn to novelists of commensurate magnitude—to Dickens or to Henry James or to Proust—we are aware in each instance of strong continuities with specific literary cultures. *À la recherche du temps perdu* is a work of the most profound and powerful originality, and yet, at the same time, and by one of literature's familiar paradoxes, we can also trace its roots backward through the history of the French novel. But *Ulysses* seems by contrast to have sprung rootless and unancestored into the fullness of its being. There are many reasons for this; to name them all would be to name Joyce's imagination and his conception of his craft. One of them has perhaps not been given sufficient consideration. Joyce's task—certainly that one of his tasks which lay at the forefront of his canvas—was the representation and evaluation of his culture. A culture which thought its thoughts, conducted its affairs, with borrowed words. His response was to cast its words anew, to contrive for his picture of his city a form which owed nothing, or next to nothing, to literary traditions of the imperial power. Throughout *Ulysses*, as we have seen, he mocks the rebellious traditions of Irish history, but it may be that, in the course of doing so, he accomplished an Irish rebellion of the deepest and the subtlest kind, a rebellion within the word, within language itself.

18

DUBLINERS

DUBLINERS, WHICH IS one of the crucial books of modern literature, is the work of a very young man. A version of "The Sisters" was published in 1904, when James Joyce was twenty-two, and within three years all of the stories had been written. They express a young man's angry and contemptuous rejection of his native city, a provincial backwater which served as capital of "the most belated race in Europe." The theme of the stories is paralysis, both moral and psychological, and the style is that of a "scrupulous meanness." But in fact these explorations of paralysis are alive with the unsettling energies of art, and the scrupulous style holds in so precise a balance the presumably opposed techniques of naturalism and symbolism, that however often we read them, we read them each time anew.

Dubliners has drawn to itself a considerable body of criticism, which is by now in substantial agreement that although each of the stories has its local integrity, the book exists also as a web of echoes, refractions, correspondences, subversive ironies. Indeed, one of the pleasures of this text is a slowly strengthening awareness that the stories are bound together by links of syllable and image. So assured, so finished is their mastery that one remembers with astonishment not only their author's youth but also the wretched conditions of his life when he began them.

In April of 1903, Joyce had been summoned back from a first flight
abroad by a telegram: "Mother Dying Come Home Father." He traveled back on francs borrowed from one of his language pupils in
Paris. Mrs. Joyce lingered on until August, and for some months after
her death Joyce stayed in the crowded, heavily mortgaged Cabra
house with his drunken, violent, self-pitying father, priggish brother,
and bewildered, grief-stricken sisters. Most of the furniture had been
pawned, and at times there was not enough to eat. Late at night the
father would come home, drunk, to revile them all as "an insolent
pack of little bitches." Joyce himself, then and later when he had
moved into lodgings, was leading a disordered life, drinking almost
as heavily as the father, visiting the brothels, cadging money from
acquaintances, and dressed in clothes handed down to him by his
friend Gogarty. It was not, one would suppose, an atmosphere con-
ducive to the composition of intricately wrought prose.

In June or July of 1904, George Russell, editor of the *Irish Homestead*, asked Joyce: "Could you write anything simple, rural?, live-
making?, pathos?, which could be inserted so as not to shock the
reader. If you could furnish a short story about 1800 words suitable
for insertion the editor will pay £1. It is easily earned money if you
can write fluently and don't mind playing to the common understanding and liking for once in a way. You can sign it any name you
like as a pseudonym." Russell, a generous and kindly man, well knew
Joyce's arrogance and intellectual pride, but he also knew the desper-
ateness of his circumstances. And Joyce, for his part, accepted so
swiftly that "The Sisters" by "Stephen Daedalus" appeared in August,
to be followed by "Eveline" and "After the Race." He received for
them a total of three pounds.

He wrote nothing more in Ireland. In June he had met Nora Bar-
nacle, the young woman who was to share his life and to enter all of
his books in unexpected ways. She first makes her presence known in
"The Dead," the culminating story in *Dubliners*. In October they left

Ireland forever, their fares being secured by another series of begging notes. "I have absolutely no boots," he hinted to a friend on the day of departure. In Trieste, where they settled, he wrote the other stories.

By 1906, the book save for "The Dead" was finished and in the hands of Grant Richards, an English publisher. It would not be published until 1914, however, the delay being caused by Richards's exaggerated fears that various passages were indecent or otherwise offensive and Joyce's stubborn refusal to tamper with his text. The delay maddened Joyce into an obsessive fury, of course, but from our own comfortable distance, it can be seen as serving an accidental purpose.

At the beginning of 1914, Joyce was unknown and almost unpublished. In the preceding December, however, Ezra Pound had approached him by letter, and Joyce responded by sending him the first chapter of *A Portrait of the Artist as a Young Man*. Thanks to Pound, the novel was published serially in the *Egoist* from February to September. Midway, and coincidentally, Richards relented and published *Dubliners*. By the end of the year, Joyce had earned recognition in literary circles as a member of that extraordinary generation of innovators which included Eliot, Gertrude Stein, and Pound himself. Suddenly, as it were, a provincial Irishman, impecunious, self-banished, and not entirely respectable, had moved out from the shadows into a life of accomplishment and literary legend.

"I call the series *Dubliners*," he wrote to a friend in 1904, "to betray the soul of that hemiplegia or paralysis which many consider a city." Two years later he was writing to Richards: "My intention was to write a chapter of the moral history of my country and I chose Dublin for the scene because that city seemed to me the centre of paralysis." A disingenuous claim: it was Dublin which had chosen him, a writer as urban as Kafka. But there can be no doubt that paralysis is the central, organizing image. The first paragraph of "The Sisters" offers as narrator a boy for whom the very word *paralysis* sounds like the name of "some malificent and sinful being," and at the center of the story sits the enigmatic and disturbing figure of a paralyzed priest. Eveline, in the second story to be written, is held so firmly in the grip of a sterile and repetitive existence that she rejects her chance for a husband and a new life in South America. (Above the harmonium in the dusty house which she shares with her bullying father hangs a colored print of "the promises made to Blessed Margaret Mary Alacoque," a saintly and paralyzed virgin of the seventeenth century: the most casual-seeming details in these stories have a way of resonating.)

In these two instances, an actual paralysis, one physical and the other emotional, is dramatized, but all of the other stories engage the condition, more obliquely and therefore perhaps more powerfully. Routine, a choked-off life, an ambition denied, a life dulled by whiskey or church incense, all these are forms of paralysis. At the close of the party in "The Dead," Gabriel Conroy describes an old mill horse of his grandfather's, so broken by routine that once, pressed into service as a carriage horse, it walked round and round and round the statue of King Billy in College Green. His listeners break into "peals of laughter," for how can they recognize in this an emblem of their own existences?

In that letter which describes Dublin as a center of paralysis, Joyce says that the stories present the city in four of its aspects—childhood, adolescence, maturity, and public life. But the stories of childhood, "The Sisters," "An Encounter," and "Araby," are set apart from the others by having an "I," a dramatized, first-person narrator. This unnamed boy possesses a remarkable sensitivity to words, their powers, reticences, ambiguities, mysteries. Almost the first thing he tells us is that certain words, *paralysis, gnomon, simony,* fall strangely upon his ear, and that one of them, *paralysis,* has come to fill him with fear. He has found *gnomon* in his Euclid and *simony* in his Catechism, but *paralysis* has come from elsewhere, from the airless room of the dying priest, a figure at once repellent and seductive.

Father Flynn, paralyzed, his tongue lolling, coat dusty with spilled snuff, is an image of the Church he had once served. The Catholic Church was for Joyce a bullying immensity, hoary with years, massive with rituals, dogmas, sacred vessels, altars, brocaded vestments, liturgies and litanies, and utterly destructive of human freedom. But its power, however abundant may have been its energies in the past, was now the power of inertia, of weight. A mysterious disability has come upon this priest, symbolized, as his ignorant sisters tell us, by an incident with a dropped chalice. Now he has but one disciple, the boy whom he instructs in matters of the spirit. But the matter which he chooses for discourse is chillingly abstract, inhuman, designed, as the boy says, to show him "how complex and mysterious were certain institutions of the Church which I had always regarded as the simplest acts."

The boy has also, faintly at first but growing more vivid with time, a secret place of the imagination, remote and exotic. A confused dream about Father Flynn lingers as a memory of "long velvet curtains and a swinging lamp of antique fashion. I felt that I had been very far away, in some land where the customs were strange—in Persia, I thought.... But I could not remember the end of the dream." In "An Encounter," the boy and his chum Mahony escape school for a day, and watch a Norwegian ship, "a graceful threemaster," discharge her cargo at a Liffey quay. "I went to the stern and tried to decipher the legend on it, but failing to do so, I came back and examined the foreign sailors to see had any of them green eyes for I had some confused notion...." There the sentence breaks off: silence is a part of Joyce's language. Later, as he lies on a bank of the Dodder, "chewing one of those green stems on which girls tell fortunes," he is approached by an elderly homosexual, "shabbily dressed in a suit of greenish-black," who makes ambiguous, veiled advances. An ordinary experience of boyhood. But this man, the boy suddenly observes, is peering at him through "a pair of bottle-green eyes." The boy seeks constantly to read "legends," whether on shop fronts or the sterns of vessels, or in faces, or in newspapers and books. And the elderly stranger is linked by a legend of green eyes to ships and sailors and distant places. (When a London printer refused to set "Two Gallants" into type, Joyce remarked that a more subtle inquisitor would have recognized "the enormity" of "An Encounter.")

In "Araby," the remote, glamorous, and unattainable place is announced by the title. The boy, we now learn, lives in a house where once a priest had died in the back drawing room. Not the priest of "The Sisters," and yet the association is strong and unavoidable. Now, however, the boy has a different center for his emotions and imagination, the sister—we are never given her name—of his play-fellow, Mangan. Only once do they speak, when she asks if he will be going to *Araby*, a charity bazaar with an Oriental theme. If he goes, he promises her, he will bring her something. She cannot go herself, she tells him, as she twists her silver bracelet and as lamplight falls on the curve of her neck and the white border of her petticoat, because there is to be a spiritual retreat at her convent.

But on the Saturday night it is after nine before the boy is able to set out for Araby, holding a florin tightly in his hand. When he arrives, the bazaar has almost shut down. Most of the hall is in dark-ness, and there is "a silence like that which pervades a church after a service." Before a curtain, "over which the words *Café Chantant* were written in coloured lamps," two men are counting money on a salver. At one of the few open stalls, a girl and two young fellows are flirting, their language flat and vacuous. The boy turns away slowly and the story ends:

> Gazing up into the darkness I saw myself as a creature driven and derided by vanity; and my eyes burned with anguish and anger.

An economical and neatly turned account of youthful disillusionment. Yet surely the language of that concluding sentence is excessive—*driven . . . derided . . . vanity . . . anguish . . . anger?* But the meaning of *Araby* is embodied as fully in its language as in its fable, and from the first the language has been heightened, intense. "Her name was like a summons to all my foolish blood," and "her image accompanied me even in places most hostile to romance."

> On Saturday evenings when my aunt went marketing I had to go to carry some of the parcels. We walked through the flaring streets, jostled by drunken men and bargaining women, amid the curses of labourers, the shrill litanies of shop-boys who stood on guard by the barrels of pigs' cheeks, the nasal chanting of street-singers, who sang a *come-all-you* about O'Donovan Rossa, or a ballad about the troubles in our native land. These noises converged in a single sensation of life for me: I imagined that I bore my chalice safely through a throng of foes. Her name sprang to my lips at moments in strange prayers and praises which I myself did not understand. . . . But my body was like a harp and her words and gestures were like fingers running upon the wires.

When the boy speaks of his "confused adoration" of Mangan's sister, we might accept this as the conventionally extravagant language of erotic yearning, were not an actual confusion at work in his language. The language of religious, indeed of specifically Catholic experience has been transposed by innocent profanation into a secular key. The ugly sounds of city streets have been softened into litanies and chants, and the name of the unnamed girl springs in prayers and praises to the lips of her worshiper. Her image is a chalice which he will carry safely, unlike the guilty and failed priest of "The Sisters," who had dropped his chalice, and whom we last saw in his coffin, his large hands "loosely retaining a chalice."

With imagination set at such a pitch, disillusionment must bear the colors of anguish and anger. "The syllables of the word *Araby* were called to me through the silence in which my soul luxuriated and cast an Eastern enchantment over me." The girl and the exotic-sounding bazaar are linked in his intense reverie, and it is proper that it should have, as he approaches it, the appearance of a shrine, bearing a "magical name"—the last of those legends which he sets himself to read. But it proves to be a church after its service, near-empty, dark, drained of mystery. Its tabernacle bears the words *Café Chantant* in colored lamps, and before it sit the money-changers in the temple. And the mincing, genteel flirt at the booth is not so different, we must assume, from Mangan's sister.

We are told insistently that "her name" was like a summons, and that "her name" sprang to his lips in strange prayers. Why, then, are we never told her name, and why is her brother named Mangan? As to the latter, some pedantic readers of Joyce, myself included, have been lured into speculation. James Clarence Mangan was a mid-nineteenth-century poet who lived and died in wretched poverty and in the ugly slums of Dublin. Penniless, a drunkard, he was intoxicated also with Araby, with the golden and mysterious East, and sought to palm off poems as translations from the Arabic or the Persian or the Turkish. Joyce had celebrated him in a 1902 lecture written in elaborate, Paterian cadences, "a stranger in his native land, a rare and bizarre figure in the streets." Mangan—or rather, the Mangan of Joyce's imagination—endured the ugliness of his life and world by worshiping in his art an ideal lady, "his virgin flower, and flower of flowers." His ideal lady is, in his poetry, given a variety of fanciful Oriental names, or else, and more often, no name at all.

The narrator of "Araby" had set off for the bazaar with a two-shilling piece. As he walks away from it, in anguish, he allows "the two pennies to fall against the sixpence in my pocket"—exact change from a third-class railway ticket and a one-shilling turnstile. From this point on, *Dubliners* will take precise and remorseless notice of small sums. Eveline makes eight shillings a week. Farrington, in "Counterparts," pawns his watch for six shillings: we track them, shilling by shilling, through the Dublin pubs. Lenehan, in "Two Gallants," buys hot peas and ginger beer for twopence halfpenny. The symbolic weight of all this silver and copper is set, transmuted, in the final sentences of that story:

> Corley halted at the first lamp and stared grimly before him. Then with a grave gesture he extended a hand towards the light and, smiling, opened it slowly to the gaze of his disciple. A small gold coin shone in the palm.

The characters of *Dubliners*, like those of *Ulysses*, are drawn from a narrow social range—minor functionaries of government or trade, shabby but conscious of rank, fond of drink, boastful about the past, furtive about the present, adroit at dodging creditors and improvising excuses. They are clerks, cashiers, journalists, agents, small commercial travelers, shop assistants. Men, that is, with a vivid sense when sober of how much change is left in the pocket and how much a round of drinks will cost. It was the class which Joyce knew best, shabby-genteel son of a shabby-genteel father. But he could not have been presented with richer material, for the great modern city was to be the theater of his art, and precisely this class had become one of its characterizing populations. Melville's Bartleby and Kafka's Joseph K. are the unlikely cousins of the Dubliners, and so too is the government clerk in Gogol, in his handsome, transforming overcoat.

A surprising number of these Dubliners are connected with the law and the police. Mr. Mooney, of "The Boarding House," has been "obliged to enlist himself as a sheriff's man." Corley, of "Two Gallants," is the son of an inspector of police, and "was often to be seen walking with policemen in plain clothes, talking earnestly." In

"Grace," a commercial traveler named Kernan falls drunk down the lavatory stairs of a public house, is helped to his home, and then is persuaded by friends to attend a spiritual retreat which a Jesuit named Purdon is giving especially for businessmen. Of the three friends who rally round and bring him to the retreat, one is a secretary to the City Coroner and the other two are employed in the Royal Irish Constabulary Office in Dublin Castle. Joyce had a cautious disdain for policemen and soldiers, and "Grace" seems delicately to suggest the appropriateness of one bullying institution turning poor Mr. Kernan over the other one.

In Joyce's original intention, "Grace" was to have been the concluding story of *Dubliners*. It is a mordant story, bitter and funny. Father Purdon, a name borrowed by Joyce from a street in the brothel district, is a Jesuit and therefore, as Mr. M'Coy says, caters for the "upper classes." The text which he has chosen for his sermon, the parable in Luke which counsels us to make unto ourselves friends out of "the mammon of iniquity," is notoriously a difficult one. And, one would suppose, a delicate one to present to a congregation of moneylenders, pawnbrokers, and city councilors. But Purdon, who has come to them as their "spiritual accountant," subverts it to his uses, and the story ends with the word "accounts" echoing and re-echoing.

But in fact *Dubliners* closes with a story more rich and complex, and more generous in its response to life. "The Dead" is one of the great stories of our literature. It reaches backward, drawing up and affirming themes and images from the earlier stories, but it also transcends them. The spiritual paralysis of the earlier stories is so deadly because the paralyzed are unaware of their condition, or else, like Little Chandler, are brought to a limited and useless self-knowledge. Gabriel Conroy, as he comes from snowy Dublin to the Misses Morkan's annual dance, smiles and jokes and moves "vigorously," but the language which presents him suggests a paralyzing cold, with "a light fringe of snow" on the "snow-stiffened frieze" of his overcoat.

But the story turns upon a powerful reversal. At its close, as he lies beside his sleeping wife in their hotel room, and as snow taps upon the windowpane, his eyes fill with tears. They are for himself, to be sure, but also for Gretta and for Michael Furey, her early lover, who had died years before, perhaps for her. The tears, the text tells us, are "generous" tears.

One other story Joyce projected for the book, but it would not take form and remained unwritten. It was to deal with a Jew and his wanderings through the streets of Dublin. But after thinking about it, Joyce finally admitted to his brother that he had not got beyond the title. He had thought of calling it "Ulysses."

—Introduction to James Joyce, *Dubliners*
(Limited Editions Club, 1986)

19

SEAN O'CASEY

IN THREE PLAYS, the two-act *Shadow of a Gunman* (1923), *The Plough and the Stars* (1924), and *Juno and the Paycock* (1926), Sean O'Casey shaped an extraordinary fusion of tragedy, comedy, and knockabout farce out of the dramatic years which brought modern Ireland into bloody birth—the Easter Rising of 1916, the guerrilla war against Britain's armed forces in 1920–1921, the bitter, murderous Civil War which followed the disputed "treaty" of 1922.

In 1927, for a variety of reasons, he moved to England, and until his death in 1964, he continued to pour out a stream of plays, manifestos, essays, pronouncements. What seems beyond dispute, however, save among tenured scholars of the drama, is that nothing in those long decades came close to the triumphant, the almost mysterious triumph of those three plays about "the Troubles." By the 1940s, he had settled into a career as a world-class bore, pontificating and rhapsodizing.

The roots of O'Casey's politics and of his art lie buried, intertwined, in the Dublin of his young manhood. He was born in 1880 into a Dublin family which was Protestant for a generation or two and which was clinging desperately to the bottom rung of the lower middle class. The father's early death forced the children downward socially. Two of O'Casey's brothers joined the British army and he himself, plagued by wretched eyes and a poor physique, became first a stock clerk, then a laborer.

As a young man he had four consuming interests: the theater; the Gaelic League, which was dedicated to restoring the falling fortunes of that language; and the Irish Republican Brotherhood, a legendary —but in those years minute—semisecret organization dedicated to the establishment of a free Ireland by armed rebellion. The fourth commitment, which came a bit later but was to prove the decisive one upon his spirit, was to the Dublin- and Belfast-based Socialist movement, led first by Jim Larkin, and then by James Connolly.

O'Casey's commitments were rich with paradoxes and potentially explosive tensions. For example, Protestants (like O'Casey but of higher social status) had played shaping roles in both the Gaelic League and the Irish Republican Brotherhood. By his day, however, the circumstances of Irish culture had made both groups overwhelmingly Catholic in composition, and he was situated within them in the kind of prickly awkwardness upon which artistic creativity thrives. He was the quintessential Irishman who is always "agin" whatever movement he is a part of.

His apprenticeship to the drama was different in kind. The Dublin of his day, as, earlier, of Shaw's, was mad for theater, not especially the esoteric and lofty theater of Yeats, Lady Gregory, and Synge, but the popular melodramas of which the Victorian Irishman Dion Boucicault was a leading craftsman. In understanding Shaw, as Professor Martin Meisel long ago pointed out, the role played upon his imagination by the theaters of his Dublin youth should not be neglected, and far more is this true of O'Casey. If both men wrote plays which (unlike those of Yeats) gripped and continue to grip large audiences, this may well be because they learned parts of their craft by sitting in Dublin galleries at countless matinees.

But it is even more to the point that O'Casey's imagination and spirit were strained to the rending point and then ripped open by the extraordinary events preceding and following the Rising on Easter Monday of 1916. His role in the events preceding it was small but not entirely insignificant.

Grossly to oversimplify a complicated situation: in early 1916, there existed in Dublin two bodies of armed (more or less) militants, intent upon wresting control of Irish life and destiny away from the British Empire. The larger of these groups, the Volunteers, led by Patrick Pearse and Tom Clarke, was essentially middle class and espousing a simon-pure nationalism. The other, which had once claimed O'Casey's fierce loyalty, was the Irish Citizen's Army, Socialist in orientation and led by James Connolly. The very possibility of an alliance between these ideologically divergent groups had led to O'Casey's forced resignation from the Citizen's Army. And on Easter Monday, in confirmation of his misgivings, he saw the two swing into action side by side.

Adding insult to injury, he watched Connolly's men hoist above headquarters the flag of Irish nationalism, rather than his beloved Socialist banner, stars and a plough against a field of blue. Hence, of course, the title of his most famous play, applauded in these days by Irish-Americans, at once bellicose and tearful, who do not understand its significance. For O'Casey, the Easter Rebellion was a bloody and shameful waste, and, in his magnificent play, the heroes are not the swaggering blowhards who go out to fight, but a working-class Protestant woman, Bessie Burgess, loyal to king and creed, rough-tongued but great-hearted. Her Catholic counterpart in *Juno and the Paycock* is Mrs. Boyle, "Juno," who cries out in the last scene, "Sacred Heart o' Jesus, take away our hearts of stone, and give us hearts o' flesh! Take away this murtherin' hate, an' give us Thine own eternal love!"

When *The Plough and the Stars* opened at Dublin's famous Abbey, there was the riot which by tradition attended the presentation of works of genius in that venue. The ostensible grounds were that he had brought the Plough-and-Stars flag into a public house, and that he had suggested that whores might be plying their trade in holy Ireland. The deeper, unformulated ground was that the play, like the other two in the trilogy, expressed his bitter, angry, hilarious, sobbing despair at the wrong rebellion fought at the wrong time by the wrong people.

As Seamus says in *The Shadow of a Gunman*, and he speaks for O'Casey: "I believe in the freedom of Ireland, an' that England has no right to be here, but I draw the line when I hear the gunmen blowin' about dyin' for the people, when it's the people that are dyin' for the gunmen! With all due respect to the gunmen, I don't want them to die for me."

O'Casey's long life after that was anticlimax. Gary O'Connor tells the story soberly and well in this biography, judiciously and generously.[1] He has a sense of O'Casey's many imperfections, and of his stubborn, remarkably narrow streak of genius.

—*Newsday*, May 29, 1988

---

1. *Sean O'Casey: A Life* (Atheneum, 1988).

20

FRANK O'CONNOR

I

FRANK O'CONNOR and I became friends in the last years of his life, and for one of those years, in the early Sixties, we were neighbors in Dublin. We would meet most days for a glass of wine before dinner or a pint of Guinness in the late evening. Our block of flats stood next to the eighteenth-century Grand Canal, in the south of the city, and we would cross a narrow footbridge beside one of the locks to Mooney's, a pleasant, nondescript public house with a long bar, its red marble polished by the elbows of generations of porter drinkers.

Michael O'Donovan—"Frank O'Connor" was his pseudonym— was a temperate drinker, two glasses of claret or a single pint of stout, but a magnificent talker. His language was vivid and unexpected, wide-ranging and yet precise; his intelligence and his sensibility were alert, quirky, and inebriating. He had returned to Ireland after a long, self-imposed exile, and there had come a truce in his embittered lover's quarrel with his society. In America and England and on the Continent, he had won recognition as one of the masters of the modern short story; the fame had spread at last to his own country.

Dublin is a city where writers are known even to people who are little given to reading, and Michael was an unmistakable presence, a handsome, strong-featured man, white moustache and shock of white hair, quick brown eyes behind thick-lensed glasses. Mooney's regulars—clerks and laborers and minor civil servants—recognized him from newspaper photographs. Radio had made them familiar with his voice, dramatic and intense, with the rich cadences of a Cork accent. He was aware of their recognition—he did not lack vanity—but would be entirely intent upon our conversation.

Despite his travels, he thought of himself as a provincial intellectual and always argued to win. Much later, I jotted down some of the topics of those informal seminars: Chekhov, Joyce, eighth-century Ireland; Stendhal, Turgenev, the ruined abbeys of Munster and Connaught; Dickens, the art of bel canto; Mozart and Schubert, Goethe and Kafka. His erudition had been hard-earned. He had grown up in poverty, the son of a hard-drinking ex-soldier and a maidservant. His formal education ended at fourteen, when he counted himself lucky to find work as a messenger on the railway. He was proud of the academic honors that had eventually come his way, the appointments to Harvard and Northwestern and Stanford, the courses in Shakespeare and Joyce and Jane Austen. And his attitude toward those writers was at once sensible, outrageous, and ruthlessly independent, as when he would argue to me that Joyce was not a novelist at all but rather the last of the great medieval rhetoricians.

But he would speak also, some evenings, of his own craft, and then the manner changed, became quiet, tentative; the pyrotechnics vanished. Like his friend the sculptor Seamus Murphy, who never forgot his beginnings as a journeyman stonemason and carried to the end his bag of tools, he was a meticulous craftsman. Everything he wrote, from a story to a review for a Dublin Sunday newspaper, went through its several drafts, the tone modulated, at times deliberately roughened so that it would ring with what seemed to him the essence of style, "the tone of a man's voice, speaking."

He was especially pleased by his stories of middle-class Ireland, with its teachers and priests and auctioneers. He said once, a landlord surveying his small, measurable demesne, "I prefer to write about Ireland and Irish people merely because I know to a syllable how everything in Ireland can be said." Writers should never be trusted when they say such things. Ireland and its people were his delighted, exasperated obsession. "Merely" indeed.

O'Connor was thirteen at the time of the abortive 1916 uprising, which gave inspiration to the guerrilla war that came three years later. He was old enough to carry messages and to help set up roadblocks. That war, as he came to believe, was a marvel of improvisation, an act of the imagination that allowed a handful of young men to pit themselves against an empire. The treaty with England that was worked out in December 1921 was a compromise, and fact and imagination were placed in conflict. Some of those young men, O'Connor among them, remained faithful to the imagination, and war was followed by civil war. They were defeated, and O'Connor, like many others, wound up in jail. In his autobiography, *An Only Child*, he writes:

> And what neither group saw was that every word we said, every act we committed, was a destruction of the improvisation and what we were bringing about was a new Establishment of Church and State in which imagination would play no part, and young men and women would emigrate to the ends of the earth, not because the country was poor, but because it was mediocre.

The work that held a particular fascination for me was the one that established O'Connor's reputation in 1931, *Guests of the Nation*. In that book of stories, issuing directly or obliquely from the guerrilla war against England and the civil war that followed in its wake, imagination and history hold converse.

Imagination—for which "improvisation" is the mildly ironic synonym—is the quality to which, above all others, O'Connor gave reverence. But he was aware of its ambiguities and treacheries, the random corridors that it opens upon both farce and tragedy. "Guests of the Nation," the title story, explores a tragic corridor and is as fine a story as any he was later to write. It does not contain a wasted word, and yet there is a deceptive tone of leisurely anecdote that is maintained almost to its shattering conclusion.

Two young Irish Volunteers, Noble and Bonaparte, the narrator, are holding under guard in a cottage in the mountains two British soldiers—a perky, opinionated cockney named Hawkins and a large, quiet man called Belcher. The four have become friends, after a fashion, playing cards together, arguing about the Bible, Hawkins learning to dance to "The Waves of Tory" and "The Walls of Limerick." What none of them realizes, at first, is that the Englishmen are being held hostage against the threatened execution of Irish Volunteers in Cork. The men in Cork are killed, and the orders come to kill Hawkins and Belcher. "You don't understand me," Hawkins shouts at a man named Donovan, who has come to fire the shots, "but these lads do. They're not the sort to make a pal shoot and kill a pal." Then Donovan, with Hawkins dead at his feet, turns the gun on Belcher and says, "You understand that we're only doing our duty?" And Belcher says, his head raised like a blind man's, "I never could make out what duty was myself. I think you're all good lads, if that's what you mean. I'm not complaining." Noble raises his fist at Donovan, and at that moment Donovan fires. The two bodies are buried in the bog. Bonaparte reflects:

> Noble says he saw everything ten times the size as though there were nothing in the whole world but that little patch of bog with the two Englishmen stiffening into it, but with me it was as if the patch of bog where the Englishmen were was a million miles away, and even Noble and the old woman, mumbling behind me, and the birds and the bloody stars were all far away, and I was somehow very small and very lost and lonely like a

child astray in the snow. And anything that happened to me afterwards, I never felt the same about again.

It is a simple story and yet unyielding in its refusal to simplify our response. Years later, in a bar far different from Mooney's, a San Francisco bar at one edge of an immense continent, O'Connor's daughter, Liadan, said suddenly, as though she had hit upon a way of defining him, "My father hated violence." But our response to the violence in this story is more complex than hatred is. In Cork, the British army, with the logic of all armies, has executed rebels in arms, and the guerrillas, who have created for themselves a mirror image of that army, are compelled to respond in kind. These country lads are at once soldiers and fellows playing at being soldiers. There is a faint air of masquerade. The very words they use have been requisitioned from the "real" army, for whom they have been worn smooth by centuries of use—"platoon," "brigade," the word "enemy" itself. O'Connor's characters, Irish and English alike, are ordinary, decent men caught up in the indecency of history.

The effect is quite different from that generated by the magnificent images of violence in Isaac Babel's *Red Cavalry*. Babel's response to violence may perhaps have been moral, but emotionally he conspired with it, endowing it with a shimmering, aesthetic energy. Different also from the mannered, dandyish neutrality of Ernest Hemingway's early stories. At one point, Hawkins is explaining the World War as a capitalist plot, and the old woman in whose house they are quartered says:

> Mr. Hawkins, you can say what you like about the war, and think you'll deceive me because I'm only a simple poor country-woman, but I know what started the war. It was the Italian Count that stole the heathen divinity out of the temple of Japan. Believe me, Mr. Hawkins, nothing but sorrow and want can follow people who disturb the hidden powers.

Capitalist greed, Irish patriotism, British imperialism, the theft of a Japanese idol—frivolous abstractions when set beside the four men playing cards, or Belcher carrying a load of turf for the old woman, or the bodies stiffening into the bog. Murderous abstractions.

It is the taciturn Belcher, incapable of eloquence, who speaks for us when he says that he cannot make out what duty is. From the story, we learn that when the hidden powers of life are violated, even by such good lads as these fellows, the violators pay a heavy price.

Frank O'Connor died in 1966. A few years later, the proprietors of Mooney's gutted its interior and created a cocktail lounge festooned with livid neon tubing. If you went in there, you would not recognize it, and serious conversation is difficult because of the television set. But on the evening news from the northern corner of Ireland you would be able to watch them playing soldiers in the streets of Belfast, British Tommies and Irish patriots.

—*The Dial*, February 1987

II

The intellect of man is forced to choose
Perfection of the life or of the work,
And if it take the second must refuse
A heavenly mansion, raging in the dark.

The lines are by W. B. Yeats, who was the friend and patron of the youthful Frank O'Connor, and therefore stand with a particular appropriateness above a review of this biography. But in fact they came several times to mind, as I was reading the biographies of Robert Lowell and Delmore Schwartz and John Berryman and Katherine Anne Porter—insatiable, like other readers, for specifics of madness, alcohol, infidelity, waste, bitchiness, manic narcissism. It is because these four were among the finest writers of our time that the books had come into being, and the same reason seemed to justify my curiosity. Had they been rock stars or diet doctors or sanctimonious politicians, my curiosity might have been no less, but it would have lacked a particular justification. Art is a mystery, I assured myself, but perhaps a few of its secrets rest among the roots of these disordered lives.

But now there has come to me for review the biography of a friend. James Matthews brings considerable gifts to this *Life* of Michael O'Donovan,[1] the Irish short-story writer who became famous as "Frank O'Connor." Matthews's criticism of O'Connor's fiction is properly directed toward the establishment of links between the life and the art, but it is unwaveringly sensitive and shrewd, never reductive. And for the work of a biographer who never met his subject, his portrait of O'Connor's vivid, almost theatrical public personality is astonishingly accurate. The heart of his enterprise, however, is a search for the man who moved and acted and felt beneath that self which was presented to the world.

Hovering above all such literary biographies in the modern mode is Lawrance Thompson's many-volumed life of Robert Frost. It was in 1939 that Frost chose the admiring and then-youthful Thompson as his biographer. Decades were to pass and Frost to die before the work was completed, and by then a sadder and wiser Thompson had discovered that the magnificent poet of hired men and snowy woods was also a monster of ruthless and mean-spirited calculation. The result was a massive curiosity—an authorized biography within the paragraphs of which an author struggles with the appalling human implications of his researches.

Matthews, I hasten to say, was not presented with a similar problem. Whatever the messes of O'Connor's life, it was never a life of

---

1. *Voices: A Life of Frank O'Connor* (Atheneum, 1983).

calculation. Quite to the contrary, he was a man of fierce loves and hates, impetuous and reckless, blundering through vigorous innocence into cat's cradles of domestic and social entanglements. The crucial decade of his life, the 1940s, was given over, in part, to strange, Laocoön-like threshings within the coils of an entire society. And, in part, to the composition of short stories which are miracles of shapely craft, the narrative voice casual, colloquial, never striving for effect, but the design lovely, intricate, and poised. He was a compulsive, almost a possessed rewriter, who thought nothing of devoting twenty drafts to a story. And like other obsessed writers, he was capable of laying waste the lives of those joined to him—wives, lovers, children, friends. Matthews has spoken at length with most of these. And, in particular, the first two of the women who bore O'Connor's children have been generous with their memories, if not always generous in their memory of O'Connor.

"Writing a life of Frank O'Connor," Matthews says, "is like circling a stranger's house, circling and peering into that house from the outside, circling to know something of who or what is inside, never able to enter but content with momentary glimpses from many angles." Well and honorably said. These are words which any biographer, of any man or woman, should take to heart, and without failing to note the nervous, disturbed moral tremor within them. Matthews, I suspect, was drawn toward the composition of this biography by two joined impulses—an admiration of O'Connor's art and a liking of the immensely attractive personality which O'Connor, in his final years, presented to the world. What he discovered, in the course of his researches and his interviews, was a flawed, passionate man, mercurial and vehement, with just enough of the genius in him to make him a delight and a trial.

When O'Connor and I became friends, in the last decade of his life, the public image, though recent, was firm. He had sailed home to Ireland from his exile, attended by a loving, witty, and resourceful American wife. In America he earned what had also been granted to him in Ireland with grudging and at times savage reservations—acknowledgment as a man who had written some of the finest stories ever written in English. "Only a major prophet," a Dublin journalist had written in 1951, "could have achieved such reeking unpopularity in his own country. Few Irish writers have managed to maintain at sullen heat, and for so long, such personal antipathies against themselves: fewer still extracted such sweet-savored bemusement from doing so."

The O'Connor whom I knew was, as they say, larger than life, a handsome man, at once charming and imperious, with a crest of thinning white hair, a bristling mustache, piercing brown eyes behind thick glasses, and the manner of a wary conquistador. He was a bit of a dandy, conscious of the effects of dress, and his jackets of Donegal tweed and Galway bonin were offset by a single exotic touch—a leather-thonged bolo, dark-hued, fiery Navajo turquoise. As if saying, "Damn your eyes, I am back home with foreign decorations." He had long since returned to the appropriate Irish authority his medal as a veteran of the War of Independence.

At one point, I saw him almost daily, for a quiet and very moderate drink in the evening: the poet Patrick Kavanagh described him with disapproval as "a *bun* man, not a *pub* man." But although we became close friends, I never disturbed his fiercely guarded reticences. I was one of his new friends, the friends of his self-assured final years. But because many of the Irishmen whom Matthews has interviewed were also friends, or acquaintances, I was aware of him as a man who in earlier years had attracted fierce loyalty and fierce dislike. And Dublin being Dublin, I was proffered gossip, malice, and oblique, knife-edged anecdote.

It had been an extraordinary life, linked with the life of modern Ireland in ways which created curious resonances. Michael O'Donovan was born in a Cork slum in 1903, the son of a drunken ex-soldier and a servant girl, and educated, after a fashion, by the Christian

Brothers. Inspired by one remarkable teacher, Daniel Corkery, novelist, faltering poet, and ferocious, sectarian patriot, he joined the Irish Republican Army, chose the side of the irreconcilables during the Civil War, fought, was captured, and spent a year in prison. In prison, a brilliant autodidact, he read the Russians, studied German, translated Goethe. After prison, and for almost twenty years, he worked as a librarian. And he wrote stories and poems which caught the attention first of AE and then of Yeats. By the time of World War II, in 1939, his reputation as a writer was established, he was with Yeats a director of the Abbey Theatre, and he was shortly, with his Cork friend Sean O'Faolain, to found *The Bell*, which was to be the most distinguished literary journal ever to appear in Ireland.

Then, all at once, everything came unstuck. As he explained it to me once, "I was living with a married woman, Yeats died, I resigned from the Abbey Theatre, and Hitler invaded Poland." It was clear that he had ranged these events in a descending order of importance. Within three years, he was, quite literally, an outcast, working in England, and by various open and covert pressures from government entirely banned from the radio and the newspapers of his own country. "Blast Ireland," he wrote to a friend. "I spent ten years trying to save this country from itself when I should have been trying to save myself from the country."

This was the crucial period of O'Connor's life. Despite Matthews's best efforts, what happened and why remains mysterious, save in outline. The rigid Irish puritanism of the period cannot be exaggerated, and O'Connor, never a prudent man, had affronted it by openly "living in sin." And was later to affront it again when he established a second liaison with an Englishwoman whom he brought to Dublin with him. He had also made public his detestation of the mediocrity of Irish life, first in a BBC broadcast and then in the English pages of Cyril Connolly's *Horizon*. Ireland, doggedly and precariously neutral in the war, moved against him with those massive, oblique, and genial instruments for silencing of which, preeminent among nations, it possessed a secret mastery.

And yet, when all has been allowed to O'Connor's moral bravado, his bellicose integrity, and to the sullen, fearful vengefulness of his society, an impression remains that he had knowingly courted disaster. In this period, his friend Sean O'Faolain, fellow writer, fellow Corkman, fellow ex-rebel, sent him a Corkman's hot-tempered but shrewd letter: "To me, your irascibility is sheer nihilism. To me you are a magnificent anarchist.... I begin to believe, enfin, that you are just a bloody genius, and your notion that you are a man of action is a gigantic delusion, and you should be told to go away and write masterpieces—as, I have not the least doubt, you will do, and are doing." It may be that he took the injunction to go away more literally than O'Faolain intended, and in more senses than the geographical: at the close of O'Connor's life, relations between these two boyhood friends, the two best Irish prose writers of their generation, were distant and strained. (Alert students of the niceties of Irish counties will have noticed O'Faolain's "enfin": Cork has always felt itself closer to Paris than to Dublin.)

In his autobiography, *Only Child* (1961), O'Connor has written movingly of those Republican soldiers who came out of the prison camps in 1923 to discover that the Ireland of their imagination had somehow shriveled beneath the unromantic sun of actuality. Some emigrated, some made their peace with the sunlight. O'Connor stayed at home, at least until the 1940s, but refused to make his peace. While Yeats was there, there was always a presence to assure him of the possibilities of magnanimity, heroism, and literary splendor.

A mother's boy, rejecting a father of brutal and hard-drinking flesh, he had sought fathers of the spirit—Corkery, AE, the ghost of Parnell, and at last he found Yeats. The Yeats of O'Connor's memoirs is a majestic giant—the old wizard had worked his magic on young Michael O'Donovan. But the hero-worshiping portrait does credit both to Yeats and to O'Connor—the portrait of a writer unwilling to accept from the world anything meaner or less splendid than his imagination of the world. O'Connor, in his quarrels with Ireland, adopted Yeats's lordly fighting stance, his pen a saber. His difficulty may well have been defined in a letter from the good-tempered but always shrewd O'Faolain: "The people are our people, our fathers and mothers. They will take it from Yeats—from Parnell—but not from Mikey Donovan, nor even from Frank O'Connor, unless Frank is prepared to follow Yeats, and never, never, never go down to the gutter where familiarity breeds...familiarity." O'Faolain knew his countrymen.

O'Connor was a bit of a genius—the only one I have ever known. And if you first met the man years after reading and rereading the stories, the man was startling. The stories come to us through a complex narrative voice, the development of which Matthews traces with great sensitivity. It was a voice deliberately relaxed, sinuous in its responsiveness to the many voices of its society, rich in its colors and modulations. But the man lived in a blaze of intellectual and emotional fire—generous, fearless, sullen, candid, devious, fierce, gentle. A tangle of what would in others have seemed contradictions, but which came, in him, from some constant center of being. Bookreviewing has its own ironies: a mother's boy myself, my feelings toward this mother's boy were filial.

Matthews has written a biography worthy of his subject. The biography that counts most of all, Frank O'Connor's *Collected Stories*, was published in 1984.

III

Fame had come to him long before his death in 1966, in his native Ireland, and in England and America. It was not precisely the same fame. Irish readers responded to the delicate preciseness, the generous and yet sardonic realism with which his stories embodied and interpreted their social world. But American and English readers, for whom, perversely, Ireland always seems somehow picturesque, responded, rather, to his extraordinary craftsmanship, his meticulous wedding of a full and intricate narrative design to a style which was deliberately colloquial, even slangy when the occasion demanded it, yet capable of moving with ease to the formal and to the lyrical.

And there was another difference. The nature of literary life in Ireland makes it almost impossible to separate the man and the work—not when you are certain to meet the man at a turning in Grafton Street, or to find yourself arguing with him in an unlikely pub. And the man was as extraordinary as his work. Upon this friend and foe were agreed, and he had plenty of each. After his death, some of his friends contributed to a commemorative volume. In almost every instance, the attempts at measured critical judgment break off, the wish to define the vibrant, energy-crammed man pushing itself to the surface. My own words there will serve as well as others: "He was an impressive man—tall and erect, with the head of an old king, piercing brown eyes behind glasses, a shock of white hair and a bristling mustache. When he argued, the great handsome head was thrown back imperiously, and the effect was likely to daunt the most seasoned debater."

He had emerged from poverty into Ireland and into Irish literature—from a cottage in Cork's Blarney Lane, son of a maidservant and a hard-drinking ex-soldier, from service with the Irish Republican Army during the Civil War, from a year in a Free State prison. To say merely that he was self-educated misstates the fact. His friends knew that he was a man of great erudition, whose learning, at once exact and imaginative, ranged easily from Jane Austen to medieval architecture, from Chekhov to Mozart. In his youth, as a good nationalist, he learned Irish: before his death, he had mastered Old Irish, which is as remote from the modern tongue as is Anglo-Saxon from modern English.

That story of his which probably is the one best known among American readers is "Guests of the Nation," a chilling, deliberately low-keyed, and unforgettable story of two IRA lads who become friends with two British soldiers they are guarding, and then, on orders from headquarters, execute them. But it is not a characteristic story. The Ireland into which he emerged from his prison had had its partial revolution, and was settling down with the long hangover which followed upon its heady bout of violent idealism. Like many other veterans, he viewed postrevolutionary Ireland with bitter scornfulness. It was, as he says in his autobiography, an Ireland from which "young men and women would emigrate to the ends of the earth, not because the country was poor, but because it was mediocre."

But this bitterness, although it found abundant expression in his prose and in sulfurous conversation, did not offer him either subject matter or mood for the great stories he was to write. These stories, although some of them brim with anger against wasted lives, turn their back, casually but totally, upon polemics. "They describe for the first time," he was to say, "the Irish middle-class Catholic way of life with its virtues and its faults without any of the picturesqueness of early Irish writing which concentrated on color and extravagance." They do indeed. He knew to a syllable how things are said in Ireland, and to a gesture how things are done. How friendships are made, and alliances, and enmities, within what is less a culture than an enormous extended family. The stories are filled with lonely people, but it is the kind of loneliness which is experienced only within large families, and not the kind visited upon someone who is, as was O'Connor himself and as the title of his autobiography emphasizes, *An Only Child*.

He was an exacting craftsman, capable, as Richard Ellmann says in his introduction to O'Connor's *Collected Stories*, of reworking a story fifty times. "When I write, when I draft a story," O'Connor told the *Paris Review*, "I never think of writing nice sentences.... It is the design of the story which to me is most important, the thing that tells you there's a bad gap in the narrative here, and you really ought to fill that up in some way or another. I'm always looking at the design of a story, not the treatment." But it is equally true that he was committed to a specific notion of style. "Generations of skillful stylists," he wrote elsewhere, "from Chekhov to Katherine Mansfield and James Joyce had so fashioned the short story that it no longer rang with the tone of a man's voice, speaking." Much of his scrupulous care was devoted to the restoration of that voice.

And yet now, reading all the stories together, it seems to me that during his lifetime we missed the design in the carpet. For O'Connor, this was a reader's cardinal sin.

In *The Lonely Voice*, his study of the short story, he offers conscientious and astute analyses of the style of Turgenev and Chekhov, Joyce and Babel, but his impulse in each chapter is to cut through to the living center of a writer's being, to the vision which informs his work and makes it a coherent whole, radiant with idiosyncratic meaning. And in his own case, we may find a clue in the title which he gave that book. He had the notion that the story-writer's voice, as against the novelist's, is a lonely one, "romantic, individualistic, intransigent." It is a dubious generalization, but perhaps it defines his own center of being.

The communities which exist in O'Connor's stories, communities of families or priests or pals growing up together in provincial Irish towns, are tied together by strong ropes of affection, bickering, shared memories and traditions, shared habits of speech, unspoken shared assumptions. But the voice of the man, speaking, the voice which brings them to life within the ear, comes at a slight distance apart from those communities. The voice aches to join them, almost does, but finally does not. It is, in his own words, a lonely voice, romantic in its longing for the thick, blanketing warmth of Irish life, but held apart from them by its own intransigence, its own awareness of the exacting virtues of individualism.

Perhaps it is, and to the end remained, the voice of the young man who left behind him slum and ambush and prison camp, determined to make his own values, to remain faithful to his own vision. It is in any event the voice of a very fine writer, pure, full-bodied, and fully human.

21

CONSCIENCE OF KILKENNY

IN 1985, HUBERT Butler, who was then eighty-five, a child of the century, published *Escape from the Anthill*, a first collection of his essays and journalism. And Irish readers discovered, belatedly, that their countryman was a writer of rare elegance and grace, and with an even more rare moral and intellectual courage. He lived to see through the press two other books of essays, *The Children of Drancy* and, in his ninetieth year, *Grandmother and Wolfe Tone*. A final volume, *The Land of Nod*, appeared after his death in 1991. *Independent Spirit* is a generous selection of these essays, edited by Elisabeth Sifton.[1]

Over the years, literary Irishmen had come upon many of the essays in Irish or English journals or had heard them given as broadcasts, although others were written in his final years and the prose of these is as musical and as finely honed as ever. But it was with their appearance in books that readers became fully aware of Butler's stature—a writer, as Roy Foster said, worthy to take his place in "an intellectual tradition which takes in Montaigne and Turgenev as well as Swift and Shaw." It was as though the disparate essays, those written in contemplation and those written in the heat of controversy,

---

1. Farrar, Straus and Giroux, 1996.

with their varied subjects and tones, had needed to be placed against each other, reflecting aspects of his mind and spirit.

He was born into the Protestant small gentry of County Kilkenny and, like others of the Anglo-Irish who could afford it, was educated at English schools and at Oxford. He was old enough to remember the state visit of Edward VII; he was passing through Dublin at the time of the 1916 Easter Rising; he returned from Oxford in 1922, after the Black and Tan war against the Empire had been fought and when the country was at the brink of its civil war. After that war, many of his class packed up, sold out (if they had not been burned out by the rebels), and crossed the Irish Sea to what they thought of as "the mother country," even though their families may have been settled in Ireland for centuries.

But Butler knew that he was Irish. For a time he was a county librarian. Then he left the country to make his living in Egypt and Moscow as a teacher. He was gifted in languages and made highly regarded translations of Leonov and Chekhov. He spent 1938–1939, "one of the happiest times of my life," working in Vienna with a Quaker organization to get Jews out of Austria. He was in the Balkans for three years on an extended scholarship, becoming proficient in Serbo-Croatian and also an appalled, fascinated student of Balkan entanglements, political and cultural.

But in 1941, when his father died, he came into the family property of Kilkenny, a Georgian house in the town of Bennet's Bridge and a few hundred acres on the River Nore—enough to give him security. And there, apart from travel when opportunity arose, he spent the other half-century of his life.

He was an Irishman of a special kind, savoring his social rank in the gentry and fiercely proud of what was best in his Protestant tradition. And he was especially proud of Kilkenny, a county richly textured in archaeology, history, legends, traditions, and a past woven of both Catholic and Protestant strands. This was not a mix calculated to make life easy for him in the Ireland of the 1920s through the 1950s, especially given his stubborn insistence on discovering truths, however unlovely, and publishing them, however awkward the consequences.

A newly self-liberated people, mostly rural, had grown up thinking of the Anglo-Irish gentry as their oppressors and were inclined to feel that the time had come for them either to go back home or else to take their place docilely in the new political order. Most of the gentry were Protestant, which made them a minority within a culture now dominated by a triumphalist and at times bellicose Catholicism. Butler had returned from his travels with a far-ranging mind and imagination. He saw Ireland in a European context, but, almost equally, he saw the world as it was imaged in the river of a quiet Kilkenny town. He was both cosmopolitan and intensely local.

A controversy of the 1950s brought him into the national spotlight. In Ireland, faraway Croatia was honored and mourned as a victim of communism's jackboot and her imprisoned Archbishop Stepinac as a hero of resistance to communism. But although this was the case, more or less, there was an untold earlier story which some Irishmen did not know and which others were interested in concealing. During the Second World War, Hitler's puppet in Croatia, Anton Pavelitch, had waged a savage campaign, ostensibly in the name of Roman Catholicism, against Orthodox Serbs. Many thousands of them were slaughtered, in what Butler was to call "the most bloodthirsty religio-racial crusade in history, far surpassing anything achieved by Cromwell or the Spanish Inquisitors." With respect to this crusade, Archbishop Stepinac and his Church remained silent or slippery-tongued.

So too had Pope Pius XII, with regard to this and to the other catastrophes of our century. In a different context, Butler passed a haunting and crushing verdict upon that pope: "The gospels say that a darkness fell upon the earth when Christ was crucified and when a new era began. Surely the Silence of Pius has the same symbolic quality. It was mysterious and ominous, like the silence of woods and fields that precedes a total eclipse of the sun."

Butler's attempt to make these facts known and accepted in Ireland brought down upon him the wrath of conservative Irish Catholicism, down to and including his forced resignation from the local Archaeological Society over which he had presided and which had done much to nourish relationships between the two communities. As the *Standard*, a Catholic newspaper, jubilantly reported: "If he has any regard for public opinion, he must know by now that his action has met with not alone local but national disapproval. That is sufficient." Boycotting, that is, sufficed; no need for the stake. "I hope," he was to write in mild summary, "I have not appeared to diagnose for my Catholic countrymen a unique susceptibility to a disease with which we are all more or less infected."

And he could be as harsh—well, almost as harsh—with his own co-religionists, who often, he thought, in the interests of peace and sociability, forfeited the great Protestant virtue of private judgment. He was that rarest of beings, someone with a genuinely independent mind.

"Make no mistake," Joseph Brodsky wrote in introducing a French edition, "Hubert Butler was no Nazi hunter or Protestant crusader against the Vatican: he was a dishonesty hunter. He just happened to know Serbo-Croatian better than the gentlemen in the Roman Curia, and was more aware of the bloody record of some of the Croatian prelates retained by Rome for an otherwise worthy cause. But then he happened to know several things better than others did, apart from languages."

All this would make him a most interesting and socially valuable oddity, a prickly, slightly anachronistic country gentleman, venturing out of his house beside the quiet Nora to denounce bigotry, intolerance, cruelty, as practiced in Croatia or Nazi Germany or the small towns of Ireland. But this leaves out an essential fact: he was a literary artist of vivid and often exquisite prose. This is seen the more readily when his interests confront each other in the collected essays—in Kilkenny, in the Balkans and the Baltic, in Russian literature and the English novel, in the history of his family, in the contrasting textures and landscapes of the Irish past and present, in the conscienceless horrors of our century and the quietness of a rural road. Out of such confrontations, a literary personality emerges—shrewd, generous, at once civilized and fierce.

"For all his elegance," Maurice Craig wrote in the forward to *Escape from the Anthill*, "Hubert Butler is no belletrist. For him an essay is a projectile, aimed at a particular target and freighted with what it needs to do his work, no more and no less." But this is slightly off the mark, taking no account of those essays in which he lets his fancy move among his pleasures, his delight in nature, society, a well-written book.

He was himself, and in what he wrote he gave us what he tried to make an honest version of that self. That is how he judged others, and how, I think, he would want us to judge him.

—*The Washington Post Book World*, November 10, 1996

22

A GHOST OF THE OLD *NEW YORKER*

BEHIND THE SEXY Versace glitter, vermilion nail polish, and jungle-red lipstick of Tina Brown's *New Yorker*, there lurks the ghost of an earlier *New Yorker*—hair caught up in a bun, Mongol pencil tucked into bun, sensible shoes, salt-and-pepper skirt from Peck and Peck. The ghost, cherishing a wry attitude toward experience, whispers phrases as it polishes and repolishes sentences for "The Talk of the Town." Occasionally it wanders the halls of the old *New Yorker* office, across Forty-third Street from the present one, hoping to hear the laughter of Brendan Gill, reading a note slipped under his door by the waggish Wolcott Gibbs. This is no wind-grieved or anguished ghost, for such emotions were too strong for the old *New Yorker*, which was, above all, civilized, its civility reaching perfection of form in what became known as "the *New Yorker* short story."

It might be the ghost of Maeve Brennan, who died in 1993. More than fifty of her contributions appeared in "The Talk of the Town" as communications from "our friend the long-winded lady." In his introduction to *The Springs of Affection: Stories of Dublin,*[1] which republishes many of Brennan's short stories, William Maxwell describes some of the topics of her prose sketches—the light from the sky at a

---

1. Houghton Mifflin, 1997.

certain time of day, a cage full of birds for sale in the basement of a
five-and-ten-cent store, a young man waiting for his date in the bar
of the wrong hotel. In 1969, these casual pieces were published as
The Long-Winded Lady. I think I remember them, dimly; they are
an acquired taste, like olives stuffed with blanched almonds. But
Maxwell, with characteristically unobtrusive skill, points toward
moments of a sort that haunt Brennan's more substantial fictions: she
was an artist of the evanescent.

Her background was slightly out of the ordinary. She was born in
Ireland, where her father, Robert Brennan, took the Republican side
during the Civil War and for a time was a hunted man. One of her
earliest stories describes a police search of their house; the tone is
muted, deliberately lacking in drama. When De Valera, her father's
leader, took office, the father came out of the political wilderness with
him, and was made ambassador to Washington. After his term in that
office, Maeve, who would then have been in her early twenties, did
not return to Ireland with the rest of the family.

She soon found her proper place at *The New Yorker*, where, beyond
the "Talk of the Town" sketches, she produced two volumes of justly
admired short stories. In her mature years she married another
New Yorker writer. It was not a successful marriage: he was an alcoholic, a field for which *The New Yorker* of those years offered numerous candidates.

Her final years, however, were very much out of the ordinary. I
myself heard occasional stories but nothing any more specific than
Maxwell's tactful and brief account. Living helplessly alone, she
became destitute and psychotic, and began haunting the *New Yorker*
office, which provided her with shelter. "During the last decade of her
life she moved in and out of reality in a way that was heartbreaking to
watch and that only hospitals could deal with," Maxwell writes. She
had violent spells.

This awful fate makes my opening description of her as the ghost of *The New Yorker* seem vulgar and unfeeling, but it cannot be resisted. In her prime, she had a large framed photograph of Colette, which once, as a mark of silent approbation, she hung above Maxwell's desk. Afterward she removed it, apparently because he liked the novels of Elizabeth Bowen, whom she resisted, on political grounds, as Anglo-Irish. On other days, she would write quotations from Yeats on his wall. There was so much hilarious note-exchanging between Brennan, Gill, and Maxwell that the editor moved her to the other side of the building.

But art is willful, capricious, and captivating, and the fiction that emerged at her hands is extraordinarily good, moving, and strange. Of the stories set in Dublin, there are three groups. First, stories clearly autobiographical, set within a family living in Ranelagh, a quiet and respectable middle-class section of Dublin. They are, as Maxwell says, "written with great care and radiant with the safety and comfort of home." That cherished comfort gives the stories their center, contrasted with which an outlaw father and a house raided by the police are incidentals. Then come stories about a couple named Rose and Hubert Derdon, who live in what would seem to be the identical house. Hubert is a salesman in a shop in fashionable Grafton Street. A son is studying for the priesthood. The Derdons are bound together by familiarity, anger, and craving for a kind of domesticity that takes anger as one of its elementals: "When Rose appeared in the doorway Hubert felt such dislike that he smiled." In the third group, another middle-aged couple, Delia and Martin Bagot, are living—if that is the word—in that Ranelagh house, with their children. They are less unhappy than the Derdons, although they are desperate in ways that they themselves do not know about. Martin lives a bachelor's life within the family, while believing that his is a family strengthened by ties of warmth and love.

The language in all of the stories is clear, simple as glass, apparently as transparent—and they record disappearances of feeling, losses, life-sustaining illusions. They assume that families come into being, are sustained, by manifold unstated magic thoughts, attitudes toward objects. Small happinesses come without warning, leave quickly. They are stories that quietly, without airs or pretenses, challenge the stability of being itself. In the story called "The Carpet with the Big Pink Roses in It," the carpet has a solidity denied to Delia Bagot as she walks across it.

Nothing in the earlier stories prepares one for the final one, a novella, "The Springs of Affection," which Maxwell may well be right in calling one of "the great short stories of this century." In its dissimilarities but also its resemblances, and especially in its placement within the volume, it is suggestive of "The Dead" in Joyce's *Dubliners*. In this story, Delia and Martin Bagot are dead, but live in the memory of Martin's twin sister, Min, who in life had hated Delia, who has inherited their furniture, and into whose rooms her own dead are welcome:

There was a place here for all of them—a place for Polly, a place for poor Clare. A place in the middle for Bridget. A place for Martin in his own chair. They could come in anytime and feel right at home although the room was warmer and the furniture a bit better than anything they had been used to in the old days.

—*The Washington Post Book World*, January 11, 1998

23

BRIAN MOORE

I. Dangerous Amusements

A SEQUENCE IN a Canadian Broadcasting Corporation documentary on Brian Moore shows him sitting in the backseat of a car which is moving through a slum section of his native Belfast. Someone—perhaps a British soldier, perhaps a child with a toy rifle—points a gun at them, and his wife asks why. "Don't ask me," Moore says in a middle-class Belfast accent which decades of absence have not altered, "I'm not an expert on these troubles."

The moment seems to reinforce the opening words of the film's narrative. Moore is jogging along the beach at Malibu, where he has lived for some years, and the narrator begins: "He was born in Belfast and left. Now he says that he is at home everywhere and nowhere. But the one place where he is truly at home is at his typewriter." And the film, faithful to the platitudes of its genre, shows us, at that instant, Moore's hands poised above his machine.

It is something more than a platitude, though. For a long time, writers as diverse as Graham Greene and Christopher Ricks have been describing Moore (rightly, in my opinion) as one of the finest living novelists. But the terms of their praise hold a puzzlement, however muted, as to just how he is to be placed in either a literary or a spiritual or even, as we shall see, a geographical sense. "He is my favorite living novelist," Greene writes. "Each new book of his is unpredictable, dangerous, and amusing. He treats the novel as the tamer treats a wild beast." And Ion Trewin, in *The Times* of London: "He is one of the best novelists writing, never travelling the same ground twice."

On the face of it, these are terms of unqualified praise: All novelists hope to travel new ground with each book, and most of them secretly nourish a wish to be seen as a tamer of dangerous beasts of the imagination. But there is also an implication of something more disquieting: the absence of a figure in Moore's carpet, to use the threadbare Jamesian image. And this literary possibility finds, for some, an explanation in the objective facts of his career, a kind of homelessness, a kind of being at home with homelessness.

His first novel, *The Lonely Passion of Judith Hearne* (1955), is a fierce, almost a heartbreaking portrayal of a lonely woman in one of the loneliest cities in the world: Belfast before the new Troubles, as physically grim as Victorian Manchester, bullied by sects and churches, stale politics and staler pieties, enlivened only by the tiny venoms of bigotry and snobbishness, by alert distrusts of others and of the self. As it happens, religion may seem to have an even more central role in his novel *The Color of Blood*,[1] thereby supplying fresh evidence to those who mistakenly call him a "Catholic novelist" and to those who mistakenly call him an "anti-Catholic" one. Its subject, however, is not religious faith, but rather the politics of religion, relationships between religion and power, religion and the spirit.

In an unnamed country that is clearly Poland, a cardinal named Stephen Bem has dexterously—perhaps too dexterously—been playing off against one another the demands of an irreligious police state and the fierce and violent demands of a right wing within the structure of

---

1. Dutton, 1987.

the Church's hierarchy and clergy. There is an attempt by, it would seem, fanatics on the right to assassinate him. And he is placed under protective custody, evidently by the state security forces. But nothing is quite what it appears on the surface—including Bem himself, son of a servant in the old prewar regime and proud of his cardinal's robes, which are the color of blood.

Small wonder that Graham Greene likes Moore, the reader may be inclined to say, for here is a plot which places us squarely in Greeneland. But this is so only in atmospherics, and in the deliberate, almost playful manipulation of what have become the conventions of that sort of spiritual thriller. In fact, Moore's real subject, in this as in many other of his novels, is the fragility of the self.

Moore's 1968 novel *I Am Mary Dunne* states its subject in its title. *Memento ergo sum*, the narrator says to herself, half hysterically and half in defiance, revising the slogan from Descartes written by a nun on the blackboard of a long-vanished classroom. "I remember who I am," she says in the closing lines, "and I say it over and over and over, I am Mary Dunne, I am Mary Dunne, I am Mary Dunne."

"You lose your past," Moore says in the documentary, in deliberately quiet, throwaway tones. "That seems to be one of my themes." But the film will show us Moore talking with his sisters, his brother, show us a photograph of the surgeon father, silk-hatted, monocled, overwhelming. The film will tell us that we may lose the forms of the past but not its power over our imaginations.

At times, Moore's theme finds expression as an exploration of the artistic imagination itself, which he sees as the self constructing— perilously and mysteriously—artifacts which are lovely, necessary, and absurd. In *The Great Victorian Collection* (1975), for example, a young Canadian professor who has been attending a conference in Berkeley checks into a Carmel hotel and wakes up to discover outside his window, where there had been a large, empty parking lot, an elaborate and intricately detailed collection of Victoriana housed in stalls, showrooms, model (and scandalous) boudoirs, and given focus by "the selfsame crystal fountain which I recognized now as the work of F. & C. Osler, a marvel of casting, cutting and polishing of faultless blocks of glass, erected originally in the transept as the centerpiece of the Great Exhibition of 1851."

The collection is really there. Other people try to exploit it, to turn it into a Disneyland. Rival scholars (read literary critics?) explore its recesses and argue as to whether or not it could be an amassing of incredibly exact forgeries of the originals, which may or may not be missing from such places as the Victoria and Albert Museum in London. There are dangers, of course. The collection of Victorian oil paintings could fade under the metal sun of California and their claim to authenticity be by that much diminished.

The Great Victorian Collection is a stunning parable of the imagination, told with subtlety, charm, and great wit. Moore's subjects are at times so bleak and frightening that readers may forget that he can be a very funny writer. But certainly there was nothing funny, although much that was deliberately grotesque, in his novel *Black Robe* (1985), the story of a seventeenth-century French Jesuit moving deeper and deeper into the Canadian wilderness, as two cultures, European and Indian, come closer to their mutually incomprehensible centers. It can be read, chillingly, as an exploration of what existence the self has when the certitudes of its civilization have been stripped away.

The customary unsettled, even uncertain view of Moore is reinforced, perhaps created in part, by the outlines of his biography. Born and raised in Belfast, in an upper-middle-class, conventionally pious and conventionally nationalist Catholic family, he escaped by accepting overseas service with the British Ministry of War Transport, seeing duty in North Africa, Italy, and France. In 1948 he emigrated to Canada and lived there for ten years, working as a journalist. He still holds a Canadian passport. He lived at various times on Long Island

and in Manhattan, before moving to California to work briefly for Hitchcock and settling, finally, in Malibu.

Like his work, Moore is difficult to pigeonhole. There are (so far as I know) two book-length studies of him. One is in the dreadful Irish Writers Series issued by Bucknell in the 1970s, and the other was written by a Canadian professor for the equally jejune Twayne series, subsection Canada. In each case there is an implicit, if gingerly formulated, effort to stake a claim upon Moore—as an Irish writer, as a Canadian writer. Who in the world, save a writer for whom the self is problematical, would voluntarily travel with a Canadian passport? Canada, that lumbering giant in search of a self, rolling anxious eyes toward the Atlantic, the Pacific, the Arctic, Chicago, London, Paris—and Malibu! Its very syllables carry the sounds of an enormous marine emptiness breaking against expanses of sand, traffic on a ribbon of freeway.

Louis MacNeice, like Moore a Belfast-born writer in self-imposed exile, once bade goodbye to Ireland in the closing lines of a poem which, taken from their context, do not disclose their ironies and reservations. Ireland, MacNeice says,

> ... *gives her children neither sense nor money*
> *Who slouch around the world with a gesture and a brogue*
> *And a faggot of useless memories.*

Like MacNeice, Moore has traveled the world without a slouch, and his accent could never be described as a "brogue." He has never avoided Belfast as a setting, but neither has he planted the flag of his imagination upon it. All of Moore's novels center upon a single character—the wife of a Belfast doctor, a woman nervous and restless in Manhattan, a seventeenth-century Jesuit, a Polish cardinal, the obscure husband of a famous actress, a Belfast-born scriptwriter in Hollywood, a Canadian academic, the abbot of a monastery. His ability to move inside their skins—the women as well as the men—is little short of dazzling. He is pure novelist, at home, as the film has told us, only at his typewriter.

But the film has one quite startling moment as the car drives through Belfast. It is a city of graffiti, either alphabetical (I.R.A. RULE O.K.) or in advocacy of an improbable mode of ecumenism (FUCK THE POPE). We see some of this as the car moves along. But then it turns into Camden Street, where Moore, thirty years before, had situated the boarding house of his fictional Judith Hearne. And on the gray gable end of the corner house, someone has painted, in large black letters, the words JUDITH HEARNE IS ALIVE AND WELL. Who painted it? The Creator of the Great Victorian Collection, perhaps. It is a Brian Moore moment.

—*The Nation*, October 3, 1987

II. An Appreciation

BRIAN MOORE WAS a wonderful writer, one of the few genuine masters of the contemporary novel. He has left us as legacy some twenty novels, eleven of them distinguished and a handful of them unique, isolated triumphs. "Isolated" because they seem like the work of twenty different writers, almost entirely lacking those explicit or subterranean bonds which, so we have been taught, constitute the coherences in a writer's work—continuities of setting, tone, attitude, style, theme. Nothing wrong with this, of course, but when we stand back to think about his work as a whole, it is a fact which inevitably draws our attention.

This apparent lack of thematic or technical continuity does not seem to have bothered him, although it may have helped to make him, as Christopher Lehmann-Haupt has noted, "one of the best known obscure writers alive." There is no Yoknapatawpha County in his assembled novels, no plowed and tilled acres to claim as territory, no burdens of guilt or innocence passed forward from one generation to the next. There is, in short, no typical Moore novel. And this is one of the deliberately offered pleasures of his art.

His early novels, to be sure, are set in his native Belfast, and the first of them, *The Lonely Passion of Judith Hearne*, has acquired its own fame as a portrait, at once humane and unsparing of a spinster's harrowing life in a harrowing culture. He removed himself to a safe distance from Belfast and Northern Ireland long before any literal shots were fired there, and his return visits were wary. His later novels might be set in the wild forests of seventeenth-century Canada, Paris, the beaches of the Riviera, London's West End, California, North Africa. And the theme, in any given novel, might be adultery, religious doubt, political guilt, the disintegration of tradition, lies, the pleasures of sexual passion. (I know of few writers who can evoke such pleasure with greater vividness or less fuss. Whether this is a major or minor accomplishment, it is most impressive.)

And with an equal lack of fuss, he became one of Ireland's "wild geese" in that country's tradition of self-exile, the tradition of Wilde and Joyce and Beckett. But his travels carried him far beyond Paris, the usual destination. He was in North Africa and Italy during the war and later moved to Canada, where he became a journalist and took out citizenship. And then, finally and for many years, to Malibu. Clearly, he thrived there and certainly his work did, those novels which stood on their own feet, without leaning on their predecessors. Each of them is unexpected and idiosyncratic, filled, each one of them, with its own energy, color, and scents. Each one launches itself afresh upon an exercise in fable-making.

It is difficult, Anita Brookner wrote a few years ago, to think of another writer these days who is "taking risks of such unfashionable magnitude." Perhaps that is why he has never been quite fashionable. He had a sense of magnitude and a confidence in his own skill. Confident, also, in the power of fable, a story well told, to sustain the writer on his tightrope and to entertain, perhaps to dazzle, the audience.

He always impressed me, on the rare occasions when we met, as that rarest of creatures, a good writer who enjoyed writing. He was a slight, trim man, with great reticences and great courtesy. His literary style resembled him—lean, direct, undemonstrative, and exact. The style resembles that of two other contemporary masters of story— William Trevor and Graham Greene. A late novel, *The Statement*, about a war criminal on the run with the help of Catholic Church officials, is like a deliberate tribute to Greene's manner—a swift, breathless thriller which is also a serious moral exploration of guilt. And the compliment has been matched. Greene once wrote of him: "Each book of his is dangerous, unpredictable, and amusing. He treats the novel as a trainer treats a wild beast." Magic, very rarely the literal magic of the occult but more often simply the stage magic of the prestidigitator, is used in Moore's fiction as a metaphor for a combination of skill, dazzlement, and illusion. But he worked his own fine effects with one of fiction's earliest resources—a seductive story told with a spare elegance of language. His final novel, set during the nineteenth-century French conquest of North Africa, is called *The Magician's Wife*.

—*The Los Angeles Times Book Review*, January 17, 1999

24

THE POETRY OF SEAMUS HEANEY

SEAMUS HEANEY IS our modern poet of territory. He is also, as every poet is, but he to an extraordinary degree, a savorer of words, their roots, sounds, valences, faithful to a belief that they contain deep-packed, inexhaustible equivalences for feelings, passions, landscapes, weathers, histories, communities. He began with a search for words with which to express a territory, and his art, as it developed, turned language into territory.

The word "territory" itself, which I have used to name his art, has a history which would confirm his faith in language's magical appro-priateness, so aptly does it define him for us. Like his art, it has widen-ing circles of meaning, moving outward from a constant core. It comes into English from the Latin, but its ancient etymology, says the *Oxford English Dictionary*, is "unsettled." The poet of bogs would approve of this. Its root is usually taken as coming from *terra*, meaning earth, land, but the early Latin form suggests a different derivation, from *terrere*, meaning to frighten. Thus, a *territorium* may once have been a place from which men were frightened away, because it belonged to others or was sacred to a god or goddess.

But in English, it most often means a specific place. As when a seventeenth-century writer speaks of "a circuit of ground, containing a liberty within itself wherein divers men having land within it, and yet the Territory itself doth lie open and is not enclosed." It can also mean a specific place whose boundaries are undefined: the OED offers here an example from a writer named Yeats, although not the poet. It can mean land or country "belonging to or under the dominion of a ruler." Here the OED example is taken from Sir William Petty, the surveyor general of Ireland, whose maps and tables defined the sub-ordination within the land of the Gaelic, Catholic stock from which Heaney is sprung. Figuratively, it can mean the domain or space which pertains to a particular art. And, finally, the printer Caxton, in the fifteenth century, used the word as a mistranslation of the French *tertre*, a rising ground, a hill, an eminence.

For Heaney, the central territorial core is the farmland of south Derry, which lies in Ulster, the northern of the four Irish provinces. It is a specific place indeed, and his poetry has taught us how specific, for it celebrates the intimate textures, noises, weathers, memories of the land. But it is also, as the dictionary would have it, a specific place whose boundaries are, in a sense, undefined. Derry lies within that part of the province of Ulster which is the colony or ministate of Northern Ireland, belonging to or under the dominion of the United Kingdom. Diverse men have land within it: Ulstermen loyal to the British Crown, and Irishmen, like Heaney, whose loyalty is to an older power, a territorial goddess, sacred and frightening.

From its beginnings, from *Death of a Naturalist* in 1965, his work has balanced a twinned fascination, with the natural world and with the man-created world of language. He speaks, in his prose, of words as bearers of history and mystery, and remembers hearing, when very young, his mother's recitation of lists of affixes and suffixes and Latin roots with their English meanings. It is a memory of language set within nature, a Mossbawn kitchen beyond which lay farmland, pastureland, bog. Two kinds of root, of farms and of verbs, which later went to the shaping of a poetic voice, joined upon the rooted tongue. But those first poems are also hedged, to use a word from nature, by an alert awareness that language is and yet is not a part of nature. In "Digging," the poem which opens *Death of a Naturalist*, he watches from the window, pen in hand, as his father spades the potato field. "I've no spade to follow men like them," he says, and then concludes:

> *Between my finger and my thumb*
> *The squat pen rests.*
> *I'll dig with it.*

Standing there upon an opening page, the metaphor seems a shapely, witty conceit. Witty, because the poem's body holds the knowledge, present but unspoken, that there is a sense in which spading is heavier work than writing poems. It is only when the pages are turned, of this book and the ones that followed, through *Door into the Dark* (1969) and *Wintering Out* (1972) to the great culminating poems of *North* (1975), that its exact seriousness is revealed. His art, through that book, has been an art of digging in a sense so literal that when one turns back to the first poem, it is the father, and not the son at the window, who has become the figure of metaphor.

Fortune and Art, Aristotle splendidly if mysteriously tells us in the *Ethics*, foster one another. "There is a sense," he says, "in which Chance and Art have the same sphere." Thus, for example, it was decreed within that sphere that Heaney should grow up with an intimate knowledge of bogs, and that bogs should for a time be one of his central, controlling images—bogs rendered accurately in look and smell and feel beneath the boot, and yet also great, mythological repositories of the past. The image first announces itself in "Bogland," the final poem of *Door into the Dark*:

> *Our pioneers keep striking*
> *Inwards and downwards,*

Every layer they strip
Seems camped on before.
The bogholes might be Atlantic seepage.
The wet center is bottomless.

These pioneers do not move outward, as American pioneers once did, horizontally across a vast unhistoried land toward where prairies slice a big sun at evening. Their operations, cutting turf for fuel, are downward, and into a literal history, for pasts have been preserved by the juices of the bog. Men on a bog, a familiar sight in Heaney's territory, but here defining a psychic condition, a relationship not with space but with time.

Equally, Chance and Art conspired to place him within a countryside where the ear was quickened by the sound and shape of words which held within themselves a tangle of histories, reaching back through vowels and consonants to old divisions within the land—Gaelic, Scottish, English. The poets of Northern Ireland know that usages, shapes upon the tongue, carry freightages of community, express, paradoxically, inarticulate loyalties. Heaney's art, even when most intimate, even when the voice is musing, even when the subject is love or solitude or a hidden place, touches community through language.

It is thus, as I have said, an art which can be defined as that of territory, but only if we hold in mind the fullness of meanings which cluster about that word. After *Door into the Dark*, the art deepens, keeps its hold upon its core, but moves outward to accept new challenges. And by a kind of inevitability, the challenges arose from within the territory. By 1969, Heaney, who then was teaching literature at Queen's University in Belfast, was an established poet. And in that year the Troubles in Northern Ireland quickened to the bloody violence which still continues. "From that moment," he has written, "the problems of poetry moved from being simply a matter of achieving the satisfactory verbal icon to being a search for images and symbols adequate to our predicament." His concern was not to give voice either to liberal, evenhanded lamentation or to "public celebrations or execrations of resistance or atrocity." His task, rather, was to draw both from within himself and from what he saw around him, a poetry equal to history's occasion and yet faithful to his private muse, to poetry's stubborn particularity. "I felt it imperative," he says, "to discover a field of force in which, without abandoning fidelity to the processes and experience of poetry as I have outlined them, it would be possible to encompass the perspectives of a humane reason and at the same time to grant the religious intensity of the violence its deplorable authenticity and complexity."

He was looking, he says, for what Yeats, in "Meditations in Time of Civil War," calls "befitting emblems of adversity." But this seems to me slightly off-key. Yeats's art is emblematic—a silk-sheathed sword, a rose, a tower, abstracted out of the natural world. Heaney's is not. He cannot be imagined as sharing Yeats's wish never to take his bodily form from any natural thing. And for his central image of those years, he returned to the bogs, and to a man who had, quite literally, been married to nature.

At about this time, "the year the killing started," he discovered P. V. Glob's book *The Bog People*, which is "chiefly concerned with preserved bodies of men and women found in the bogs of Jutland, naked, strangled or with their throats cut, disposed under the peat since early Iron Age times." Some, like the Tollund Man, as he is called, "were ritual sacrifices to the Mother Goddess, the goddess of the ground who needed new bridegrooms each winter to bed with her in her sacred place, in the bog, to ensure the renewal and fertility of the territory in the spring."

In the earlier poem, "Bogland," the bog is kind, holding within itself nothing more menacing than the skeleton of an elk, "butter sunk under/more than a hundred years." The bogs of the poems which now follow hold different trophies of time. "The Tollund Man," in *Wintering Out*, initiates the new series and continues as one of its psychic centers. It juxtaposes by layering, as a bog does, its ancient victim, ageless, "Naked except for the cap, noose and girdle," and the modern killings in Northern Ireland, "four young brothers, trailed for miles along the line." Some day, the poet says, he will visit Jutland:

> *Out there in Jutland*
> *In the old man-killing parishes*
> *I will feel lost,*
> *Unhappy and at home.*

To feel both unhappy and at home within man-killing parishes is one definition of the Irish, but more especially the Northern Irish, condition. Sir Walter Scott, visiting the country in 1825, had noted in his journal: "Their factions have been so long envenomed, and they have such narrow ground to do their battle in, that they are like people fighting with daggers in a hogshead." "Hogshead" is good, but it is a visitor's word, harsh, disdainful, lurid. "Parishes" is better: local, ironical, and consoling.

Each of Heaney's books contain seeds which will later flower. In *North*, the accreted powers and meanings of the bog are deployed against a geography of history and identity. Ulster is in the north of Ireland, but all Ireland is part of a larger North. It knew Viking raids: Norse queens lay buried in Irish bogs, and bone fragments of Norse syllables are embedded in familiar place-names. But that is all that is left of them in Ireland—a legend of savagery, a few bodies preserved in bog-juices, some place-names. For Heaney, these vanished raiders, men of blood-feuds, murders, revenges, are icons of a violence so pure it need not be named.

North balances images of an intense and pure affection

> *And here is love*
> *like a tinsmith's scoop*

sunk past its gleam
in the meal-bin

with images drawn from the present violence and set within the perspective established by the ritual violence of the Iron Age. He is so fully humane a writer that it is easy, perhaps tempting, to overlook another aspect of his poetic character—an ability to confront violence with the tough equanimity of a tribal bard. At times, he holds these aspects in a deliberate equipoise, to achieve a disturbing moral complexity. In "Punishment," a girl of the Jutland bog, killed by her people as an adulteress, is juxtaposed against the Derry girls who in the 1970s were cropped and tarred for having fraternized with the enemy:

I who have stood dumb
when your betraying sisters,
cauled in tar,
wept by the railings,

who would connive
in civilized outrage
yet understand the exact
and tribal, intimate revenge.

If *North* expresses a historical and political attitude, it is one which Heaney himself has named with an explicitness more full than a critic would risk. "To some extent," he has written, "the enmity can be viewed as a struggle between the cults and devotees of a god and a goddess. There is an indigenous territorial numen, call her mother Ireland, Kathleen Ni Houlihan, the poor old woman, the Shan Van Vocht, whatever; and her sovereignty has been temporarily usurped or infringed by a new male cult whose founding fathers were Cromwell, William of Orange, and William Carson. What we have is the tail-end of a struggle in a province between territorial piety and imperial power."

(He might have added that the fatality of a male cult lurks within its arid abstractness. Of the three paternal deities of Ulster loyalism, not one was an Ulsterman, but rather, an Englishman, a Dutchman, and a Dublin opportunist who privately disliked the province.)

This is an explicitness beyond a critic's risk because one of the book's powerful generative centers is the tension between historical vision and a poetic determination to keep an eye clear as the icicle's bleb, faithful to the actualities of a lived and felt experience. With *North*, Heaney won recognition within Ireland and beyond it as a voice through which a culture was defining itself. But he earned it precisely because of his refusal to admit encroachments upon his private, poetic self of historical or political generalizations. Rather, that self has moved outward, to negotiate with history.

North is a culminating volume, an exploration downward into old territory, and outward into new. It brings to a close the first, long sweep of Heaney's art, and contains intimations of the next. "Exposure," its final poem, is set in rural Wicklow, in the south of Ireland, to which he moved with his family in 1972, "neither internee nor informer; / An internal emigre, grown long-haired / And thoughtful." It anticipates the lovely series of "Glanmore Sonnets" which are the center of *Field Work* (1979). Here he explores his two territories, that of earth and that of verb, but with new emphases and confrontations. The first, the originating territory, speaks now through a sibyl, whose words are ominous and bleak:

> *The ground we kept our ear to for so long*
> *Is flayed or calloused, and its entrails*
> *Tented by an impious augury.*
> *Our island is full of comfortless noises.*

Art's territory is music, the silent antagonist of noise:

There are the mud-flowers of dialect
And the immortelles of perfect pitch
And that moment when the bird sings very close
To the music of what happens.

In *North* and in *Field Work*, his two territories stand toward each other in ways that are at times dialectical. Two poems artfully frame the first half of *North*, "Antaeus" and "Hercules and Antaeus." They are playful poems, and it is always well to read serious poets with particular care when they are being playful. The first one was written by a younger Heaney, in 1966, and here it is carefully dated for our instruction.

If Heaney is the modern poet of territory, Antaeus is the ancient, mythological embodiment of its power and its fatality, giant and demigod, son of Poseidon and Gaea, who could outwrestle all strangers, for if he was thrown down, he would draw fresh strength from Mother Earth. The earlier poem celebrates his voice, boisterous and confident within territory:

Girdered with root and rock
I am cradled in the dark that wombed me
And nurtured in every artery
Like a small hillock.

There is here but a hint of his fate, a reference to a hero seeking "golden apples and Atlas." For Hercules would one day come and defeat him, not by casting him down, but by lifting him high off the earth. In the second poem, Hercules arrives, "sky-born and royal," his future hung with trophies, and

Hercules has the measure
of resistance and black powers
feeding off the territory.

He lifts his arms "in a remorseless v," and lifts and banks Antaeus,

> *high as a profiled ridge,*
> *a sleeping giant,*
> *pap for the dispossessed.*

Heaney, of course, is the Antaeus figure, nourished by the powers of his territory, and Hercules, imperialist adventurer, remorseless and cunning, is the invader. But it would misread the poem not also to see him as another aspect of Heaney, the bearer of trophies and awards, traveler to New York and London, and to California and Mexico, the lands of golden apples. The poems are an overheard dialogue of the poet with himself—bantering, self-mocking, yet edging toward a concern which is best approached on the oblique. The concern has its shadowy presence within "Digging," the poet secure within his territory, yet separate from it by a window's depth, the pen which distances as it digs. It is proper that he should confront such concerns, but they need not concern his readers. "Etymologist of roots and graftings," he is an Antaeus strong within his territory, but as artful as much-traveled Hercules.

Caxton, the father of fine printing, and godfather, therefore, of the present volume, may have wrought better than he knew when he used the word "territory" to mistranslate a foreign word which means a rising ground, a hill, an eminence.

—Introduction to *Seamus Heaney, Poems and a Memoir*
(Limited Editions Club, 1982)

25

FAMILY SECRETS

STAIRS
February 1945

On the stairs, there was a clear, plain silence.

It was a short staircase, fourteen steps in all, covered in lino from which the original pattern had been polished away to the point where it had the look of a faint memory. Eleven steps took you to the turn of the stairs where the cathedral and the sky always hung in the window frame. Three more steps took you on to the landing, about six feet long.

"Don't move," my mother said from the landing. "Don't cross that window."

I was on the tenth step, she was on the landing. I could have touched her. "There's something between us. A shadow. Don't move."

I had no intention. I was enthralled. But I could see no shadow.

"There's somebody there. Somebody unhappy. Go back down the stairs, son."

I retreated one step. "How'll you get down?"

"I'll stay a while and it will go away."

The opening page of Seamus Deane's *Reading in the Dark*[1] suggests, in its deliberate spareness, qualities which in the unfolding will
more fully reveal themselves. It is a childhood experience, but the
voice speaking across the years is poised and literary—"a plain
silence," "the look of a faint memory." We learn that it is a working-
class house—the staircase brief, the lino pattern rubbed away. It is
a house across which shadows fall that may be supernatural, visi-
tants. This is a culture, we soon learn, in which spirits are given a
half-credulous, half-skeptical acceptance. "People with green eyes
were close to the fairies, we were told; they were just there for a little
while, looking for a human child they could take away."

The novel's short, crisp chapters, carefully dated and intricately
linked by image, carry the narrator from childhood, in 1945, to the
beginning phases, in 1968, of Northern Ireland's most recent Troubles.
By then, what had earlier seemed emanations from another world
have resolved themselves—perhaps too neatly—into occurrences of
another kind, natural but just as sinister, as menacing to the minds
of the living. Near the novel's close, brusquely and almost as afterthought, the "Troubles" as we have known them from headlines and
television enter the story: "We choked on CS gas fired by the army,
saw or heard the explosions, the gunfire, the riots moving in close
with their scrambled noises of glass breaking, flashing petrol-bombs,
isolated shouts turning to a prolonged baying and the drilled smashing of batons on riot shields." But it is not afterthought. *Reading in the
Dark*, as might have been expected of its author, is a book centrally
and subtly historical and political, and offers evidence that, at least in
Northern Ireland, the political and the private are bound together.

This is his first novel, but Seamus Deane, who was a schoolmate in
Derry City of Seamus Heaney and Brian Friel, has long been established as one of Ireland's most challenging literary critics. His criti-

1. Knopf, 1997.

cism, whether of literature or of public life, is acerb, shrewd, independent, and enlivened by a brisk and not always genial wit. In Ireland's always-lively culture wars, a significant event was the publication, in 1977, of "Literary Myths of the Revival," his sardonic demythologizing of the movement led by Lady Gregory, Synge, and, first and foremost, Yeats: "Yeats had demonstrated throughout his long career that the conversion of politics and history into aesthetics carries with it the obligation to despise the modern world and seek refuge from it." His harsh strictures are not entirely palliated by his deep responsiveness to the beauty of Yeats's verse. Deane himself is an exact and probing poet, angular and lean. *Reading in the Dark* had been long in gestation and execution, and bears the marks of this: it is polished, adroit, and deeply disturbing.

For one thing, it deliberately subverts two modes of fiction. One is formed by the novels—so numerous as almost to constitute a genre—that have sought to express the atmosphere and terrors, the emotional scars, the crippled lives, which constitute a portion of life in present-day Northern Ireland. Deane's novel, set in the decades before the present Troubles and convincingly displayed as their inevitable prelude, quietly establishes a historical perspective lacking in most of those novels. And Deane stands apart from these writers in a second way: his identification with his nationalist community is guarded from sentimentality by the formal severities of his structure and language.

The other mode, the bildungsroman, has as its great Irish instance Joyce's *Portrait of the Artist as a Young Man*. It is a central text for modern Irish literature, and Deane plays off it, sometimes for comic purposes, and at other times to mark the distance between Stephen Dedalus and his own unnamed narrator. (Almost nameless: by detective work one discovers that he is named Seamus Greene.)

Three of Deane's chapters ("The Facts of Life," "Retreat," "Religious Knowledge") deliberately and almost jokingly echo Joyce's in setting and even in imagery. Deane's narrator is in a Christian

Brothers school in Derry, and Stephen far to the south, first at an elite Jesuit boarding school and then in the clerically dominated Royal University, but they have similar encounters with the clergy. Stephen is summoned to the room of the dean of studies, who is having trouble with his fire; Deane's narrator is summoned to the room of his spiritual director, who has a fire blazing even though it is a warm day. In each novel, the fire is given a little useful life of its own. Deane's encounters, though, allowing for the element of parody, itself a Joycean technique, possess a warm-blooded humor far removed from Stephen's Byronism and Joyce's icy distance from his protagonist.

A *Portrait*, with its suavities and ambiguities, expresses the progressively more severe separation of Stephen Dedalus from his culture. "When the soul of a man is born in this country," Stephen tells his nationalist friend Davin, "there are nets flung at it to hold it back from flight. You talk to me of nationality, language, religion. I shall try to fly by those nets." As Deane has written elsewhere, Stephen supplants the language of the tribe with his own, so that the subject of the book becomes its author:

> In that light, the novel is a series of carefully orchestrated quotations, through which we see a young mind coming to grips with his world through an increasing mastery of language. Further, we recognize that this is a moral not merely a formal achievement.

In one of the diary entries, theatrical and faintly ambiguous, which bring the *Portrait* to its close, Stephen writes: "Mother is putting my new secondhand clothes in order. She prays now, she says, that I may learn in my own life and away from home and friends what the heart is and what it feels."

The mother's prayers in Deane's novel arise from her perception of a guilt which cannot be lifted. His is a close, warm family, despite crippling strains that are nursed in bitter silence, in partial truths and half-revelations, in multiple misunderstandings of what lies in the past:

> I felt it was almost a mercy when my mother suffered a stroke and lost the power of speech, just as the Troubles came in October 1968. I would look at her, sealed in her silence, and now she would smile slightly at me and very gently, almost imperceptibly, shake her head. I was to seal it all in too. Now we could love each other, at last, I imagined.

It is a family that is close even as it shatters.

For the mother, the shadow at the window has several identities, but chiefly it is that of her husband's brother Eddie, who disappeared in April of 1922, after a big shoot-out at a local distillery between the IRA and the police. By some accounts, he fell into one of the exploding vats of whiskey when the burning roof collapsed. But rumors have placed him abroad, in Chicago or in Melbourne. One winter's day, the boy overhears the matter discussed as his father and his mother's brothers repair the boiler in his small house. Eddie's story blends in with other tales of disappearances, returns from the dead, exorcisms.

We are given no direct historical information, and are expected to know that 1922 was a crucial time in the history of Northern Ireland —was in fact the time that marked its creation as a political entity. The Black and Tan war against England had ended in a treaty, of which the most disastrous consequence was the partition of the island, with Ulster's Catholics hived off into what would in short order become a police state, in which they were bullied and severely discriminated against by an armed Protestant majority. The conflict had dark, tangled roots stretching back into earlier centuries, but now it was to bear poisonous fruit. The new statelet, memorably described by one of its prime ministers as "a Protestant state for a

Protestant people," kept a vigilant control over its minority, within which a few—the IRA—attempted from time to time a futile armed resistance. The others kept their sullen, sardonic distance from a state whose very reason for existence would have made ineffective and humiliating any vow of allegiance.

The economy bore down heavily upon Catholics. The narrator's father is an electrician's helper who, when times are good, works at the British naval base: "going out foreign," it is called. His Aunt Katie works in the shirt factory, the traditional women's job, from which the women stream home, "arms linked, so much more brightly dressed, so much more talkative than the men, most of whom stood at the street corners." The neighborhood police informer, Fogey McKeever, is "a young, open-faced man of twenty or so with a bright smile and wide-spaced, rounded eyes." It is Fogey whose information sends into the narrator's house the RUC men who beat up the father and his sons. And he is far from being the novel's only informer: this is a police culture in which informers thrive.

For the Catholics, there are two spiritual resources—the Catholic Church and the neighboring county of Donegal. The city of Derry (which British cartographers insist on calling Londonderry) is separated from the rest of its county by the River Foyle, which empties into a great lough and thence into the Atlantic. It is embedded into the flank of County Donegal, which politically is not part of Northern Ireland at all but rather is the northernmost part of the Republic of Ireland (or, as it is known in the north, the Free State). It is a great, mountainous, sea-girt reservoir of what remains of Ireland's Gaelic life. Both sides of the narrator's family came into Derry City from Donegal, carrying with them songs, folk beliefs, tales of fairies and revenants, music, the memory of dark, unspoken betrayals. Donegal is a repository, also, of the Irish language, of which the parents can recall only school-learned rudiments. Later, when the narrator thinks he knows the family's secrets, he writes them out, for his own satisfaction, in Irish. The parents cannot understand this account of their own secrets when he reads it out to them.

Near a lost farmhouse in Donegal lies "the field of the disappeared," where the souls of those who never had Christian burial return on Saint Brigid's day and on the festival of Samhain, "to cry like birds and look down on the fields where they had been born." On a high hill commanding both Lough Foyle and Lough Swilly stands the Grianan of Aileach, an ancient and enormous stone fort, built, tradition holds, by the ancient gods, but more likely in some early Christian century. The Fianna, Ireland's heroic warriors, lie sleeping below, waiting for the special person who will rouse them to make final war on the English. All this lies a day's walk from Derry City, behind its border. It has always offered easy refuge for rebels on the run. Early on in the novel, alone or on visits to his ancestral Donegal with friends, the narrator encounters them all—the ruined farm, the field of the disappeared, the fortress. By the close of the novel, he has unriddled their meanings in the life of his family. They have held, for the narrator at least, the unwinding and ironical mysteries of what happened to Eddie, the IRA uncle, in 1922.

The Catholic Church plays a pervasive and deeply ambiguous part within this subjugated Derry culture. It shares with its people a sense of injustice and a conviction that beyond the borders of the United Kingdom it is recognized as the true church. But the priests, negotiating with the governing power, are complicitous with it. Brother Regan, delivering the Christmas address in primary school, counsels the boys in acceptance and inner peace as they prepare for a world of "wrong, injury, insult and unemployment, a world where the unjust hold power and the ignorant rule." Sergeant Burke of the Lecky Road barracks of the Royal Ulster Constabulary, brutal by profession and an associate of the policemen who beat up the narrator and his father, is himself a Catholic. When he dies in bed, his priest-sons concelebrate the Requiem Mass. It is attended by the bishop. "'How dare he do that,' hissed my mother." But it is received wisdom that "the police and the priests were always in cahoots," a knowledge that cohabits easily with a deeply held Catholic faith.

In 1957, at the height of the cold war, the boys at secondary school are addressed by a priest, a chaplain in British army uniform, who has been sent by the government's Ministry of Education. He reminds them that Derry, a naval port, is "part of the Western world's preparations for the defeat of the international Communist threat, . . . a battle of cold atheism against the genial warmth of that Christian faith that has lit so many Irish hearts down the centuries." Our internal disputes are no more than family quarrels, local troubles, transient divisions. This inspired chain of cold war platitudes runs on through long paragraphs, reminding us, and perhaps by Deane's intention, of the famous sermons on Hell in *A Portrait*.

Next day, in history class, Father McAuley reveals to the boys that this was no true Catholic priest, but a class of English heretic called Anglo-Catholic. Nevertheless McAuley is at one with him, sharing a global vision which looks beyond troubles in "our little streets toward the approaching world conflict." Outside the classroom, the narrator's tough chum, Irwin, clarifies matters as seen from those streets: "Propaganda. That's all that is. First, it's the Germans. Then it's the Russians. Always, it's the IRA. What have the Germans or Russians to do with us? It's the British who are the problem for us. McAuley's a moron."

The British officer concealed in priestly robes is an old theme, running from the rebel ballad of 1798 to the pyrotechnic of *Ulysses*. Ben Dollard, in *Ulysses*, sings the ballad: "The false priest rustling soldier from his cassock. A yeoman captain." And Bloom reflects: "They know it all by heart. The thrill they itch for." But of all the traditional themes which this novel touches upon, one dominates over all the others, and sets the key for both the theme and the music.

A pair of contrasting icons can be used in a rough-and-ready way to separate out two shaping motifs of the Irish novel—the Ruined Big House and the Informer. Deane himself has written of the former: "The Big House surrounded by the unruly tenantry. Culture besieged by barbarity, a refined aristocracy beset by a vulgar middle class—all of these are recurrent images in twentieth-century Irish fiction, which draws heavily upon Yeats's poetry for them." In fact, this specifically Anglo-Irish tradition stretches back far beyond Yeats to the very first novel of Irish life, Maria Edgeworth's *Castle Rackrent* in 1800. The Protestant Ascendancy, in a move that would have won Faulkner's admiration, began to mourn its own passing when it was at the very height of its political, economic, and cultural power. And thus forward through the Victorian Charles Lever and the Edwardian Somerville and Ross into our own times, with the derelict gardens and gates, the burned-out big houses of Elizabeth Bowen and Jennifer Johnston.

The Informer, who betrays to the conqueror the secrets of a submerged people, is the theme that runs through the songs, legends, history, art, even the folk beliefs of that "other" Ireland from which Deane comes. The hulking shadow of a drunken and remorseful Victor McLaglen, flung across rain-glistening Dublin slum walls, falls from John Ford's *The Informer* into the dark bog of the Irish past. "The indispensible informer," so the incorrigible Stephen Dedalus calls the breed.

Reading in the Dark dramatizes the shattering consequences for a family of informing, suspicions of informing, constructions of the past by which a supposed informer's face, pressed against window glass, carries to the generations of a family the conviction of tangled sins against the heart of a community. Near the beginning of the book, the narrator discovers that Eddie may not have died in the 1922 shoot-out, or vanished into Chicago or Melbourne. More probably, he was killed as an informer, and upon orders of the narrator's grandfather, an old Republican stalwart. But only a part of this is true: truth, the narrator discovers as he grows up and goes off to the university, is complex and twists back upon itself. Just possibly, it may at last become fully known, but it can never be fully communicated.

One can only read Deane's fine novel with admiration. It has much to say about families, about a beleaguered but tenacious culture, about a compulsion to unravel the riddles and misheard language of the past and the pain which this can engender. And it does so with a skillfulness which never diminishes its emotional power. One's only reservation has to do with its very skillfulness. Everything in the book, everything, is put to work as symbol, from a cathedral framed by a window to a Chekhovian German pistol to the tinted darkness of a church interior. But this may be what happens when poets write novels. And it is this heavy structuring by images that allows the book its triumph, which is to impose order and the loveliness of meaning upon disorder and violence.

—*The New York Review of Books*, October 23, 1997

III

Irish and Irish-American History

26

GREEN REVISIONISM

AS THE IRISH historian Robert Fitzroy Foster remarks in the preface to his masterly, mildly sardonic history, *Modern Ireland 1600–1972*,[1] "The tradition of writing the 'story of Ireland' as a morality tale, invented around the seventeenth century and retained (with the roles of hero and villain often reversed) until the twentieth, has been abandoned over the last generation. A vast number of special studies have appeared, revolutionizing long-held views in several key areas."

We therefore begin with a melancholy paradox. A profound revolution in Irish scholarship has indeed overthrown the simple (and several of the more sophisticated) narratives of the Irish past. Chiefly, though, it has been a revolution within university lecture halls and journals, although its general assumptions have altered into the urban middle classes, guided by "revisionist" and "de-mythologizing" writers of whom the exemplar is Conor Cruise O'Brien.

The traditional "story of Ireland" or, rather, stories—one Catholic and one Protestant—are still vivid within the general population and still bloody in the streets of Belfast and Derry. Real issues of justice and human rights are at stake in Northern Ireland, but a genuine conflict has been contorted into savagery by these disparate stories,

---

1. Allen Lane/Penguin, 1988.

ancient yet lethal. Students of those galactic distances that now separate scholarly elites from their containing communities need look no further than Northern Ireland.

One of Foster's chief concerns in *Modern Ireland* is to demonstrate that the central effect of contemporary scholarship has been a liberation "from the Anglocentric obsession that once led the study of Irish political and economic history so far astray." The meanings of that adjective "Anglocentric" are multiple, but they may be subsumed within the general notion that the several conflicting stories of Ireland have all had Ireland's relations with England at their core. And reasonably enough, it could be argued: for many centuries the history of Ireland was its history as a colony of the British Crown. But Foster, and other recent historians, argue forcefully that the consequence has been a digression into one ideology or another, the nationalist or the loyalist story, and away from a steady, unillusioned consideration of what was actually happening in, and to, Ireland.

Foster has chosen appropriate dates. In 1601, the Tudor reconquest of Ireland was consummated by the defeat on the Cork coast of the rebellious Hugh O'Neill, Earl of Tyrone. In 1972, the Republic of Ireland voted to join the European Economic Community; that same year Britain, its petulant fury masked as statesmanship, suspended its puppet government in Northern Ireland, having recognized, rather belatedly, that its Parliament existed entirely to serve the interests of Ulster's Protestant majority. Britain chose instead to govern the province by direct rule from London. Within a single year Ireland had entered modern Europe and had opened a new chapter in the history, at once dismal and bloodshot, of its relationship with its "sister" island.

In the nationalist story of Ireland, Hugh O'Neill was the heroic champion of Gaelic, Catholic Ireland against Protestant England. So he was, from time to time, and as it suited him. He was in fact a wily territorial magnate defending his turf, a man by political education as much English as Irish, moving into rebellion against or alliance with various lords deputy in accordance with what he took to be his best interests. Nationalism itself, of course, did not exist in his century, although it was to supply the mold into which all Irish history was eventually poured.

Hugh O'Neill was, as Foster makes clear, a more intricate, elusive, and culturally complex figure than the lithographed hero popularized by later propagandists. And Foster is unsentimental in his quick sketches of more recent deities of Irish nationalism. Thus "bold Robert Emmet, the darling of Erin," as the ballad has it, hanged after his abortive uprising in 1803, is to Foster not a "noble and sacrificial dreamer" but a Continental-style radical whose "ideas were those of elite separatism; neither social idealism nor religious equality appear to have figured." Wolfe Tone, the chief contriver of the calamitous rebellion of 1798 and the founding father of the Irish Republican tradition, is presented (quite accurately) as a charming, witty, and ruthless opportunist who regarded Catholicism as a "dying superstition" to be exploited for entirely secular purposes.

All this has long been known, save in such redoubts of unreconstructed piety as the bars of Queens and South Boston. When Foster speaks of a revolution in Irish scholarship, he refers not to such superficial emendations of patriotic folklore but rather to deeper research and more sweeping interpretations.

A crucial example is provided by his consideration of the horrific Great Famine of 1845–1849, which, as he says,

> opened an abyss that swallowed up many hundreds of thousands of impoverished Irish people: the poverty-stricken conditions of rural life in the west and south-west, a set-piece for astounded travel books in the early nineteenth century, apparently climaxed in a Malthusian apocalypse.

It has traditionally been seen as a watershed in Irish history, cata-clysmic in its effects upon the society, and having as a subordinate consequence the creation of "an institutionalized Anglophobia among the Irish at home and abroad."

To put this latter point less gently, it has traditionally been held as having entered the folk consciousness of the Irish, and still more the folklore of the grandchildren of those forced into American exile, that the Famine was an act of genocide visited by England upon Ireland. That the causes were at once more complex and morally more terrify-ing we have known at least since the publication in 1962 of Cecil Woodham-Smith's magnificent *The Great Hunger*. It is indeed the case that, as Foster says, Sir Charles Edward Trevelyan, the "final arbiter of famine-relief policy," inclined toward the view "that the Famine was the design of a benign Malthusian God who sought to relieve overpopulation by natural disaster." But this was a theory uni-versally held among Whigs. The Famine was an abomination that flowed not from malignity but from an iron economic ideology, a his-torical point often lost on those who urge the unqualified beneficence of free trade. Trevelyan was no Eichmann; he is proof not of the banality of evil but of the evil of banality. As Foster puts matters, per-haps with too heavy a decorum, "Within both the government and the Treasury...there was also an attitude, often unconcealed, that Irish fecklessness and lack of economy were bringing a retribution that would work out for the best in the end." Rhetoric falters into silence before such brutal complacency, beside which Voltaire's Dr. Pangloss seems gloomy and saturnine.

The *effects* of the Famine, however, have been less thoroughly can-vassed until recently. One of these, as Foster says, is that, the landless and the near-landless having been swept away by starvation, disease, and emigration, there remained a population of small-scale but sol-vent farmers which, in coming decades,

would underpin the mass movements that challenged land-
lordism.... The values, beliefs and influence of the farming class
in post-Famine Ireland entered their own ascendancy, mediated
through Church, social institutions and, eventually, politics.

In the post-Famine years, that is, modern Ireland took its present
shape. The ruling Anglo-Irish social caste and the government alike
found themselves confronted not by incoherent multitudes but by an
adversarial social class, aware of its own interests and capable of
fighting to secure them, through instruments like the Land League
and political machines such as the one worked at the end of the century, with cold and enthralling brilliance, by Charles Stewart Parnell.

It was also a social class distinctly aware of its supposed cultural
and intellectual inferiority to the "Ascendancy" Ireland of its Protestant Anglo-Irish rulers, and increasingly determined to meet its adversary upon cultural as well as political grounds. It sought to assert,
that is to say, the superiority of its own culture—peasant, Gaelic,
Catholic, newly arisen from bondage, and truculent. Such a celebrated
instance as the riot that attended the opening at the Abbey of J. M.
Synge's *The Playboy of the Western World*, in 1907, speaks for itself.

It is along this thread that Foster assesses the "new" nationalism of
the new century and the years of armed struggle, 1916–1923, out of
which emerged the modern Irish state. For a very long time it had
been more or less the case that to be Protestant was to be loyalist, to
be Catholic was to be nationalist. Exceptions on both sides provided
delectable footnotes. What was new about the new nationalism was
its exclusivist nature: to be truly Irish was to be Gaelic (and, if possible, to speak that language) and, by implication, to be Catholic. The
new nationalism was prepared to accept the Irishness of Protestants
who could pass a kind of ethnic literacy test. And Protestant patriots
of the past (beginning and almost ending with Tone, Emmet, and
Parnell) were revered and ritualistically hauled out as totems of

nonsectarianism. Indeed, Patrick Pearse, the rather odd leader of the 1916 Rising, was given to speaking of Tone in language that bordered on the idolatrous.

We are familiar, even in the United States, with the dreary Protestant bigotry of the Reverend Ian Paisley. Less so, perhaps, with the corresponding rant that in the not-too-distant past lay available as fuel for his paranoia. Thus, from the extremist *Catholic Bulletin* in 1924:

> The Irish nation is the Gaelic nation; its language and literature is the Gaelic language; its history is the history of the Gael. All other elements have no place in Irish national life, literature and tradition, save as far as they are assimilated into the very substance of Gaelic speech, life and thought. The Irish nation is not a racial synthesis at all; synthesis is not a vital process, and only what is vital is admissible in analogies bearing on the nature of the living Irish nation, speech, literature and tradition. We are not a national conglomerate, nor a national patchwork specimen....

The contemporary twenty-six-county Republic of Ireland has come a very long way since the publication of such sinister racial gibberish. But I do recall that when a scholarly book of mine was published in 1958, I was taken to task by a Catholic paper for having approvingly quoted the brilliant, large-minded Catholic writer T. M. Kettle to the effect that Ireland had once been "an unimaginable chaos of races, religions, ideas, appetites, and provincialisms; brayed in the mortar without emerging as a consolidated whole." In chiding me, the newspaper charitably withheld its ace: Kettle was of Viking descent, the offspring of tenth-century carpetbaggers as are hundreds of thousands of other Irishmen. In the debates over birth control and abortion in recent decades, though, the occasional odd phrase has popped out to remind us all—liberal Catholic, non-Catholic, and agnostic—that the old spirit is still lurking at the church gates. Cathleen ni Houlihan, the ballad reminds us, has four strong sons: no believer, she, in planned parenthood.

Foster fittingly points out that the *Catholic Bulletin* was a grotesque extreme. The state that came into being in 1922, and its successive governments, have always been solicitous of the rights of the (steadily declining) religious minorities. But it is also fitting that he reminds us that the Constitution presented to the Irish Free State by Eamon De Valera in 1937 granted the Catholic Church "a special position...as the guardian of the faith professed by the great majority of the citizens." It is not difficult to deduce a cast of mind in which the non-great minority of Irishmen might find themselves somewhat ill at ease—or one that Ulster Protestants nobler in mind and being than Ian Paisley might not find especially seductive.

As Foster puts the matter, in a tone that contrives to be at once bland, angry, and amused,

> If de Valera's constitution spoke for an overwhelmingly Catholic Ireland, to claim that it also spoke for a thirty-two-county Ireland including a million Ulster Protestants might seem like trying to have it both ways. But that is exactly what the 1937 constitution did.

Happily, 1972 was also the year in which the clause in the Constitution granting the Catholic Church its special position was abolished by referendum. But Foster, a writer not given to an unballasted optimism, reminds us that

> Ireland's Catholic ethos would be defended by a majority of the population as well as a politically powerful Church leadership. And here again what must be emphasized is the low priority

given to making reunion with the Republic attractive to Protestant Ulster.

In his closing paragraphs he remarks, rather moodily, upon how striking it is that "the *soi-disant* 'revisionist' school of Irish historians" has had so little effect on "the popular (and paradoxically Anglocentric) version of Irish history held by the public mind." He might also have remarked that it has had precious little effect on the version held in the public mind of Protestant Ulster.

"To have an opinion about Ireland," Thackeray wrote in his *Irish Sketch Book* of 1842, "one must begin by getting at the truth; and where is it to be had in the country? Or rather, there are two truths, the Catholic truth and the Protestant truth.... Belief is made a party business." That verdict remains largely true to this day; in *The Death of the Past*, J. H. Plumb argues that the academic study of history has one invaluable civic upshot: it is the solvent of what he calls "the past," that repository of myth, legend, and dogmatic (because unexamined) opinion, a realm in which belief is indeed a party business. Ireland badly needs history like this to save it from a past that continues to exact murderous tribute from the present.

—*The Atlantic Monthly*, April 1989

27

WOLFE TONE

AT TWO O'CLOCK on Christmas morning in 1796, Theobald Wolfe Tone, described with some irony by Marianne Elliott as the "prophet of Irish independence,"[1] was pacing the deck of the *Indomptable*, an eighty-gun ship of the line that was straining its anchor in windswept Bantry Bay, off the coast of Cork. He was swathed against the foul weather in a greatcoat, beneath which he wore the uniform and insignia of an adjutant general in the army of the French Republic. The *Indomptable* was part of the weather-battered remnant of an expedition of invasion that had been launched upon Tone's assurances to the French that his country was ready for rebellion.

As he paced the deck, he was "devoured by the most gloomy reflections," but these he expressed in his journal with a characteristic wit and bravado. Should they land and fail, "I may be reserved for a trial, for the sake of striking terror into others, in which case I shall be hanged as a traitor and embowelled, etc. As for the embowelling...if ever they hang me, they are welcome to embowel me if they please. These are pleasant prospects."

It was two years after this aborted landing that Tone was taken prisoner in a second attempt at invasion and almost realized the fate

---

1. *Wolfe Tone: Prophet of Irish Independence* (Yale University Press, 1991).

he had described in his journal. Seized off the Donegal coast, he was taken to Dublin in chains, tried, and sentenced to death, but cheated the hangman by slashing his throat in his cell. By then he had learned an ugly truth: in the months preceding, some of the Irish people had indeed rebelled, but the rebellion had turned into sectarian violence at its most savage, Catholics and Protestants murdering each other under the banners of their rival creeds. For Tone, to whom the unification of his people had always been more crucial than political independence from England, the irony was utter and bleak.

Long after his death, Tone was almost deified by the hot-gospelers of advanced Irish nationalism. The process reached its climax in the perfervid oratory of Patrick Pearse, poet warrior of the 1916 Rising, who saw in Tone's end a martyrdom that provided precedent and legitimacy for the one he envisioned for himself. Carefully selected passages from Tone's pamphlets and journals were passed down from one generation of Irish Republican to the next as though endowed with the authority of Scripture.

As well they should have been. Tone was a prose writer of remarkable strengths—lucid, terse, remorselessly logical, and yet gifted with a wry, alert eloquence. And the journals reveal a most attractive person—witty, generous, graceful in thought and speech, an accomplished musician with an eye for the ladies, and a deep, rollicking, unabashed thirst. These are aspects of his character that were downplayed in the construction of the nationalist saint, whose soul was described by Pearse as "a burning flame." One can almost imagine Tone scribbling, "Ouch! Heartburn!"

The creation of Tone as a relic, however, required that he be wrenched out of his historical and political context. The great virtue of Marianne Elliott's biography is that she has placed him firmly back within it. Thus, for example, in her pages of final appraisal she reminds us:

Tone was passionately Irish. But he was part of an elite and had a very Protestant perception of the Irish masses. He thought them vulgar, lacking in spirit and prone to graft and deceit. He had little sympathy with the romantic cultural nationalism which was beginning to develop in his own day, and would have decried the additional barrier erected between Irishmen by the new Irish state's emphasis on Gaelic culture and language.

In the mythology of popular Irish nationalism, the figure of Wolfe Tone and the Rising of 1798 are blurred together. Tone, as we have seen, learned only in his Dublin prison what had actually taken place, and in his final speech, at his trial, passes judgment upon the events. "For a fair and open war I was prepared; if it has regenerated into a system of assassination, massacre, and plunder I do again most sincerely lament it, and those few who know me personally will give me I am sure credit for the assertion."

The words are well worth quoting, because, strikingly, they did not become part of the scripture, although the sentences preceding and following them did. They are worth quoting also because today, in one part of Ireland, the sectarian killers on one side of the divide imagine that they act within a tradition of patriotic murder and martyrdom for which Tone laid down the terms, both by word and by example.

It is quite true, as Elliott says, that

Tone did seek Irish independence, he did dislike England, he did resort to arms to achieve his aims.... However, the movement which Tone helped found had already, before he died, acquired aspects quite alien to his own ideals. His ideals were of an age which had already passed, and one suspects that his own militant republicanism might not have outlived that recognition. For his reputation as nationalist hero, his death was perhaps timely.

Ireland is far from the only country to have provided its heroes with such timely deaths. We are today separated by the thickness of two centuries from the world in which Tone, that gallant, admirable, and fallible hero, thought and acted. And in all countries the ways in which the present learns from the past are devious, complex, ambiguous, and at times deeply ironical.

Elliott, like Roy Foster with his brilliant *Modern Ireland 1600–1972*, is one of a number of young Irish historians who offer to their countrymen the lenses of actuality rather than the mirrors of mythology. Mirrors, alas, are on the whole more attractive than lenses.

—*Newsday*, March 11, 1990

28

LORD EDWARD FITZGERALD

THE IRISH REBELLION of two hundred years ago—it broke out in May and was crushed within a month or so—was fought in scattered patches by the peasants of Antrim in the north and Wexford and Kildare in the south. The rebels, untrained, virtually leaderless, ill-armed with homemade pikes and plundered muskets, were easily disposed of by loyalist militia and yeomen, strengthened by the garrison of British regulars. They had fought bravely, confusedly, and finally with despair.

For a time, though, the rebellion had posed a formidable threat, with 100,000 oath-bound members and a promise of help from France. It failed in good part because it was honeycombed with spies, informers, traitors, and double agents. The British rulers at Dublin Castle knew the names of the leaders at the top and middle levels, and even knew that May 23 was the date fixed for action. But the authorities held back from arrests until the final months, while the yeomen goaded the peasantry into premature violence. The Lord Lieutenant wrote to London: "I shall not lament the attempt at insurrection. It will enable us to act with effect." The most deadly arrests came on March 12, when the government, alerted by an informer, scooped up the leaders, save for one latecomer, Lord Edward Fitzgerald, who was to command the attack on Dublin.

The United Irish leaders, forced by government repression into conspiracy and then treason, were middle-class radicals—barristers and solicitors, a few doctors and editors, a country gentleman or two. Lord Edward, however, although more radical than most of them, was anything but middle class. He came from the most powerful family of the Anglo-Irish aristocracy, one that in the Middle Ages had virtually ruled Ireland. His older brother became Duke of Leinster on their father's death. Their mother, a daughter of the Duke of Richmond, joined them to the greatest of England's Whig families. To the end, Lord Edward remained on close and affectionate terms with his cousin Charles James Fox, a statesman lazily devoted to civil liberty and revolution in countries other than his own.

The Fitzgeralds divided their time in Ireland between Carton in Kildare, an enormous showplace, and Leinster House in Dublin, a town mansion so capacious that today it houses both chambers of the Irish Parliament. Other properties were scattered through Leinster. Lord Edward brought his bride to a villa on Dublin Bay called Frescati, which, unlike the other properties, was charming and open to its surroundings.

Lord Edward's was for most of his life the conventional existence of a young British aristocrat. He chose the British army for his career, and had a natural aptitude for military life, delighting in hardship and risk and displaying both courage and initiative. He seemed destined for high rank, given his connections. During the American Revolution, he joined the 19th Regiment of Foot in South Carolina a few weeks before Cornwallis's surrender, and was gravely wounded. A few years later, he was in the Canadian wilds, where he made several long expeditions and developed genuine admiration for the Iroquois, as might be expected of a reader of Rousseau. Back in Europe, he had several love affairs, a few mistresses, and some casual conquests, gambled and visited the great houses of friends.

His surviving correspondence—extensively quoted by Stella Tillyard in *Citizen Lord*, as by an earlier biographer, the Irish Romantic poet Thomas Moore—is marvelous, showing him to be nervous, quick, delighted by the natural and social worlds, high-spirited, and decisive in his likes and dislikes.[1] His writing has the pauses and rhythms of speech. Portraits confirm the impression made by the letters: style and vivacious good looks, touches of humor about the eyes and mouth. He had a genius for gardening, and he looks to foliage, crops, weathers. Even in the final weeks, a hunted man, he is in a Dublin canal garden, rooting up orange lilies—a gesture as much political as horticultural. But it is just there, in the transformation into revolutionary, that the documentation fails us, and we are thrust, like Moore and Tillyard, upon speculation. The massive Fitzgerald correspondence has been weeded of letters having political import, and most of Lord Edward's that survive are to his mother; they contrive to be spontaneous but guarded.

He was a child of Rousseau, certainly: in 1792, he went to Paris, where he shared lodgings with Thomas Paine. After the French victory at Jemappes, he offered at a public dinner a toast to "the armies of France: may the example of its citizen soldiers be followed by all enslaved countries, till tyrants and tyrannies be extinct." To round matters off, he then drank to "the speedy abolition of all hereditary titles and feudal distinctions." He would henceforth be "*le citoyen* Edouard Fitzgerald." As a first consequence, he was cashiered from the British army.

Shortly after, he made a marriage at once ducal and revolutionary. Pamela Sims, as her parents wished her to be called, was the child of the duc d'Orléans, a cousin to Louis XVI and in the line of royal succession, and Mme. de Genlis, his mistress and a memoirist beneath whose pen truth became as malleable as clay. At the revolution, the duke flung aside his rank, became Philippe Égalité, and earned the detestation of respectable Europe by voting in the Convention for the death of the King. A year later, he was himself guillotined.

Descriptions of Pamela are always ecstatic: a young but practiced

1. *Citizen Lord: The Life of Edward Fitzgerald, Irish Revolutionary* (Farrar, Straus and Giroux, 1998).

beauty with unpowdered brown hair and nonchalant bearing, dressed in simple but exquisite taste. Unpowdered because powder was a mark of the old, discredited regime. Just as Fitzgerald, back in Ireland now, wore not the prescribed white silk at his neck, but rather red for France or green for Ireland. Neither did it help at Dublin Castle that he had brought back a seductive and sexy young wife whose very existence was a reminder of regicide and the guillotine.

Fitzgerald took a family seat in the Irish Parliament without concealing his belief that the house was packed on one side by the corrupt henchmen of British power and on the other by ineffectual, rhetorically florid "patriots." Revolution must have seemed to him the only answer to Ireland's deep and festering wounds, and he formed close friendships with the leaders of the United Irish. Curiously, however, neither he nor several others joined the society until 1796, after revolution had been decided on.

When he joined, though, he rose rapidly to leadership, in part because of the glamour of his name, but in part because of his military experience and his habit of quick judgment. Later that year, he and a fellow aristocratic rebel, Arthur O'Connor, traveled to the Continent and secured a pledge of French aid.

Until the proclamation against him in March, he and Pamela attended social functions at Carton and Leinster House. He walked the streets of Dublin to attend meetings in the gaunt houses and taverns stretching out on narrow, crooked streets south of the Liffey. Moore, then a student at Trinity College, once glimpsed him in fashionable Grafton Street, and would remember "the elastic lightness of his step, his fresh, healthful complexion, and the soft expression given his eyes by their long, dark lashes." That image informs his biography of 1831, when the long-ago rebellion was softened by the lights and shadows of a gentle nationalism.

Tillyard, the author of *Aristocrats*, a gracefully written study of the four Lennox sisters, one of whom was Lord Edward's mother, wishes to give us a committed revolutionary, more radical in his politics than the other Irish leaders, more resolute and reckless in action. She reminds us of Byron's cheerful comment on his friend, "Tom Moore loves a Lord," and she goes on to say, "He was also a romantic nationalist and a romantic poet, inclined to play up chivalry and neglect politics, especially where the aristocracy was concerned."

Her revised portrait is persuasive, and if it does not entirely convince us it is because she, like Moore, must interpret Fitzgerald's character and motives from scraps, fragments, gestures. We know what he looked like and how he dressed, we know what he did, but we know little of the thoughts and passions of his final years. Moore and Tillyard have set two portraits before us, and both speak of problems of evidence that will always be unsolved. Perhaps that is one of the secrets of his charm.

Moore called his book *The Life and Death of Lord Edward Fitzgerald*, and he and Tillyard have both superbly re-created those final months in hiding, as the date crept toward May 23, and the network of spies and betrayers drew closer to the warren of streets in which he moved. Francis Magan, the solicitor who finally sold him for cash, wrote to Dublin Castle's spymaster: "Lord Edward skulks from house to house, has watches and spies, armed, who give an account of any danger being near." As Tillyard puts it, he "haunted the imagination of friends and enemies alike, and he became in the ensuing months a mythical figure." He moved through the nighttime streets disguised as a farmer in from the hills, a soldier, an apothecary—legend swelled the number. Dublin Castle knew that he must be captured, and that his capture would create problems; he was a duke's brother with powerful Whig allies. Lord Clare, the chancellor, is said to have whispered to the right ears: "Will no one urge Lord Edward to fly? I pledge myself that every port in the country shall be left open to him." But Lord Edward is said to have told a well-wisher who visited one of his safe houses, "I am too deeply pledged to these men to be able to withdraw with honor."

On the evening of the 19th, four days before the rising, as he lay in a strange bed reading *Gil Blas*, a party of yeomen burst in on him. He fought like a tiger to escape, gave the second-in-command a mortal wound, and himself received two fatal bullets. He was taken in a closed sedan chair first to Dublin Castle and then to prison. It took him a long time to die, and he was alive when the catastrophic rebellion broke out, its local commanders out of touch with each other or with Dublin, blundering about their country like wounded pikemen, wrathful and bloody. He was delirious and hysterical at the end, although in a final moment of lucidity, he apologized to the attending physician: "I give you a great deal of trouble, sir." He was, in every sense of the term, a class act.

Nowadays, the figure from 1798 most likely to be thought of in heroic terms is Theobald Wolfe Tone, in part because we have his witty, shrewd, self-mocking journals, his political prose, polished as steel. But partly because the founding fathers of modern Irish nationalism, separated from each other by a half-century, Thomas Davis and Patrick Pearse, deliberately cast him, for political reasons, in a heroic mold. Tone and Fitzgerald both died in Dublin prisons in that fatal year, but they are remembered differently. Fitzgerald's life was lived first in the glittering social lights of great houses, then in the lurid flame of revolutionary Paris, finally in the deep shadows of Irish conspiracy. It is not easy to see him steadily.

The Irish writer Frank O'Connor once told me that there seemed about Fitzgerald a quality that he called Mozartean. He was inclined to see that quality in almost everything that remains of eighteenth-century Dublin, including the old Parliament building that now houses the Bank of Ireland. But about Lord Edward, he was, just possibly, absolutely right.

—*The New York Times Book Review*, July 19, 1998

29

THE MAN WHO DISCOVERED IRELAND

IN 1989, in *The Hereditary Bondsman*, Oliver MacDonagh traced Daniel O'Connell's extraordinary career from his birth into the half-outlawed Catholic gentry of Ireland's western seacoast to the triumphant political campaign by which, in 1829, he wrested religious equality from a reluctant British government. It was that very victory that allowed him, at fifty-five, to take his seat in Westminster as a member of Parliament.

In *The Emancipist*,[1] MacDonagh surveys the final quarter-century of O'Connell's life, when he retained at home the aura of a tribal chieftain, but in London was thinking and voting as an adroit British politician, for the most part in alliance with the Whigs but on occasion maintaining a strategic distance from them. It was now his great ambition to mobilize again the immense popular support by which he had secured Catholic Emancipation and direct it toward Repeal of the Act of Union of 1801, thereby restoring political independence to his island.

That final campaign crested in the 1840s and then crashed upon brutal rocks—notably British intransigence and the fractures within Irish society. O'Connell died in Italy in 1847, his health broken and

---

1. *The Emancipist: Daniel O'Connell, 1830–47* (St. Martin's, 1989).

his policies in ruins, while Ireland, by a ghastly coincidence, lay under the pall of the Great Famine.

MacDonagh's respect and warm admiration for O'Connell are at all points evident, but he is also a cool, judicious professional historian, inclined to deprecate as "magnificent extravagance" the claim by Sean O'Faolain that O'Connell "was the greatest of all Irish realists who knew that if he could but once define he would thereby create. He did define, and he did create. He thought a democracy and it arose. He defined himself, and his people became him." MacDonagh's claim, though more exact, is also a large one, that O'Connell "was in part the faithful reflector, and in part the actual shaper, of the emergent Irish nationalist Catholic culture." A nameless German horseboy put the point better than either of them when he described O'Connell to a traveler as "the man who discovered Ireland."

MacDonagh's two splendidly written and masterly volumes are very much a "Life" rather than a "Life and Times," which is unfortunate because he has demonstrated elsewhere his skill as a cultural historian and because the history of O'Connell's reputation has its own interest and importance.

At the height of his power, he was almost idolized by the Irish Catholic masses, although *The Times* of London spoke for Tories and many Whigs in the notorious doggerel that MacDonagh quotes:

> *Scum condensed of Irish bog!*
> *Ruffian—coward—demagogue!*
> *Boundless liar—base detractor!*
> *Nurse of murders—treason's factor!*

The final two of these charges, although devoutly believed in England, could not be further from the truth. O'Connell, who had once and to his everlasting sorrow killed a man in a duel, hated and detested violence, whether personal or political, and MacDonagh demonstrates that his gift to historical contexts larger than Ireland was the "development of a methodology peculiarly appropriate to colonial counterattack, in situations where violence was eschewed and the imperial power a constitutional government." And his devotion to Queen Victoria was expressed frequently with a fulsome, cloying, and fawning excess, the sincerity of which denies to his words even the thin defense of their being mere diplomacy. To the contrary, like that of most Irish patriots of his time, the "free" Ireland toward which he looked was one having a dominion status under the Crown.

But it was precisely upon these two grounds, his detestation of violence and his essentially moderate politics, that in his final years he was attacked by Irish nationalists, and with fratricidal intensity. MacDonagh does not quote the rhetorical savagery of John Mitchel, a Republican rebel of the 1840s:

> Poor old Dan! Wonderful, jovial, mighty, and mean old man, with silver tongue and smile of witchery and heart of melting ruth—lying tongue, smile of treachery, heart of unfathomable fraud. What a royal, yet vulgar soul, with the keen eye and potent sweep of a generous eagle of Cairn Tual—with the base servility of a hound and the cold cruelty of a spider.

Of the two strands that make up the political culture of Ireland, the constitutional and the violent, the rhetorical glamour of the gunman has tended to carry the day. So much has this been the case that when O'Faolain published his popular biography of O'Connell in 1938, he did so very much as an act of revisionism, a reminder to his countrymen of how much they owed to O'Connell, of how much of their aspiration had been incarnate in him. Defending his book and its subject against zealots, O'Faolain described these as people who "hate the truth because they have not enough personal courage to be what we all are—the descendants, part of the European economy, of the rags and tatters who rose with O'Connell to win under Mick Collins—in a word this modern Anglo-Ireland."

Today, as Ireland stands on the eve of her entry into the European community, she has still her zealots and gunmen, and their apologists in this country, but the main outlines and structures of the Irish past and of its bearing upon the present are being clearly and perhaps permanently established by such firm and persuasive studies as Mac-Donagh's work.

—*The Washington Post Book World*, January 7, 1990

30

THE UNCROWNED KING

And here's a final reason,
He was of such a kind
Every man that sings a song
Keeps Parnell in his mind....

— Yeats, "Come Gather Round Me Parnellites"

ON THE MORNING of October 11, 1891, a morning of heavy winds and lashing rain, the body of Charles Stewart Parnell, Ireland's "uncrowned king," was brought home from England. That afternoon, beneath brightening skies, past immense crowds, a vast funeral procession followed the coffin to Glasnevin Cemetery.

Dublin, as Robert Kee remarks in *The Laurel and the Ivy*,[1] "had long raised public funerals to the level of an art form." Parnell's loyal followers designed this one to express grief, anger, and defiance. "Died fighting for Ireland," read the legend on one wreath. For a dozen years he had towered over Irish life, but in the year before his death his power and much of his glamour had been smothered in

---

1. *The Laurel and the Ivy: The Story of Charles Stewart Parnell and Irish Nationalism* (Hamish Hamilton/Viking, 1994).

what Timothy Healy—at first a member of his party but then the most savage and scurrilous of his enemies—called "the stench of the divorce court." In the months that remained to him, he had fought a fierce, losing battle to retain control of the party he had created, one that had transformed Irish political life.

Long afterward, the grave was to be marked by a massive boulder of Wicklow granite, bearing the single and sufficient word "Parnell." Surrounded by the gimcrack baroque of Victorian mortuary art, it carried its own significance—stern and incantatory. Parnell had passed into mythology, a complex and potent legend. In Joyce's horrifying Christmas dinner scene in *A Portrait of the Artist as a Young Man*, set in the immediate aftermath of the death, Aunt Dante, Roman Catholic and puritan, screams out, "Devil out of hell! We won! We crushed him to death! Fiend!" But Mr. Casey, who might have walked behind the coffin, sobs, "Poor Parnell! My dead king."

Parnell entered the London Parliament in 1875 as neither Liberal nor Tory, but rather as a member of the small Home Rule Party, dedicated to the quixotic task of persuading England, by logic and oratory, to grant Ireland a limited measure of self-government. He seemed a merely social acquisition, a handsome and aristocratic young Protestant landlord whose previous interests had been limited to cricket, geology, and fox hunting. But he displayed an icy self-control, an indifference to English opinion, and disdain for a Parliament which he came to manipulate with a combination of shrewdness and audacity. Irishmen in Parliament were expected to be jocose, expansive, orotund. Parnell's accent was that of Cambridge University, and his manner remote and faintly taunting. Michael Davitt, the peasant-born rebel who was first his ally and then, after the divorce scandal, his opponent, was to call him "an Englishman of the strongest type, molded for an Irish purpose."

Within three years, he had moved to the head of his small party, and had earned the bitter anger of Liberals and Tories alike. But his parliamentary stance was never an end in itself. It was addressed across the water to his true audience, the Irish. "England," he wrote to a Dublin newspaper, "respects nothing but power." As he told a crowd of thousands in Dublin: "I care nothing for this English Parliament and its outcries. I care nothing for its existence, if that existence is to continue a source of tyranny and destruction to my country."

Irish history had been awaiting its Parnell. Thirty years before, famine had devastated the land, revealing its hopeless dependence upon forces beyond itself—whether those of nature, an inscrutable Providence, or a British government that had shamefully mismanaged famine relief. The armed Fenian insurrection of 1867 had been a ludicrous failure, although its rebellious tradition remained alive. So too did the far older tradition of scattered agrarian terrorism as a weapon against iniquitously high rents and eviction. Since the Great Famine, America held millions of Irish immigrants ready to provide, from a safe distance, the financial sinews of resistance. But Ireland was a land lacking in political and social coherence. It was Parnell's genius, or else his good fortune, to draw together these scattered energies and aspirations.

In 1879, a crop failure and fear of a new famine, coupled with a wave of evictions, led to the foundation of a Land League committed to reform by all means short of violence. But at times it came very close to violence. Michael Davitt, a Fenian rebel released from prison in part through Parnell's efforts, was its chief organizer, but Parnell made common cause with it. Its most memorable moments were his. "You must show the landlords," he told a Mayo crowd, "that you intend to keep a firm grip of your homesteads and lands. You must not allow yourselves to be disappointed as you were disappointed in 1847." He was referring, of course, to the Great Famine, and in speech after speech he linked the causes of land and nationality.

By the spring of 1882, charges of Land League conspiracy had landed him in Kilmainham prison, never an inconvenient address for an Irish patriot. From there, bargaining almost as an equal with Gladstone, the Liberal prime minister, he negotiated a "treaty" that partly solved the land question, and also hinted at a very tentative alliance with the Liberals. By 1885, thanks to a greatly expanded franchise, he was able to bring to Parliament an Irish party of eighty-six, all of them oath-bound to vote as a party, which meant, in practice, at his bidding. By 1889, Parnell's star fully in the ascendant, Gladstone, then in opposition, pledged a reluctant Liberal Party to support Irish Home Rule.

Just then, disaster struck. Captain William O'Shea, an Irish political opportunist, filed for divorce from his English wife, Katharine, naming Parnell as co-respondent. It was an affair of long standing. During the Kilmainham negotiations, when O'Shea was carrying messages between the prison and Downing Street, Katharine bore Parnell the first of his three children.

O'Shea might have stepped out of one of Feydeau's Paris hotel-room farces, complete with monocle, waxed mustaches, and roguish ways. Panderer, liar, blackmailer, boaster, he lacked any redeeming trait, other than a fondness for such of his children as he had reason to believe might be his. (He writes of them cloyingly, in his letters to Katharine, as his "chicks." Parnell wrote to her as to his "Wifie" and his "Queenie." The epistolary style in her little circle was not an elevated one.)

That anyone as wary and shrewd as Parnell would place himself in the power of a Captain O'Shea is surely evidence of the mysterious powers of romantic love. A dangerous love: in 1886, O'Shea compelled Parnell to foist him upon the disgusted voters of Galway, and in so blatant a manner that it should have placed on warning everyone except Parnellites suffering from terminal idolatry.

Kee's elaborate re-creation of the domestic drama is one of his strengths. An Irish journalist and popular historian, and the author of *The Green Flag*, a history of Irish nationalism, he writes intelligently and shrewdly about politics and makes good use of primary and secondary material. His use of previously undiscussed newspaper material is superb. But the political and social story has been told before: by F. S. L. Lyons in his biography of Parnell, by Conor Cruise O'Brien on the organization of Parnell's party, by Roy Foster on the Wicklow squirearchy in which he grew up, by Emmet Larkin in *The Roman Catholic Church and the Fall of Parnell, 1888–1891*, and, most recently, by Frank Callanan in *The Parnell Split, 1890–91*.

Kee's account of the other half of Parnell's life, hidden and then forced into lurid light, is matchless, and makes adroit use of Katharine's own *Charles Stewart Parnell: His Love Story and Political Life* (1914). That is an essential but understandably bizarre book: her need to make all parties to the triangle seem respectable placed a heavy burden on her slender rhetorical skills.

Katharine (she was never, save by Parnell's jeering enemies, called Kitty) is less easily brought into focus than is her egregious husband. The O'Sheas seem at first to have been two of a kind, courting Parnell for such favors as might come their way, but she came to respond fully to Parnell's deep love for her.

When the scandal broke, Parnell gave vague assurances to his followers that he had not acted "dishonorably"—meaning that the O'Shea marriage had long ago broken down. This was not a view of monogamy likely to recommend itself to Irish Catholics or to those English Nonconformists upon whose support Gladstone relied. The divorce, accompanied by the usual messy evidence, was granted on November 17, 1890, and on the 25th Gladstone made public a letter in which he warned that Parnell's continued leadership would make home rule impossible for many years. Parnell, following his central strategy, issued a "manifesto" addressed to "the people of Ireland," in which he denounced English interference in Irish affairs (soon he would be calling Gladstone "the grand old spider") and made clear his intention to retain power. In early December, the Irish party met for five days in Committee Room 15 of the House of Commons in

London, and the name of that room would have a baleful existence in Irish history and echo in Joyce's fiction.

The fierce quarrels in the room were a foretaste of what was to come —Parnell by turns icy and maddened, Tim Healy vicious and lethal. "And who is to be mistress of the party?" Healy asked. The party split, leaving Parnell with a rump, and that split, as Conor Cruise O'Brien has written, "is the most traumatic episode in the span of Irish history that lies between the Great Famine and the Easter Rising of 1916."

Parnell was able to rally the Fenian rebels, devotees by now of lost causes, but the Catholic Church was against him, and so was middle-class opinion. In the months that remained to him, he fought and lost three by-elections, traveling back and forth between Irish country towns and his English house in Brighton, which he shared with Katharine, now Mrs. Parnell. The insults hurled at him were ugly, and with each defeat his decline became more evident.

His final, mythic image hardened in these months—solitary, unyielding. It was a complex legacy to his people. For Yeats, an image of aristocratic pride ("For Parnell was a proud man. No prouder trod the ground"). For Joyce, proof that prudish respectability, political scheming, and a bullying Church would always be arrayed against the heroic. For the rebels of the 1916 Rising, a link with an earlier and nobler Ireland. His political skills in triumph and his superb fighting temperament in defeat had given his people a figure through whom they could seize self-respect in the face of imperial condescension.

I have read somewhere that Captain O'Shea, in his later years, became a crony of Major Count Walsin Esterhazy, the actual traitor for whose crime Dreyfus was sent to Devil's Island. Two of a kind.

And Tim Healy? The 1916 Rising eventually made possible for Ireland the self-government for which Parnell had fought—a Free State. Tim Healy became its governor general, representing the British Crown.

—*The New York Times Book Review*, September 4, 1994

31

THE MOLLY MAGUIRES

ON JUNE 21, 1877, in the anthracite-mining county of Schuylkill, Pennsylvania, ten men, all of them Irish and, so the state charged, members of a secret, oath-bound conspiracy to murder known as the Molly Maguires, were hanged in two batches. Four in Mauch Chunk, a town as gaunt as its name, were hanged together on a special gallows built for the occasion. In neighboring Pottsville, it had at first been intended that the condemned be hanged on a scaffold capable of accommodating all six, but it was later decided to hang them in pairs. All ten were accompanied by priests, and most of them made well-rehearsed expressions of guilt and contrition. All were buried in consecrated ground in Catholic cemeteries.

Twenty men in all would be executed, but it was the mass hangings on Black Thursday that lingered in the American imagination, like the exorcism of an immense, depraved and unfathomable evil. Great crowds had assembled in the streets of the towns and were kept in order by the heavily armed Coal and Iron Police. History, wrote the *Chicago Tribune*, "affords no more striking illustration of the terrible power for evil of a secret, oath-bound organization controlled by murderers and assassins than the awful record of crime committed by the Molly Maguires in the anthracite-coal region of Pennsylvania." And the *Philadelphia Public Ledger*, published in a city not too distant in miles from Schuylkill but dwelling, it was hoped, in a different moral universe, spoke of a "day of deliverance from as awful a despotism of banded murderers as the world has ever seen in any age."

The Mollies had acquired and were to retain a powerful, baleful, and complex symbolic meaning. Oaths, even wicked ones, were taken seriously, and the wicked ones conjured up the amorphous terrors of dark and lethal conspiracies. Ironically, and with tragic consequences, two organizations that fiercely opposed the Molly Maguires were deliberately branded as their secret puppetmasters and made to share their infamy. One was the miners' legitimate labor union, the Workingmen's Benevolent Association, which had inherited the traditions of British trade unionism, which rejected violence. In particular, it shunned Mollyism, which had acquired a national reputation for the use of murder and intimidation as weapons in industrial conflict. The other target was, to all intents, the Roman Catholic Church.

There had indeed been violence and disorder in the mining district ever since the Civil War, and it included the murders—Kevin Kenny prefers to call them assassinations—of some twenty-four mine foremen and superintendents. The killers formed a loose group that may as well be called Molly Maguires as anything else, but only if the name is used in the subtle and precise manner of Kenny in *Making Sense of the Molly Maguires*,[1] his remarkably fine work of historical research and analysis:

> The Molly Maguires always existed on two related levels: as a sporadic pattern of violence engaged in by a specific type of Irishman, and as a ubiquitous concept in a system of ideological representation that sought to explain the variety of social problems besetting the anthracite region in the mid-19th century. In other words, the violence in which the Molly Maguires

---

1. Oxford University Press, 1997.

undoubtedly engaged was put to all sorts of uses by contemporaries, most effectively by those who were opposed to Irish immigrants and organized labor. Any reinterpretation of the Molly Maguires today needs to inquire simultaneously into how the Molly Maguires were represented and what they may have been in fact.

Attitudes toward the Irish had been shaped almost from the hour of their arrival in Schuylkill in the wake of the Great Famine of the 1840s. Throughout the decades and the turmoil that followed, they were given expression and shape in the nativist pages of Benjamin Bannan's *Miners' Journal*. Bannan, of Welsh descent, held a political vision that was not ignoble: a sober God-fearing industrious republic of free workmen and their employers. His austere Protestant soul, however, was revolted by the spectacle of a "race" that seemed not to respect this vision, as the Irish, to his eyes, did not.

For one thing, they were not Welsh. Work in the mines was divided between the skilled labor and the outside tasks, such as sorting out slate. The skilled and experienced miners were from Wales, trained in mining through generations and with a strong sense of guild solidarity. The unskilled laborers were Irish and came, most of them, from West Donegal, where there were no mines nor much of anything else. The nativists—the racists of that day—of course regarded the difference as evidence of the laziness and ignorance that were part of the Irish essence. The Welsh were inclined to agree.

Muff Lawlor's shebeen in Shenandoah and Jack Kehoe's Hibernia House in Girardsville were not places to which Bannan might be tempted to repair for a thoughtful glass of claret. But of course he was never tempted. He had concluded, as had his readers, that the Irish constituted a distinct and abominable branch of the human family. To their laziness were joined other vices: drunkenness, a readiness to fight, blasphemy, primitive superstition, and a slavish idolatry of the

Pope. A fear of the Pope and his designs upon American democracy was general, but the Irish peasantry were believed to have brought over the plague in a particularly virulent form.

Elsewhere in the same county, the poverty of West Donegal was spoken of with pity, and British gazettes could scarcely describe it without a shudder: "The coast, over the greater part of the distance, is singularly broken and intersected....The sea-board is almost a chaos—a dismal wilderness of bog and pond, of barren sand and naked rock—a tract of desolation in which moors, ponds, shivering torrents, drifting sands and denuded granite are mingled in utter melee, and severally striving for the mastery." The largest landlord, the marquis of Conyngham, governed from the distant pasturelands of County Meath. He was represented on the scene by agents and overseers, who prefigured the mine foremen and superintendents of Schuylkill, first as perceived oppressors and then as targets.

In Donegal, as well as in many other regions of Ireland, a tradition of violence against agents and middlemen had been developing for a century under a variety of picturesque names—Rockites, Whiteboys, Terry Alts, Ribbonmen. And Molly Maguires. The West Donegals had taken little part in these episodes, but they knew all about them; violence was part of the texture of their lives. Violence in Schuylkill, a product of the same culture, with its tradition of retributive justice, began during the Civil War, as a savage reaction against conscription into what was seen as "a rich man's war." But it grew during the 1870s, as Kenny shows, as a response to worsening industrial conditions created by the expansion of capitalism.

It is an irony of the Molly Maguires' history, as distinguished from its historical moment, that the more capable the historian the more likely he is to conclude that we will never learn much about the actual Mollies, beyond their names and the dates of the particular murders for which they were hanged. And we may not even know that, for several of the men hanged were innocent of those crimes. We know so little partly because until recent years, we knew so little about the laboring classes and partly because we have accepted the vivid and melodramatic near-fictions of their enemies.

In October 1873, a superintendent of Allan Pinkerton's National Detective Agency reported to Franklin Gowen, president of the Reading Railroad—which under his vigorous leadership controlled mining as well as transportation—"the rumored existence at Glen Carbon of an organization known as the 'Molly Maguires,' a band of roughs joined together for the purposes of instituting revenge against anyone against whom they may have taken a dislike." Within the month, Gowen was meeting with Pinkerton.

Molly Maguire, so Gowen revealed to a supposedly horrified Pinkerton, was a "noxious weed" transplanted from Ireland. The "band of roughs" in Glen Carbon had within days expanded to stretch across the continent. "Wherever in the United States iron is wrought, from Maine to Georgia, from ocean to ocean—wherever coal is used for fuel, there the Molly Maguire leaves his slimy trail and wields with deadly effect his two powerful levers—secrecy and combination." Galvanized by this threat to an industrialized nation's very existence, which seems to have escaped the attention of the head of a national detective agency, the two men vowed to join their efforts.

Pinkerton seems not to have noticed Gowen's eccentric manner of conveying information by rodomontade, possibly because he himself, we discover, spoke in an identical way. They determined that they must send an undercover detective into the field, and as Pinkerton—or, rather, his ghostwriter—says: "It is no ordinary man that I need in this matter. He must be an Irishman, and a Catholic, as only this class of people can find admission to the Molly Maguires." And he insisted that none of his agents "shall ever be required to appear and give evidence on the witness stand." Hamlet himself faltered before the conditions his father's oath laid upon him, but Gowen, in a species of pentameter, accepted the stipulation.

The man Pinkerton chose, James McParlan, a young native of County Armagh in Ulster, entered the Schuylkill region in 1873 under the name of James McKenna and, at the same moment, entered American folklore. For two and a half years, he lived in the constant company of men who cheerfully murdered informers and left that company only to testify at their trials. Of his courage and his quick-wittedness, there can be no question, but the narrative shaped from his thrilling experiences is a different matter. Even before the final executions, Pinkerton had produced his long exposition, copiously illustrated—with crude woodcuts—*The Molly Maguires and the Detectives*. To the present day and until Kenny's study, nearly all subsequent accounts have derived from this work and from its numerous imitators. The only real attempt to break what Kenny calls Pinkerton's narrative mold was James Coleman's Marxist study in 1936.

Kenny, like most historians these days, has an austere distrust of narrative, which is regarded as inherently simplistic and, in the case of the Molly Maguires, with good reason. "McParlan's activities in the anthracite region need only be briefly summarized here," he says with a touch of donnish hauteur, "as the job of reconstructing his movements has already been done well and often."

A chapter giving some consideration to the conventions and purposes of the narrative tradition, of which Pinkerton's book is an instance, might have taken Kenny off his path, but it might have been worth the diversion. It is a bizarre but far from unique example of mid-nineteenth-century popular culture, which finds room not only for its central narrative of murder and detection but for accounts of how cocks are trained for fighting, the nature (albeit bowdlerized) of an Irish wake, the furnishings of a priest's parlor, choruses and verses of Irish music-hall songs, reports of prizefights. But it is a narrative that moves inward through layers of secrecy to the center of a conspiracy. Small wonder that Arthur Conan Doyle drew upon McParlan's adventures for one of the Sherlock romances, *The Valley of Fear*.

Who were the Molly Maguires, what did they do, and why? It is the third of these questions that the Pinkerton narrative and subsequent books fail entirely and mysteriously to answer. The currently accepted theory, expressed for example in Wayne Broehl's *The Molly Maguires*, as Kenny says in summary, holds that "on both sides of the Atlantic, the antagonists of the Irish were the same—the English. In Ireland they were landlords and agents; in Pennsylvania they were mine owners and mine bosses." A romantic notion but one that lacks particularity; the Mollies knew they were Irish all right, but they were not motivated by primordial ethnic passions.

What then? In a scene in Pinkerton's book, one among many, a Molly reveals to McParlan a plan to wreck one of the trains of the Philadelphia and Reading Coal and Iron Company on the general ground that "the Company would be greatly injured," as though Schuylkill was a kind of Sherwood Forest and the company a kind of Sheriff of Nottingham to be tormented on general principle.

Buried within *Making Sense of the Molly Maguires*, there is a counternarrative, and a most persuasive one. Its central figure is not McParlan or Kehoe, the "King of the Mollies," but Gowen, described by an admirer as "one of the great architects of industrial capitalism," and a figure straight out of Theodore Dreiser. By 1873, using the well-known methods of the robber barons, he had driven out of Schuylkill the independent mine owners and the middlemen. Two forces from the emerging labor movement remained to be confronted: the Workingmen's Benevolent Association and, distinct from it, the shaggily organized, mute, and murderous band of roughs known as Molly Maguires. They left behind them only a few badly written notes of warning, a few rough ballads, and a curiously powerful legend.

Gowen shattered or at least thoroughly demoralized the workingmen's trade union by a three-branched campaign: providing welfare benefits by which it was undercut, defeating it in the long strike that it attempted, and insinuating its identity with the Mollies. By 1875, with the strike in ruins, the Mollies alone lay in the field against Gowen. Their notions of retributive justice, as Kenny rather primly calls it, looked to less dispassionate eyes like terrorism and murder. Gowen's problem and Pinkerton's, and the problem of nativists in America in general, was to explain how these murderous roughnecks constituted parts of a conspiracy so wide that it threatened the republic.

The answer lay at hand. The Molly Maguires had taken control of the Schuylkill branches of the Ancient Order of Hibernians, which served as their front. In the world beyond, membership in the AOH was shared by hundreds of thousands of boisterous Irishmen with an array of passwords, secret winks, arcane rituals, perfervid Catholic piety, high-flying mumbo jumbo—parts of that urge to join societies that Alexis de Tocqueville had remarked upon as peculiarly American and identical to such Protestant equivalents as the Knights of Pythias and the Odd Fellows. And as innocent.

By preying upon nativist fears and paranoia, the enemies of the Mollies were able to insinuate the notion—despite the fierce and unequivocal denunciation of the Molly Maguires by the Catholic hierarchy—that the Schuylkill branches of the order were merely the entering wedge of a vast scheme. Indeed, as Kenny persuasively suggests, the Black Thursday processions to the gallows of prisoners and priests, the public admissions of guilt and prayers for forgiveness may have served, beyond religious need, the ideological function of establishing a distance between the Church and these shamefully errant sons.

By 1878, the Molly Maguires were gone from Schuylkill, never to return there but continuing to linger in the American imagination. History itself, as sometimes it does, wove that imaginative lingering. The trials were a mockery of any judicial process. As one historian put it: "A private corporation initiated the investigation through a private detective agency, a private police force arrested the supposed offenders, and coal company attorneys prosecuted—the state provided only the courtroom and hangmen." Gowen was the preeminent prosecutor, and his long closing speech is a marvel, with great swatches of verse by Bulwer-Lytton and even more dreadful poets and playwrights. In 1889, on a Friday the 13th, he took a hotel room in Washington and blew his brains out. Legend created a belated act of retributive justice by the Mollies.

McParlan became a Pinkerton superintendent and, thirty years later, persuaded a man named Harry Orchard to implicate the western labor agitator Big Bill Haywood in a conspiracy that murdered a former governor. Clarence Darrow, Haywood's lawyer, destroyed him in cross-examination, using as material the methods he had employed with the Molly Maguires. In *Big Trouble*, the late J. Anthony Lukas's book on the Haywood episode, Lukas speaks derisively of McParlan as "the Great Detective."

In 1979, the Pennsylvania Board of Pardons recommended a posthumous pardon for Jack Kehoe, "the king of the Mollies," and the governor, Milton Shapp, denounced Gowen's "fervent desire to wipe out any signs of resistance in the coal fields." All Pennsylvanians, he said, paid tribute to "these martyred men of labor."

In the pages of Pinkerton's book, Jack Kehoe displays from time to time a sardonic, indeed a mordant, wit. These recent developments may have brought a smile to his hard-bitten lips. Wherever he is.

—*Los Angeles Times*, April 5, 1998

32

SHADOW OF A GUNMAN

ON THE EVENING of August 22, 1922, as light was beginning to fade on the hills of West Cork, Michael Collins, military commander in chief of the newly established Irish Free State, was ambushed and killed on a narrow road between Bandon and Macroom. He was thirty-two years old.

The three-year guerrilla war against the British (1919–1921)—a war of shootings in city streets, ambushes on lonely roads, reprisals—had been waged by young men, many of them in their twenties. Collins, a genius of organization and equipped with boundless energy and daring, had directed it from a score or more of offices and "safe houses," traveling without disguise, by bicycle or on foot, through a Dublin of barricades and British searches.

Both the rebels and the British fought with unsparing violence, and Collins had become in British eyes the hated chieftain of a "murder gang." But he had also become, even to them, a figure of legend, and their newspapers had grudgingly accorded him a heroic stature. But he was no pasteboard hero. He was a complex man with a fatal flaw.

By 1921, both the Irish and the British were looking for a solution. Lloyd George's London cabinet, politically insecure and battered by post–World War problems, was anxious to settle one of them at least, although not by weakening Crown and Empire. As for the Irish, what was being glorified as "the War for Independence" was in fact a series of raids on police barracks and rural gunfights, sustained by brilliant propaganda and Collins's extraordinary intelligence operation. And, as he had good reason to know, the Irish Republican Army was stretched thin on the ground, ill-armed and low on ammunition.

A truce was declared, and Eamon De Valera, who was already termed in wistful expectation "President of the Irish Republic," sent to London a delegation headed by Collins and Arthur Griffith. The treaty to which they reluctantly put their signatures, though, was to give Ireland not peace but a civil war which was to prove bloodier and more savage than the war against the British. It was to lead to Collins's death at the hands of close comrades and fellow Irishmen.

The treaty gave to Ireland a larger measure of self-government than might have seemed possible ten years earlier. It was accepted by majorities in the Irish cabinet and Dail (or parliament), but by perilously narrow majorities. The treaty granted much to Irish aspirations but it withheld much. It required Ireland's continuing acceptance of the British Crown, and, more fatefully, it provided for the partitioning of the island. The north, with its Protestant and loyalist majority, would remain part of the United Kingdom.

It was rejected by De Valera and his followers, and, more strenuously, by many of the IRA commandants who had been doing the fighting. They had been killing and being killed not for a limited measure of self-government but for the almost mystical "Republic" which was proclaimed in blood and martyrdom by the suicidal Easter Rising of 1916. In defense of that "Republic"—in the cause, that is, of total independence for the entire island—they were prepared to do more killing.

Winston Churchill, a member of the British negotiating team, has described the signing of the treaty. "Michael Collins," he writes, "rose looking as though he was going to shoot someone, preferably himself. In all my life I have never seen such pain and suffering in restraint." Collins told another signatory, Lord Birkenhead, that he had signed his death warrant.

He had not wanted to go to London. De Valera, a subtle diplomatist (and student of Machiavelli) had been the obvious choice, but held that as head of state he should remain above the conference table. More to the point, he knew, as did Collins, that treaties imply negotiations and negotiations imply compromise and compromise can cause a calamity back home.

Both Collins and De Valera had fought in the failed 1916 Rising, and Collins's prison mates had nicknamed him "the big fellow." He had a farm boy's tall, muscular frame, and he was handsome in a blunt, forceful way, with a heavy face quick to smile or to snarl. Even in the prison camp, he was a man in a hurry to get things done, to take responsibilities, to give orders, to cajole, or to bully. He respected the executed leaders of 1916, but for him the Easter Rising had had "the air of a Greek tragedy about it," poetry and cloudy rhetoric leading to stone walls and firing squads. The war which he was left to take up was to be covert, lethal, tight-lipped.

It was his own life, however, which now took on the air of a Greek tragedy. He was under tremendous pressures. The treaty, he was persuaded, had extracted from the British as much as they were prepared to yield, and he regarded it not as a permanent settlement but as "a stepping stone," not freedom itself but the freedom to work for freedom. Both the British and the infuriated Republicans, however, may be excused for taking the treaty at face value. The British demanded that he keep his word, and the Republicans abandoned him because he had given it.

There was a slow drift toward the civil war which no one wanted, least of all Collins and De Valera, and then a violent eruption. The Republicans had seized a number of public buildings, including the massive and magnificent Four Courts on the Liffey. On Wednesday, June 28, 1922, at three in the morning, Collins's Free State forces opened fire on it with eighteen-pound field guns borrowed from the British army. In doing so Collins was yielding to British demands and to the implacable logic of circumstance.

There have been a number of biographies of Collins, many historical studies, and, at his centenary in 1991, numerous fresh appraisals. Tim Pat Coogan's *The Man Who Made Ireland: The Life and Death of Michael Collins*[1] can stand beside the best of these, Frank O'Connor's *The Big Fellow* (1937). As a very young man, O'Connor had served in the Republican army fighting Collins; his biography is a generous act of reconciliation. Coogan is under no such burden, and he has been able to make use of a wealth of material unavailable to O'Connor. He writes with a warm but critical admiration for this devious, impulsive, ruthless, greathearted young soldier.

That August evening in 1922, Collins was traveling in an open touring car, preceded by a motorcyclist escort and a Crossley tender holding ten Free State soldiers. An armored car equipped with a Lewis gun brought up the rear. At a place in the road called Beal na mBlath (the mouth of flowers), they drove into the ambush. Emmet Dalton, the seasoned soldier who accompanied Collins, shouted, "Drive like hell!" which surely was the correct order. But Collins, as soon as he heard shots, tapped the driver's shoulder and said, "Jump out and we'll fight them." In the brief battle which followed, as Coogan says, "he was out in an open roadway, with no cover, while in front and behind him some of the toughest and most experienced flying column men in the country were firing at him or his party."

Since then, especially in recent years, a spate of grassy-knoll theories have offered elaborate explanations of how and why Collins was ambushed, but Coogan, quite sensibly, has little time for them. Collins was killed in a Republican ambush which he should have been wary enough to avoid. And there is the beginning and end of it.

---

1. Roberts Rinehart, 1992.

The real mystery, so it has always seemed to me, is why he ignored or belittled warnings as he traveled with light protection among hills swarming with his enemies, and why he decided to fight it out in defiance of common sense and the most elementary laws of battle.

Collins was prosecuting the war with his habitual thoroughness, but there is no doubt that it was sickening him. Increasingly, he showed himself as moody, angry, short-tempered—and, as is often the case when leaders die, people were to speak later of his expressed forebodings. There is something at once willful and touching in his confidence that he would be safe in the hills of West Cork.

In the debates on the treaty in the Dail, the language used about Collins by his enemies (much of which Coogan spares us) had been coarse and almost murderous. At least one member threatened to shoot him if he ever came to Cork. Others spoke sneeringly of him as a romantic hero created by Fleet Street journalists. One charge, though, may have stung him with particular fierceness.

Seamus Robinson, an IRA commandant with a formidable battle record, asked whether in fact Collins himself had ever been in a single battle, a single ambush, whether he had ever been seen to fire a shot against an enemy of Ireland. His rhetorical question was answered by the bitterest of Collins's opponents, Cathal Brugha, a brave, desperately honest man who served as minister of defense. Time and again, Collins had got things done by riding roughshod over him. He had nursed his grievances, and now he struck back. "One of the heads of the subsections," he said, "is Mr. Michael Collins; and to use a word which he has on one occasion used, and which he is fond of using, he is merely a subordinate in the Department of Defence."

Some subordinate! But the sneers of Robinson and Brugha would have stung because they were true. There is no record of Collins literally firing off a gun against the enemy. He planned the strikes and sent out the gunmen. But to someone bred in his particular Irish school of masculinity, and to someone of marked physical courage in a land at war, this would have seemed a savage taunt. By August of 1922, Cathal Brugha had himself been dead for two months, "fatally wounded as he advanced down a Free State barricade manned by riflemen, revolver in hand, ignoring calls to surrender." On hearing of that death, Collins had written, "I would forgive him anything. Because of his sincerity, I would forgive him anything."

Perhaps, though, he was answering Brugha's taunt when he died at Beal na mBlath, firing at enemies who were hidden from sight.

—*The Washington Post Book World*, October 25, 1992

33

BORNE UP BY THE GHOSTS
OF THE FALLEN

IN 1959, Eamon De Valera, the seventy-seven-year-old *Taoiseach* (prime minister) of Ireland, was preparing to leave the office he had held, despite interruptions, for decades, and from which he had shaped an Ireland curiously close to his own image of it. He had at last been persuaded to hand over the reins to a successor, and to move "up to the Park"—to Phoenix Park, that is, and the residence of the country's president, a purely ceremonial head of state. Beside his desk stood a switchboard of brass levers by which he communicated with ministers, the army, heads of departments. His secretary came in to discover him, a tall, blind old man, with his arms wrapped around the switchboard. "Oh, Padraig," he said, with tears in his eyes. "It's awfully hard to leave the levers of power."

This is one of those moments for which biographers pray, and there are many of them in Tim Pat Coogan's *Eamon de Valera*.[1] It is the kind of biography not much seen these days, colorfully written, engagingly robust, and remorselessly, at times gleefully, hostile. All the De Valera biographies are either adulatory (*De Valera and the March of a Nation*, one is called) or rancorous. Sean O'Faolain wrote one of each, as his youthful admiration for the patriot who had defended the

---

1. *Eamon de Valera: The Man Who Was Ireland* (HarperCollins, 1995).

Irish Republic against betrayal was replaced by dislike of the narrow-minded and devious politician who flattered the timidities and prejudices of a peasant society venturing fearfully into the modern world.

Coogan, an Irish journalist and historian who has also written a biography of Michael Collins,[2] paints a dark portrait of a man driven, from youth through old age, by lust for power. But this is not unknown among political leaders, especially those who have risen through revolution. Collins, whom Coogan places against De Valera as a counterhero, may not have lusted for power, but he dallied with it most happily, and at times exerted it with ruthless and chilling efficiency. The implacability of Coogan's attack, which frequently is brightened by his delight in his subject's breathtaking hypocrisies and "bare-faced lying," itself merits examination.

An explanation may rest in the American subtitle. The subtitle to the British edition, "Long Fellow, Long Shadow," is more evocative. De Valera loyalists had dutifully concocted the name to compete with Collins's nickname, the Big Fellow. But "The Man Who Was Ireland," for all its marketing catchiness, has resonance. To understand Ireland for much of its seventy years of semi-independence, one must understand De Valera. From the 1930s to the 1950s, when Ireland looked into the mirror it saw that saturnine, long-jawed face of a mathematics teacher turned tortuous dialectician, of a rural patriot turned adroit political manipulator. Coogan's hostility may be a culture's anger against a part of itself, and his biography an act of exorcism, a slaying of the family dragon on the hearth.

De Valera was born in Brooklyn in 1882 to a Spanish man and a young immigrant woman who, when he was three, shipped him to County Clare, a place heavy with national memory and aspiration. There he was raised by her family of small farmers, amid persistent if doubtful rumors of his illegitimacy. His cleverness earned him an

---

2. See Chapter 33.

education at Blackrock College, where he was later a teacher, and he soon became a member of various nationalist organizations, especially those dedicated to native culture and the Irish language. Modern Ireland was born out of this heady mixture of rural values, Gaelic speech, the legendary history of Irish patriotism, and a devotion to Roman Catholicism. That was the culture shared by De Valera, Collins, and nearly all the young men who were to emerge from rebellion and war as Ireland's new ruling caste.

When the mixture exploded on Easter Monday 1916, De Valera was an officer in the Irish Volunteers, in command of an important position on the perimeter of the fighting. Opinions differ as to his weeklong defense of the area, with his admirers ascribing to him a martial zeal worthy of the ancient hero Cuchulain, and Coogan, predictably, seeing him as a badly rattled and nearly hysterical civilian thrust into a military role. Of his personal courage there can be no question.

He was sentenced to death for his role in the Easter Rising, and escaped death when the English called off further executions just as De Valera was about to be shot. The following year he emerged from prison as the senior surviving commander and a figure already acquiring cult stature. He was elected president of Sinn Fein, the separatist political party, and of the reorganized Irish Volunteers.

By 1919 Sinn Fein had established an underground government and parliament, the Dail Eireann, and the Volunteers were being transformed into a guerrilla force shortly to become famous as the Irish Republican Army. During 1920 and 1921, the IRA conducted a hit-and-run campaign against the Royal Irish Constabulary, the British army, and finally the Black and Tans, a special force organized by England and allowed to conduct raids and reprisals with utter lawlessness.

During the fighting, Michael Collins emerged from the shadows as a resourceful guerrilla strategist, a master of intelligence, and a genius at juggling bureaucratic structures. He was a powerful and glamorous figure, gifted at improvisation, generous, and witty, if at times arrogant and overbearing, equally at home with murder and merriment. In short, an anti–De Valera.

Irish history was now, tragically, to unroll itself between the conflicting temperaments and characters of the embryo politician and the guerrilla chieftain. During much of the war against England, De Valera was in America, raising funds and organizing public opinion. When he came home in December 1920, on a passage secretly organized by Collins, he was greeted by an emissary with: "The Big Fellow is leading us and everything is going marvelous." De Valera replied: "Big Fellow! We'll see who's the Big Fellow."

In the spring of 1921, the British government sent signals that it was ready to work toward a resolution of the Irish question, and negotiators prepared to meet at 10 Downing Street. The English team was led by its heaviest guns, Prime Minister David Lloyd George and the colonial secretary, Winston Churchill. De Valera declined to lead for the Irish, lest the purity of his symbolic status as "President of the Republic" be sullied by the tawdry compromises of negotiation. Instead, he asked Collins and Arthur Griffith, the founder of Sinn Fein, to lead the delegation.

Within the Irish Cabinet itself, within the Dail, among the guerrilla fighters on the hillsides, there were supporters who would settle for little less than a pure and utterly free republic. But this was not on offer. Any resolution would have to include some kind of oath to the British Crown, and the partition of Ireland into north and south. The trick would be to get the best terms possible within those limits, while at the same time holding off the die-hard Republicans. Whoever put his name to a treaty with compromises would be damning himself as a traitor in the eyes of some of his own people. De Valera knew that and so did Collins. Collins's acceptance of the mission was the bravest act of his career, and De Valera's refusal the most morally questionable of his. When Collins signed the treaty, he said in frustrated fury that he had probably signed his own death warrant. And so he had.

This was the central drama of De Valera's long career and Collins's short one. When De Valera was very old he talked one day in Phoenix Park to a distinguished historian, Sir John Wheeler-Bennett. His mind circled back fifty years, to the days of the treaty, when the guileful Lloyd George and the cunning Churchill outbargained and out-bluffed Collins. "He sat for a few moments in a reverie," the historian wrote, "and then broke out into almost a lament for the soul of the Sinn Fein Party as it had been 'before the British savaged it.'"

The treaty Collins brought back led to a civil war in which more were killed in battle or executed than had died in the fight against England—among them Collins, shot from ambush in his own County Cork. De Valera spent the civil war of 1922–1923 wandering among the Republican guerrillas, who did not fully trust him, suspecting him of being as ready to compromise as Collins and Griffith had been, provided appearances were kept up. And indeed they were right. During Cabinet quarrels about the treaty, he had presented to his colleagues his "Document No: 2," which differed from the treaty in ways that could be grasped only by a fellow mathematician.

De Valera emerged from the civil war as the standard-bearer of that pure republic for which other men had been shot dead, by the English or by their fellow Irishmen. In 1927, at the head of a new political party, Fianna Fail, he entered the Dail, taking the hated oath of allegiance to the Crown, but taking it behind a veil of linguistic obfuscation that would do credit to a deconstructionist. In 1933, Fianna Fail came to power, and De Valera settled down to preside over a country living on memories of the "four glorious years" of national struggle, scarred by the wounds and savage memories of the civil war, economically impoverished, bewildered by modernity, and subservient to a triumphalist Church. Its heroes were dead or on pension.

The Irish historian Joseph Lee says, in generous words Coogan quotes: "Behind the ceaseless political calculation and the labyrinthine deviousness, there reposed a character of rare nobility. His qualities would have made him a leader beyond compare in the pre-industrial world." It is a nicely "Irish" formulation—precise, gracious, and barbed.

Coogan says De Valera's wife, Sinead, once "half-humorously, half-despairingly, told friends that she could write a play about him. But, she said, she did not know whether it would be 'a comedy or a tragedy.'" The Sean O'Casey who wrote *Juno and the Paycock* would have told her that that makes it a very Irish kind of play.

—*The New York Times Book Review*, April 30, 1995

34

DISPATCHES FROM THE FRONT

"I CAN CALL up spirits from the vasty deep," says the Celtic rebel Owen Glendower in Shakespeare's *Henry IV*, but Hotspur, the play's brisk, soldierly Englishman, mocks him: "Why, so can I, or so can any man, but will they come when you do call to them?"

For Englishmen of the present day, Gerry Adams, president of Sinn Fein, the political wing (more or less) of the Irish Republican Army, seems an embodiment of their worst dreams, a specter called up from the vasty deep of Irish history. Clever, remorseless, glib, ruthless, mendacious, by turns placatory and fierce, he is everything that Englishmen pride themselves on not being. Why, they ask, using the structure of Professor Higgins's question to Colonel Pickering, why can't a Paddy be more like a Brit? They are made especially furious by his avowals, earnest-eyed behind glasses, that he has never been a member of the Irish Republican Army itself. Such an admission, by making him eligible for a return to prison, would serve the twin, indeed the identical, causes of truth and Britain. In truth, of course, few people anywhere believe his protestations, and those few are likely also to believe that there is intelligent life on Mars.

Historically, the English have always been furious with people who do not play by English rules, especially when they have access—to say the least—to guns and explosives. Indeed, they are disinclined even to speak to such people until they have handed over those weapons. Such a process, known in euphemism as "decommissioning," is at the center of the present impasse in the peace process.

When Bobby Sands died on hunger strike in Belfast's Long Kesh prison in 1981, *The New York Times* wrote that "despite proximity and a common language, the British have persistently misjudged the depth of Irish nationalism." But this fatal, at times murderous, misjudgment exists not despite a common language but because of it. In the culture within which Gerry Adams was shaped, English words do not have the meaning that they have in Whitehall and Downing Street or in the pages of English newspapers.

Adams was shaped by that culture, as he tells us in *Before the Dawn*,[1] an autobiography that is at once enlightening and deliberately opaque. It is the culture of West Belfast, Catholic and working class, instinctively non-British but with its politics shading from a conventional nationalism to the extremes of a Republicanism ready for violence should the need and occasion arise. Most Northern Catholics believed, staunchly if vaguely, that they were Irish and not British and that they were in numerous and severe ways discriminated against, in the first instance by their Protestant neighbors but ultimately by London. Those Protestant neighbors were determined, in the memorable words of one of their prime ministers, to keep Northern Ireland "a Protestant state for a Protestant people." But the Catholic community, across the province, was uncertain as to when, if ever, matters could be changed.

Adams, however, was born and raised within the Republican tradition, a minority within a larger minority. He comes from a family Republican on both sides for three generations, members of a culture that went far beyond the singing of "Kevin Barry" in a pub to include border raids, gun battles, prison terms, and harassment by Orange

---

1. *Before the Dawn: an Autobiography* (Morrow, 1997).

bullies in and out of police uniform. Their other, Catholic neighbors rejected both the violence and the intransigence of the extreme Republicans, while according them a grudging, wavering respect as keepers of the flame of Irish independence.

He was born in 1948, the year after his father, a building laborer, had completed a five-year prison sentence for Republican activities, and his earliest days were spent in the Falls Road, the very center of Belfast nationalism and a center with which he remains in close touch. A bit later, his family moved to the new housing estate in Ballymurphy: "It was badly built, badly planned, and badly lacking in facilities, but it nevertheless possessed a wonderful sense of openness, there on the slopes of the mountain." Like most of Northern Ireland's Catholic boys, he was educated by the Christian Brothers, with, importantly, summer visits to the Irish-speaking mountains of West Donegal, still in the north but politically a part of the Republic of Ireland. The Falls Road and the mountains of Ireland can be said to form the complementary centers of his political identity—the activities of a working class kept subordinate to colonial rule, and mountains of an Ireland of the imagination. Before he had completed his schooling at St. Mary's, he had become part of the Republican movement.

Matters in Northern Ireland changed dramatically at the close of the 1960s. The initial instrument of change was a civil rights movement, heavily populated by students, after the fashion of that decade. When loyalist resistance to change escalated into near civil war, local nationalist communities formed defensive strategies that included Republican groups, only to discover that the IRA, for all its swagger, was unable to deliver, so to speak, the goods. Ideological disputes within its factions had left it fragmented, disorganized, and ill-equipped. (When the IRA meets, Brendan Behan, a member, used to say, the first item of business is the Split.) It was in the aftermath of this calamity, and against the background of the disintegrating "Protestant state," that Republicans of Adams's generation came to the fore. Deeply loyal to traditional Republicanism, which for them was history itself, they were also, in their way, children of the 1960s and knew the words not only to "Bold Robert Emmet" but also to the civil rights songs of the United States and South Africa.

Before the Dawn can be read as the history of the last quarter-century in Northern Ireland, from the perspective of someone who educated himself and came to power within one of the traditions—a crucial one at the moment—of the province. One of its problems—and fascinations—is that it is written from within the center of an unresolved national conflict and therefore faces the competing needs of historical candor and political reticence. As Adams himself puts it in his preface, "It is probably an invariable rule that the participants in any conflict cannot tell the entire story until some time after that conflict is fully resolved." And it may be that the memoirs of a successful underground leader are best written in his sunset years, when he can indulge his memories. Adams, writing from the battle line, must maintain a natural talent for caginess of utterance. Thus, his account of the conflict between the Official and Provisional wings of the IRA, ending in the victory of his own faction, the Provisionals, shrouds what was in fact bloody conflict.

His efforts to supply a personal history of the Republican movement without being clear about what he, personally, was doing have carried him into techniques which bear a striking although inadvertent resemblance to those of postmodernist literature. Maureen Orth, in a recent *Vanity Fair* article, describes her efforts to learn whether he is, or was, a member of the IRA: "Thus begins a Kabuki scenario that every chronicler of Adams is forced to participate in, knowing that the truth is somewhere within the fan that conceals him."

At times in the autobiography, he emerges from workaday obscurity into a position of clear but unspecified authority, only to sink back once more into shadow, rather like Woody Allen's Zelig. In one extraordinary instance, he is released from Long Kesh so that he can be flown, with high-ranking members of the IRA, to a London meeting with British officials, although later "I was disconcerted when my name appeared in the newspapers because I was doing nothing, as I saw it, to deserve this attention." We cannot even know whether, behind the fan, he is smiling at our frustrated curiosity.

It is far more striking that two entire population groups are given in this book only a flickering, Zelig-like existence. You would never guess from *Before the Dawn* that the majority of the people in Northern Ireland are Protestants and are deeply attached to their sense of a British identity. Here they make shadowy, unreadable appearances as drinkers in a pub where Adams worked or as sashed and bowler-hatted marchers in Orange processions or as loyalist paramilitaries. They are present as cartoons—a sketch of King Billy on a gable-end, the venomous ranting of an Ian Paisley, the voice of a policeman dehumanized by a bullhorn. This is in part a consequence of the conditions of apartheid in which the two populations have lived. But it is also a willed ignorance, a refusal to enter into the imaginative life of a different community.

Neither, though, can non-Irish readers grasp firmly from the book that many more of Northern Ireland's Catholics identify themselves with the nonviolent Social Democratic and Labour Party than with Sinn Fein. But then Adams has written this autobiography to define his own position, rather than that of others. He writes not as a historian but as an embattled participant, choosing his words with wariness. In some later day of peace, writing at his unbuttoned ease, he may choose to tell us the whole story.

—*The Washington Post Book World*, January 26, 1997

35

THE DAY WE CELEBRATE

THERE WAS A time, within the memories of those now ancient, when the pubs of Ireland were closed on St. Patrick's Day, "incredible as it may seem today," as we are told by Mike Cronin of Leicester and Daryl Adair of Canberra, the authors of this lengthy book. The ban came early in the history of the Free State, and perhaps, so they speculate, "was, in part, a reflection of the close relationship between the Catholic church and the Irish State," although it also had the support of "teetotallers in both Catholic and Protestant communities."

The one exception was the dog show held that day by the Royal Dublin Society, which had a special license. Thither to their grounds on one March 17, went Brendan Behan, and in the course of the day he was tripped up by one of the finely bred exhibition animals. "For God's sake," he said, glaring around the bright, sunny grounds, "surely this is a terrible place to bring a dog." Or words to that effect. This bit of Behanology is known to many, but I first heard it from that great and grave authority on the urban lore of Dublin and Omagh, Ben Kiely. You will look in vain for this anecdote in *The Wearing of the Green: A History of St. Patrick's Day*, published with a green cover by Routledge.[1]

---

1. 2001.

But then you will find little of urban anecdote at all, whether of Dublin or of New York. To judge by their surnames, Cronin and Adair are members of what they call, with numbing frequency, "the diaspora," but they display little of that storytelling craft which tradition attributes to their ancestors. They do little to create people on the page in all their vivid particularity, and they might reasonably object that such was no part of their purpose.

But parades, after all, are made up of people—people parading and other people watching them do it. It is people, after all, who transformed the day's signifying event from a religious observance to a drinking marathon. Very few come forward from the early days, whether Anglo-Irish squireen or humble cottier, to confess that he had himself drowned the shamrock, although many are ready to snitch on their neighbors. An Irishman in Australia, Joseph Holt, wrote in 1803 that his usual time to commence sowing was the first Monday after St. Patrick's Day, "it requiring a few days to get my men sober."

Cronin and Adair found Holt's words in a book by Patrick O'Farrell. I wonder, although I lack the energy to look it up, if this could be Joseph Holt, the rebel leader in Wicklow in '98, fearless as Mickey Dwyer, who was transported to Australia where he prospered and wrote his memoirs which were "edited" by Crofton Croker. To Cronin and Adair, he is a name on an index card, thousands of index cards.

Literary gents fare less well on those index cards. W. B. Yeats is described as one major Irish writer who was not born in Dublin, and the short stories in *Dubliners* are described as "a collection of tales about the vivacity of life in Dublin around the turn of the 20th century." Poor Joyce, who thought he was writing chapters in the moral paralysis of his nation. They then leap the Atlantic to describe E. B. White—that courtliest of New Yorkers, who wrote about his adopted city as no one else ever has—as "notorious." He earned the word, apparently, with his 1949 remark that "the only event that hits every New Yorker on the head is the annual St. Patrick's Day parade."

The book is, for all that, a prodigy of research, at both the primary and the secondary level. The list of American and Australian newspaper files examined wearies the heart—hundreds upon hundreds of articles in which journalists did their best to write variations on the set themes, the luck of the Irish, top of the morning, and the rest of it. The Irish-American Club of Cleveland holds an annual Danny Boy singing competition, which was recently won by "an olive-skinned, 100 per cent Lebanese American, the first such ethnic to win a bit of the green." The river in Chicago (not much of a river, as I recall it) is dyed green for the day. Sydney boasts the world's largest fluorescent shamrock.

But what is the point of these languid urban flummeries when all the world knows that the only one that matters is the one that marches up New York's Fifth Avenue? And that of course includes the parade in Dublin, which was invented to appease the bewildered anguish of New Yorkers who had flown over on the assumption that celebrations on the home turf must soar above the merely spectacular only to discover that the pubs were closed and the thoroughfares deserted save for an industrial machinery pageant and Brendan tottering down to Ballsbridge.

In 1970, Dublin tourism took matters in hand, and the *Irish Independent* called the ensuing parade "one of the most colourful events staged in the history of the national festival." There must be some term in social anthropology to describe an annual parade invented by impoverished emigrants to a distant continent and then, a century later, imitated by the mother country and described as a "national festival." In that same year, the Irish consul general, Charles V. Whelan, declared from the reviewing stand in New York: "In Dublin they're taking a line from this one.... Indeed, they had Judge Comerford come over from New York to Dublin as the expert on this kind of thing."

"Judge Comerford," the authors explain in a terse footnote, "was the legendary organiser of the New York St. Patrick's Day parade"—

and of much else in Irish New York in the later decades of the last century. He deserves more than a footnote, but the authors, despite their devotion to index-card history, tend to leave unexplored its more colorful tributaries. Thus, for example, they hopelessly confuse the Young Ireland movement and the later and very different Fenian movement.

They do an admirable job, though, of documenting one of the key issues of nineteenth-century Irish America: the tension in the US between those of Irish descent and the powerful sentiments of those nativists who saw a nation of Protestants of English descent being overwhelmed by an alien horde who had sworn allegiance to the Pope and the whiskey still. The tension was especially high in New York City in the closing decades of that century, and had its effect on the parade. In 1886, the city elected as mayor a bigot named Abram Hewitt, who supported an "'authentic' Anglo-Saxon America," and who refused to review the March 17 parade.

Hewitt was not reelected. I should hope not. What could Tammany Hall have been thinking of?

—*The Irish Times*, March 16, 2002

IV

Historical Fiction and Personal Essays

36

ON PROUST AND TIME

IF FISH COULD think, they would think about water. If birds could think, they would think about the skies. In their far-flung migrations, it is said, they have in their small brains, imprinted, a map of the heavenly constellations, but there is no reason to believe that they move beyond this to cosmological speculations. We do think, and what we think about is time, more steadily and variously than we suppose. It is our sky, our water, our weathers; within it we live, because of it we perish. It is not a subject upon which I can claim to speak with any particular authority, and yet I am conscious, as a child of our times—you notice how easily the word slipped out there—that it is in particular a theme with those writers who, in particular, shaped the modern, although not perhaps the postmodern generations.

The three foundation works of modern literature, it seems to me, are *Remembrance of Things Past*, *Ulysses*, and *The Magic Mountain*, and in all three a concern with the mysteries of time is either a near-obsessive concern or, at the very least, an organizing principle, a technique. When the narrative voice of *The Magic Mountain* broods upon time, in its elephantine, Teutonic way, I tend, I must confess, to nod for a time—for a time!—but this is not at all the case for me with respect to the other two novels. *Ulysses* is a novel constantly alert to time, not merely in its elaborate organization about the hours of a particular day, but in its measurement of the climates which the hours create.

With Proust's novel we move within chambers, caves, colonnades, temples of time. "*Depuis longtemps*," he begins, "For a long time, I used to go to bed early." And thus beginning, his overture moves us forward to that enchanted—literally so—moment when the taste of a crumb of madeleine evokes the madeleine of his Aunt Leonia, soaked in lime-flower tea, and then, immediately the old gray house upon the street, where her room was:

> And once I had recognized the taste of the crumb of madeleine soaked in her decoction of lime-flowers which my aunt used to give me (although I did not yet know and must long postpone the discovery of why this memory made me so happy) immediately the old gray house upon the street, where her room was, rose up like the scenery of a theater to attach itself to the little pavilion, opening on to the garden, which had been built out behind it for my parents (the isolated panel which until that moment had been all that I could see); and with the house the town, from morning to night and in all weathers, the Square where I was sent before luncheon, the streets along which I used to run errands, the country roads we took when it was fine. And just as the Japanese amuse themselves by filling a porcelain bowl with water and steeping in it little crumbs of paper which until then are without character or form, but, the moment they become wet, stretch themselves and bend, take on color and distinctive shape, become flowers or houses or people, permanent and recognizable, so in that moment all the flowers in our garden and in M. Swann's park, and the water-lilies on the Vivonne and the good folk of the village and their little dwellings and the parish church and the whole of Combray and of its surroundings, taking their proper shapes and growing

solid, sprang into being, town and gardens alike, from my cup of tea.

Into this famous passage he has inserted an essential parenthesis—"although I did not yet know and must long postpone the discovery of why this memory made me so happy." C. K. Scott-Moncrieff's somewhat perverse fondness for Shakespeare's sonnets led him to give to his English translation of this immense novel the rather too flowery title *Remembrance of Things Past*. The French title, of course, is *À la recherche du temps perdu*. The difference, which brings us back at once to our subject, is crucial: *The Search for Lost Time*. We too, we readers, like Proust's nameless (or almost nameless) narrator, must long postpone our discovery of why this memory makes him so happy, as do certain other moments. The stumbling, most famously, upon the uneven paving stones in Venice, brings back the past to him, not in a fragment, however poignant, however vivid, for such memories are easily and often evoked, but rather, in such privileged moments, the entire past, an entire past, is rendered up to him, in the fullness of its particularity, and at last, by the contemplation of such moments, he has, in very fact, conquered time, lost time has been recovered, and in the recovery, happiness resides.

Proust, that is to say, puts the sensation of time at the very center of human experience, although, to be sure, the transactions between time and love, time and society, time and art, are crucial. His aching nostalgia, it has been argued, led him to be idiosyncratic in this matter. For most people, nostalgia is an emotion which wanes and waxes in intensity, but for some, Proust among them, it is a controlling passion, around which others organize themselves. It is safe to assume that few, even among the most resolute Proustians, accept literally the victory which he claims: accept, that is, that he has wrested the past from its pastness, carried it forward into the present. There is far too much tenuous and tenebrous metaphysics going on in the novel for the claim to be fully accepted. Indeed, one can be tempted to the other extreme, can be tempted to argue that the narrator's metaphysics of time serves, rather, to provide Proust with a scaffolding upon which to hang his intricacies of plot and self-analysis.

Certain it is at any rate that the kinds of feeling which Proust solicits from his reader, and which he himself makes manifest in such luxuriant abundance, is, in itself, time-bound. That is, that he is exploiting states of being and feeling, attitudes toward the past, which had preceded his own day by at most a century—attitudes which we associate with Rousseau and Chateaubriand in his culture, and with Wordsworth in our own.

37

OBSESSION

I WAS DELIGHTED to have been asked back to PEN/Faulkner, which seemed to me one of those rare literary occasions which are both elegant and humane. Ever since April, when PEN/Faulkner asked me to join with you and talk about obsession for three minutes, I have been able to think of little else.

I went first of course to the dictionary. Not the OED. I had misplaced the magnifying glass, and in any event, using it always arouses my latent feelings of social inferiority. A friend many years ago inherited a full set from his father, and I always imagine him strolling to his shelf while I crouch over microscopic type. I did go, though, to its admirable abridgment, the *Oxford Universal Dictionary*, where I discovered of course that all my life it or I had been using the word incorrectly. The word "obsession" derives, I was instructed, from the Latin *obsidere* and meant originally "to besiege," as a fortress is besieged or invested. And thence, says the dictionary, actuation by the devil or an evil spirit from without. And thence, finally, from that, the action of any influence, notion, or fixed idea which persistently assails or vexes. But this ran very counter to my notion that an obsession arises from within and seizes upon the external. A man obsessed by the notion that he is the reincarnation of Napoleon is not influenced toward that big leap by a chance visit to Waterloo, or by marriage to a woman named Josephine; it is quite the other way around. His obsession leads him to seek out the battlefield that he may relive an old sorrow, and he pays court to a woman who bears the appropriate name.

I turned to *Webster's Third*, which of course dismissed the besetting activities of devils or spirits as obsolete, *obs*. *Obs*. is an abbreviation which in *Webster's Third* always carries a chilling whiff of contempt. *Webster's* settles instead for "a persistent and disturbing intrusion of, or anxious and inescapable preoccupation with a feeling, especially if known to be unreasonable." This seemed even worse. Obsessions are indeed persistent but they need not be disturbing or a cause of anxiety, nor something from which one vainly seeks relief. Surely it all depends on the nature of the obsession. And the more I reflected on it, the more hostile seemed that word "unreasonable." Unreasonable to whom? It seems a bit nasty of external reality first to implant the obsession in the sufferer's mind and then to condemn that mind for accepting it. Dictionaries claim to be neutral judges of language, but in fact they are subtle casuists. And in fact they are subtle casuists directed against writers and artists in general, who believe that their central energies arise from within, and then confront the without.

After these two, I had no need to consult their lesser and more recent rivals, but something unreasonable and obsessive drove me on. The *American College Dictionary* speaks of the besetting or dominating action or influence of a persistent feeling, idea, "or the like." One turns to a dictionary for precision, and is fobbed off with an airy wave of the editorial hand, "or the like"!

The *American Heritage Dictionary* is the most modern, with hundreds of line drawings and little reproductions in the margin. I had hoped, as I turned to the O's to find a drawing modeled upon Fuseli or Goya of an actual obsession, crouched upon a skull and battering for entrance. I was disappointed but was able to learn that of recent years, the verb "to obsess" has acquired an intransitive usage. For illustration, the *Heritage* turns not to Walter Pater or Evelyn Waugh or Vladimir Nabokov. Instead it goes right to stylistic headquarters, to Scott Turow himself, one of whose novels contains the line, "She's dead but you're still obsessing."

After that, it took me the better part of two days to find the magnifying glass, but was it worth the effort and the dust? When the OED needs an illustration it turns to the splendidly named Hubert Crackenthorpe, a decadent of the English 1890s and a justly forgotten one, who is quoted as having said, "The thought of death began to haunt him until it became a constant obsession." One does not quarrel easily with the OED, but surely all obsessions are constant?

My task, fortunately, has only begun. *Roget's* and *Webster's Thesaurus* list among synonyms: fixations, fascination, phantom, craze, delusion, mania, infatuation, fixed idea, compulsion, and (perhaps Mr. Turow's contribution) hang-up. I am now in the process of hunting down these words and their shadings and colorations. It is a task before which everything else seems unreasonably to be fading away.

—from *Obsession* (Quill and Brush, 1994),
a collection of remarks from the
Fifth PEN/Faulkner Gala,
Washington, D. C., October 2, 1993

38

HISTORY AS FICTION,
FICTION AS HISTORY

AMONG THE BOOKS published in the British Isles in 1798, two were destined for immortality, and a third for near oblivion. The two were of course the *Lyrical Ballads* by Wordsworth and Coleridge, and *An Essay on Population* by a newly ordained clergyman named Thomas Malthus. The third, of which only a few hundred copies had been hurriedly printed and at the author's expense, was awkwardly titled *An Impartial Narrative of What Passed at Killala in the Summer of 1798*. The author, Arthur Vincent Broome, identified himself on the title page as M.A. (Oxon).

He was also, and more to the point, a Protestant clergyman with a parish in Killala, a fishing village on the coast of Mayo in western Ireland. There, in August and September, he had witnessed, first with stupefaction, then with dismay, and finally with despair, an uprising which had been occasioned by an invading army of a thousand French soldiers, veterans of Italy and the Rhine, under the command of a vigorous and skillful young general named Humbert. Humbert led an impromptu army of soldiers and Gaelic-speaking peasants to a series of victories, first against yeomen in the town itself, but then against regulars, inland at Ballina, and at last, farther inland yet, at Castlebar, where a large British army was shattered. It retreated back through the town and out into open country in such haste that the battle passed into folklore as "the races of Castlebar."

But the general, island-wide insurrection upon which Humbert and the Directors had been relying, depending upon the deceptive promise of an Irish rebel named Wolfe Tone, was not kindled. Within weeks, his army was destroyed by superior British force—horse, foot, and artillery. The French were sent home on a prisoner exchange, but the Irish, hundreds of them, were slaughtered without quarter at the site of the final battle, at Ballinamuck, the place of the pig. A part of the victorious army then moved westward upon Mayo, slaughtering as they went; a rear guard was butchered in the streets of Killala, and the army swept on, killing as they went; the avowed intention was to teach Mayo a lesson. The lesson was learned by Mayo, although it was not the lesson intended.

These had been trying weeks for the Reverend Arthur Vincent Broome. Humbert had seized his house as a headquarters, and later it was used by the rear guard of rebels, under the command of a local farmer named Ferdy O'Donnell. A curious, entangled, and doomed friendship between Broome and O'Donnell developed, and O'Donnell was killed outside the window of Broome's sitting room.

In the several years in which he had lived in Killala, Broome had come to measure the distance between two worlds—his own and that of the natives, separated by language, by religion, by culture, but above all separated by an appalling poverty, as abject as any in all Europe. The occasional small farmer, like O'Donnell, schooled and a bit worldly, was the exception. The peasants in their appalling numbers, and dependent upon a single crop, lived in crude cabins of mud, or in caves hollowed from hillsides. These were the men who had risen up, had fought, at last were killed without quarter.

Broome was by nature a mild-mannered man—he describes himself in one of his unpublished journals as a "lover of civility and buttered toast"—but what he had witnessed had disturbed him profoundly.

That Christmas, he and his wife went home to Derbyshire with his brother Nicholas, and there Broome unburdened himself to the Anglican clergyman, a young man who helpfully passed on to him a copy of his own friend Malthus's essay, in the hope that it might reconcile him to the inevitability of human misery. He passed along also, for good measure, his copy of the *Lyrical Ballads*, but these effusions Broome in his journal dismisses with near contempt. The lyrics he found pretty enough, "although strained and artificial in their very effort to appear natural, but there is also a long and ludicrous ballad or 'rime' in which a sailor slays a large bird with an arrow, for which apparently heinous offense he is pursued by all the powers of hell and his shipboard companions perish miserably, all this set forth in a wearisome style of false innocence and simplicity." But it was Malthus who truly horrified him, and especially so in view of his experiences in Ireland:

> Mr. Malthus began simply enough, by demonstrating that populations will always grow at a rate swifter than that of the food which they require, unless checks be placed upon their growth. These checks he divided between the positive and the negative, of which the former included famines, plagues, and pestilences. What an awful vista his words opened up! I could not force myself to accept the inevitability of his argument, yet try as I would I could not escape from it. It was as though, like some darker Newton, he had hit upon a formula which had for centuries lain hidden just beyond the edges of men's minds. Clear and cold as iced water, it clarified and chilled the brain. And all set forth with an air of unimpassioned calm which contrasted most vividly with his abominable conclusions.
>
> I would have thought that Ireland, with its centuries of recurring famines, was well suited to his thesis, but I sought for it in vain. His first volume ranged over the entire world, and brought

before our consideration the naked wretches of Tierra del Fuego and Van Diemen's Land, the yet more wretched savages of the Andaman Islands, the paint-bedaubed warriors of North America, the furry Laplanders, the horsemen of the Asian steppes. But of Ireland, which lay at Mr. Malthus's doorstep, there was not a word, until I came to the very last page, where tersely he informs the reader that the natives are too barbarous to admit of counting up their numbers. And then he adds: "The checks upon the population are of course of the positive kind, and arise from the diseases occasioned by squalid poverty, by damp and wretched cabins, by bad and insufficient clothing, by the filth of their persons, and occasional want. To these positive checks have of late years been added the vice and misery of intestine commotion, of civil war, and of martial law." He says not a word more, and his disdain was painful to contemplate. All that I had witnessed, all that tumult and passion, that confusion and blood, were but checks upon population. The dead in the streets of Killala, the obscene weights upon the Castlebar gibbet, the peasants hunted down in the Belmullet wastes, had contributed their lives to an equation. The Irish, it would appear, were doomed to an endless sequence of spawning and starving, spawning and starving.

"It is a most salutary and Christian work," young Mr. Clifford assured him, when he returned the books. "Mr. Malthus reminds us that man is not a perfectible creature. He strives blindly to propagate his kind. There is no salvation within nature or within society." He then described to Broome a tract society, newly founded in London, which proposed to distribute New Testaments in the west of Ireland.

"But they cannot read," Broome said. "They do not speak English. What folly is this, what new folly? It would serve as well to cram pages of the Testament in bottles and set them adrift to be carried to Africa or the Sandwich Islands. Better still, let them translate Mr.

Malthus into Gaelic, and thus instruct the poor that they starve by theorem, and die to conclude a syllogism."

I have thus far been speaking of actual personages—Coleridge and Wordsworth, Thomas Malthus, Lord Cornwallis, General Humbert, even Ferdy O'Donnell, the rebel leader who was bayoneted to death outside Broome's window (one of his descendants is a distinguished Irish archaeologist, exploring, most appropriately, a bog in Mayo). The exception is Broome himself. He never lived, save as a character and one of the narrators in my novel, *The Year of the French*.

When I began work on the book, I knew that I would need some outsider to the scene, who could establish the setting and orient the reader, someone to whom Ireland might at first have seemed, as he says, an "island which might for all purposes be adrift on the South Seas, rather than at our doorstep." A conventional device in fiction. But although Broome never existed, his book did. If you consult the catalogs of elaborate libraries, you may find it there. *An Impartial Narrative of What Passed at Killala in the Summer of 1798*. No author's name is given on the title page, although we know that it was, in very fact, written by a Protestant clergyman resident in Killala. The clergyman was Joseph Stock, the bishop of Killala, although he modestly refers to himself throughout in the third person. He it was in whose house, properly if grandiloquently termed his "palace," that General Humbert installed himself, and, later, Ferdy O'Donnell.

When the idea of writing a novel about the Mayo uprising first occurred to me, and I began assembling material, I discovered, from the sparse material then available, that Stock had written an account, and he was described as a man of generous spirit, devoid of the passionate political and religious bigotries of the time, although of course a loyalist to the British Crown. The book was essential for me, and I located a copy in a midwestern library and sent off for it. Interlibrary loan was in those days—the mid-1970s—a branch of the overland stage, and while it was traveling to me, the voice, not of Bishop Stock but of Arthur Vincent Broome, had begun to echo in my ear, and I had begun to write. In the meantime, I had discovered that Stock was not English but Irish, of a distinguished Anglo-Irish family, a Fellow of Trinity College Dublin, and a mathematician of some celebrity. And when his book arrived, I discovered that the earlier references to it had been entirely mistaken. His tone was querulous rather than generous, and understandably so, the tone of a man whose life had been turned upon its head by an outlandish invasion, and whose life had been put at risk and his very house commandeered. He did make one exception, and well he might. He and the other loyalists in the town owed their lives to Ferdy O'Donnell, who protected them against mob fury after word arrived of the disaster at Ballinamuck and the approaching British army of vengeance. Accordingly, there is a sensitivity to his language when he speaks of O'Donnell, whose cause he abominated, but whose character won his reluctant respect. And as for this being what he calls "an impartial narrative," this is true only in the special sense that he made distinctions among the French, whom he loathed, the rebels, whom he despised, and the loyalist militia, members of his own church, whom he dismissed as blundering poltroons. There was the stuff there out of which to create an interesting narrator—brisk, sardonic, a trifle bilious—but not for this book.

"Like others of my projects"—this is Broome speaking—"my earlier journal stumbled to a halt after months and long lay gathering dust upon a shelf in my library. Where these notes are now, I cannot say; perhaps they served to start a fire, this being the fate which locally befalls paper upon which words have been written. They would have served no larger purpose, however, for my early impressions were all, as I now know, misleading, this land being as treacherous as the bog which stretches across much of its surface. It is, in the most exact sense, an outlandish place, inhospitable to the instructions of civilisation. . . . Were I to have the colouring of this island's map, Mayo would appear upon it in browns and blues, the brown of hillside and bogside, arched over by an immense sky of light blue."

Stock would never have spoken so or written so or felt so. A footnote upon the poor man, before he vanishes into history's trapdoor. His "cathedral" survives to this day, but as a simple parish church, open one Sunday a month for the area's now-small Protestant population. But his "palace," Broome's rectory, was knocked down in the 1930s. The stones were tossed into a crusher, and eventually saw service in pebble-dash local housing. But there is a local legend. Stock, like many of the Anglo-Irish gentry, had pride of family, and he had set into the wall above the fireplace a block of Portland stone, elaborately carved with the family's coat of arms. So handsome a stone that a workman called it to the attention of the foreman, who shook his head, "Toss it into the crusher." It was as though he spoke with the voice of history, and when I heard the story, in one of Killala's public houses, it was as though my own reaction had been anticipated. There is a happy ending of a sort. After the success of the novel which carries my Arthur Vincent Broome's *Impartial Narrative*, an enterprising Mayo printer reprinted Bishop Stock's *Impartial Narrative*. It has gone out of print.

My subject has not so much a thesis as it is a meditation upon curious points of juncture within historical fiction between fact and fiction, a collection of junctures, some serious, some trifling. And if I use a book of my own at the outset, it is not from vanity but simply because I have been in the kitchen. It is a trifling matter, perhaps, that I used occasionally to worry about my near obliteration of Bishop Stock, worry, that is, that I may have violated one of the tacit protocols of historical fiction, a contract between writer and reader, between writer and the actuality of the past.

A more serious but not an unrelated matter arises from the way in which historical novels bring forward upon the page actual figures from the past. Examples of the problem can be found in almost any of the historical films made in Hollywood from the 1930s through the 1950s. In, for example, a 1954 film called *King Richard and the Crusaders*, Richard is played by Rex Harrison and his bride, the Princess Berengaria of Navarre, by Virginia Mayo. In the final scene, Richard, on horseback, is accosted by his bride, who has hoped that he will stay around Navarre for a while. But he reminds her that he must hurry off to liberate the Holy Land. "Oh," the Princess says, shaking her golden locks, "fight, fight, fight, that's all you ever think about, Dick Plantagenet." To hear the word "Plantagenet" spoken by lips shaped by service as a cheerleader at Beverly Hills High is to experience, in a manner almost erotic, the crash against each other of vast historical plates.

And yet it may be that such films have given away the game. Historical novelists place upon the page with seeming confidence personages from whom they, and we, are separated by deep and bottomless gorges. Lord Cornwallis is a subordinate character in *The Year of the French*, his words and actions, his very thoughts reported to us by a soldier writing in his old age, who as a young officer, a half-century earlier, had served as aide-de-camp. I read the biographies of Cornwallis, his official correspondence as viceroy of Ireland, the memoirs of some of his contemporaries. But the novel's Cornwallis is given to us filtered through the language of an old man remembering his own hero-worshiping youth. Whence then comes the novel's Cornwallis— by turns generous and haughty, witty, overbearing, satirical, by turns shrewd and self-satisfied? I suspect that I may have owed less to my research than to my recollections of General Burgoyne in Shaw's *The Devil's Disciple* and even his Julius Caesar and his Napoleon in *Man of Destiny*. But this may say little more than that novels have worked out conventions by which to dramatize certain kinds of beings—in this case, a man of political and military power and skill who loves the power and has no thought to relinquish, yet can stand aside from it, wise yet narcissistic.

Historical fiction is an especially *writerly* kind of fiction. Arthur Vincent Broome did not come into the world an orphan. My recollection of other clergymen of fiction must surely have gone into his making—the Vicar of Wakefield and even poor Mr. Causable in *The Importance of Being Earnest*. A few years before beginning my book, I had seen, at Dublin's Abbey Theatre, Cyril Cusack in a dramatization of *The Vicar of Wakefield*, and his black-clad figure and fuddled benevolence lingered with me.

Broome is not the only character in the novel to leave behind a historical record, and one of them deserves notice at this point. In Mayo south of Killala there stands the ruins of what in 1798 had been a handsome mansion of cut Portland stone, the house of a family of the half-outlawed Catholic gentry named Moore. In that year, the founder of the family fortune in the Spanish wine trade was dead, and Moore Hall was shared by his two sons, George and John. Of John we know little save his extraordinary fate. He was swept up into the rebellion—most unusually for a landowner—was made, grandiloquently and fatally, president of the short-lived Republic of Connaught, was captured when the British retook Castlebar, and died, conveniently, of jail fever while awaiting trial for treason.

But we know more about George, who was the grandfather of George Moore the novelist. He had been educated, as John had been, on the Continent, higher education at home being then denied to Catholics, but in London had been a member of the Holland House set, a friend of Fox and Sheridan, and he wrote, but never finished, a history of the early years of the French Revolution, his sympathies being with the Gironde.

Here, for a moment, there is a complication. Broome is an imaginary character who has written an actual book, as it were, but Moore is real. His fragment of historical writing, a preface in which he speculates, in a strikingly modern way, upon the ways in which histories can be written, survives in the manuscript room of the National

Library of Ireland. I was fascinated by the idea of a man thinking about the French Revolution in the wilds of Mayo when suddenly it is dropped upon his doorstep, destroying much that he valued and loved, including of course his brother.

I had known Moore Hall for years. Whenever I was in that part of Mayo I would find myself drawn back to it. In 1923, during the Civil War, it was burned by the IRA and now stood a ruin out of Piranesi, ivy-covered, its windows empty eyes staring sightlessly toward Lough Carra. The IRA had done a thorough job—they used petrol, paraffin, and incendiary bombs—but above the blackened portico could still be read the motto of the family: *fortis cadere, cedere non potest*. It always seemed to me emblematic—Ireland is scattered with ruins, stretching back over many centuries, Anglo-Irish, Elizabethan, Norman, Celtic. Once, I talked with a man who had known the fellows who burned Moore Hall. It made the past seem recent.

And so I concocted a journal for George Moore to keep, in which we slowly discover that behind the frigid ironies and wit of his prose lurked a very different kind of man. I had not planned to construct a novel composed in good part of imagined documents, but once I had the words of Broome and Moore, the bit was between my teeth, and there was no stopping me. There are about eight—I haven't checked. Beside these, and the memoirs of Cornwallis's aide-de-camp, there is a Castlebar poet and schoolmaster whose journal, in Gaelic, is translated a half-century later by a condescending Victorian editor, the memoirs of a sentimental widow of one of the rebels, and beside these, government reports, the reports of informers, letters, pseudo-documents of various kinds. In what may well be the greatest of modern historical novels, H. F. M. Prescott's *The Man on a Donkey* (1952), the author says in her prefatory note that her theme will emerge only when "the different stories which it contains run together and are swallowed up by the tragic history of the Pilgrimage of Grace."

I intended something like that. The novel seeks to suggest that for

Ireland, in the summer of 1798, history swung upon a long, decisive blade. And it is true that in one sense an Irish world came to a close then. The London government seized upon the rebellion as a pretext to abolish the Kingdom of Ireland and, by an act of Union, to merge, legislatively, the two countries. And from this, much would follow. In 1798, the west of Ireland's peasant population was Irish-speaking, as would not, one hundred years later, be the case. The language had suffered two shattering blows—the Great Famine of the 1840s and a system of state education in which English was designated as the sole vehicle of instruction. But even as late as 1798, poetry was written in Irish, the poets were aware of one another, and aware of the very old traditions out of which their art had come. And in that art, however far it may have fallen from its once-high estate, was vested the values of the old Gaelic culture. These poets maintained themselves as small farmers, tavern keepers, teachers in hedge schools, sometimes—as was the case with the most celebrated of them, Eoghan Ruagh O'Sullivan, as day-laborers. One such, entirely fictitious, I made a central character, and I endowed him with an insight and perhaps also a faculty for prophesy, which allow him to know that his world is closing.

Owen MacCarthy is a most reluctant rebel, is captured in the final defeat, and is carried back to Castlebar and hanged. The fellows being carried back with him in an open cart are simple peasants, as he himself would seem to an outsider. Beside the cart march British militia who are in fact Irishmen, Gaelic-speakers, Catholics like MacCarthy, and from his native county of Kerry:

> "That is my own country," MacCarthy said. "I was born and reared outside Tralee."
>
> "Well enough I know who you are, Owen MacCarthy, and it is a great disgrace you have brought upon yourself and upon Kerry."
>
> Awkwardly, arms pinioned, MacCarthy got himself back onto the floor of the cart.

Kerry head beneath stiff tricorne and lobsterback coat.

"'Tis far we are now from Kerry, the two of us," MacCarthy said.

But the Kerryman, thin-lipped, looked at the road before them.

"'By Killarney's fair lakes where I oftentimes strayed,'" Mac-Carthy said. "Do you know that one?"

"I know that one," the militiaman said, and then fell back to let the wagon rumble past him.

What harm was there in a fellow like that, doing his landlord's bidding, proud of his red coat? Never again would he have a coat so fine, the cloth smooth and rich.

Beside pastures rich in the September sun, autumn a subtle presence in the air, the wagon moved north towards Mayo. Norman keeps guarded distant hills, fairy mounds kept silent sentinel. Labourers watched them, motionless as mountain hares, by nightfall a tavern tale. Provisions and sacks of grapeshot travelled with them, soldiers and militiamen thick as blackberries on the bush, wide-mouthed cannon. Edmund Spenser and Oliver Goldsmith travelled with them, and great bulging libraries of books and statutes printed in English, bills of lading and proclamations, John Milton and Richard Steele, white-wigged orators and a new alphabet. An image filled MacCarthy's mind: General Trench's army carried northwards into Mayo a great handsome clock, the wood of its casing shining and polished, its delicate strong springs ticking off the final hours of his world.

In that passage, to speak only of its rhetoric, past and present are conflated, although I trust more felicitously and more knowingly than was the case with Virginia Mayo and the Princess Berengaria. The basic awareness, the awareness of a world's ending, is MacCarthy's, and MacCarthy, as we have had reason to know, has read Milton and

Steele and Edmund Spenser. But the presiding sensibility is not his. It is a modern sensibility, translating his perception into a modern key.

L. P. Hartley's novel *The Go-Between* opens with what was to become a well-known observation: "The past is a foreign country. They do things differently there." It gives a title to a wonderful book by David Lowenthal, which examines ways in which the past has been thought about, felt about, imagined, invented, reinvented. For our culture, the historical novel has been one such contrivance, and it seems to me that it has been the chronological twin of romantic history, children, the two of them, of the nineteenth century, when, in certain ways, we began to imagine the past as being simultaneously remote from the present and continuous with it. We are separated from the past by an abyss of time, to appropriate and misuse the title of a great historical novel by Marguerite Yourcenar. And yet we have had also the contradictory feeling that human nature is woven from a single cloth, that the passions, vices, and virtues of the past could not have been that different from our own.

It was in the romantic decades of the nineteenth century that our culture came into possession of a particular sense of historical time, of its weights upon us and its meanings for us. This awareness was to create the great histories of Michelet and Thierry in France, of Macaulay and Froude in England, of Parkman and Prescott and Motley in this country. It has become fashionable to speak of the great romantic histories as fictions, as novels, and God forbid that I should object. It may be, to sound a morbid note, that as the academy has passed a death sentence upon narrative history, so also, by inadvertence, it may have done so upon the historical novel. History itself has schooled me to accept this with serenity.

The great historical novels were the exact contemporaries of the great histories—Walter Scott in Britain, Balzac and Hugo in France, Manzoni in Italy, Fenimore Cooper in this country. Both the histories and the novels turn upon historical, cultural, political contrast and crisis. In Parkman, for example, the conflict for possession of the North American continent between the Protestant culture of England, of the north, and the Catholic culture of France, a conflict given a truly novelistic intensity by the complexity of Parkman's feelings, by his projection upon the conflict of warring aspects of his own psyche. Indeed, to our present-day tastes, the conflicts in the histories are all too dramatic. Someone once said of Macaulay that his was a style in which it was impossible to tell the truth. The reference was not simply to his habit of rummaging through archives to find evidence in support of his own feelings about things, but also, we may assume, to his rhetorical practices. Thus, Macaulay describes the chief justice before whom Warren Hastings was tried, in accordance with his fondness for triple modifiers, as "rich, quiet, and infamous." The effect is one which any novelist should envy.

The serious novels of those decades, those that both established and defined the genre, depend upon historical oppositions of culture, and of cultures caught in a crucial moment of change. In Scott, Englishman and Scotsman, Highlander and Lowlander, Whig and Tory, merchant and nobleman. In Fenimore Cooper, the opposition of city and forest, settled land and prairie.

So too did the central energies and impulses of both the histories and the novels derive from a common source, a confidence, almost religious, that the past could in fact be recovered. Not more and more facts, but the past itself, its colors and smells, its walls and pavements, the very air itself. And this recovery was more than merely possible, it was obligatory, a moral task laid down for our performance. Thus, Michelet, writing of the victims of the French Bastille, says of them that the worst was not merely that they should have died within that prison but that they should have been forgotten.

"Forgotten!" he writes. "O terrible word! that a soul should perish among souls! Had not he whom God created for life the right to live at least in the mind? What mortal shall dare inflict, even on the most guilty the worst of deaths—to be eternally forgotten?... No, do not believe it. Nothing is forgotten, neither man nor thing. What once has been cannot thus be annihilated. The very walls do not forget, the pavement will become accomplice, and convey sighs and noises; the air will not forget." The Bastille is emblematic of Europe, indeed of the world, which Michelet equated with Europe. "The world was covered with prisons, from Spielberg to Siberia, from Spandau to Mont St. Michel. The world was a prison!" He ends with an exclamation point, which was by far his favorite device of punctuation.

The embarrassing fact is that the number of prisoners set loose from the Bastille on July 14, 1789, was exactly seven, as we are sardonically reminded by Simon Schama. One was the comte de Solange, a competitor with the marquis de Sade, whose family hoped that they had seen the last of him. Four were convicted forgers and two were lunatics who were sent off to an asylum. One of the lunatics, I am proud to report, was Irish. His beard was waist-long, perhaps in tribute to the spirit of forgetfulness, but he seemed the most reputable of the *libérés*, and he was carried in triumph through the streets of Paris. He took this as his due, having long been under the belief that he was the reincarnation of Julius Caesar.

Michelet's superb confidence not merely in the knowability of the past, of its continuing voices in pavement and air, has long since been drained away from us. When we listen, so we now believe, we think we hear voices, but those are our own voices. More than twenty years ago, when I first began to think about the form I wanted my novel to take, I was thinking about it in an office in this building, and, a few doors away, my friend Steve Greenblatt was thinking about history in other ways. But at some points, the two ways touched, and one of these is relevant here. "I began," Greenblatt was to write some years later, "with the desire to speak with the dead." And he goes on: "Even when I came to understand that in my most intense moments of straining to listen all that I could hear was my own voice, even then I did not abandon my desire. It is true that I could hear only my own voice, but my own voice was the voice of the dead, for the dead have contrived to leave traces of themselves, and those traces make themselves heard in the voices of the living." At the cost of twisting askew a bit what he is saying here, the words themselves may be taken as speaking to whatever it is that emboldens historical novelists. Not that we possess any longer the Michelet-resembling confidence of a Victor Hugo. A great modern historical novelist, the Faulkner of *Absalom, Absalom*, for example, knows that the past, even the past of his own roots, is shot through with dubieties, false corridors, is in the end the intense, conflicting, high-flown rhetoric of voices speaking into the air of evening, into night air.

Nowhere does the modernity of *The Year of the French* betray itself more fully, deliberately so I trust, than in the self-consciousness of my handful of narrators, their intermittent suspicion that they speak only to themselves and neither to past nor to future.

Of my handful of narrators, only Sean MacKenna thinks otherwise, the poet-schoolmaster turned draper, with a shop in Castlebar. But I leave the final words to him:

Nothing worthy of record during my return to Castlebar, which I reached at nightfall. The soldiers have for months been gone from Mayo save for the garrison here in the town, and they are but memories, like the French. As I rode past Stoballs Hill in the darkness, I attempted to imagine what the great battle there had been like, the drums and bright banners and cannon shot and shouting. I could not. I told myself that the battle already lay with the Norman keep upon the far shore of that sea which separates past from present. But that is not true, there is no such sea, it is but a trick of speech. All are bound together under God, mountain and bog, the shattered fortress and the green pasturelands of death, the drover's eagle that took wing upon the eve of battle, memory, history and fable. A trick of speech and of the blackness of night, when we are separated from one another and from the visible world. It is in the brightness of the morning air, as the poets tell us, that hope and memory walk toward us across meadows, radiant as a girl in her first beauty.

You will recall that Edgar Allan Poe, in his *Philosophy of Literary Composition*, reasons out, by a process he would have us regard as ice-cold in its rationality, that the ideal subject for a poem is the death of a beautiful woman. So, by analogy, I may be suggesting that the proper subject of a historical fiction would be the death of a beautiful culture. And such an argument might, at least, be mounted. And that despite the evidence to the contrary of the powerful tradition of what might be called "the novel of cultural reconciliation," of which the most relevant instances would be Walter Scott's *Waverly* novels. Scott's purpose, a high Tory purpose, was to celebrate the reconciliation of Britain and Scotland, of Highland culture and Lowland culture. But whatever his formal intentions, the images likely to remain in the reader's imagination, from the title novel of the *Waverly* novels down through *Redgauntlet*, are those of the defeated and historically convicted Highland chieftains and their Jacobite supporters. In his presentation of their fatality, he walks constantly and not always with success the thin line between sentiment and sentimentality. It is instructive to recall that the last of the Stuarts, the self-styled Henry IX, Bonnie Prince Charlie's brother, ended his days in Rome, living on a pension from George IV. George IV, under the direct influence of Scott's novels, which he eagerly devoured, had become a devotee of the cause of the pretenders to his own throne, and had gone so far as on occasion to wear the Highland kilt, a mode of attire which ill became him. Thus does art sentimentalize the defeated, once that defeat is absolutely certain. There is almost a law for such matters: "Weep and the world weeps with you, laugh and you laugh alone."

I have spoken of Poe as employing a manner which he would have us take as ice-cold in its rationality, but of course it is no such thing. Poe's emotional and passional concerns, his near obsessions, run like red-hot wires just beneath the decorum of his manner. And so, again by analogy, I may have been misleading in describing the choices which led me toward some strategies and away from others when writing my own novels. Of course there was much going on in my mind that I did not properly understand, and much that I did not know about, as is the way with every novelist and every novel. At this distance from them—or at least from the earliest of them—I think I have a fair notion of some of the things that were going on in my mind, but I have no intention of talking about them in public, you will be relieved to hear. With one exception and that, I think, an important one.

For a long time, it had seemed to me that the French landing and the Mayo uprising which it sparked would make a good novel, although I had not the most remote wish to write it. There had been two earlier uprisings that year—one in Ulster, the result of a short-lived alliance between the Catholic and Presbyterian country people, and one in the south, in Leinster. They were far better known, and they did not interest me at all. Over the years, a kind of sentimental nationalist cult had grown up around them which, if anything, I found disturbing. The rebel ballads and banners, the iconography concealed what had in truth been ugly and brutal, at the end degenerating into sectarian butchery. But Mayo fascinated me, and from time to time I would look into its slender records, I would hear a bit about the surviving folklore. Once I walked along the long road into Ballina, which terminates in the town with a street called Boher-na-soper, the road of straw, because it was a night march, and the peasants came out from the cabins and lit torches of straw to guide Humbert's rebels. And I took the trouble to read the preface to the unfinished history which George Moore wrote in Moore Hall, in which he says that histories are matters of arrangement, placement, and juxtaposition. And once, with a friend, I measured out what must have been the final battlefield at Ballinamuck, and walked into the bog where the defeated rebels had been killed without quarter. By lucky accident, my friend was knowledgeable about bogs.

Then, one day, I realized that for a long while I had been haunted —that seems the proper word—by an image. It was a man, tall, lean but heavy-shouldered, in dark clothes save for a neck cloth, walking a bit unsteadily, as if he had had too much to drink. Darkness is gathering on a summer night. He is walking along a narrow path beside a strand, the sea on his right, gray and still. I kept seeing him. Then, one day, in an office around the corner from this room, I picked up a pencil and began to write:

> MacCarthy was light-headed that night when he set out from Judy Conlon's cabin in the Acres of Killala. Not drunk at all, but light-headed. He carried with him an inch or two of whiskey, tight-corked in a flask of green glass, and the image which had badgered him for a week. Moonlight falling upon a hard, flat surface, scythe or sword or stone or spade. It was not an image from which a poem would unwind itself, but it could be hung as a glittering, appropriate ornament upon a poem already shaped. Problems of the craft.

That became, unrevised, the first paragraph of *The Year of the French* and from it the novel with all of its strategies, multiple narrators, mirror ironies, and the rest of whatever I hauled from the bag of tricks spun itself out. In the novel, it may well be that I handle the poet MacCarthy with too great and too partial a tenderness, shielding him from those icy showers with which the other characters are drenched from time to time, in accordance with the rules for the construction of romantic irony as laid down in the handbooks. If that is so, it is so, I think, because the memory of that image and of what it seemed to be releasing in me remained with me for a long time. It probably is so that when we hold to our ears the convoluted shell of the past, what we hear are our own voices.

But there is a dialectic between shell and voice. The voices which only seem to be speaking to us, being in fact our own voices, have been instructed by all that we know about the past, all the contradictory things that we feel about it, all that we have imagined about it. Those voices make possible for us imaginary selves, imaginary opposites, imaginary others. Historical fiction licenses these imaginings in ways that history itself, history proper, does not.

—unpublished lecture, delivered at Berkeley, February 29, 1996

39

LISTENING TO THE DEAD

IN BOSTON A few months ago, a friend, an editor, and I were remembering another friend, one of my oldest and closest ones, who died in New York last year at about this time.

Some of you will remember Kevin Sullivan as the author of *Joyce Among the Jesuits*, which yet another friend, Richard Ellmann, always spoke of as belonging to the slender shelf of essential Joyce scholarship. This is so, I think, because of the preciseness with which Kevin locates Joyce in the context of a Jesuit education. But also because, moving beneath the comely and supple surface of his prose, lending it energy and complexity, is his allegiance to his own education by and in the Society of Jesus, of which he spoke always with a mingled respect, affection, and irony.

Our Boston friend was describing an amiable, disputatious evening, many years ago, at Kevin's house above the lordly Hudson, fueled by deep drafts of John Jameson's whiskey. At last Kevin, moved toward definitional eloquence, said, "And I, sir, am a humanist." "Are you, indeed, and do you mind telling me what the hell a humanist is?" Without need for reflection, Kevin said, "I don't know what it is, but that is what I am." Floating somewhere in his mind, I am certain, were a few sentences which he was fond of quoting. They are from a letter that William Butler Yeats wrote, in the month of his death, to Lady Elizabeth Pelham: "Man can embody truth but he cannot know it.... The abstract is not life and everywhere draws out its contradictions. You can refute Hegel but not the Saint or the Song of Sixpence."

If, taking my friend at his word, we draw some definitions from his own practices, we would say that it is a part of the humanistic enterprise to savor language, words in their sounds and seemings, their exactnesses, their ambiguities, their gravities and colors, their permanent, shifting positions in the spaces of the imagination.

I remember a day, more than thirty years ago, at lunch in the Columbia Faculty Club, when he handed me a slip of yellow, lined paper on which he had copied a passage that he had composed the night before. It was to become part of *Joyce Among the Jesuits*. "In Ireland it is seldom possible to escape the past. It is like the turf of the country, everywhere under foot, the stuff of fire to warm old memories at the hearth, or to lend a flame to passions that have burned out the hearts of men and cities." He was proud of that passage, and was right to be: try shifting its clauses about, however slightly, and see what happens.

Now, the word *past*, as it happens, closes the first paragraph of my novel *The Tenants of Time*. Of Patrick Prentiss, the young historian, it says: "He had fallen in love with the past, a profitless love." Some readers have taken that phrase, "a profitless love," as registering a failure on Prentiss's part, a disappointment, a futility. As to be sure it does. It is part of the novel's pattern that he comes to accept the impossibility of the task he has given himself—that of writing a full, resonating, answerable chronicle of the Fenian uprising in March of 1867 in a town in West Cork called Kilpeder. Too much is being withheld from him by witnesses, by survivors, by loyalties to people, to memories of the dead. More serious yet, he has come, in some modes, to perceive all of the past as a shifting sand, its colors and textures treacherous. But if this is the case for him, it is not simply so, and the phrase "profitless love" is not simply a dismissive one. Prentiss himself knows that, and so does the dictionary. Profitless loves are the very best kinds. The dictionary has words for profitable loves, many of them unkind words.

Now, I would like this evening, taking a slight liberty with the given title of my lecture, to explore a bit what has become an accepted truth, a truism, and therefore a bit of an untruth, about Ireland, about the Irish, about, in particular, what is written about the land and its people. It is a truism lying everywhere at hand, no need to search for it: that the Irish are shaped by their past, by history; more so, by implication, than other peoples. Thus, this very day, the advance galleys of William Trevor's marvelous new novel, *The Silence in the Garden*, came to me, and with it jacket copy which speaks, quite accurately, of "his deep understanding of the tragic patterns of Irish history." Why this should be so, and the question of whether indeed it *is* so, is not my direct concern, which is, I am afraid, a far less modest one. It has to do with my own apparent obsession with the past, and my texts, in part, are drawn from what I have myself written.

I say this with embarrassment, indeed, with a mild shame. Once, this same Kevin Sullivan and I were on our way to West Cork—ourselves, the novelist Benedict Kiely, and a young journalist, weighty men crammed into a car of modest proportions. There had been a long, liquid lunch in the public house in the Glen of Aherlow, and Kiely and I were favoring the company with our wisdom and eloquence, occasionally as duet, but mostly as simultaneous and competing arias. At last, the unmistakable Sullivan baritone shattered the melodies. "Oh God! To be trapped with one Lord Byron would be bad enough. Two are unendurable. And we won't reach Glengariff for hours." Scott Fitzgerald somewhere describes Edmund Wilson as his intellectual conscience. Kevin is mine, and whenever I talk myself into talking about my own work, I hear that "Oh God!" echoing against the hills of Cork. Nevertheless...

Many kinds of people tend to be obsessed by the past, or curious about it, or in love with it, or in a lover's quarrel with it—not only Irishmen, not only historians. Historians, of course, have gone through a form of marriage with the past, although there have been recent signs of infidelities and discords, on one side at least. In that same opening chapter, young Prentiss meets another historian, a historian of sorts, a retired schoolmaster named MacMahon, living among hills and books. You have a great appetite for books, Prentiss tells him. And MacMahon, testing the word, says, "You have the right of it, I think. For years, I thought I was gathering up knowledge and wisdom in double handfuls, but in the end, 'tis but an appetite, like any other." That is why those of us who work with words or with the shapes of the past are so often angry with ourselves, nagged by the suspicion that what we do serves neither the glory of God nor the advancement of the human race but simply gratifies an appetite. A harmless enterprise, no doubt, but not an especially noble one.

We historians occasionally claim, but more often it is claimed for us by helpful others, that the study of history redeems itself because we learn from that study how better to conduct our own affairs, arrange our public existences. This appeal to social redemptiveness, whatever may be its force with respect to pornography, does not work for historical literature—and is advanced, I suspect, as part of a parallel strategic casuistry. The assumption is that unless we know the past, we are condemned to repeat it. An epigram to that effect seems alone to have survived out of the immense corpus of Santayana's writings. It has the truth of epigram, which is never negligible and always suspect.

In Ireland, in fact, it could be argued that it is knowledge of history, history speaking in ancestral voices, rather than ignorance, which enforces its repetition. "History," Stephen Dedalus tells Deasy, the schoolmaster who employs him, "is a nightmare from which I am trying to awake." It is probably the most quoted sentence in *Ulysses*, save of course for the very long one in which Molly remembers having entered history by saying that yes, she will Yes. Stephen, as we know, is thinking about history in its largest terms, of the chains of inexorable event by which the soul is bound upon the rack of contingency: history is the "art" which Joyce has assigned to that episode in his scheme, and its language is soaked with historical reflection and refraction. The context of that particular utterance, however, makes clear that at the moment it is Irish history that Stephen has in mind.

Nevertheless, the notion that one can learn from history, or at least that one should try to, is as old as Plutarch. In the epilogue to *The Year of the French*, Arthur Vincent Broome puts the question directly. Broome is a fussy, worried, scrupulous Protestant clergyman. A natural Christian, Sullivan once called him. He calls himself, more exactly, "a confused clergyman with an indifferent education, a lover of comfort and civility and buttered toast." Here is the question, as he puts it, and the answer he receives:

"Does man learn from History?" I once asked a scholarly and sagacious friend. Rather than dismissing the question with the scorn which doubtless it merited, he reflected upon the matter, and said at last, "No, I believe that we do not. But it is possible to learn from historians." I have upon occasion given thought to this; when, for instance, reading the capacious works of Hume and Gibbon, and the most that I can make of it is this:

Gibbon gives to us the breadth of the classical world, from the Hellespont to the pillars of Hercules, a vast temple with colonnades and recesses, glowing white marble beneath a blazing Mediterranean sun, and displays to us then its hideous and shameful destruction. How firm a sense do we derive of all its constituent parts, of their intricate relationships! How certain is its destruction, with alien creeds subverting its powers and alien races wearing away its far-flung frontiers. Each cause and reason is locked securely into place. And over all the mighty drama presides the awesome authority of Gibbon's splendid language, his unimpassioned rationality. Here, we think, is the chief civil drama of human history, in which tens and hundreds of thousands played their parts, but a drama compelled by the human mind to yield up its uttermost secrets. Great was Rome and catastrophic was its fall, but great too is the energy of the historian's mind, the cool deliberation of his judgment.

But then! We put the volume upon the table, and go out for a stroll in the garden or to visit a sick parishioner or perhaps only to pare our nails, and doubt seeps in, a Gothic tribe at the frontier. Perhaps it had not been like that at all. Perhaps all had been chaos, chance, ill-luck, perhaps even Providence, perhaps the ancients were indeed punished for their sins, as was once believed. Perhaps Gibbon is but a master magician, a sorcerer of language, a Simon Magus of stately paragraphs. Perhaps it is not Rome that we have seen, but Gibbon's imagination bestowed capriciously upon the past rather than upon mountaintop or sunset or ruined abbey or other Romantic flummery. And the past remains therefore unknowable, shrouded in shadow, an appalling sprawl of buildings, dead men, battles, unconnected, mute, half recorded. Perhaps we learn nothing from history, and the historian teaches us only that we are ignorant.

Like much else in my presumably fictitious novels, that passage was taken from life, as it were. When I was teaching at Berkeley, another friend, Conor Cruise O'Brien, came to the university as a visiting Regents' Professor, and I put the question to him as we drove across the Bay Bridge from the airport. The answer he gave—"it is possible to learn from historians"—is the one which I entrust to Broome's "scholarly and sagacious friend." It is a fact highly pertinent to my present discourse that Dr. O'Brien has no recollection of the conversation, and denies, most courteously, that it ever took place. This is the sort of thing which persuades Patrick Prentiss, in the final pages of his novel, to leave history for a life of political action: politicians find memory an encumbrance.

Now that I can stand back a bit from the two novels, I can see that they have been aswarm with historians: all of the narrators are at work upon narratives of one sort or another, and several of these can be called histories in the formal sense of the term. Broome persists with his: his *Impartial Narrative*, as I have him call it, in a play upon an actual work of that title by the Anglican bishop of Killala in 1798, whose misfortune it was to have the episcopal palace seized by the French general, Humbert, to serve as his headquarters. Broome persists: we are to imagine it as constituting a part of the novel we are reading. But he has his doubts, and his last words to us are these: "Then I will turn and walk back to my residence, where tea will be awaiting me before the fire. Heavy curtains will be drawn, to hold back the limitless silences of the Mayo night. We know parts of a world only, parts of a history, shards, bits of broken pottery."

But my George Moore at last abandons his ambition to write a history of the Gironde, and his final perception of his abandoned work and of himself is more savage and more self-lacerating:

> He never completed his history of the Girondist party in the French Revolution. For several years after his marriage he continued to work upon it, but each year he felt less interest in the task, and less confidence in his ability to complete it, or in his ability to understand the mainsprings of politics and history. The first two manuscript volumes survive, the prose polished but perhaps too formal and too still, the handwriting an elegant copperplate, the ink brown and faded. Beyond these are drafts of chapters, revised, scratched out, partially rewritten. And notes for other chapters, clumps of names and dates, broken-backed

epigrams and faltering generalizations. He had been left at last with a frozen puddle of history, muddy water frozen in the depression of a woodland path, dead leaves and broken twigs dim beneath its filthy surface.

Perhaps Moore's mistress, Sarah Browne, is wiser than any of them, a woman a bit tarnished by history, with a tarnished-silver voice. "I never read histories," she says; "poetry and novels. More novels than are good for me. But not histories. All those sorrows and dates."

In the final pages of *The Tenants of Time*, Prentiss visits the two men who in a sense have become fathers to him, MacMahon in his cottage in the hills of West Cork, and Lionel Forrester, by profession a writer of both novels and popular histories, by avocation, a gentleman. Prentiss tells Forrester of a school which has arisen on the Continent that claims "that the past can never be known, history never be written, the histories we have mere pleasant narratives, pathetic, whatever." And Forrester, an unflappable chap, says, "They may be right. A history is a kind of narrative, a fiction."

But MacMahon, when Prentiss reports this to him, cries: "And so Lionel Forrester and yourself have decided that history is little better than a novel. And what am I supposed to do with all my books, my Gibbon and my Lingard and the handsome set of Motley that you have brought to me this day? Am I to suspect that the Dutch republic never did rise? A sorrowful time it will be for schoolmasters, if that sort of nonsense is allowed to walk abroad." In fact, he is not at all naive as to such matters. Years before, he had said to Prentiss: "'Tis my own great love, history. But there are times, do you know, when I will sit in this chair on a winter's evening, with a good fire and a jug of heated spirits, and my Macaulay open on my lap, and I will ask myself how in God's name does he know what he tells us he knows. There will be little notes at the foot of each page, like brambles in a field, but they fail to persuade me."

With respect to Macaulay, MacMahon's suspicions are dead-on, and perhaps with respect to Motley as well. We have come to suspect those written histories that are too comely, too graceful, shaped with too controlling an artifice. And, too, there is a compelling practicality to his question. Must he be compelled to witness the devaluation of the books on his shelf, for which over the years he has paid down hard cash? Must he conspire with a skepticism that could place in jeopardy the gainful employment of schoolmasters and professors? To profess the past, to profess merely to love it, is to invest in it, in various practical ways: it may not be, after all, so profitless a love.

But for Ireland a special condition obtains, for there a living present, a living culture coexists with a past which most vividly presents itself as ruined. Yet another of my historians, another schoolmaster, Sean MacKenna in *The Year of the French*, reflects upon this:

> We are a land of ruins. Norman keeps and towers, and the queer round towers of which no man knows their antiquity, shattered manor houses of the Tudor times, the roofless monasteries and abbeys savaged by the men of Cromwell, their broken arches gaunt arms against the tumbling clouds, strongholds of O'Neills and O'Donnells, Burkes and Fitzgeralds, bashed and battered away, moss and ivy creeping over their stumps as they lie dreaming beneath the great sky of Ireland. Strangest of all, the great cairns and fairy mounds, ruins of some race perished long before the Sons of Milesius led the people of the Gael to these shores. As though in this land all, everything, has been sentenced from the beginning to break apart, fall into pieces, powerless against our harsh divinities of rain and wind and weed and tall grasses. All in ruin, the ruin of a world, sacked and burned and smashed by Danes and Normans and Irish and English.

A good-hearted fellow, MacKenna, but a bit given to striding upon tall stilts of rhetoric, as he now seems to me. But Patrick Prentiss is a different sort of fellow, yet his thoughts run along those lines. He has been visiting with a friend from Oxford days who now is an Anglican clergyman in a village in Devon. And all about the skies, the weathers, there seem reminders to Prentiss of what his own island is not: "The warmth of the Devon summer was almost palpable, a thick blanket of settled air. Church, bridge, stream, path, the motionless ferns, delicate deep-green embroideries, the sound of bees like the heavy air given voice, all spoke to him of an ordered world, an ordered history. The scene, with its unctuous harmonies, reproved the tattered narrative which he had been trying to piece together. Tea would soon be waiting in Dick Leese's parsonage, set at its discreet distance from the church; the table spread in the garden, near beds of roses, red, pink; and young Eleanor Leese's hands, white birds, moving swiftly above the cups." Dick Leese tries to argue Prentiss out of his project, his history of the Fenian uprising in 1867. "Try the War of the Roses," he says, "the court of the Sun King. Not gunmen and Irish police barracks and constables shot down from behind hedges. Good sensational stuff, that, but it isn't history." "We have no other history," Prentiss says. "Ambushes, demagogues, famine graves. That is our history." "We," Leese says. "Our. Now we are getting to it."

Of course, this sort of thing can be overdone. There is a volume of photographs of "the once great houses of Ireland," bearing the terse title *In Ruins*. I lack the technical knowledge to explain or describe the wizardry by which the photographer has contrived to bathe in melancholy splendor such improbable edifices as "Mr. Godwin's Palace of Damp," built in County Limerick in 1867, and abandoned in 1921–1922. Interesting dates, as Sarah Browne might say. The jacket copy tells us that the photographs "give us exquisite ghosts of a privileged and vulnerable society." An interesting word, vulnerable, as Ned Nolan might say. And after all, there are rose gardens in Ireland as fine as those in Devon; Hugh MacMahon has a very fair one, and so do several other, more palpable friends of mine. And there are stretches of England which commend themselves to the attention of other photographers of what might be called "the grotesque crumble."

More to the point, and especially so in a country like Ireland, where history, politics, and literature notoriously meet at that notorious crossroads, a concern with ruins—with, for example, the Georgian mansion in ruins—can nourish impulses which are pious and benign, and yet serve ideological and political programs which are neither of those.

It might perhaps therefore be more helpful if I turned from the general problem to the specific example—myself, to wit, and what would seem clearly to be my own obsession with the past, with history. It has been a bit unfair of me to cite, as witnesses to my argument, Hugh MacMahon and Patrick Prentiss and Sean MacKenna and Lionel Forrester. I cannot entirely disclaim responsibility for their existences, let alone their obsessions. And I should perhaps look for a bit, setting aside Ireland, history, scholarship, and the inventions and subterfuges of fiction, at this obsession.

MacMahon, for his part, fears that it may after all be "but an appetite, like any other." But it may also be the case, perhaps, that some appetites, for language, for example, for friendship, for order and energy, are far from ignoble, are parts of our human and humanizing inheritance. In which case, of course, they require no justification save that offered by the exercise of their powers.

I began by quoting from one friend, and moved forward to a second. Now I will depend upon a third. The first chapter of Stephen Greenblatt's magnificent book *Shakespearian Negotiations* opens with an account of the motives and impulses which led him to take up a career in literary studies. The first sentences, characteristically of Greenblatt's rhetorical strategies, are dramatic, complex, and intellectually alluring. "I began," he says, "with the desire to speak with the dead."

This desire is a familiar, if unvoiced, motive in literary studies, a motive organized, professionalized, buried beneath thick layers of bureaucratic decorum: literature professors are salaried, middle-class shamans. If I never believed that the dead could hear me, and if I knew that the dead could not speak, I was nonetheless certain that I could re-create a conversation with them. Even when I came to understand that in my most intense moments of straining to listen all I could hear was my own voice, even then I did not abandon my desire. It was true that I could hear only my own voice, but my own voice was the voice of the dead, for the dead had contrived to leave textual traces of themselves, and those traces make themselves heard in the voices of the living. Many of the traces have little resonance, though every one, even the most trivial or tedious, contains some fragment of lost life; others seem uncannily full of the will to be heard.

When I read that passage by my friend, a short while ago, I was struck forcibly by the power and accuracy, the both of them unexpected, springing as it were from ambush, the power with which they seemed to be defining hopes and energies which lay behind my own first book. That one is not a novel, but rather about novelists and *their* words—the Irish novelists of the early nineteenth century. Its final sentence names them: "The foolish enthusiasms of Lady Morgan and the wisdom of Maria Edgeworth—it was all written down, as Yeats was to say, in a fiery shorthand, that it might never be forgotten."

Yeats had edited, in 1890, a book of stories taken from these novelists, and had composed as its dedication to them a poem which he continued to print, in all the editions of his poetry. But poets are no more to be trusted than novelists and historians, to say the least. The poem had ended with these lines:

Cabins gone now, old well-sides, old dear places,
And men who loved the cause that never dies.

One may suspect that this reference to "the cause that never dies," perhaps also the muted reference to cabins that had vanished with the Great Famine, were composed beneath the vigilant eye of his patron, the old Fenian, John O'Leary. At any event, in 1924, another interesting date, and in the less clamorous pages of AE's *Irish Statesman*, he published a rewriting of the poem, which now ends with the lines

We and our bitterness have left no traces
On Munster grass and Connemara skies.

Traces. Curiously, Yeats, listening to these dead Irish voices, hears from them the word that Greenblatt uses, a word that since Yeats's day has gathered up burdens of meaning without losing the one that lies at its core. And it now seems to me possible that in my book on these writers, there lay buried, beneath layers of professional alertness and bureaucratic decorum, a wish to speak with the dead. Even, perhaps, a wish to speak with my own dead forebears, who in that century had been not American but Irish.

My training had been as a literary scholar and also a cultural historian of sorts, in what is now thought of as the heyday of what is now thought of as the "New Criticism," or the "Old New Criticism," or whatever. (It seems to me, even now, to have been excellent training, and with certain advantages over the present "New New Criticism." It had, for example, the advantage that the criticism in French was written in good French, the criticism in English in good English. For the most part. And perhaps because its ablest practitioners were, in this country, distinguished poets with a professional knowledge of when they were writing poetry and when they were writing prose. Be that as it may.)

But I was in one sense a bad pupil, because although I learned the rules of the game, I constantly, if at times secretly, violated them by a hunger to know the men and women behind the words they wrote, to touch the hands which had made the inscriptions. Not equally or indiscriminately so. In the case of *The Irish Novelists*, for example, it was two of them in particular, Gerald Griffin and William Carleton, men different from each other, the one middle-class, romantic (until his final years), dark, ambiguous, contradictory, a writer who could traffic almost casually in images with buried lives, in legends with startling resonances. The other, a large, heavy man, heavy in spirit as well as flesh, puzzled, violent, parts of his life a mess. He came, as it happens, but perhaps not merely as it happens, from the same part of Ireland as did my grandparents—although mine from a neighboring county which has been accurately described as being half in the north and half under water. And I well remember, across thirty years, a sense, the sense that Greenblatt speaks of, that I was straining to listen to the dead, that it was important to me that I should hear them.

It requires no great feat of extrapolation to see ways in which what I (following Greenblatt) have been saying about the reading of literature can be extended to the reading and writing of histories, and, more especially so, of historical novels. So easy a feat, indeed, that I will not burden you with its performance. I might sketch for you a moment, a precise autobiographical moment, when the image came to me out of which *The Year of the French* elaborately evolved itself, and a different one in which *The Tenants of Time* emerged as a germ or a seed or whatever. The image for that one, incidentally, came powerfully from Ireland but indirectly so. It came as I was standing one evening at the window of a hotel looking down upon the Thames, with the Houses of Parliament on my right, and Tower Bridge on my left.

There is, of course, a catch within Greenblatt's formulation: he reminds us that even in our most intense moments of straining, we hear only our own voices, and these moments come, for novelists, when they least expect them—when, that is, they feel confident that they have found voices, voices other than their own, for their characters.

Why one might wish to speak with the dead is of course an unanswerable question, and may well be also one of those questions which should be unaskable. But perhaps the literary arts, the arts of history and the past, are valuable to the human enterprise because they have commerce with the almost unaskable, and bring back to us provisional, qualified, nervous answers. What we learn from history, finally, are ways of feeling about the past and ways of instructing those feelings with intellect. Ways of listening to voices which are no longer speaking, or speaking in voices that we hear haltingly and confuse with echoes of our own. That may have to suffice us.

(*circa* 1988)

40

KEVIN SULLIVAN

I SPOKE THIS above the grave of Kevin Sullivan as I stood with his family and with other friends in Saint Raymond's Cemetery on April 1, 1987:

> Our dear friend, Kevin Sullivan, was a scholar and a gentleman. As I speak these words, I can hear him reproving me for the use of cliché, but it is a necessary one. In Kevin, certain of the scholarly virtues, certain of the virtues of gentility, were conjoined and intermingled, strengthening each other.
>
> He had a scholar's delight in language, in its elegances and eloquences, its ability to be precise, exact, provocative, evocative—whether the language was English, Latin, or Greek. And he had a gentleman's sense of the ways in which language can be used to make life larger, wittier, more humane. I am hearing, in the ear of memory, voices, some of them American, some of them Irish, saying, variously, "Kevin Sullivan was in the room that night and he said, once he had heard that...." And what followed would be precise, witty, not always untinged by malicious wit, but always large-spirited, never mean or grudging, always humane, tolerant alike of the imperfections of others and of himself.

Despite the depth and length of our friendship—and I think of him as a brother—I was myself not always immune. I remember that he once found himself in a crowded car which included myself and another very close friend, the distinguished novelist Benedict Kiely. Ben and I had been treating the other inmates of the car not so much to a narrative duet but rather to competing and simultaneous solo performances. Then the unforgettable depth of the Sullivan voice filled the air: "To be trapped with one Lord Byron is bad enough. Two are unendurable. And we won't reach West Cork before dark."

To his life as scholar, writer, teacher, companion, gentleman, only one thing was lacking, and it was added, a little over five years ago, when he married Fran Murphy in the church from which he is being buried. Always now, I will remember Kevin in Greenwich Village and Gramercy Park, in Fitzwilliam Street and the Shelbourne and Sligo and Mayo and Rathgar, but my central image will be of the sun-filled living room of the gracious and hospitable apartment in Brooklyn which he had come to love. Especially, I will remember him in the final weeks of brief, valiant recovery when, with Fran's untiring and unwavering care, he greeted friends with his customary aplomb and courtesy, putting aside for the hour the task that he had set himself—rereading the *Iliad*. In Greek of course.

A scholar, a friend. *Requiescat in pace.*

Those words were composed in haste, of course, but I will let them stand, and for that reason. What we write in haste often carries a special truth. But I would like to add this to it. One day, in the 1950s, Kevin and I met for lunch, as we did once or twice a week, in the Faculty Club at Columbia. He handed me a slip of yellow-lined paper on which he had copied down a sentence written that morning as part of what would be an early chapter of *Joyce Among the Jesuits*:

> In Ireland it is seldom possible to escape the past. It is like the turf of the country, everywhere under foot, the stuff of fire to warm old memories over at the hearth, or to lend a flame to passions that have burned out the hearts of men and cities.

He said nothing by way of explanation, and he expected nothing but a nod of approbation. It was, as he knew, a damned fine sentence—he lacked any false modesty—and he was passing it along to someone who, as he knew, shared his respect for the decencies of English prose, and equally for its self-assured half-rhythms and inevitabilities of sense and sound. That kind of respect for the resources of English prose—those particular kinds of resources, at any rate—often seemed to us to be dying out. To be expiring, if blunt truth be told, upon the tables of some of the colleagues who surrounded us. Although, of course, not all, and it was a matter of considerable vindication to the two of us that Columbia figures of the day—Jacques Barzun, Lionel Trilling, Mark Van Doren—were scholars who combined erudition with literary grace and power. It was what we hoped for ourselves.

It is not an accident that Kevin's book of 1958, *Joyce Among the Jesuits*, maintains its place of unique honor amidst the mountains and cataracts of Joyce studies which have appeared. It is, quite simply, a necessary book. No biographical study has accomplished Kevin's feat of illuminating the precise nature of Joyce's Jesuit education, and of marking out, delicately, suggestively, at times with a deliberate offhandedness, the consequences upon Joyce's work. Not even the magnificent biography by Richard Ellmann, as that other great gentleman of modern scholarship happily allowed. In two, at least, of his commentators, Joyce, who himself of course was quite a gent, has been well served.

Joyce Among the Jesuits; an extended, witty, shrewd monograph on Oscar Wilde, filled with unexpected and precise judgments; a sheaf of handsomely written essays and reviews; a long-contemplated, unfinished study of the Irish Victorian novelist Sheridan Le Fanu. Many of Kevin's friends and admirers—myself at times—would express wonder, bewilderment, annoyance that he did not publish more. The answers lie buried, most of them, within Kevin's psyche, and to probe would be intrusive. One, though, is evident, I think. He was a master of style, and he held himself to standards more rigorous even than those by which he judged others.

The last time I saw Kevin in St. Vincent's Hospital, near the end, he was on a gurney, being taken out of his room for treatment. "Have you read So-and-So's new novel?" he asked, naming a stridently Irish-American novelist and newspaperman whom neither of us held in high regard. I said that I had not, and Kevin fixed me with those unyielding eyes. "He's getting worse. He used to write like a goat. Now he can't write like a goat." It was an oft-used phrase. Goats always seemed to him the nadir of literary awkwardness, some Jungian image conjured up, perhaps from the Puck Fair of his ancestral Kerry, perhaps from the poetry of Hesiod.

A man of rare wit, learning, grace, and just judgment.

41

BENEDICT KIELY

I CAME TO IRELAND for the first time in the early summer of 1960 and booked into the Shelbourne. That afternoon, I saw George Yeats, the poet's widow, having tea in the lounge. That evening, Frank O'Connor strolled up to have a drink with me from his flat on the Grand Canal. And then, until closing time, I was talking about Ireland, Irish history, and Irish landscape with Ben Kiely and Sean White in the above-stairs bar of the White Horse on Burgh Quay.

It was an auspicious introduction to the island. The widow of the greatest of Ireland's poets, the short-story writer who was also Ireland's short-tempered and salutary conscience, and, after nightfall, the writer who was to become, and has remained, one of my closest and most valued friends.

The windows of the White Horse look out across the oil-dark Liffey toward Eden Quay, with the Custom House to the right and Bachelors' Walk to the left. It had long been under the genial but firm management of Michael O'Connell, white-haired and upright, and it was the port of call for journalists on the *Irish Press*, where Ben was then literary editor. It was, although none of us knew it then, the end of the great days of writers' pubs and journalists' pubs—the Palace, the Pearl, the Tower, the Swan, the White Horse.

Ben was also the *Irish Press*'s "Patrick Lagan," with a weekly column of local history, archaeology, travel along byways to remote towns in Munster or Connaught or his native Ulster. His readers, as I have written elsewhere, "envisioned a russet-bearded enthusiast drinking tea after a hard day's journey, trouser-cuffs of salt-and-pepper tweed held by bicycle clips as he lingers over a lamb sandwich." In fact, he was a firmly built northern Irishman whose most vigorous exercise was leaning over a bridge to study the water. He knew, and knows, all the rivers, all the bridges and battlefields, all the good public houses and hotels.

I came to him armed with two kinds of introduction. Ben had liked my book on the Irish novelists of the early nineteenth century, a book much influenced by *Poor Scholar*, his study of William Carleton. That book had shown me ways of relating novels and tales to their social and political culture.

Equally to the point though—because Ben is one of those rare writers who believes that people are as important as books—a year or two before, my friend Kevin Sullivan had gone to Ireland for the first of what would be many visits, and he and Ben had become immediate friends. Over the decades which followed, we were to become close friends, the four of us, Ben, Kevin, Sean White, and myself.

It had its moments. I remember a week-long journey into deep Cork made by Ben, Kevin, David Hanly, and myself. Ben's account, written with suavity, warmth, and circumspection, is included in his *All the Way to Bantry Bay*. The project was Kevin's. He had formed the notion of writing an account of the epic march to the north made by his namesake, Donal O'Sullivan Beare, after the defeat of the Irish at Kinsale in 1602. Long before, a young writer and patriotic journalist, Ben had himself followed that march, and he had forgotten nothing—the ridges, the legends, the anachronistic ballads, the complicated historical actuality.

I remember—we all remembered—a magical, golden late afternoon in the public house in the Glen of Aherlow, for Ben a special place, because the aboriginal (so to speak) Kielys came not from Omagh in the north but from this Glen. It was a long afternoon, the arts of poetry and song were displayed, and toward the end, almost as surrealism, an Inland Revenue official arrived upon business, sized up the situation, opened his official leatherette briefcase, took out a bugle, and joined the party. Ben describes it in his book, and it is the sort of thing which some readers may regard as romantic Kielyite embroidery. But I was there. They may not realize that Ben is the kind of realistic writer about whom the romantic accretes, drawn by the sonorous, hypnotic voice, and especially when he is reciting "The Man from God Knows Where" or singing "The Captain with the Whiskers."

And a night, equally magical, in Eccles's Hotel in Glengarriff, where Ben recited to us, virtually verbatim, paragraphs from Thackeray's visit there in 1842, and reminded us that in Edwardian days, Glengarriff was described in tourist guides as "a group of houses and shops gathered about Eccles's Hotel." The great days of Eccles's Hotel are long past, but they were briefly rekindled.

I remember us standing, the four of us, the next day, on the foreshore of West Cork, beside the ruined castle of Dunboy, exploded in that tumultuous Elizabethan conflict, as we tried, the four of us, to imagine, in midsummer, that bitter December day on which O'Sullivan Beare and his people had set off. And I remember thinking how fortunate that we were remembering it with Ben, in whose imagination the Irish past burned like the gorse of autumn.

And I remember, some days later, over pints in the public house in Limerick Junction, phoning ahead for rooms in Cruise's Hotel in Limerick City. O'Sullivan Beare had not included this in his itinerary "so far as we know," but travels with Ben often involved elaborations and at Cruise's he held us spellbound with an account of Patrick Sarsfield's brilliant raid on the Williamite camp at Ballyneety.

I knew even then that travels with Ben, whether in his own right or as Patrick Lagan, were giving me a matchless apprenticeship into Ireland. Some years ago in an essay introducing some of his short stories to an American audience, I began with this sentence: "Benedict Kiely, a writer in whom are joined magnificent lyrical and comic gifts, is one of the most admired of literary figures in his native Ireland." And went on to say that "his art begins with a profound sense of place, of both physical and human geography, and of the integuments by which people and landscape are bound together."

But the present occasion is not, as I take it, one for literary criticism, but rather for the celebration of a friend. Kevin's favorite among his novels was *The Cards of the Gambler*, and many would agree with him, but my own choices are *The Captain with the Whiskers* and *Carmincross*, of which another close friend who is also, perhaps, his most perceptive critic warned him that "no-one will know what that book is about except yourself and Tom Flanagan." And, by a general agreement, the most powerful of his works, tragic and enraged, is *Proxopera*, with its unflinching look at his native province. (But as I write this paragraph, I can hear Ben reminding me that going on to talk about what you have said you would not discuss is a rhetorical figure as old as Cicero. There is even a Latin name for it in that long list of rhetorical devices which Ben alone, now that my mother is dead, still has at his fingertips.)

Perhaps I can make a bridge back to the personal by reminding us that one of the most admired and cherished of his short stories is "The Dogs in the Great Glen," which is about the first of the journeys which he and Kevin had made, in the 1950s: "The professor had come over from America to search out his origins and I met him in Dublin on the way to Kerry where his grandfather had come from and where he had relations, including a grand-uncle, still living." What the professor remembers is a story told to him by his father "that one night coming home from the card-playing my grandfather slipped down fifteen feet of rock and the only damage done was the ruin of one of the two bottles of whiskey he had in the tail-pockets of his greatcoat. The second bottle was unharmed."

Kevin told that story to me as well, and it worked its deep way into the opening chapter of *The Year of the French*, in which Owen Mac-Carthy, a bit drunk, walks along Kilcummin Strand with a tight-corked flask of whiskey in the pocket of his coat. Imaginations move in mysterious ways, especially when they move among writers who are friends.

Benedict Kiely is one of the finest writers of fiction of our time. But I began by calling him a writer for whom people were as important as books, and that, I think, is the most valuable of the lessons that he taught to me. I secretly admire a saying by the aesthete and epigram-matist Logan Pearsall Smith: "They say living is the thing, but I prefer books." Ben showed me the error of that, not by preaching—he never preaches—but by example. To be sitting with Ben among friends, in a public house in Nenagh or Clonmel, or at home over coffee and wine, or at lunch with friends in Dublin, at the Clarence or the Gresham, is to know that books are wonderful and enriching, but that life—if properly lived, if lived with style—is the thing.

—*The Recorder*, Summer 1994

42

EVENING DRIVE TO BALLINAMUCK

WHEN I LOOK upon my long friendship with Seamus Heaney, I think of journeys we have made together. To Belfast. To his family's farm in County Derry. Along the highway south from Berkeley to visit friends in Carmel. To the Thomas Hardy country in Dorset, with side visits to Oxford and Devonshire and Cornwall. A drive one St. Patrick's Day, with his friend the singer David Hammond to Galway Bay and Yeats's tower at Ballylee. I cannot recall a single thing said, though, but only the long, companionable silences which are possible only when those traveling together are friends.

But I remember one in particular and for selfish reasons. In the summers of the 1970s, I was in Dublin adding summer by summer to an immense typescript which became at long last the historical novel *The Year of the French*. Without quite understanding what I was doing, I was turning myself from a university professor into a novelist. It seemed a wildly transgressive thing to be doing in one's middle years, and outside the family I let no one in on the secret save Seamus and Marie and our friend Kevin Sullivan. Many nights, Seamus would drive over to our house in Rathgar. He would read for us a poem or two on which he had been working, some of which were to become famous. And I would listen, torn between wonder and impatience, until such time as I could read until late into the night from my own manuscript. My academic colleagues at Berkeley would, I suspect, have regarded the enterprise as an amiable eccentricity, but Seamus was wonderfully supportive, as were Marie and Kevin, and those Dublin summers seem in retrospect, golden.

But there came a time when I needed help of a more practical kind. My novel, which was based as closely as I could make it upon history, concerned a peasant uprising in the west of Ireland in the late summer of 1798. After initial successes, the rebels and their French allies moved desperately southward. At last, outside a village in Leitrim called Ballinamuck—the place of the pig—they were crushed by a powerful army under the command of Lord Cornwallis. The French, given the honors of war, were sent to Dublin to await repatriation. But the Irish were crowded back into a bog where they made a final stand, and there, save for a handful who were sent back to Mayo for hanging, they were butchered as they stood, by bullet, bayonet, or musket butt.

I needed of course to get a sense of that battlefield and bog, and being a nondriver I turned to Seamus for help. It should have been a two-hour drive out of Dublin, but we contrived to make it into an expedition which included the crossroads in Sligo where the rebels made their fatal decision to move south, and the hill of Cloone where they made their final encampment beside a now-ruined church, and Carrick-on-Shannon, where the prisoners marked for a Mayo hanging were held, and then, several days later, we went to Ballinamuck.

There, or more precisely on the road leading into the village, we encountered an elderly gentleman, heavy-shouldered and corpulent, blue and watery of eye, whom we will call here Bobby Leahy. At first Bobby seemed an invaluable cornucopia of local folklore about the battle. Only slowly did we realize that we had stumbled upon the town drunk, his mind a boggy morass of misinformation. Ballinamuck, tiny though it is, boasts two public houses, the Pikeman and the Ninety-Eight. Bobby had been barred from both of them, an impressive accomplishment. It was impossible to disengage from him, his imagination inflamed by the pints which we somehow procured for him. At the battlefield itself, Bobby hovered in the background, gesticulating and describing the exploits of Gunner McGee, a semi-mythical hero of the rebellion.

But it was there, at the site, that I realized my unconscious craftiness in bringing with me someone who knew more about bogs than writers usually do, and who was able to hazard informed guesses as to this one's shape and extent back on that dreadful afternoon. But nagging at the two of us—and that was to be the strangest aspect of the experience—was a sense that we had ourselves some kind of tangential relationship to it. It was impossible: we had no relation either to the Mayo rebels or to the Sligo and Leitrim men who had joined them. Seamus is of course a northerner, from Derry, and my own people had emigrated from the adjoining county of Fermanagh. And yet the feeling persisted as we walked down the hill to the field and along the edge of the bog. Blackberries were heavy on the bush when the battle was fought; after the slaughter, the British soldiers filled their tall helmets with them. They were growing now—it was close to the battle's anniversary—and we snapped off branches to bring home with us.

If you care about folklore, the person to consult is not the local schoolmaster, but always the retired schoolmaster, and so we did. He was away that day, but I left my address, and the day following he sent down copies of pamphlets he had written, on the village and on the battle. Early in the 1790s, I learned, these acres had been settled by people from the north, fleeing the Orange persecutions of those years. He gives a list of names, and among them are Heaneys and Flanagans. Distant kinsmen?

And there you are. It had been spattering rain, off and on, all day, and it was raining now as we said goodbye to Bobby, standing in the rain and swaying a bit, beside a late-Victorian statue of a rebel, brandishing a pike. He came to seem to us, on the long drive back, a kind of muse of Irish history, engaging and unreliable. It was easier to joke about him than to talk about our inexplicable—as that evening it was—sense of connection with that bog.

—from *Seamus Heaney: A Celebration*,
edited by Stratis Haviaras
(A *Harvard Review* monograph, 1996)

43

DARCY O'BRIEN

CASA FIESTA

I would not change the beginning for anything. I had an electric car, a starched white nanny, a pony, a bed modeled after that of Napoleon's son, and I was baptized by the Archbishop of the diocese. I wore hats and sucked on a little pipe. I was the darling of the ranch, pleasing everyone. One day I was sunning myself in the patio, lying out on the yellow and blue tiles, contemplating the geraniums and sniffing the hot, clean air. A bee came up and stung me on my bare fanny. The response to my screams was wonderful. Servants everywhere, my mother giving orders. Don Enrique applied an old Indian remedy and my father took me down to the beach house to let the salt water do its work. Oh what a world it was! Was there ever so pampered an ass as mine?

When my father was away on location, I would go to the tack room where Don Enrique sat polishing the saddles and the bridles and the boots and get him to tell me more stories about my father, how he became an honorary Apache and shot crocodiles on the Amazon, how he was good to his horses and courted my mother making Wrong Romance. *My father said that Don Enrique's stories were true and wasn't I lucky having such a wise old man around. Then he would tell me more stories and I would go to sleep on his big shoulder with my arms around him.*

By the age of five, I could amuse my parents and their friends after dinner, when they would sit before the great eucalyptus fire drinking café diablo.

I WOULD PAY hard cash, silver dollars on the barrelhead as the cowboy star father would have put it, to have written that first page of Darcy O'Brien's first novel, *A Way of Life, Like Any Other.* After he had become a practicing novelist, he would occasionally teach what are called "fiction workshops" at the University of Tulsa, and because he always delivered value for money, I am sure that he told his apprentices what good first sentences and good opening paragraphs should do—ways in which tone and distance are established, in which clues as to setting and cast are worked in, attitude, point of view, hints as to what kind of world will change for us. He would never have used his own work as example, but it is all there: eucalyptus trees, "on location," an old Indian buddy from the early cowboy times, the movie industry and movie money.

The smart-ass in the workshop—there is one in every workshop, never one of the promising writers, but occasionally a future critic— would ask about something called "voice," and Darcy would almost certainly have said, "I don't know about that." He knew, as did one of his favorite artists, Louis Armstrong, that if you have to look for it, you'll never find it. Nobody can help you find a voice, neither in workshop nor in bed. When Darcy found the first of his voices, he found his career and his discipline, and he took them, as he did everything, with wit and style and—in the Ivy League way—well-concealed seriousness. "They're always looking for their voice," he said once, "like some damned lost dog."

"Oh what a world it was! Was there ever so pampered an ass as mine?" A rhetorical question. History has provided thousands of more pampered asses—Madame de Pompadour's to name but one. The voice is there in that seemingly offhand sentence, the voice of a knocked-about Huck Finn pretending to be young Tom Sawyer, hopeful and illusioned. A quizzical, forgiving, self-mocking voice. The mother gives the orders, but it is the father who takes the boy down to the healing salt water. In that first moment rests the seed of that marvelously constructed pair, the beautiful, vain, theatrical mother, and the father with his own theatricality, the son of a San Francisco police chief who had transformed himself, with John Ford's help, into a cowboy star of the silver screen. "Oh what a world it was!" So the world isn't like that now, and if we are responsive to the voice, we guess that the story will be about how it changed for the speaker and his father and his mother. "Very clever, Professor," I can almost hear Darcy saying to me, his voice heavy with malicious affection.

Darcy's hero (and mine) Scott Fitzgerald had a celebrated exchange with Ernest Hemingway once about whether the rich are different from us. (Actually they didn't; another of Papa's lies. In the literary wars, Hemingway's strategy was to come on the battlefield the next day to pistol the wounded.) We have a different puzzle here. Are the children of famous movie stars—or rather, to use the novel's text, the children of former movie stars who have fallen on bleak days, personally and professionally—different from us? The answer perhaps is the one given to Darcy by an Irish friend in a Czech restaurant in California: "It's a way of life, like any other."

George O'Brien, the father, starred in a film which makes every *cinéaste*'s list of the ten greatest silents, Murnau's *Sunrise*, and it deserves to be there, a goofy, bizarre, wonderful fable. But for two of Darcy's later friends, Ben Kiely and myself, the great George O'Brien classic is *Riders of the Purple Sage*, with George as the laconic, quick-draw gunfighter, Lassiter. George may not have been the world's

473

greatest actor, but he had mastered the art of being laconic. Ben saw it with his father in Omagh, County Tyrone, and I saw it with mine in the Pickwick Theatre in Greenwich, Connecticut. For all three of us—Darcy, Ben, myself—the film is recalled with complicated memories of fathers and movie matinees.

There was a time, an incredibly long time ago, when Darcy had been my graduate student at Berkeley, but neither of us could really recall it, because in the decades that followed we had become fast friends, consulting each other on the things in life that really matter—delayed advances, royalties, book tours. In the final years we were on the phone to each other about three times a week, and occasionally we would talk about other matters—the nature of evil, for example, which his books about conscienceless murder had made for him a vivid actuality.

Ireland had been for us the instrument of bonding, and although we would visit each other in Los Angeles and Long Island and Tulsa, Ireland was for both of us the true dwelling place of our friendship. Darcy was a very fine writer, talented in a half-dozen ways, but he had a genius for friendship, and his Irish friendships were especially close —Ben, Seamus Heaney, Conor Cruise O'Brien, and he was just beginning one with Christopher Cahill, the editor of *The Recorder*. But there were, also, even stronger roots sunk into his past.

The study which his wife, Suzanne, helped him to create in Tulsa was in every sense what his friend Seamus would call a place of writing—with its photographs of those extraordinary glamorous people, his parents, and the poems and novels of his friends, and the father's ornate saddle with its silver-chased pommel, and the memories of John Ford, and the signed letter from John Wayne. And the typewriter on which he wrote those graceful, often hilarious letters to his friends. One evening in that room, I was holding one of his father's .45s, and saw that he was looking at it curiously: for him it was not a weapon but part of his artillery of the imagination. At Darcy's funeral mass in the Tulsa cathedral, his stepson, Brent, read from *The Great Gatsby*. And most appropriately. There was a lot of Nick Carraway in Darcy, and something of Fitzgerald, and a touch of Gatsby himself.

—In Memoriam Darcy O'Brien,
a supplement to *The Recorder*, Fall 1998

44

ONE AMERICAN IRISH IDENTITY

I AM DEEPLY conscious of the great honor done me by the American Irish Historical Society in choosing to bestow upon me this medal. Conscious because of the distinction of the Society, but also for more personal reasons.

The Society's distinction is in part one bred by age, for its roots extend back into the nineteenth century and the roll call of its members carries the names of men of Irish ancestry illustrious in the spiritual, the military, and the public life of our nation. Admirals, statesmen, judges, and, as at present, men of medical eminence have been its presidents-general. Its greater distinction, however, derives from its animating spirit, a spirit proclaimed by the words on its seal: "That the world may know." And by its name. From its foundation, the Society has been concerned with two intertwined subjects, the history of Ireland and the history of the Irish in America. Each is a subject rich in its complexity; joined, their richnesses—and at times their ironies—are inexhaustible.

In its early years, the Society was saluted by President Theodore Roosevelt, who was the friend of Yeats and Lady Gregory, and who followed with sympathy Ireland's Literary Revival in the 1890s, in words which remind us, less by what they say than by what they assume, that the history of the Irish in America, as of the Irish in

Ireland, is woven of many strands, both Munster and Ulster, both Catholic and Protestant. If, in the nineteenth century, the Irish contribution to American life was predominantly a Catholic one, then in the eighteenth century, it was more strongly a Protestant one. And, over the past two centuries, cutting across that distinction, Irish-Americans have differed greatly among themselves in the ways they have related themselves to their ancestral heritage, in the ways in which they have looked toward Ireland, in the hopes for Ireland which they have entertained, in their political fealties. It is so at the moment.

But this Society has distinguished itself, by the principles of its foundation, steadfastly maintained, in holding to notions of Irish identity so broad and so generous in spirit as to welcome the allegiance of all. None have held more resolutely to this principle than did one of its founding members, John Devoy, the fierce and splendid old Fenian rebel. And, as a member of the society has written, it is almost certainly the only circumstance of Devoy's life in which he chose to stand above conflict.

Over its years, the Society has developed into a rich repository of Irish-American history and tradition, and a fact of significance in the cultural life of the nation. Especially has this been so in recent years under the presidency of Dr. Kevin Cahill. Under his careful, imaginative, and vigorous direction, it has moved outward, to become for all of us not merely a historical but a cultural and a humane resource, hospitable to the arts, to literature, to scholarship, to social thought. It is difficult to measure not only what the Society has been achieving in the past few years, but more specifically, what he has himself, through it, been achieving.

There are, then, many reasons why I should hold in honor the Society and its medal, but some are personal, and I would like to specify them. Conventional wisdom holds that the effect of an honor is to make humble its recipient, and, as often, conventional wisdom is wrong. To judge by my response to the present occasion, its effect is

considerably to expand the ego, and to encourage a tendency to rem-
inisce. I would ask you to indulge this tendency for a few minutes,
with my promise that I will use it to make a point.

In the early 1950s, I was a member of the English faculty at
Columbia, and I was living on the far east side, in a section of York-
ville which, as it happens, was still partly Irish. In the morning, I
would walk over to Fifth Avenue, and wait outside the Metropolitan
Museum for the bus to Morningside Heights. (In those days, as some
of you may remember, Fifth Avenue buses ran both north and south.
And on time.) I was teaching a humanities course, the great books
of the Western tradition, from the *Iliad* to the *Aeneid* in the first
semester, and from Saint Augustine's *Confessions* to Dostoevsky in
the second—my favorite among the courses I have taught. My general
commitment was to the cultural history of modern Europe. I had finished a study of the novels and the politics of André Malraux, and
was at work on a study of the English writers who had ventured into
the Middle East in the nineteenth century.

As I waited, occasionally in the company of a very great cultural
historian indeed, who lived far closer to Fifth Avenue, I stood facing a
handsome, five-storied mansion out of the days of the robber barons,
ducal in its disregard for cost, but winningly chaste and elegant. I
would often study the building and its brass plate, which named it as
the American Irish Historical Society. My feelings were at once mingled and curiously intense, feelings which even now I cannot specify
with precision. For most of my life, the words "Ireland" and "Irish"
have had for me a special resonance, striking, somewhere within me,
a faint clear bell. But that bell sounded more easily for me in York-
ville, reverberating against railroad flats and bars whose neon signs
said "Clancy's." Not, with the beaux-arts grandeur of the Metropolitan at my back, against that gracefully bowed front with its wide,
shimmering windows, behind which might have moved a Henry James
hero, or an Edith Wharton heroine. And yet there also seemed to me

something about it fitting and proper, a kind of assertion of pride. I should perhaps have remembered that Henry James, that celebrant of spacious and sunlit avenues, was himself an Irish-American, the grandson of an immigrant from County Cavan. James himself never forgot it.

Once, long after Henry James had left his native New York to take up permanent residence in England, he visited Ireland, and recorded his pleasure at being in the home of his ancestors. He stayed in the Phoenix Park, at the Vice-Regal Lodge, and his host was his friend, the Lord-Lieutenant. Now, my grandparents had also come to this country from the north of Ireland, from County Fermanagh, although his came from the Presbyterian and mine from the Catholic side of that province's tangle of traditions and loyalties. But, and probably for that very reason, his grandfather and mine assimilated themselves to this country in very different ways, and at very different rates.

That eldest of the American Jameses, by reason of those conjunctions of creed and race by which identity is constituted, wove himself easily and with the connection of ease into the fabric of native American life, and his son and his grandsons were to be ornaments of what is properly regarded as a distinguished American family. My own grandfathers, like Henry James's, achieved considerable material success in this country, and, like his, thought of themselves as, and were, American. But they also thought of themselves as Irish, and indeed were staunch and fierce Irish nationalists. But my father's shade of green was far paler. He was sent to a very distinguished and very American university with a library at that time specializing in the history of the Reformation, and also, presumably in an effort to be even-handed, the history of superstition. He was conscious of his Irish origins and knowledgeable about them, but did not hold to them with any special zeal. To be candid, he had no choice but to be conscious of them: some entirely Irish names have to American ears an ethnically neutral ring—Martin, Redmond, Powers, Prendergast, Joyce—but

Flanagan is not one of them. And I in my turn, the green now pale to the point of translucency, was sent to a most excellent college which had developed as a part of the New England Protestant tradition. Where, to round matters off, I was seduced by the elaborate periods of Henry James's prose style. To the extent that America may be thought to hold within itself a distinctive Irish-American community, we had contrived in three generations to move rather far away from it.

Why then, I wonder, did the word "Ireland" sound that bell for me, amidst the cosmopolitan urbanities of Fifth Avenue, and why was it to sound with an increasing sonority over the years? A few years after those Fifth Avenue mornings, I was to turn away from those English travelers to the Middle East, and publish a study of the Irish novelists of the nineteenth century. And thereafter, the greater part of my scholarship was directed to the history and the culture of Ireland. I began to spend my summers there, as I still do, and I have lived there for five sabbatical years scattered across the last twenty. My first novel, *The Year of the French*, is set in Ireland at the close of the eighteenth century and my present one is set in Ireland of the nineteenth. The greater part of my close friends are Irish, and there are certain inexplicable ways in which I feel more at home there than I do in my own country.

I put the question "Why?" but I do not propose to answer it here. I am not certain of all the reasons, and they would in any event be more personal than the occasion warrants. I put it for a different reason.

My location of my Irish-American identity and that of my family is typical only in the sense that there is no such typical experience. "Ethnic identity," as it is currently called, is, like all other identity, a personal matter, complex, slanted, convoluted. Nevertheless, and to speak of the matter in the broadest possible terms, it can I think be held that we have had in this country, throughout its history, a general culture, an official culture, what is sometimes called, with suspicion, an establishment culture. To this culture, over the two centuries of our existence, the various immigrant groups have made a series of developing and at times paradoxical accommodations. Indeed, their histories have been the histories of such accommodations or reluctances to accommodate. And, although to a far lesser extent, the history of the general culture may be read as the history of the accommodations, or reluctances to accommodate, which it, in turn, has made. To put it another way, America possesses both an official and an unofficial history, and of these one is far better known than the other, for the quite sufficient reason that it is within the official history that books are written and read. There has been of recent years an attempt to redress the balance, but as yet it has lacked, for the most part, either scholarly or intellectual sophistication. The unofficial history would be that of the tensions, rich and creative tensions, between the official and the immigrant cultures, including, perhaps especially, those unwilling immigrants who are our black population. Their culture, in particular, has, until recently, existed within the official culture only as that culture has elected first to misperceive and then to define it.

Take what is for our present purposes a large example—the history of the city of Boston for the past one hundred and fifty years. It has been, until recently, and to the knowledge of everyone, a history of the tension, amounting at times to covert warfare, between the Brahmin culture of the settling families and the culture of the Irish immigrant, the latter being of course defined by the former as a lack of culture in either the honorific or the neutrally anthropological meaning of the word. But although much attention has been given to the political and some to the sociological intricacies of that conflict, almost none has been paid to it as an important chapter in the cultural history of the country. It lies, by definition, outside that official piety which regards our culture as uniform and homogeneous, and which views ethnic differentiations as attractively picturesque superficialities, chiefly in evidence in parades and festivals.

There is here an immense loss to our conscious recognition of the enriching actualities of the American cultural experience. And the official, the establishment culture has not been the only loser. The experience of America for most of our immigrant-descended populations has been for the first, perhaps the first two generations, a ghetto experience. Until fairly recently, however, this has often been succeeded by a process which I would call self-ghettoization, that is to say, a withholding of the self from the establishment culture, which the ethnic populations perceive as more elitist, more culturally harsh and uninviting than it has, in fact, become. Here, the ethnic communities, including perhaps the Irish-American, find themselves caught in a double bind. If they enter the establishment culture, they do so, they feel, at the expense of cutting away their roots, those sources of strength, vitality, and communal warmth. If they do not, they are sentenced to life within a cultural province, with all the disabilities which attend the provincial. The remedy, perhaps, lies with an Irish poet, as always. Patrick Kavanagh once reminded his readers that all true culture is at once parochial and cosmopolitan, but never provincial.

Something like this proper confidence, one which maintains a healthy tension among competing cultural expectations, has begun to take root precisely where, after all, one would expect to find it, among the young, for whom the social warfares of earlier generations have receded. With respect to the Irish, there are clubs and programs of study in all of the colleges and universities of this city and others, an interest in the history and culture of Ireland—in particular its musical and literary culture—and an interest in the experience in America of the immigrant generation and those which followed it. The American Irish Historical Society, as might be expected from its history, has been zealous in the fostering and in the support of this quickened interest among the young. In general, and I speak for the moment as a university professor, it is a generation whose lack of interest in history is frightening. But in this one particular, there is a quick, historical nerve—a sense that the meaning of that particular moment in time which is their own existence is shaped and colored by the conflicts and triumphs of earlier moments. It is likely both to temper and to enrich their sense of that complex and almost boundaryless culture of which we are all of us a part.

Now I have touched upon a strand or two only of a rich and densely woven fabric, and I would like to say a word, finally, as to how I stand with respect to it. To be an American conscious of his ethnic identity—but I speak for the occasion as an American conscious of his Irish identity—is to exist within complexities, paradoxes, contraries, ambiguities, ironies, and, perhaps, a few pitfalls. But this seems to me a condition not grim but, rather, exhilarating, a continuous challenge to intellect, imagination, sensibility, on occasion a challenge to conscience, choice, action. Our fellow Irish-American, Henry James, once wrote, memorably, that it is a complex fate to be an American. He said this not mournfully but with relish, for he relished complexity, and so, I think, do I. Ours is a culture of paradoxes, and I am grateful to those circumstances which have allowed me to be alive to some of them, curious about them, responsive to their nuances.

I began these remarks on a Manhattan street, looking across traffic toward the building which houses the Society which has seen fit to bestow upon me tonight this great honor. That scene has for me the power of the emblematic. Northward of us, northward of me and northward of the building, lay the great university, American and cosmopolitan, which was that day's destination. Eastward of us, red bricks of an earlier generation, American and parochial, where our people had taken one of their early positions. Emblems of the official and the unofficial cultures. By temperament and circumstance alike, I have taken bus rides backward and forward, across what was once their no man's land, I hope not as spy but as emissary.

But I will close with a scene at once far distant from the Society and yet very close to it. When I was first able to visit Ireland, almost a quarter-century ago, I was on the faculty at Berkeley, in California. I had a two-hour stop in New York, and an old and close friend, Kevin

Sullivan, came out to have a meal with me. He had been my colleague at Columbia, is a fellow member of the Society, and is here this evening. Noticing a certain distractedness on my part, he asked about it, and I said, "Kevin, all my life I have been dreaming about Ireland. What if I don't like the place?" He remembers the words slightly differently: such are the perils of Irish scholarship.

But a day or two later, with the adventurousness of what I now know was youth, I was walking on a road on the coast of Kerry, Kevin's ancestral county. Rain, fine as a heavy mist, shrouded the scene at first, but it was a long walk, and presently the mists drifted away. Rocky fields lay to my left, the rocks a wet, intense black. The small black cattle grazed upon grass so perfectly and deeply green, so fully a kind of platonic essence of green, as to belie language. The upland slopes were dotted with sheep. To my right, still half hidden by lingering mist, lay deep waters and the hills of the Dingle peninsula. Before me, the road wound toward a village. That moment was a moment clear of those paradoxes and ambiguities of which I have spoken—a clear, breathless, unified moment. I was at a far end of the island from the farms in Fermanagh which my grandparents had left, but I had a powerful sense, never afterward to leave me, that some deep and essential part of my being had found its way to its home. And a sense also, that I would be, thereafter, more completely at home in America.

—*The Recorder*, 1984

Acknowledgments

The editor wishes to express his gratitude to Daria D'Arienzo and the staff of the Amherst College Library Archives and Special Collections, where the Thomas Flanagan (AC 1945) Papers are held, for their gracious assistance in locating many of the previously unpublished essays included in this volume. He also wishes to thank William Cobert and the officers, Executive Council, and staff of The American Irish Historical Society. Personal thanks are due to Caitlin Flanagan, Seamus Heaney, and Elizabeth Cahill for a variety of suggestions and directions which helped to bring this book to fruition.

Michael Donovan?" in *The Dial*, February 1987. Reprinted courtesy of Thirteen/WNET New York.

"Dangerous Amusements" is reprinted with permission from the October 3, 1987, issue of *The Nation*. For subscription information call 1-800-333-8536. Portions of each week's *Nation* magazine can be accessed at www.thenation.com.

"Brian Moore: An Appreciation" copyright © 1999 *Los Angeles Times*. Reprinted with permission.

"Wolfe Tone" copyright © 1990 *Newsday*. Reprinted with permission.

"Lord Edward Fitzgerald" copyright © 1998 by The New York Times Co. Reprinted with permission.

"The Uncrowned King" copyright © 1994 by The New York Times Co. Reprinted with permission.

"The Molly Maguires" copyright © 1998 *Los Angeles Times*. Reprinted with permission.

"Borne Up by the Ghosts of the Fallen" copyright © 1995 by The New York Times Co. Reprinted with permission.

"The Day We Celebrate" reprinted courtesy of *The Irish Times*.

"Obsession" reprinted with permission of the PEN/Faulkner Society.

All other essays are reprinted courtesy of the estate of Thomas Flanagan. For previously published material, the place and date of original publication is indicated at the end of the chapter. Every effort has been made to locate published versions of manuscript material.